Daniel Aaron Salomon

**Confessions of an Autistic Theologian:**

**Doing Theology in Pictures-A Contextual, Liberation Theology for Humans on the Autism Spectrum**

**By**

**Daniel A. Salomon**

*To my late mentor Dr. Philip Bosserman who gives new meaning to the word "temporarily able."*

*A brilliant sociology professor, ordained Christian minister and lifelong peace activist who died tragically within the last two years of dementia but who was the first friend I have had who has been faithful to me till the end and whose soul survived dementia.*

*His peaceful temperament, his patient personality and his love of life and humanity remained "in-tact" tell the end, showing to what degree disability is not a character issue but a biophysical condition grounded in biophysical reality.*

*And that one's immortal soul exists "beneath and beyond" ones disability, even one's neurological disability.*

*That disability, even mental disability is just another form of human suffering, integrating disability and mental disability into the rest of the human condition.*

*I especially thank Dr. Bosserman for giving me the sociological alternative to psychological reductionism (sociology, social change and nonviolent political activism), the frameworks of (peace studies, conflict resolution and anti-oppression) which I have employed in my own liberation and the liberation of my group and for providing a coherent model of liberal-progressive Christianity.*

*He provided me with a liberal-progressive alternative to Christian fundamentalism and apolitical passivity. That one can be a pacifist without being passive, that one can challenge society without being anti-social, that one can still be a faithful Christian but still engage other world religions and a secular society and that one can have a rich spirituality, even a vibrant religious faith, outside of organized religion and official channels. That the Living God exists "beneath and beyond" perverted institutions and human precepts.*

*My wish is for this project is to help preserve some of his ideas and take his ideas into the new territory of autistic pride and disability justice.*

*That peoples with all kinds of disabilities and neurological differences will receive the solace- that there is another way to feel in control of your own life and your own body other than psychologically adjusting to worsening and worsening conditions, overfunctioning in an unsympathetic society, or lashing-out at society in ways which are anti-social, violent and self- destructive.*

*That way is the way of nonviolent resistance!*

Table of Contents...................................................................................................

### Preface: Making My Book Accessible

Written by one Christian theologian living on the autism spectrum, this project is my attempt to liberate all peoples on the autism spectrum, including myself.

This project can also serve as a model for those with physical disabilities, as well as those who have learning disabilities or struggle with a mental illness.

This project will also provide fresh insights and new resources to the ecological and animal movements, as well as various minority rights movements around the world--- especially the anti-colonialism movements in the Geographic South and the anti-patriarchy movements in North America.

My project also attempts to educate temporally able, neurotypical human beings.

My goal for my **non-disabled**, **neurotypical readers** is:

*To help sensitize temporally able, neurotypical people to my world and to people like myself--- the growing number of people around the world diagnosed with autism spectrum disorders or other cognitive challenges such as learning disabilities and mental illnesses.*

Up to this point, to my awareness, there has yet to be a person on the autism spectrum who has written about their experiences from a Christian liberation theology perspective (anti-oppression) or even from a Christian contextual theology perspective (telling our story).

There has not even been an attempt by a person on the autism spectrum to engage in theological reflection (a sympathetic critique of the Christian faith).

Yet, there has been much ink spilled in Christian theology and practice---showing patronizing, paternalistic, even chauvinistic "segregationist charity" to peoples with autism and their families, such as myself and my family.

In otherwords, many Christians are currently offering intellectual arguments, modest curriculum reforms and special religious rituals ---arguing that one has a Christian duty to be "kind" to peoples with autism and their families.

There is even much Christian literature in recent times showing why peoples with autism must be included in some (but not all) of the Christian Church's activities, as well as being given some (rudimentary) pastoral care and spiritual formation, mainly to instill a spirit of passivity in the neurodiversity community.

None of this normal disability literature is A) written by a person on the spectrum themselves and B) is written from the abelist bias of "segregationist charity."

An "inside-out" perspective written by a person who has to live with this condition themselves is radically different than an "outside in" perspective such as a family member or a well-meaning professional who might be personally affected by the situation, but does not have to live the autistic person's life and is subsequently subjected to project even misinterpret my own self-understandings, or even my own desires and needs.

Social justice---giving people what they actually need---is revolutionarily different than "segregationist charity"---doing nice things for a person just to appease your liberal guilt, while having no intention of fully including that person in your world as an equal.

Tragically, public discussions about autism and disability in religion and society automatically switch from justice to charity whenever autism or any other disability issues are addressed.

This is no more the case in organized religion!

Where religious institutions are the only institutions which can legally exclude, discriminate, or refuse to accommodate all peoples with disabilities.

This is because religious groups have lobbied our political leaders for this "special treatment."

The government cannot get away with this!
Private colleges and universities cannot get away with this!
Even-corporations cannot get away with this!

This is because religious institutions such as churches are exempted from the Americans with Disabilities Act (ADA).

Only religious institutions which take government money such as theological schools, seminaries and Christian colleges, still have to comply.

To make this more personal and concrete, I as a person with a disability lose all my ADA (Americans with Disabilities Act) protections whenever I walk into a church, synagogue or mosque.

I literally have to say "Peace to this house" (Luke 10: 5) every time I enter a house to worship to practice my religion.

I am a persecuted Christian right here in North America, right here in the United States of America, a country which claims to have "freedom of religion."

This is because I have absolutely no legal guarantee that I would not be "discriminatorily harassed," excluded, asked to leave, even have the police called on me---just for practicing my religion---because religious institutions are ADA exempted.

A religious exemption to ADA also means a church I happen to walk into on a particular Sunday has absolutely no legal obligation to give me "reasonable accommodations" for my disability.

Reasonable Accommodations which I take for granted in schools, universities, parks and employment agencies around the country.

As a result of this "legal loophole"--- I have been discriminated against and spiritually abused, repeatedly by ---- Christian and Jewish groups alike. And, I have absolutely no legal recourse.

Yet, I, as a person with autism, am a spiritual being with spiritual needs. I have a soul, "in the image of God he created [me]" (Genesis 1: 27) and I am a first-class Christian, in God's eyes.

I also want a Christian church community to "live-out" my Christian faith with like any other Christian.

My autistic identity even informs and blesses my Christian faith.

Autism is not a mere disability or mental illness but autism is also an *alternative phenomenology*, "a non-ordinary state of consciousness," "a different way of seeing," even an *alternative lifestyle*.

Autism gives me a unique perspective and special gifts!

I am no-longer ashamed of my condition!

Although it took me many years to get to this point, because of how society, even myself, has responded to my unique condition.

Peoples with autism, like all peoples with disabilities are a legitimately oppressed minority group desperately in need of healing and liberation.

This project is an attempt to redress this injustice.

To celebrate autistic culture!

To learn from the tactics and experiences of other minority rights movements!

To dialogue with other oppressed minority groups!

To break-down shame and stigma with information about ourselves and others!

To put a face on the autism spectrum!

To understand where autistic people are coming from, from our own point-of-view!

To see the world through our own eyes!

But ***most importantly*** affirm in no uncertain terms--- that all peoples on the autism spectrum do in fact--- ***have a spiritually even religiously meaningful inner life***.

That we are full human beings like everyone else!

We *are not* "others." We *are not* curiosities. We *are not* cute childlike characters. We *are not* "tragedies." We *are not* "marginal cases." We *are not* complicated machines.

We *are* full human beings with desires and feelings, with a proud history, a profound legacy, a bright future, who have just as much right to exist in this world and in the Body of Christ as anyone else.

The Christian Church believes in a Loving God and advertizes a house of worship "where everyone is welcome at the table." For this reason---the institutional Christian Church *does have a* Christian obligation to seek justice for peoples with autism, now.

Any Christian Church worthy to call itself Christian has a moral and theological obligation to ***fully include*** all peoples with physical and intellectual disabilities *not only* in catechism or other Sunday school classes *or even just in* worship services, ***but also in leadership positions, missionary opportunities and even in religious orders.*** Anything less is from the Evil One!

*Unfortunately, organized religion more than any other social institution discriminates,* oppresses and abuses peoples with autism and other disabilities because they can, legally speaking.

Organized religion has also tapped into two bigoted ideologies--- neurotypicalism and abelism.

*Neurotypicalism* is the belief that everyone and everything must conform to the norms, taboos and standards of peoples with a fully functioning vermis. Any other ways of knowing and experiencing are dubbed inferior and must be patronizingly controlled. Neurotypicalism also impacts human-animal relationships and human-Earth relationships.

*Abelism* is the belief that the world "should" be geared-up to people without disabilities. Abelism also impacts human-animal relationships and human-Earth relationships.

Yet, that does not have to be so!

Legalized spiritual poverty---neurotypicalism and abelism are a profound betrayal of the tenets of world religions, especially Judaism and Christianity with which this series will deal with.

You will discover as you read this work that the foundations of Western religion are very affirming to peoples with autism and other disabilities. And, to ignore this factor is to breech the integrity of these religions.

## How to Use This Book:

In each of my books I have attempted to address an issue not being addressed in the secular environmental or animal movements:

In *Creation Unveiled* (USA: Xulon Press, 2003) I challenged many of the anti-Christian attitudes found in the secular environmental and animal movements. In *Christian Environmental Studies* (Amazon.com: Kindle Edition, 2008 and Amazon.com: Create Space Independent Publishing Platform, 2012) I provided critical analysis, systematic theology and curriculum development for the fledging Christian ecotheology, animal theology and science theology fields. In *Human-Animal Reconciliation* (Amazon.com: Kindle Edition, 2008) I offered a practical application of Christian ecotheology---using Franciscan interspecies communication techniques to nonviolently resolve wildlife pest problems. In *Have Mercy on me, an Ecological Sinner* (Amazon.com: Create Space Independent Publishing Platform, 2012) I revealed my social location, ecological autobiography and vegetarian testimony and opened-up about my own personal struggles with

"Compassion Fatigue." Here--- I also identified "compassion fatigue" and the increasing polarization in our society as a legitimate issue which the ecological and animal movements must address candidly.

Now in *Confessions of an Autistic Theologian* (Create Space Independent Publishing Platform, 2013) I plan to address my autistic Christian ecological identity directly---where in this book I plan to reveal my method for theological reflection as a Christian on the autism spectrum, share more of my Aspie "wild space," tell more of my story including my spiritual autobiography and continue to "break the silence" on neurotypicalism and abelism in the Christian Church and in society. Most importantly, in this latest work I begin to articulate my own theology versus deconstructing or popularizing someone else's theology.

This book is meant to be an ecological catechism and moral manual for secular environmentalists and neurodiverse peoples alike--- which are following my career--- giving my readers basic background information about theology, spirituality, ethics and critical theory. As well as my personal positions on major issues in religion and society.  To better understand where I am coming from!

In other words, in this book I am going to give my readers--- the long awaited book--- my autism story!

Realizing that I only have the authority to talk about my own experiences being on the spectrum, I cannot speak with authority for the experiences of all peoples on the spectrum.

**The Liberation Theology Tradition and This Project:**

This project will follow the ***liberation theology methodology*** for asking theological questions, *the three Ps*, effectively used by other minority rights movements:

*Praxis:* What is true is what is useful to the oppressed. The truth of the oppressor cannot be trusted and is not inherently objective, absolute, universal, or stands on its own. It cannot be assumed that the knowledge and wisdom of the oppressor is done in good faith, out of ignorance, and that it is not inherently self-serving, possibly even malicious, at times. A "hermeneutic of suspicion" will need to be employed, as a result, in certain situations. Truths found in the oppressor's culture can be utilized though, but needs to be contextualized and translated into the context and strategy of the oppressed.[1]

*Preferential Option:* The oppressed must always be sided with over the oppressors. The oppressor has to be assumed to be in the "wrong" and the oppressed have to be assumed to be in the "right."[2] Nuance will need to be granted in cases involving when "a poor man who oppresses the poor is like a beating rain that leaves no food" (Proverbs 28: 3, NKJV).

*Prophetic in Nature:* Will "speak the truth to power!" Will not compromise on truth-telling! Will question authority! Will question social institutions! Will question cultural norms/taboos! Will question doctrines, narratives and other human precepts! Will deconstruct misinformation and disinformation, corruption and deception and things which are plain wrong. Nothing is above or below, interrogation, while at the sametime, realizing that "truth-telling" does have a "relationship context" though.[3]

This series will also use the ***liberation theology formula,***[4]

*Judeo-Christian Theological Reflection:* The theology, religion, and spirituality derived from the foundations of the Abrahamic religions of Judaism and Christianity.

*Marxist Analysis:* The sociology derived from the foundations of Karl Marx and other Marxist-like thinking. Other useful sociologies, anthropologies or philosophies might also be employed.

*Social Location:* Takes into consideration both the social and cultural context of the group being liberated and takes into consideration the group's "pragmatic experiences"[5]- needs, desires, wants, situation and relationship to the oppressed.

Finally, ***other principles*** this liberation theology will abide by:

*Accessibility of Materials:* Information will be legible to the target audience-the oppressed group in need of liberation. A non-elitist approach will be taken. As much as possible, considering the scope of the work and the make-up of this population.[6]

*Sensitivity to Language:* Language, metaphor, and structure *will not* be the language, metaphor, and structure of the oppressor, but that of the oppressed and will be sensitive to the feelings, experiences, histories and social location of the oppressed group.[7]

*Humility of Experience:* The liberation theologian will only speak authoritatively about his own feelings, experiences, history and social location. The liberation theologian doing the reflection *will not* assume that he knows or understands other peoples' feelings, experiences, histories and social location in this group. The liberation theologian will only speak from his feelings, experiences, history and social location with authority. It will be up to the other members in the oppressed group to come to their own conclusions, recover a model for their own purposes, make relevant generalizations, application to their own circumstances and be empowered ultimately to write their own personal liberation theologies. The liberation theology only promises a starting-point, for further acts of resistance and discourse. The liberation theologian will draw from the experiences and insights of other peoples with autism, other neurodiverse humans, those with physical disabilities and other oppressed minority groups, though.[8]

**Introduction-A Spiritual Testimony: My Faith Life Being an Aspie**

Historian and Cognitive Scientist, Rab Houston and Uta Frith, in *Autism in History: the Case of Hugh Blair of Borgue* writes about what they understand the religious capacities of peoples with autism to be--- based on their recovery of Hugh Blair of Borgue. An eighteenth century nobleman whom the authors contend was on the autism spectrum. The following is based on a legal proceeding where Blair was on trial to determine if he was "stupid" and not be allowed to marry.

> It was not enough that Hugh Blair knew the whole of the catechism and attended church regularly. Thus, Mr Gordon succinctly stated he could not see Hugh's heart...
>
> Clearly, the behavioral signs suggested that Hugh appreciated religious feelings and participated in the proper religious activities. Nevertheless, the final verdict of the court implies the judge did not believe that Hugh had the same sense of God as other member of his community. This matches our interpretation of Hugh having a diminished awareness of mental states.[9]

Steven Shore, a man living with Asperger, counters these incorrect conclusions about the spiritual life of a man with autism in the eighteenth century, recovered by the above historian and cognitive scientist, when Shore makes the statement, "people with designated disabilities have the same needs, wants and potential for a fulfilling life as everyone else."[10]

Shore's principle can also apply to spirituality and religion. Even though, like Hugh Blair in the eighteenth century, I have a different sense of God, than the surrounding community, that does not mean that I do not still greatly desire God, like any other Christian, like the authors above have already alluded too.

As I will demonstrate to you in this section, I, as a full human being with Asperger, have an extremely active, vibrant faith-life, which is every bit as valid as the neurotypical faith-life in my surrounding community. Hopefully, once you finish this volume you will be assured that a person with autism can have a meaningful inner faith-life, despite his/her limitations. That one does not need a certain "theory of mind," to have a "sense of the divine." As you read this narrative, you will get a rare window into the faith-life of a person like Hugh Blair, from his perspective, in his own words and be affirmed that you or a loved one, can in fact, or has already obtained a meaningful spirituality or religious faith. Living a spiritually-rich life is something you can do, or if you are a parent or loved one of a person with autism, this is something you can pursue with your child.

You can trust that your child's spiritual and religious experiences are very real, despite the ambivalence you might read from some researchers and skeptics in newsletters or other publications, which you might come across.

I know in my case, as a person with Asperger:

- I *do* believe in God, I have a relationship with God; He talks to me through direct, unmediated communication---through "auditory voice" or to put it in more psychological terms, through stimulating my consciousness---my "God neurons"[11]--- liken to echolocation in bats. God is the best mentor, teacher, consoler, friend and lover I have ever had!

- I *also* have a close friendship with Saint Francis of Assisi in Heaven and his fellow comrades (Saint Anthony, Saint Bonaventure, Brother Rufono, Brother Juniper, Brother Bernardo, Brother Leo, Brother Sylvester, Friar Wolf, the Archangels Michael, Gabriel, and Raphael, along with Sister Moon, Sister Water and the Sabbath Queen) through the "Communion of Saints," mediated by my Lord. Francis and the Brothers are also some of the best friends I have ever had. I desired a relationship with Francis of Assisi for many years, before making contact with him in Heaven.

- I *also* have undergone a powerful conversion experience from Judaism to Christianity, meaning I made a conscious choice to choose a particular religion, including receiving believer's baptism at age twenty-two.

- I *am* a graduate of Andover Newton Theological School, outside of Boston, earning both a Master of Arts in Research and a graduate certificate in "Science and Religion" from the Schools of the Boston Theological School in the Spring of 2006. Graduating with a 3.7 GPA.

- Since I *graduated* from theological school in 2006---I have published in the peer reviewed academic journal---*Journal of Critical Animal Studies* (JSAS), where an abridged version of my journal article was published in the on-line activist publication, *The Scavenger.* I was invited to have a web-page on Reverend Frank Hoffman's website, www.all-creatures.org. I have self-published four other books on Amazon. In 2012, I was invited to be on the panel discussion on "Disability and Animals" at the annual Society for Disability Studies (SDS) conference in Denver, Colorado--- which I did. I am now a member of the society. I have been invited back to SDS's annual 2013 conference, this time in Orlando, Florida, to serve on a follow-up panel discussion on "Animals and Disabilities."

- *More recently* over a one-and-half year period, I initiated a restoration of a local wild area---Deer Ridge, in the neighborhood where I lived for two years in the bioregion of my birth, legally protected as a designated "common area" by the city. I cleaned-up litter in Deer Ridge's three streams and surrounding upland forests, even in Deer Ridge's own freshwater marsh. I ecologically surveyed Deer Ridge, where I documented the diversity of plants and animals found in Deer Ridge, interpreted Deer Ridge's unique landscape and waterscape and even attempted to recover the human history of Deer Ridge. I collaborated with a local community activist and a former biology professor from undergraduate to help motivate the neighborhood and local government agencies to take better care of Deer Ridge. Deer Ridge is a rare place of phenomenal biodiversity, ecological health, natural beauty and recreational potential. Literally right across the street from the apartment where I lived for two years.

- I pray, I fast, I read Holy Scripture and I serve *like* any other Christian.

- I *have been* on religious pilgrimages to the Franciscan Holy Sites of Italy (Rome, Assisi, and the Rieti Valley), the Holy Land (Israel and the West Bank) and Chimayo in New Mexico. I also have traveled to the Pacific Northwest multiple times and the American Southwest twice. I have been to Waterton-Glacier International Peace Park on the Montana-Canadian border, Rocky Mountain National Park, the Colorado Plateau and the Bahamas. Just to name a few.

- I *feel* most spiritual when I am in the Natural World.

In other words, I have a very active spiritual and religious life.


Although, some might see it as different and strange or question its validity, I find my faith to be personally meaningful and life-giving. I cannot live without it.

I even struggle with doubts, longings, disillusionments and a sinful nature, like other Christians.

So as you embark on this journey with me, you will finally learn what that eighteenth century doctor was not able to do, "see Hugh's heart."

Where you will learn that Hugh's heart is good! Loving! And, very human! In otherwords, that heart *is not* a broken, complicated machine. But a living soul! A soul in need of salvation!
▪▪▪▪▪▪▪▪▪▪▪▪▪▪▪▪▪▪▪▪▪▪▪▪▪▪▪▪▪▪▪▪▪▪▪▪▪▪▪▪▪▪▪▪▪▪▪▪▪▪▪▪▪▪▪▪▪▪▪▪▪▪▪▪▪▪

**Chapter One---My Soul's Journey into God: My Tasks for Spiritual Development Being a Human with Asperger**

*Finding Vestiges of God in the Natural World: Finding an Authentic Religion*

Dawn-Prince Hughes, a primatologist and a women living with Asperger, writes in her autobiography, *Songs of the Gorilla Nation: My Journey through Autism,*

> I had never been a religious person. I felt uncomfortable in most churches, finding no comfort in those buildings. Perhaps, I thought after watching these gorillas and coming to love them and learn from them, I needed to expand into God rather than being enclosed by a church. On reflecting upon gorilla ritual, I realized that my conception of God-as a great spirit living in things that could absorb me as I flung myself outward-was probably much the same as the gorilla's experience of God.[12]

Prince-Hughes needed to find an authentic religion, a religion that was consistent with both her spiritual experiences being on the spectrum and something which could help her to grow as a human being, at the same time.

A religion which contradicted her spiritual experiences and undermined her spiritual development was not a religious tradition which she could authentically embrace. And, she would ultimately end-up rejecting that religious tradition. The religion of the gorillas was a religion which she could authentically embrace. This is because, the religion of the gorillas both affirmed her spiritual experiences being a person with Asperger and helped her to grow and achieve her full potential in life.

To be more specific, the gorillas engaged in religious rituals which made sense to her, they engaged in religious rituals to ameliorate fear, yet at the sametime, helping her to open herself up to the reality of a larger world. And, on my spiritual journey, that was my first task-to "choosing a religion."

Find a religion which can A) embrace my unique spiritual experiences and B) help me to grow in new directions, opening up new reality and new possibilities.

That religion for me turned-out to be Christianity!

Choosing Christianity was a surprising, even ironic choice for me, considering my background, upbringing and interests.

For starters, I was born into a Reformed Jewish family. Both my parents are Jewish. My sister is also Jewish. My grandparents on both sides were Jewish. All my aunts and uncles and cousins are Jewish. I am a third generation immigrant. My father's sides were Jewish immigrants from Ottoman Turkey. My mother's sides were Jewish immigrants from the former Soviet Union. This makes me as Jewish, as I could possibly be according to Jewish law. I come from generations of unbroken Jewish linage, even down to being a direct descendent of the Vilna Gone, a very famous rabbi from late-Medieval Eastern Europe.

I was raised Jewish. Growing-up, we celebrated the Sabbath service every Friday night; we preformed the Passover Seder each year, we attended Synagogue at the High Holidays, Jewish New Year and Yom Kipper. We even celebrated Hanukah each year with a menorah, potato pancakes, presents, games and gelt and a brief religious service.

I grew-up on Challah, mitzvah, apples and honey and many other Jewish delicacies. And, it expanded beyond mere food and religious observances. I grew-up in a heavily Jewish neighborhood, in a heavily Jewish part of the country. I was not the only Jewish person at my school. I had teachers and professionals, which were Jewish, too. My parents are both very well educated, my father has a Ph.D. and my mother has a Master degree. Both of them put a great premium on education and have tremendous faith in its power. Both of them are very politically and socially liberal-progressive, "bleeding-heart" Democrats. Both of them are staunch Zionists, major supporters of the right of the state of Israeli to exist, as both the ancestral homeland and place of political sovereignty for the Jewish people, displaced by over two millennia of exile, colonization and genocide at the hands of foreign European conquerors.

My sister even more strongly Zionist, having made Aliyah (dual Israeli citizenship), she now lives in Israel and is married to an Israeli man where she also is finishing-up her master's degree at an Israeli university and is currently working for a Zionist organization.

I was brought-up to "question authority," "think for myself," be curious and inquisitive, be politically engaged, talk intelligently and most of all I was sensitized from a very young age, to the Holocaust and the many centuries of Anti-Semitism which have plagued the Jewish people, having had extended family members, as well as personally knowing elders in the community, who were Holocaust Survivors and Survivors of Soviet Labor Camps, even having family members and knowing of stories of people, who died in the Holocaust.

Choosing Christianity as my most authentic religion was also even more ironic considering that I was also an environmentalist and animal rights person, a scientist, who felt most spiritual in Nature and a person of autism. How in the world, did I ever find Jesus?

It is nothing less than a miracle and a testimony to the power of evangelism. First of all, my idyllic Reformed Jewish existence was not at all as authentic as the statistics about my life, would indicate. First of all, I was never Bar Mitzvah, because the synagogue which my parents attended at the time refused to train me to become Bar Mitzvah, because I had autism. As a result, I never learned how to read Hebrew and my Jewish identity was severely weakened as a result.

Growing-up in the shadows of the memory of the Holocaust, having a child with a disability was considered a great shame. That is because certain elements of the Jewish community wanted to replenish the Jewish ethnicity with all who were lost during the Holocaust. So when I was first diagnosed, even through my parents were active in the young married of their local synagogue, everyone in the synagogue stopped talking to them, once I was diagnosed. Our Jewish neighbors cut us out of their lives. One neighbor even refused to let me play with or be around her daughter. And, as a result, our next door neighbors are virtually on no-speaking terms with us, even though we have lived next door for years.

This was compounded by the fact, that I never really felt spiritual in synagogue, like Prince-Hughes, I hated being in those places. They did nothing for me, spiritually or religiously, except bore me to tears. I dreaded going there. I felt much more spiritual in the Natural World. So, before God entered my life, I was spiritual feed in His Creation. By anything and everything natural! And, as a result, showed very little interest in religious matters!

Yet, looking back on it, I realized that I was always spiritual, but experienced God in Nature and in my savant world, instead of in synagogue. Although I do remember being in awe of certain Biblical stories as a child, particularly Noah's Flood, drawing pictures of Noah's Flood. I also liked playing Jewish songs over and over again, while I was a child too, for a brief period. It is also important to note that the first question which I asked as a child after recovering from my loose of speech-"When you multiply a million times a billions do you get infinity?" And, I remember getting affirmation from a sixth grade teacher, when I said-"God is not a being but a spirit."

I also went through a phrase when I was fascinated by the paranormal such as aliens, UFOs and other unexplained phenomena. I was always fascinated by the unknown and unexplained. In addition, I also went through a Native American and indigenous peoples' phrase, too. But, God and religion were always intimidating. Even going into Churches made me feel uncomfortable. And, pictures of Jesus used to freak me out. All this changed in about eighth grade.

First it is important to note that my mother was also about this time going through with disillusionment with her Jewish-ness, because of how the Jewish community treated our family. She already was moving in the direction of making psychology her religion, not Judaism. We never found a synagogue we liked and our family was going from synagogue to synagogue. Eventually, instead of going to synagogue for the High Holidays, we would go out into the wilderness, usually to a local state park, for our observances, a ritual reenactment of these Biblical stories.

That is about the stage in our family's spiritual development that my middle school special education English teacher walked into my life. He was a very inspiring teacher and extraordinarily knowledgeable and caring, for a special education teacher in those days and at that school.

He even did much to protect students from abuse from administration, which often had policies or did actions which were not in the best interest of the students-particularly me, being a student on the spectrum. Where for example, I *should not* have been forced to eat in the cafeteria, where I was a constant target of bullies and overstimulation and where the young man who hit me over the head with a backpack for no reason, should have gotten two days of in-school suspension. He let me eat my lunch in his classroom and made sure that that student who assaulted me was punished.

My middle school was the very essence of a dysfunctional organization---from an abusive and out-of-control student body which could not be controlled by the teachers, to apathetic, unsympathetic even abusive administrators, to where I became the merciless target of bullies and abusive relationships, as a result.

This lone teacher and a handful of other brave and committed teachers and aides actually taught and made learning interesting and challenging, where the "hidden curriculum" of the learning center, I believe and my parent's believe, was to "warehouse" students with special needs, throwing people with all kinds of disabilities into their mix, because the school did not know what to do with us.

This group of teachers were committed Christians. And, one was Jewish. The English teacher was a very devout Southern Baptist and evangelized to the students and parents despite separation between church and state probations. And, he did the right thing, for I would not have found salvation in Jesus Christ any other way, or more importantly, find my authentic religious expression, which was not necessarily "the religion of my birth."

He befriended me and became my advocate. He also befriended my mother and my whole family. Here, I was introduced to the Christian religion. We would spend hours after school talking and praying. He would come to our home, even visit us on vacations. And, he respected our family's Jewishness, encouraging me to attend synagogue, worked with my mother to create a unit on Holocaust Remembrance, he even embarked on a special study course on the Holocaust where he visited Poland and Israel and became a gentile spokesperson for the Holocaust. He even transferred to my high school, in part to be near me.

At first, his language and practices were very strange to me and intimidating and even frightening. Particularly talk of Satan and spiritual warfare. But, he "set everything in motion."

Shortly afterwards, God began to talk to me. I began to hear the Voice of God. And, I began to have conversations with my new friend. They started-out short. Then they gradually expanded, until my mysterious friend took over my whole being. And, I could not live without God. I began to supplicate to God, through intercessory prayer. I began to watch Biblical archeological shows on television with my family. Our family went to lectures on spirituality. Yet, at this time I was not attending Church on a regular basis. It was literally, just me and Jesus. I heard lots of revelation, some of it I know from God, some of it; I am a little less sure. But, one thing it became evident, I was on the verge of a massive religious conversion. I found the authentic religion, which could encompass my new spiritual experiences. That is why I ended-up believing. What my English teacher introduced to me was beginning to jive with my spiritual experiences and I was actually growing spiritually. But, before I could go any further in my faith-journey as a Christian, first there were some issues which needed to be worked-out, to make Christianity "accessible" and "relevant" to my personal socio-symbolic life (autistic culture). To this we now turn.

### Finding Vestiges of God In Myself: God Translating Religion into My Personal Socio-Symbolic Life:

The late sociology professor at Emory College and author of *The Disabled God: toward a Libratory Theology of Disability* Nancy Eisland writes,

> Persons with disabilities must gain access to the socio-symbolic life of the church, and church must gain access to the socio-symbolic lives of peoples with disabilities.[13]

I definitely was a person with a disability, who was not "at home in the Christian Church," for the reason's Eisland mentions in her book: I could not access the socio-symbolic life of the

Church (the life of the church). And, the Christian Church would not access my socio-symbolic life being a person with Asperger (my autistic identity, culture and experiences). The Christian Church in recent years has definitely "universalized, rationized, and homogenized" human experience with over-generalizations, projections and partial truths. And, my self-understanding has not been affirmed by Christians and the Church at-large, as a result.

This concretely manifested itself in my teen-years on several different levels. First, I could not access the socio-symbolic life of the Christian Church because my public school education did not affirm my newly found Christian faith once I was mainstreamed into honors classes. In fact, the curriculum was downright hostile to Christianity. And, because of my diagnosis, I did not have the opportunity to go to religious schools.

Second, the church would not access my socio-symbolic life being a person living with Asperger, when I was a teenager, by forcing me to be in a youth group instead of attending adult Sunday school. Adult Sunday school was more "relevant," "accessible" and interesting to my experiences and spirituality, having been able to sit in on a few classes, before being not welcomed. While, local secular environmental and animal rights groups, allowed me to participate on adult fieldtrips and other adult functions. I never really had a concept of being a child, I always felt like an adult, even as a small child. I always felt like a miniature adult.

Most of the issues covered in the youth group which I attended were not "relevant" to me, boy-friend-girl friend relationships, drugs, alcohol and the like. And, I got very little individual attention and there was much conformity. Fear of "getting in trouble" and being morally and religiously deviant--- ran deep. Even when I almost broke out into tears after hearing a testimony about Jesus Christ on a retreat, no one had time to talk with me about my powerful religious experience. I was bored out of my mind. I hated being there. I did not feel like I belonged.

In this youth group, human experience was definitely "universalized, rationalized, and homogenized." They used as the basis of their module, a popular "myth" about Generation X, that we were all a bunch of depraved, amoral and out-of-control "punks" where "everyone was doing sex, drugs, smoking and drinking." When in reality, I came from a sector of Generation X, which was very serious, studious and chivalrous. I was not out there having lots of sex; I never did drugs, smoked or drunk alcohol-- my entire time in high school. And, most of teens there were not, either. That was not my reality! Or, their reality--- for that matter! But, I was particularly "hard hit."

Most disconcerting was the church's need to "force" me to make friends with peers my own age, which I had nothing in common with and was not "fitting in"--- instead of my usual custom of befriending adults, with the youth pastor there saying, "the bridge to adulthood is through your peers," contradicting decades of research in human development and men's studies which argues the exact opposite---that it the elders in the community--- ceremonially and pragmatically initiating me into manhood through a structured, ritualized mentoring process involving the Natural World, which is my real "bridge to adulthood."

Finally, during this period, my "self-understanding" was not affirmed or validated either, by individual Christians and the Church at-large, particularly my very special insights into nonhuman animal nature. I kept on getting into debates with religious people over the question, "Do animals have souls?" I strongly believed they do, many Christians I came into contact with, strongly believed they did not. Also, many did not support my views on animal rights, particularly on being strongly against hunting for population control--- where I did some activism in high school, trying to stop local hunts in my home county--- testifying before local governing bodies.

God found a way to make Christianity "relevant" to my personal socio-symbolic life.

First, in terms of accessing the socio-symbolic life of the Church, I was able to access it, through our family's Bible. For example, onetime with God, on a semester break, we did a Job 38-42 retreat and studied Job 38-42, from an ecological perspective within the context of the beautiful five-acre McGrillis Gardens in the bioregion of my birth (the Piedmont Plateau) and the Smithsonian National Zoo.

My mother would oftentimes read to me from the Hebrew Bible before going to bed, soothing and calming me down, where I experienced deep, mysterious peace. I would watch shows on television like "Mysteries of the Bible" with my family. I was also a big fan of "Touched By An Angel" when it was on air. We would have lively religious discussion in our Jewish household, at this time now in creative turmoil, because of my mother's decision to accept Jesus as her Jewish Messiah and her decision to start attending Christian Bible studies making some new Christian friends in the process, as a result. Some of the best friends, she has ever had. And, my mother would often give me Christian interpretations of the classics I was reading for High School Honors English. Such as making the argument that John Valjean in Victor Hugo's *Les Miserable* was a "Christ-like figure" or going to the National Cathedral to read, *Hunchback of Notre Dame*. I even picked-up some Christian philosophy of life at the youth group, which largely influenced what I understood the essence of Christianity to be. So, the youth group was not all negative.

If the Christian Church did not access my socio-symbolic life, my Lord did. We used to have long talks on my family's front porch, well after dark or in my bedroom. Or, even during times of crisis. Or, just plain have fun together. God would always tell me when I thanked him, "That I have all the time in the world." This really was the "honeymoon period" of our relationship. The Lord gave me an outlet to talk about theological questions important to me and surprisingly I found Him very sympathetic, even to my questions about animals and ecology and He provided a shoulder to cry-on when I felt overwhelmed by the popular opinion of the world, which was contrary to my convictions. God would literally spend hours with me at a time. Also, the Lord brought other spirits in Heaven for me to commune with.

The late-Rachel Carson, mother of the environmental movement, tutored me in Honors Biology, for a short while. And, we did some fieldtrips together--- until she disappeared from my life. A twelfth-century monk tried to tutor me in Latin, but on the first try, he failed at it and I never heard from him again. And, God Himself tutored me in Honors Anatomy and Physiology. It became God's custom afterwards to tutor me in all my subjects in school, once I went to college.

I also had some powerful religious dreams, then too. One time when I was sick, I had a dream that I became a spirit and I was in Heaven with all these great spirits, including Albert Einstein, and the largest blob was God. We were all wondering around this white landscape, than we wondered into a basement, which was identified to me where Hell was, an incinerator-like device. My mother also appeared in my dream, dinning on a dinner table which looked liked the torso of Jesus Christ and when God came to take her, she was so grateful to get saved.

I also had another dream where I was in Heaven, a large conservatory with plants of all kinds. At the base of the garden, was a giant on a giant throne, it was God and in my dream, God spoke, if I remember right, "All go to Heaven who respect me" or something to that effect.

Even through my unique human experiences were not honored by the church at this time, I did have individual Christians in my life who did serve as conservation partners and theological stimulation; these experiences gave me my Christian environmental commitments. I also had the opportunity to attend Christian environmental conferences and retreats in high school and college.

During this period, I also had the opportunity to watch the movie "Brother Sun, Sister Moon" about Saint Francis of Assisi. After watching that movie, I found Christianity to be "cool."

Finally, I found an outlet to affirm my "self-understanding" about nonhuman animal nature with, through my involvement as a teenager in the fledging Christian environmental movement and shortly with the Jewish environmental movement. Here, I began to develop a theological and spiritual basis for reconciling my views on animals and the environment, with my new Christian faith. And, I met other people who were also trying to do the same thing. This is where I made the decision to become a Christian, where I met Christians just like myself, with the same passion for the environment. Making my Christian faith that much more authentic. Now I could reconcile my Christian faith with my Idea of Nature.

So in essence, I made my commitment to become Christian and the obstacles for me becoming a Christian were overcome and transcended through the grace of the Holy Spirit and a few special people and groups. I was now able to continue on my "Soul's Journey Into God" having translated Christianity into my personal socio-symbolic life.

With Christianity becoming increasingly important in my life, now having accepted Jesus Christ as My Lord and Savior and personally Baptized by the Holy Spirit in a local creek, in my own bioregion (the Piedmont Plateau). Now I wanted to join my place in the Body of Christ, becoming an evangelist to the environmental and animal movements. Preaching the Good News, that God cares about His Creation. That environmentalism/animal rights can in fact be reconciled with Christianity. That Christianity is not inherently a foe to the Earth or the movement. This is where I got burnt! To this we now turn!!!

### *Finding Vestiges of God in Knowledge: Accessing Religious Socio-Symbolic Life*

In the early Christian Church, there was a Christian convert named Clement of Alexandra. Education historians Reed and Prevost describe his conversion process,

> He was born to pagan parents in either Athens or Alexandra. He received the standard education typical of a relatively wealthy boy and young man of his day. Converted while he was in his teens, he spent several years on a series of journeys searching for Christian scholars from whose discourses he could develop a better understanding of Christianity. His travels took him to southern Italy, Palestine, Greece, and the Near East before he settled in Alexandra.[14]

This describes the journey; I had to embark upon to access the socio-symbolic life of the Christian Church, as a person with Asperger. I definitely identify with Clement of Alexandra, in his quest to travel the entire ancient world, "searching for Christian scholars from whose discourses he could develop a better understanding of Christianity."

I ended-up going to my state university, which again was secular, because the Christian college of my choice which I applied to was negative about my disability and my family could not afford its tuition. As a result, I ending-up searching the entire country, looking for Christian groups to participate in and to fed and educate me in the faith. I had a greater selection of Christians to choose from, once I matriculated into the state university, however.

For the first time in my life, I came into contact with mainline Christian groups, such as the Wesley Foundation, the Student Methodist fellowship, which I promptly joined; even though I was not a Methodist. Here, I met Dr. Phil Bosserman (who this book is dedicated too), who wrote the forward and sponsored me for my first major treatise, *Creation Unveiled* (USA: Xulon Press, 2003). Allowing me to both study and do research in theology and earn academic credit at the time same. I liked the fellowship's focus on social issues versus the high school youth's narrow focus on personal purity. It was small and I had wonderful leadership opportunities which I was able to take advantage of, where my gifts were used and appreciated too.

Going to *Celebrity III*, before the change of the millennia, was a real "mountain top experience" for me, where I met politically progressive yet religiously sincere Christians, from all over the country. Here, I experienced a whole different approach to Christianity which defies straight-laced stereotypes of Christians being narrow-minded, personalistic and conservative.

I attended workshops on vegetarianism, science & religion and anti-fundamentalism. The whole conference was filled with protest & ethnic music, a New Years Eve disco party and many other multicultural worship experiences. With the highlight of the event, having a chance to hear, speak and personally meet former South African anti-Aparte political activist and Noble Peace Laureate, Anglican Archbishop Desmond Tutu. Archbishop Tutu gave an empowering, life-affirming speech. I felt like I was a part of the future of Christianity and that this was the future of Christianity in the twenty-first century.

I also explored other fellowships including The Newman Society, which was the Roman Catholic Fellowship on campus. I also liked this fellowship because it was very intellectual and very small. I was able to ask questions and get intelligent answers. I even for a short-time joined the African-American fellowship, where I was accepted as I was. Even, though I was white.

I also attended the Spirituality lecture series offered by the school, which also had a Christian speaker, a Roman Catholic priest. I also had a chance to walk a Labyrinth, which was brought to the school's art gallery.

My school, although it was a state university, with a separation between church and state, was unusual in that a certain core group of professors thought that students also needed to get their spiritual side fed too, along with their intellectual-side and must have an opportunity to learn about, talk-about, explore and experience different religious traditions, defined as spirituality, to not be exclusive or privilege one tradition over another or overly define spirituality to the students. One of the outcomes was this Spirituality lecture series, which I faithfully attended most of the talks.

I also supplemented, my secular, if sometimes anti-Christian education, with studying at the Au Sable Institute of Environmental Studies headquartered in Michigan, a Christian training center for Christian students going into environmentally-related fields. I attended two-summers and a winter at Au Sable where I earned my Naturalist Certificate. At the Au Sable Institute I had the opportunity to explore my Christian environmentalism through taking such courses as "Environmental Ethics" and "Ecological Issues in Science and Religion." I also had access to an incredible library on ecotheology; I had the opportunity to attend special weekly Vespers Services sponsored by the Au Sable Institute and received transportation to attend Christian religious services at local churches.

Back at my secular university, my sympathetic advisor said, "The moment you walked into the room, I knew you were not a biologist, but you were a theologian or a philosopher." So, she worked with me to change my major from Biology to Liberal Studies, where I would still be able to pursue a Minor in Biology, but also pursue courses more of my interest, including my undergraduate research for my book, *Creation Unveiled* (USA: Xulon Press, 2003), adding Environmental Studies and Conflict Analysis/Dispute Resolution as my other minors for my Liberal Studies degree.

I also tried to take courses with Christian professors when possible, including a Roman Catholic history professor, whom I really respected, whom I took my required World Civilization Courses with, where I learned much about Christian church history and I also completed a directed study on "Christian Environmental History" with an environmental history professor, all of which prepared me to write my first major academic book, *Creation Unveiled* (USA: Xulon Press, 2003).

Still I wanted to go deeper in my Christian identity and I needed more support and formation.

This is where I got "burnt" on both ends:

***First***, my secular university discouraged me from making positive connections between Christianity and environment/animal rights, because of the anti-Christian bias found in the environmental/animal movements towards Christianity, at the time. ***Second,*** in the Christian world, because I was not a "cradle Christian" and because of my autism and because of my unique interests and beliefs, as a result, I still had trouble "fitting in." Not the least of which--- ***a regular church community***. I also wanted a faith community that not only included me, but also included Animals and the Earth, or at-least was neutral toward them.

The later I have talked extensively in other works, so I want to elaborate on the former.

The *first resistance* I encountered with the Christian Church---involving directly and overtly my disability related issues, since I was an adult, was when I attended a conference on Christian environmentalism, my sophomore year of college. The people there were constantly trying to control me, because of my young age, from "over participating" in the conference and instead wanted me to be "meek and humble," something that I was not at the time. One of the leaders, no matter what I said, kept shooting me down, constantly criticizing me and overall being very negative towards me. This started even before the conference. He eventually "drove me crazy" and I got angry at him and his response was to say--- "You are not a very loveable person." Till this day, I have not recovered from this wound. I was absolutely traumatized and devastated as a result, a natural, normal human reaction to being "poorly treated."

The *second resistance* I encountered is when I attended a Roman Catholic mass on campus, for I wanted to be a Roman Catholic like Saint Francis of Assisi and maybe even become a Franciscan friar. During this period in my life, I was struggling with a powerful "holy longing" and wanted to give my entire life to God like Saint Francis did, many centuries ago. I went with a friend of mine at the time and I asked my friend if I could take the Eucharist and before my friend even had a chance to respond, this middle-age Roman Catholic woman "chimed in," which I never met before, who was not even a member of the campus fellowship community, blurted-out bluntly, "Are you a Catholic?" "No-but I am a Christian?" "Well, you can't receive the Eucharist!" She said sharply, in a cold, unwelcoming, tone of voice.

I was so devastated and upset that I stormed-out of Mass, in almost tears. I learned later that the Roman Catholic Church has this policy, that only Roman Catholics can take the Eucharist. A policy, which I will argue later, must be changed, to accommodate peoples with disabilities and anyone who has felt like an outcast by society, for any reason.

I also had another Eucharist "run-in" on a school trip in Florida. I went to take the Eucharist with the other Roman Catholic students and a professor and I did not know how to hold my hands. So this woman "chimed in," "Are you Catholic?" Blushing, then the Roman Catholic professor lied for me, "He just hasn't been to Mass in a while!"

Then, there were the "run-ins" with religious institutions. Part of my "holy longing" was that I wanted to engage the Franciscan world. So, I applied to this retreat center, which was recommended to me by a Franciscan friar, but the guesthouse brother at the retreat center quickly "in automatic" made the decision, to reject me. Without consulting me, talking with my required references, or even offering me an explanation, just a vague, "This is not the right expression of Franciscanism for you." Acting like there was much prayer involved---which there was not---I felt hurt and angry.

I also approached a different Franciscan friar at another time to look into the possibility of becoming a friar; he took down my address and never got back to me. I learned from my Roman Catholic History Professor that "they wouldn't take someone like you very seriously. They would just see you like a bee going to flower to flower, to get nectar." I began to feel like a "second-class Christian" because I was not born into a nice Irish or Italian Roman Catholic family. All these experiences were absolutely devastating to me and absolutely "broke my heart." They were very wounding!

Some of my worst "run-ins" with religious institutions happened when I was applying to graduate school. The first graduate school, I applied to, was a Roman Catholic institution--- I was "unexpected" after I was "accepted." When a professor from a different department, whom I met with more informally--- "backstabbed" to the director of the program, posing as an "expert on autism," being only the parent of a child with a disability, "freaked-out" the director, by telling them that I have autism and all the terrible things that could happen. Then my therapist at the time had to call the program director and tell them that making my reacceptance into the program, contingent on my "diagnosis" was "unethical," "possibly even illegal," educating her about the "Americans with Disabilities Act," where my therapist would have no part in "disclosing confidential information."

I was promptly "reaccepted" back into the program. Yet, I was so embittered by this experience that I eventually decided not to go, especially since I was not given on-campus housing and I could not do the program "distance-intensive" at home with my parents.

The next program I applied to was handled even more disgusting than the last. First of all, it was a Quaker institution, a religion which preaches tolerance. I found this place to be more like George Orwell's *Animal Farm*, "where all animals are equal, but some animals are more equal than others."[15] If I were "gay" or some other "deserving minority" I would have been accepted with absolute "open-arms." Instead I was dealt with--- with absolute suspicion, even fear. They "freaked-out" when my mother dropped the "A-bomb"[16] (autism) and said I was "autistic"--- disregarding my good grades, strong interest and positive letter of recommendations--- even the positive portrayal of my autism by my letter of recommendations. They even made their decision without even bothering to contact my psychiatrist or even my letter of recommenders, to get more information and instead on their own--- made an absolutely patronizing decision, which was even worse than "not accepting" me "at all"--- which is what they should have done. They accepted me "conditionally."

I was accepted "conditionally," "on probation" for "one-quarter," when I desired to do a "whole year." I would have to see "an external councilor" at my "own expense." I would have to "be on a schedule" or "routine." I would have to meet "manual labor requirements." If I did not meet "these requirements," I would be "asked to leave."

I was so infuriated, a totally understandable reaction to being unjustly excluded, humiliated and made to feel powerless, by a hypocritical organization, I ended-up getting angry on the phone, I told the middle class, privileged white male on the phone that "Not only does this reflect badly on the retreat center, but also the entire Quaker religion." He bureaucratlically responded, "cold-as-ice," "We don't want someone here with this attitude about Quakers." He then promptly rejected me from the program all together.

Did I tell you, he wanted my parents on the phone with me, here I was twenty-two years old and just graduated from college, Cum Laude and I was a full adult, my parents *are not* my legal guardians, yet he would only talk to me on the phone—if my parents were on the line. How paternalistic, insulting and degrading?

I know many people "in the left" like to idealize the Quakers, for their nonviolence and sense of social justice. I saw a different side of the Quakers, as a person with autism. Although I cannot speak for all Quakers or all Quaker institutions, my personal experience of Quakers is that they are anything but "nonviolent" or "tolerant," they are basically sanctimonious Northern bigots, who are emotionally violent, passive aggressive and cannot deal with anyone who is not like themselves.

*However* the tenets of Quakerism are all about "peace and love." The foundations of the Quaker religion are all about social justice and tolerance. George Fox was! William Penn was! Yet, I learned that sadly certain sectors of the Quaker-world have turned into *Animal Farm.* As a result, I cannot give today's Quaker religion a good letter of recommendation, for I have yet to have a good experience with a living, breathing Quaker. Most of them use their religion to "blue wash" their bigotry and "get there way." "Blue washing" is passing something off as "social justice" when it is anything but, like "green washing."[17] They are spiritual abusers of the worst kind! They need to be held accountable for their behaviors!

*Finally*, after another rejection, this time from a Franciscan school, I finally was accepted to Andover Newton Theological School, in the spring of 2003 to their Master of Arts in Research Program. I can now say that as of the spring of 2006 that I now have both my Master of Arts in Research and my Graduate Certificate in Science and Religion from the Schools of the Boston Theological Institute. ***I have even accessed the socio-symbolic life of the Church***, in the process.

Unlike my first choice, something better did come along. And, because of the flexibility of this program, there were no required courses, just a certain amount of credit hours in preparation for my thesis and a number of free electives and of course, writing and defending my thesis, this program was "an excellent fit."

Other benefits which made this program a "good fit for me," why "it worked" academically and spiritually for me, is that I could take a certain amount of my courses off-campus in the Boston Theological Institution Schools, offering a wider selection of courses. I was able to take courses at Boston College, Boston University, Weston Jesuit Theological School [now part of Boston College], even Harvard Divinity School-*which I did*. I took two courses at Boston College, one course at Boston University, one course at Weston Jesuit and even one course at Harvard Divinity School. The rest of my courses---were at Andover Newton.

That way, I could access different theological traditions and perspectives to "help find myself" and learn about the full diversity of the Christian religion. I was even able to take a course on Franciscan Studies at Weston Jesuit Theological School.

I could also take a certain amount of my courses on-line so I would not have to have complex "face-to-face" social interactions and have more time, flexibility and energy to pursue my own academic interests, related to my course materials. I was even able to do many independent studies, where I could go deeper exploring my own interests. I even got academic credit for going on a twenty-three day "Study Pilgrimage" to "the Franciscan Holy Sites of Italy" (Rome, Assisi and the Rieti Valley). I was even able to do an independent study on "animal rights theology."

Most importantly---I was able to live on-campus. I had a base. In addition, to being in close proximity to public transportation, I was within only a short-walking distance of the train and a beautiful, wild area called Webster Conservation Park where I could go-out to walk, study, pray and spend time alone with God.

In addition---I was also able to "weed" out classes which were not "good fits" for me, once I discovered what they were all about, because I was not burdened with an inordinate amount of requirements. And, I could add new classes in at the last minute. I fully took advantage of "add and drop periods."

I also was not so burdened down with a heavy course load that I could not pursue other interests and necessities such as be active in a local church community where I would receive additional support, pursue friendships, work on improving independence skills, take advantage of the many exciting and enriching opportunities in the Boston area, go deeper on my schoolwork---with God as my teacher--- adding additional readings and exercises and pursuing projects for my own growth, development and edification. This also gave me time--- to get my book *Creation Unveiled* published and distributed, as well as some time to promote it including presenting at an academic conference on Ghost Ranch, out in New Mexico.

Ghost Ranch was the magnificent, enchanted, Painted Desert ranch that inspired Georgia O'Keefe, now a spiritual retreat center of the Presbyterian Church. A land marked by blooming cactuses and gigantic rock formations the color of rainbows.

I also received "reasonable accommodations" for my disability--- mainly extended time for papers; there were no tests in the courses I took.

I also got an exemption for a required course called "Engaging Oppressions" which was required for all students at the theological school, but considering my history and psychology would have been inflammatory and redundant. Mainly, because they did not include the experiences of peoples on the spectrum and only briefly discussed physical disabilities and focused extensively on privilege. I could have easily been lumped into the category, "privileged white male." The courses main purpose for existing was to make sure the seminarians, particularly the older seminarians, had some knowledge of –isms, so to be aware of these issues when they graduate and work in the ministry field.

A course such of this could easily be expanded to also include neurotypicalism and abelism; anthropocentrism and speciesism; anti-Semitism, First Nation oppression and classism; men's liberation; generational issues; and critical social theory---for any oppressed minority group still being defined, so a group not included on "the agenda" would have the framework to engage in their own anti-oppression campaign.

Most people are now familiar with and are sensitive to racism and sexism, most racism/sexism today is really classism (e.g., the oppression of women in the Geographic South and lingering poverty, "de facto" segregation issues in America), covert racism/sexism (e.g., Northern racism repackaged as "globalization," having token women clergy or having Southern bigotry repackaged as "states rights") or "brown" racism---such as racism toward Latino-Americans, Muslim-Americans, Indian-Americans, Jewish-Americans and Native Americans.

Therefore, students to be socially just--- also need in the twenty-first century--- deeper social analysis which also includes discussion of unconscious narratives, academic sociology, political economy, intercultural communication, activism training, an understanding of democratic principles, opportunities to tell their story and practical guidance. Mere sensitivity training is not "good enough."[18]

Many Generation Xers, which I fall under have already been "sensitized" to these issues since a young age and as a result were also exempted or given an alternative curriculum, which allowed them to go deeper. One peer friend of my mine, who was a professional artist, was able to do a project which involved painting local people who were homeless in a particular neighborhood in Boston.

In terms of housing, when a room became available, I was able to have my own studio-with my own bathroom and kitchen--- which was absolutely necessary for my success in housing.

Finally, I had an excellent major professor which I worked very well with, which was "no small blessing" in today's "cut-throat" academic world. He was very sympathetic, patient, understanding, respectful, open-minded and dedicated. He also met frequently with me, while I was in the program, sponsored me on independent studies, he would write-out summary points at the end of our meetings so I would know exactly what was discussed. No confusion!
Even till this day, I am still in contact with him!

Another one of his strengths is that he was not a perfectionist, in that he still maintained strong academic standards, but he was also reasonable and fair---if something met minimum academic standards for the field--- that was fine with him. Nothing additional was needed or expected. And, there was room for creative thinking, too. You did not have to be "scrupulous" in most cases—this reduced unnecessary anxiety in my life. He was definitely a "good enough" guy!

Yet, he was one of the most respected and esteemed professors in the school, a tenured professor who has published extensively in his field, is constantly presenting at academic conferences, is on all-kinds of committees and has traveled around the world including living in India and China for extended periods of time.

His classroom lectures are very dense and erudite. Students have to work very hard in his classes to complete the material and receive a good grade. So, he is a testimony, that one can still be a strong professor and still accommodate the various needs of a person with Asperger or anyone else with a learning disability.

So a student with Asperger can come to a Belief in God, even study and understand academic theology too. For example, my professor let me do my thesis topic of my choice, but just reframed it into the right form, so that it would be more academic. It worked-out for the best, for I produced a much better thesis and in the process, created my own systematic theology, my own "sacred canopy," which I can still use to "put-the-world-together" and make meaning from.

Because of the "good fit" of the program I was in, I was able to access the socio-symbolic "life of the church," forming my Christian identity.

During this period, I was also baptized officially into the Christian Church, at a beautiful baptism which I was allowed to design by the church I was attending at the time--- which was preformed with total emersion in Walden Pond. The same Walden Pond, whom early preservationist Henry David Thoreau lived for two years in a simple cabin. I made my focus, the symbolic baptism of the environmental movement, based on Lauren Pope's (president of the Sierra Club) well-known speech "Apology to the Church."

This was also the period in my life, when God arranged for me to go into covenant with Saint Francis of Assisi in Heaven and I was able to talk with my beloved Saint Francis like I was able to talk with God. I also had the opportunity to meet some of Saint Francis's companions in Heaven too including Brothers Bernardo, Leo, Rufono, Juniper and Sylvester (later followed by Saint Anthony, Saint Bonaventure and Friar Wolf and more recently several of the Angels in Heaven).

This was the period when I was able to go on pilgrimage to the Franciscan Holy Sites of Italy: Rome, Assisi and the Rieti Valley.

I have found memories of sitting with the friars on a hillside above Assisi, looking down upon a landscape unchanged since the Middle Ages and I felt myself sitting peacefully with the brothers and for those few short moments, I felt like one of them. This was an experience, I will never forget. This was one of the highlights of my entire pilgrimage.

Here on a fallen, broken Earth, I was still struggling with belonging in the living Christian Church and if I were to make any continued progress on my "Soul's Journey into God"--- I would need to confront my past, not continue to run from it, "pretending to be normal," for my past was catching-up with me. I would need to embrace who I am and what I am--- a person living with Asperger. To this we now turn.

### *Finding Vestiges of God in Autism: Embracing My Autistic Identity*

Physical disability theologian Nancy Eisland writes,

> Living with a disability is difficult. Acknowledging this difficulty is not a defeat, I have learned, but a hard-won accomplishment in learning to live a life that is not disabled. The difficulty for people with disabilities has two parts really-living our ordinary, but difficult lives, and changing structures, beliefs, and attitudes that prevent us from living ordinarily.
>
> In American society, the temptation to hide our difficulties from others is endemic. For the person with a disability, denial has dangerous consequences. Physically, denial seduces us to ignore glaring physical warning signs. Emotionally, denial leads to atrophy. Ignoring disability means ignonoring life; it is the precursor to isolation and powerlessness.[19]

This definitely was the story of my life and a lesson, which I unfortunately have had to learn the "hard-way." Because of my intelligence, my longsuffering parents, the PCP toxic narrative that my mother was given when I was first diagnosed, "these kids do not get any better. Stick him in an institution and move on with your marriage."

Such disparaging advice to a young mother was coupled by the abelist special education system of the 1980s and 1990s which I grew-up in. Special education in those days was an abusive, boring even dangerous experience for me which held little promise for being college bound--- so my parents made a bold move.

My parents completely mainstreamed me into all honors and college preparatory courses. After tremendous success being mainstreamed in World Studies and Creative Writing in Middle School, in the middle of my first semester of my freshman year of high school, I was moved from a "level-four" (special education) to a "level-three" (inclusion) program, dumped "sink or swim" into Honors English and Regular Algebra. Alongside Honors American History and Environmental Science-which although a regular course, a college text was used.

My freshmen year of high school, I was completely mainstreamed into honors and regular classes, with only an hour of "resource room" and "reasonable accommodations." Getting only "bare-bones" accommodations mainly aimed at a person with mild learning disabilities--- such as untimed tests and the ability to take tests in a quiet room.

Even through the head of the learning center told my parents I would not succeed, by the end the first semester, I earned a "B" for the first semester in Honors English, with one of the most difficult teachers in the school.

I also earned "A's" and "B's" in my other classes too, only struggling in Regular Algebra, getting a "D," the first semester, but still passing.

With the help of an excellent math tutor, who was a retired math teacher, I was able to raise my grade up to a "C" by the time I graduated from high school.

After that initial semester, I never looked-back!

I went onto to successfully complete the second semester of Honors English, staying all four-years of high school in "Honors English." I completed all three years of my required history courses in honors classes. After acing "Regular Environmental Science," I went onto to take "Honors Biology." And, my senior year, "Honors Human Anatomy and Physiology." I made it all the way through "Pre-Calculus" in Mathematics. I successfully completed two-years of "Latin." I even made the "Honor Role," almost every semester and was inducted into the "National Honors Society," my senior year.

By the time I graduated, I was also a published author; I published an official publication for the Rachel Carson Council Inc… entitled *Rachel Carson In Carteret County, North Carolina: A Journey To The Edge Of The Sea* (1997) the non-profit organization where I did my required community service--- for the state of Maryland--- high school graduation requirement.

During this period, I also had the opportunity to stay in Rachel Carson's summer cottage in Maine and set-up my microscope at the very same desk where Rachel Carson wrote her environmental classic *Silent Spring*. My focus being for my community service--- visiting places which were important to "mother of the environmental movement," Rachel Carson.

The Rachel Carson Council Inc. offered me this volunteership, when on my high school's Earth Day Fair, a representative from the Rachel Carson Council, Inc. found my project on "Famous Environmentalists" which I did as part of my "Environmental Science" course.

I also was accepted into multiple colleges, including one where I received a scholarship. I ended-up going to Salisbury State University, now Salisbury University, in Salisbury Maryland. I achieved much success there too, graduating Cum Laude, writing my first major intellectual treatise *Creation Unveiled* (USA: Xulon Press, 2003) and for the first time in my life, I actually had peer relationships, even friendships.

I also had tremendous success, volunteering at the Salisbury Zoo, where I met Wounded Healer, the Canada goose with an injured wing whom some of you might have read about in *Creation Unveiled* (USA: Xulon Press, 2003). I, in addition, had the opportunity to study at the Au Sable Institute of Environmental Studies in Michigan where I earned my Naturalist Certificate. I also presented at the 2001 National Undergraduate Research Conference and most importantly, I did not have to "worry" about my disability issues.

I was fully accommodated for all my disability related issues in undergraduate. Including getting extended time on tests, having the ability to take tests in the test taking center and I was even able to take essay tests on the computer. The Vice President Of Student Affairs and my academic advisor, the people who dealt with my disability issues when they came-up, even gave me accommodations which I did not even request, but where essential for my survival and thriving in college, including Priority Housing and Priority Registration.

Priority Housing guaranteed me on-campus housing. Priority Registration guaranteed me that I would be able to take courses of my choice-without having to "worry" about classes I needed or wanted, being closed. My advisors also looked-out for me, such as reminding me to wear a coat when it was getting cold. I also had the option to receive free counseling and my parents hired a private tutor for me.

My freshman orientation, held in Algonquin Provincial Park, in Canada, allowed me to bond with other students and faculty members and got my freshman year off to a "good start"--- socially.

As a result, I adopted a view of my disability-which God has entitled-the "*shame-overcome-assimilate*" approach. I saw my autism as something which I was secretly ashamed of, something which I have successfully "overcame" and I was moving on with my life, something which I did not want to talk about, or dwell on. Something which I did not consider to be a major part of my identity. Something which I was deeply embarrassed about, every time I or someone else talked about it. These were the years I "*pretended to be normal.*"

I could get away with it, for I had the necessary support systems in place. This mentality was reinforced by the reality that my survival was based on "overcoming" as much as possible. The alternative was unthinkable. This created a profound sense of pressure to succeed. *No matter what the impact would be on my psyche or my physical heath*.

Even God *at this time* did not want to focus in on my autism, seeing me as "Whole in Christ" and was subsequently very taken aback at how society, particularly the Christian Church, responded to my autism, later on in life.

Yet, during this time, my Lord *was addressing it "behind the scenes"* without using the *label "autism."* Such as making sure that I made it to class and my other responsibilities, helping me get out of abusive relationships, preparing me for a major disappointment which I will talk about later and even showing much "grace" – even after my aggressive reactions.

Yet, there were some foreshadowing that *my secret was pursuing me*.

I was accepted to a Christian college, but that Christian college also had serious concerns about my ability to succeed in the program, based on a previous negative experience with a person with a disability. As a result, I was discouraged from enrollment. I never went!

My resource room teacher really tried to "cram" necessary "life skills" to be successful in college, my senior year of high school, even to point of being excessively hard on me, in frustration, calling me, "selfish" or that "you are the most selfish person in the world." Wounds which I have still not recovered from. "Selfishness" and "lacking empathy" is a common neurotypical misconception, even stereotype about peoples with autism.

Once I arrived in college, the faculty sponsor for the Outdoor Club, did not let me go on anymore climbing trips, after I almost fell, when mountain climbing. Some of my secondary disorders include issues with low muscle tone, motor coordination, motor planning and multitasking. It gave him a scare!

I had a mentor for about a year that absolutely insisted upon the Socratic Method and refused to agree with me. We had a vicious falling-out, over his inability to find "common ground" with me. Which I knew he had. At the time, I thought it had to do with my Christian faith being an environmentalist, which was certainly a major factor, but I learned latter that the Socratic Method was not a good model for learning for me, being a person with autism, because I am at a tremendous disadvantage "social-emotionally," because I all too often feel isolated and under attack from all fronts, by an unsympathetic society.

My best mode for oral intellectual discourse is "the dialectic" which is more of a "thoughtful conversation" than a "debate." The dialectic method also includes provisions for individuality, respectful disagreement even mutuality. Although, I can oftentimes hold my own in debates, what people do not realize is that I am an "outgoing-shy person" and although I might appear to be confident and firm, later I pay for it, through becoming what I used to call "tortured." I would be flooded with negative emotions. And, suffer greatly as a result. And, I would internalize too.

Then I was susceptible to horrible verbal reactions which would come out of nowhere. Onetime when I took a course on "Marine Mammals," this was a summer course, meaning long hours of field-work which began at 4:30am in the morning and ending about 10pm at night, not to mention lecture time and time to complete homework assignments and prepare for tests, "on-top-of" a cafeteria which only served "whites" to vegetarians--- one afternoon, we were having a class discussion about whale hunting. I got tired of defending my possession and the professor would "not back off" until I agreed with her. So I just "stormed away" from the picnic table. Later, the professor was so furious with me, that when talking about the incident, she had another middle age student, converse with me, about how she does not like my animal rights views. Then, the professor proceeded to call my validity as a Christian into question, because I did not have a faith community and did not have the "correct" Christian doctrines. I told her I could not find a faith community. She gave the most, cold and cruel response possible, "This might sound harsh, but you do things which make other people not want to bother to get to know you."

She then marched over to the dean's office after I did not do well on a test, the excuse she needed and got me "thrown-out" of the class. She continued to stalk me, while I was completing another class at the same time. By asking me to write a diary about my perspective, which I did, and then she ripped it to shreds with strident and judgmental comments. Causing me to react again--- aggressively. I have not totally recovered from this wound either. And, I was completely traumatized in the process…

One of the most devastating of these experiences was when I arrived my first semester in graduate school and learned upon taking a course on Franciscan Studies--- *that I can never become a monk or a friar because I have autism.* And, this is--- *despite all the progress I have made*. *My diagnosis alone would disqualify me from being included*.

This embittering revelation absolutely "broke my heart" and I was filled with much uncontrollable anger and rage as the result.

I felt like I have been "cheated out" of devoting my entire life to God. That, I would be condemned to a miserable "life in the world." I felt--- patronized, dehumanized and excluded. It made me feel like a second-class Christian.

Unlike other acts of oppression which have been targeted towards me--- my whole life. This time I was beginning to discover what academic sociologists call one's "*sociological imagination*," "*discovering ones place in history*." I was beginning to see the injustice and unfairness of it all. I was beginning to make the connection between my early childhood autism diagnosis and being excluded and discriminated against as a grown man.

Not because I was a Christian environmentalist, not because I was not a cradle Christian, but because of my diagnosis when I was three years old. This possibility enraged me to no end! After all I have tried to overcome, after all I have persevered through, after all my "hard work" and my diagnosis was still "holding me back." Not letting me pursue my dreams. I also concluded that *I did not deserve to be discriminated against*. *That this was contrary to the founders of these orders and their beautiful teachings*.

I also confronted them on this. Every time I meet a monk or a friar. I confronted them, trying to verify whether what I learned was true. Every time, I confronted one of them, they would "neither confirm nor deny it," "give me run-around," "get defensive," or even "shut-down" on me, all-together. This happened consistently.

So not only, was my rejection from being a first-order religious, a powerful example of my past continuing to haunt me and why embracing my past and my autism was essential to my own personal experience of peace, love and happiness. But this was both coupled and compounded by more pragmatic issues which I encountered, when I moved to Boston, to attend theological school.

Graduate dorm life which was radically different than undergraduate dorm life. Graduate dorm life involved sharing a communal kitchen and bathroom, dealing with people who could not deal with my disability and being reminded at every turn that I have a disability. Whether it was people stopping on the street and asking me, "Are you okay?" and not letting up. Or, having nasty "run-ins" at different churches. To getting nasty "social cues" from other neurotypicals which seem to come out nowhere, to having people just plain "freak-out" or "explode" on me. It was a non-stop barrage of abuse and humiliation. I could not even go out on the town and have fun and not be reminded. No matter where I went. People were always making me feel self-conscious of my autism. I felt like the persona in Ralph Ellison's Harlem classic, *Invisible Man*.[20] No matter what gifts I could share, no matter what my "content of my character" was, I was still seen as an autistic, as disabled, as different, as other.

I was even seen as a threat, something to be "scared" of. A problem! This was despite many years of trying to "overcome" my disability and trying to "become normal." It was like the book, *Ain't No Making It*[21] which I read in one of my college sociology courses. That just because you "work hard," there is no guarantee of success, if you were disadvantaged to begin with. You still remained poor. No "bringing yourself up by your bootstraps." In other words, ***the "shame-overcome-assimilate" approach was not working.***

It took me so far, but it could not take me no further. I reached a "glass ceiling." And, I kept banging my head up against it. Then, I had this very strange dream.

It all happened my third semester of theological school, when I was taking an on-line course called "Life as Pilgrimage." I had recently studied about different types of pilgrimage dreams for one of my required texts and then one night I went to bed. I had the strangest dream.

I dreamt that I was with my mother and father in my hometown of Rockville, Maryland. We stopped at a local city park. I was dragging a vacuum cleaner through the park which my father was trying to get me to let go of. I was walking down a path with all kinds of different people through an arid landscape of white rocks and sand. Then we walked down a path to a stone monastery on-top-of a massive rock promontory overlooking a vast rugged valley below. We walked into the stone monastery, the same color as the surrounding rocks, built from the same surrounding rocks.

I remember feeling so happy in this place "for the artificial and the natural were one." Inside the monastery were two paths. One path took you to cells shaped like grottos. Inside each grotto--- there were taxidermy displays of wild animals liken to what sees in Nature Centers. The other path took you to an overlook of the valley below, where there were encampments in the distance- little tiny wooden houses. And, unlike the surrounding landscape, the valley was actually green and verdant from this overlook.

Then just as I was really having a good time, my parents called me, telling me-that it is time go. I remember in my dream-them taking me to this dinner and ordering malts, then having an argument and then waking-up.

God revealed to me--- that this dream embodied all major archetypes of pilgrimage dreams (common human experiences).

Later that year I presented at the "Colloquium on Religion and Violence" at Ghost Ranch, in New Mexico, on a paper based on my earlier book *Creation Unveiled* (USA: Xulon Press, 2003) I had a major disillusioning professional crisis-where I learned from God that I do not "fit into any of the boxes" and that it is okay to encompass all of the boxes and embrace all my different facets and commitments.

I saw both A) a Mosque on an arid promontory in Northern New Mexico in "real life" and B) I visited a Pueblo where Native Americans, Roman Catholics and the Natural World were living in peace and harmony with each other. The Native Americans---is my ecological side. The Roman Catholics--- is my Judeo-Christian side. The Natural World--- is my autistic wild side. Thus began my process of "letting go" of trying to "fit in" and my pilgrimage of healing from "compassion fatigue."

No more will I try to seek salvation in ideology, in a particular movement or research program. Pigeonhole myself into a particular perspective. Be "force-fit." Define my identity by a particular figure, ideology, or movement. But, embrace all which is true. Embrace all my different facets.

Different sides. All my loves. All my passions. In other words, be myself. Taking what is true from different figures, ideologies and movements and leaving the rest behind.

I was ready to "loose [my] life for [God to] save it" (Luke 9: 24). To find my true identity and embrace it, instead of my past pattern of relying on different personas or charisms, to form my identity. And, I felt a kind of "emptiness" as I went to give my talk. As a result. A type of Pascal Death had occurred within me.

After a while, I began to lose interest in the conference. Opting instead of listening to papers, spending time with my Lord and Saint Francis, out in Creation. I attended a talk or two, some special events. I kept my "mini-pilgrimage" to the Franciscan Holy Sites of Chimayo, which I signed-up for. I sold a few more copies of my book, but mostly I befriended a domestic donkey, whom I named Brother Ass. I went birdwatching, hiking, I walked the outdoor labyrinth, exploring some of the most beautiful scenery in the world, away from some of the snobbish people I have ever met.

After returning from the conference, during this same season in my life, I found a brochure for a conference sponsored by a Roman Catholic group on the topic entitled "peoples with development delays." God recommended that I pick one up and sign-up, for God thought this would be a good place to work through my autism issue. And, that this would be an opportunity to get justice for Daniel.

My entire academic career I have been learning about how to get justice for every group imaginable and all this time, I was still being oppressed. I had still not seen Martin Luther King's Promised Land, for myself. I was continuing to be oppressed and excluded, as other groups were enjoying much liberation and justice, at least in certain circles, mostly the circles that I was most interested in associating with, the liberal-progressive ones.

So I signed-up and went-out and it turned-out that this conference was scheduled right after I had my final disenchantment experience in New Mexico, having "given-up" on the "shame-overcome-assimilate" approach to my life and my disability. I was ready to work through my autism issue.

I went to the conference and shortly later, I fired my creepy childhood psychiatrist. I got re-diagnosed from Pervasive Development Disorder to Asperger's Syndrome with anxiety and depression (a less stigmatizing diagnosis). I found a new psychiatrist in Boston. I advocated to be moved out of an abusive, dysfunctional dorm situation to a new dorm with my own bathroom and kitchen. I advocated to be taken off the school meal plan which was not equipped to deal with vegetarians and was making be ill. I started taking ownership of my independent living skills and my health for the first time in my life. I started researching neurodiversity including how the oppression of Aspies such as myself and that of nonhuman animals are linked. But most importantly--- I finally accepted that I was a person with Asperger's living in a hostile, unsympathetic neurotypical society. I was finally able to embrace my autistic identity, including discovering the strengths of autism.

Now I was able to begin to start the task of redefining myself in light of this new revelation. Continuing my "Soul's Journey into God."

### *Finding Vestiges of God in Neurotypical Society: My Initiation into Manhood*

#### *Self Formation*

Richard Foster (a popular Christian writer) describes the spiritual self-formation process,

> Perhaps we could think of spiritual formation as a pattern, a series of concrete actions that will gently move us toward transformation in Christ. The disciplines themselves, however, are not transformative. The transformation in us is God's work. It is a work of grace. The deep transformative grace comes to us not through our own doing but as pure gift.
>
> And yet something is demanded from us; the free gift of ourselves, our submission, our willingness to change, our ascent to God's grace. In the end our yes is what's required. In our own words and in our way, we need to say, 'Speak Lord, your servant is listening.' We need to say, 'Be it done to me according to your will.'[22]

Yet, I needed time and space, to engage on this necessary spiritual task being a person with Asperger. I needed to engage on this task, for all my life being a person with Asperger, other people have been forming me with their own exceptions for my life, mainly to make me "normal." Be like everyone else, so I can "function" in the world, regardless of its impact on my self-esteem, my personal happiness or my sense of dignity or even my human rights.

For example, when I was a boy, I used to draw pictures of stoplights and maps. My parents would come into my room and take my pictures away and throw them out. Then my mother would break-down and cry. My mother was lead to believe by respectable experts in the 1980s that my savant-like behaviors were a sign that they were not able to "cure" my autistic ways. She believed what the professionals told them, that autism was a terrible disease which needed to be cured or I will end up in an institution the rest of my life. My parents did this out of love, it is just that as a family, we did not have many options and were given an extremely "toxic narrative" to work with. They as my parents wanted me to live a normal, functioning, productive life, as any parent would want, but did not realize that there is a major difference between "being functional" and "being happy."

I asked myself the questions. What is the point of being "functional" and being "a walking dead person"? What is the point of being able to take showers and wash my own clothes and keep-up friendly relations which I did not even care about and having an empty life---vocationally and spiritually? The answer was---no point! So for many years, I did not take attempts to work on my social and independence skills very seriously.

I was put in daycare as a child, not because my mother worked, for my mother wanted me to see what "normal" children were like. I spent most of the time, by myself stemming, sleeping and being in my own world and overall being bored out of my mind. The movies which they played every Friday used to frighten me and I never watched them. Hiding from them. I also remember being grossed-out by a doll of E.T. I only occasionally reached out to other children or participated in some of the structured activities.

I was also thrown-into a neurotypical Boy Scout troop. It was bearable, while it was run by a very gifted, caring and sensitive scoutmaster with an excellent sense of humor, but once he left, it degenerated into a very abusive and negative experience. Where I became a constant target and overall it was becoming all-around "junk" in my life and I languished there for many months, until my parents and I were able to finally let go of it.

From the beginning, the other scouts used to poke fun of my deep personal spiritual connection to the Natural World. I was mocked, humiliated and abused-constantly. Throughout my experience. By both other scouts and even other parents. Even the way the Natural World was experienced by them, was alien to me, "Point-A to Point-B" hiking--- most of the time, instead of stopping to savor every bird, flower or tree. Expect for special activities. I was so glad to get out and do activities which were more authentic and life-giving.

I learned within the last year while reading a book on male child abuse that the "real reason" why I was not accepted by the other boys was that this fun-loving, "cool" scoutmaster was showing us pornography and sexually explicit movies which portrayed women in naked, sexually provocative, objectified roles, while helping us to divide women up into "mothers," "bitches" and "prostitutes." He also made many homophobic slurs to argue why homosexual boys and youth should be excluded from Boy Scouts. I most likely never "fit in" for I came from a very progressive family which never taught me to objectify women or homosexuals, I *was not* sexually active and some of my autistic behaviors could easily have been mistaken for what are now called "Queer" behaviors (straights that have homosexual-like behaviors).

Nevertheless, an adult exposing minors to pornography, explicit adult movies and homophobic thinking creates a climate of bullying for both gays and straights alike and socializes children and youth to a life of abuse and bigotry. This is why such behavior by adults is technically classified as "childhood sexual abuse." It's against the law!

Whether it was daycare or Boy Scouts, there was but one standard, one expectation, for my life- "becoming normal." To use hyperbole and taken to its logical conclusion, being a drug dealer was okay, as long as it was "normal." Regardless of whether it was moral, virtuous or even made me happy.

For example, the replacement scoutmaster took me fishing one-day while away on a week-long Boy Scout camp. We caught fish and the fish were promptly killed. I began to feel very guilty, about whether what I was doing was wrong, "a sin." His response, "Sin a little!"

It was often the custom in special education to pick the "coolest" kid in class and use him as an example, of what good social skills look like. Not taking into consideration that I might not have anything in common with that person, or might not want to be like that person, or even want to spend time with that person. More "junk" in my life.

The adults in my life were filling my life with "junk" left and right. Relationships which I did not want to be in. Groups which I did not want to be a part of. Taking precious time away from me exploring my interests and passions. Forcing me to live my life, by other people's expectations. Mainly be "normal." As a result, my sense of self, suffered as a result. And, it backfired too.

For many years I *did not* take opportunities to work on my social or independence skills, for I equated them with taking my identity away from me. Professionals would not address my emotional life either, even when I requested it, instead opting only to focus on social and independence skills. Not getting to the roots of my problems, where I continued to suffer. For example, I had a psychiatrist who when I onetime got passionate about something in a family meeting, his response, "O-that is just OCD!"

In the process, leaving untreated very serious anxiety and depression issues, at their own peril, for not only has this caused me much grief over the years, it has even impacted my relationships with other people, the very thing they were trying to work-on with me. For example, "the fear and the dread" were put into me by professionals about getting negative "social cues" from neurotypicals, even telling me that people could be quietly rejecting me, making me scared every time someone gives me a social cue. Even till this day. I live in much fear of rejection.

It was only many years later that these issues were finally dealt with. And, I can now say, that I have an excellent psychiatrist, who is beginning to address some of these issues. But, I needed to engage in much "self-formation" to reach this point.

The desire to engage in spiritual formation, was codified my junior year of college, when I took a course called, "History of Violence and Nonviolence In American History," where I had the opportunity to study Martin Luther King's Jr. four models for engaging in direct action: "Data Collection," "Dialogue," "Self-Purification" and "Direct Action."

God translated this model to my process of human development, my first two years of college (undergraduate)-I engaged in "Data Collection," I was currently engaging in "Dialogue," so after I graduated college, it would be time to engage in the third stage, "Self-Purification." Liken to the experience of the prophets and Lord Jesus Christ going out into the Desert or the Forty-years the Israeli Lights wondered in the Wilderness, God promised me an "Intellectual Promised Land," a place where I can engage in "self-purification," in preparation to go-out "into the world" to do "Direct Action." God also advised me, that I would not be ready to work for paid employment, until I completed a "self-purification" process.

Then, I turned twenty-one years old and God said my birthday present for turning twenty-one, was attaining "self-agency." It was not until many years later, that I realized the full significance of what God was offering me. My life at twenty-one did not feel like I had self-agency. What God did do, was plant a very significant idea in my head. An idea, which allowed me to engage in spiritual formation, which eventually lead to an authentic and powerful sense of self-agency in my life. And, embracing my autism and learning about and forming that side of myself was an essential part of that process.

We both decided that this place would be a graduate school environment. We both agreed that a Bachelor's degree would be insufficient preparation for employment and life. That something was missing. We agreed on this particular graduate school-which unfortunately did not work out. Although, God was very positive at the time, that this was my "Intellectual Promise Land." It took me several tries until I found Andover Newton Theological School.

God did finally follow through and found for me an "Intellectual Promised Land" and I ended-up going to Andover Newton Theological School in Boston. Here, I started to engage in my self-formation process. I was in Boston, while my parents were in Maryland. This gave me some "breathing room" from my family to make progress in my spiritual self-formation.

I gained much self-knowledge, which I could not have gained anywhere. Knowledge, I needed to be both happy and functional, for I actually had time to think things through and find myself.

This was also the time in my life, where I also embarked on a twenty-three day pilgrimage to the Franciscan Holy Sites of Rome, Assisi and the Rieti Valley. A dream of mine-which I was waiting for and trying to make possible for many years. This was another major growing experience. Here, I learned additional self-knowledge: First of all, I learned that all my problems will not go away if I move to another country. I came to peace with the reality that I live in America. My sister believed that the "root of my problems" was the fact that I live in America and American culture was a misfit for me. I came to realize that reality was not better in Italy. That Italy was not my home, but America. Yet, I do need "healing spaces," I do need the right socio-physical environment to survive, thrive and be happy.

I learned that I would be happier living in a small town or rural environment, possibly, in a Mediterranean climate such as New Mexico, Arizona or California, though.

I learned that I must not be traveling in groups to get the full pleasure of an experience because of my alternative phenomenology--- being a neurodiverse human.

I need to be traveling alone--- with just God, Francis and the Brothers.

This is because I have a very different "spirituality of place" than other people. And, this caused interpersonal conflicts. This became painfully apparent on this pilgrimage. Where my times alone, where my highlights. And, least stressful. This trip codified this reality---although after some experiences in colleges, I was becoming apprehensive of group trips.

I learned that my plight was very similar to the lepers of the Middle Ages, that the lepers were my "archetypal ancestors."

I learned that I am to look forward to the Messianic Age, instead of backwards to the Middle Ages and here I would find everything I am looking for.

I felt before, if only I lived in the Middle Ages, if God put me in the Middle Ages, I would be happy. But I learned otherwise, at Lagos Trasimeno, the island where Francis fasted for forty-days. I saw the manor of the man who let Francis stay on the island, in absolute ruins. And, the remains of the manor were being used as a garbage dump and its once beautiful garden were overgrown with weeds. Francis in Heaven revealed to me, that all his people had to offer me as a legacy was "a bunch of buildings being used as a garbage dump, and an order, which I cannot even join. He wished "as a father, he could provide more for his children. Then he pointed to the Lord's Creation and showed how our Heavenly Father could do a much better job providing for me, than he could." Francis also encouraged me "not to look back to the Middle Ages but forward towards the Kingdom of God where I will get everything I am looking for."

Finally, I learned that the pilgrim miracle promised to all those who visit Lagos Trasimeno was for me to be comfortable in "my own skin."

I even developed a new appreciation for taking care of my living space upon visiting the Monte X community in Italy, who provided a safe-haven for outcasts and addicts who get healed without psychiatry or medication, through long hours of manual labor, daily supports groups, fraternal living and a mission to create beauty. Although, Monte X "turned-out" to be the wrong community for me at that time, I did take their teaching of creating beauty and applied it to creating beauty in my own personal living space.

I also received much support and affirmation from other pilgrims including one Franciscan Sister (Sister Helen-who I mentioned in the acknowledgement section of my book *Have Mercy on me, an Ecological Sinner*) who wrote a poem about me. I would like to share it with you, for it describes my charism being a person with Asperger, what I have to offer the Christian Church and The World, being a person with Asperger and how my new identity which was forming in me, as the result of my self-purification process which I was engaging in.

I *do not* include this poem to be pampas or boastful and it is important to contextualize some of the language and values of this poem. Some language might come across as the language of "virtuous suffering," but knowing this woman personally very well and her cultural context being a Roman Catholic, she meant more than mere pious pity, she certainly *did not* mean it to be patronizingly in anyway. Sister Helen more saw the good, that there was and is, in my autistic identity, my subsequent gifts and witness, as well as the Holy Spirit working through my autism.

Also, some language might come across to some as the language of conformity, but it is important to take the advice of my tenth grade Honors English teacher that "everyone conforms." Even those who are "non-conformists are conforming to not conforming" or to a subsequent sub-culture.

In my case, what she was referring to was trying to "conform to things" I wanted to be a part of. Not just conforming for the sake of conforming. This was the type of conformity she witnessed in me on the pilgrimage. With this guidance, below is her poem, in her own words.

> Please meet my friend Daniel.
> A volcanic heart erupting with the love of Francis.
> An energizer mind filled with questions
> And ideas stumbling over one another
> As they escape; and sometimes sprinkled with laughter.
> (Are the answers given really questions for my heart?)
> Eyes that mischievously draw you into another world.
> A captivating smile intermingles with a pondering frown.
> Dancing feet and gesturing arms signally excitement and restlessness
> As he scans the horizon.
> Abstraction is a foreign land.
> Creation is the homeland needing to see, feel, touch, sit on, walk on and be with.
> Reality is not his strong suit yet <u>his</u> reality is a strong suit.
> A bruised spirit searching for a home within and without-
> Desiring desperately to fit in.
> Shackled by the pain of rejection.
> Conversing with Francis and God,
> He dons his straw hat, picks-up his water bottles, and dragging his jacket, he continues his journey.

If on your travels your heart meets Daniel, know you have been given a gift.
Personally, he has taught me the meaning of unconditional poverty.
I have met the poor suffering Crucified Christ who is in each of us.
Thank you. Daniel.

Finally, during this last year at theological school, I took a number of other steps which could be defined as "fleshing-out" my spiritual self-formation process.

First, with my graduation date approaching and losing my precious studio apartment, returning to Washington D.C. to move in my family--- for I did not have the money to live elsewhere. And, with the pressure for me to work, brimming from my parents. God decided to help me discern what my trade was--- I had not even identified what my trade was. I was completely clueless on what to do after I graduated in terms of paid employment, outside of getting a doctorate degree.

I did not care for the employment options available and most of them played into my disability and very seldom took into consideration my strengths and my interests. Many required me doing things against my conscience. I had also developed this fear over the years that a job meant "selling your soul." I picked this up from my environmental studies days. So after a number of exercises, we identified my trade as being a professional writer/researcher. That I can work as a writer for an organization which I believe in.

This was before Amazon.com special self-publishing program for authors.

Now I am able to work full-time as an *independent professional writer* and *government disability services* allows me to live independently in my own apartment where I no-longer have to worry about going hungry, thirsty or "ending-up on the street," nor do I ever have to choose between eating and a "right livelihood" ever again.

Also, *during this period*, by fate, I woke-up at 6 AM, one Saturday morning; I hardly am ever up at that time on Saturdays for I observe the ritualized Jewish Sabbath. By fate, I just happened to turn on the television. Being advertized was Lucinda Basset's *Attacking Stress, Anxiety and Depression* program. God encouraged me to go to the phone and order her free tape. Which I did, it turned-out that the tape was just an advertizing for her program. So, I ordered the entire program, for a free trial basis. Since, I was also fasting from television during this period; we thought this would be a good thing to listen to, while I ate my meals. Also, I ordered the month supply of vitamins, which came with the program.

The vitamins and tapes absolutely changed my life forever. While listening to her tapes and doing her homework exercises, I began to work through the issue of "worry" and began to deconstruct all these destructive habits which I have learned over the years, which has lead me to suffer from very serious anxiety and depression, unnecessarily. I began to develop strategies for confronting my chronic worrying and was able to name the different things causing my worrying whether it was obsessive scary thoughts, "what if" thinking, panic attacks, anger, guilt, negative thinking, etc.

She was very helpful in giving me a good framework for addressing negative thinking. Oftentimes people have used the term "negative thinking" as a way to simplify, whitewash over, and trivialize my problems. But, she helped me to reframe the categories of negative and positive thinking. "Positive thinking is really empowerment thinking." And, that one must develop empowerment or possibility thinking, along the lines of what is believable, something that the negative mind would actually believe.

I learned that I was "passive assertive" and needed to be more assertive versus passive aggressive or just plain aggressive. It took me a number of years, to gain mastery of this. Mainly because of the social skills involved. And, I have a ways to go. But, I feel that I am getting better.

I also developed a better appreciation for the importance of exercise and a good framework for developing a viable exercise program, how food impacts my moods and since Lucinda Bassett is a Christian and the program was very sensitive to Christian issues--- I was able to integrate this program theologically. Unlike other psychological interventions in my life. For example, I learned that I do not have to feel guilty for putting myself first, because I need to fill-up myself, so I can give to others.

Although this program was designed for neurotypicals--- in mind, God helped translate these exercises and insights into relevancy for my life experiences. With God's help, I learned to separate the concept of realism in psychological contexts from political contexts. That "realism" at the psychological level---- is a good thing. It means being reasonable.

God contextualized the principles and exercises which were not relevant or contradictory *to* my experiences and value-system. He also added additional exercises too, which were particularly relevant, using the framework of the last week's lesson. For example, we spent hours writing out strategy sheets and hanging them up in my apartment. I could not have done the self-talk component without my Lord "whispering sweet words in my ears."

Still till this day, I sometimes listen to her relaxation tapes, whenever I take a nap, go to sleep at night, or become stressed. I also for a brief while became active in the free on-line support group, where I learned about the difference between therapy and psychopharmacology and that I must not go to a psycho-pharmacologist for talk therapy. I was actually doing this for a while and getting hurt in the process. The psychiatrist, whom I saw in Boston at the time, when I came to him about my "fear of punishment," response was that it is legitimate to be scared about going to jail, "that when you commit murder, you go to jail." Another time I was having dorm problems and his response was, "Too bad, there is not a pill, which can solve this problem."

"Obsessive scary thoughts" were more complicated and till this day, I struggle with chronic obsessive scary thoughts. But, I know how to counter them and manage them, with God's help. Although it can be an arduous process though. I also struggle with what Basset calls "growth spurts" where my whole anxiety and depression comes backs, but I am now able to "fight back." And, refute it, even though I cannot completely eradicate it. And, some experiences I have gone through just challenges the limits of what "positive thinking" can explain. So it requires some work to "stay positive."

In terms of the vitamins, I even got more amazing results. This was the closest to a miracle I have ever come. Between the fasting from food and television, the healthy practices, the Bassett program and the vitamins, I was never healthier in my life. I lost weight, I engaged in a massive yeast die-off which caused me to get rashes all over my body-until they disappeared and never returned. I had more energy. My thesis advisor even remarked at how productive I was and how quickly I was getting my thesis chapters out. I ended-up acing my defense and getting an A on the graded portion of my thesis. All on just one meal of day!

I have never gotten the results or the progress, like I did that one Lent. All these things have plateau out, the vitamins, the Bassett program and the other healthy practices. God believes that these things are still "buoying me up," though. And, that "difficult life situations" have interfered with my treatment and that I would be in much worst shape without them. Also, God contends that the fasting might have played no small role in these almost miraculous results.

I also read two healing books during this period. One was on "post-traumatic stress disorder" and another on "toxic churches."

God contended that I suffer from "post-traumatic stress disorder" because of how society has responded to my disability--- which was overwhelmingly negative, dysfunctional, abusive and all-around hurtful and tacky. We were finally vindicated when my latest psychiatrist was willing to test to see if I had Post Traumatic Stress Disorder. I tested positive!

Getting a PTSD diagnosis changed radically how I was treated by medical professionals, an even greater "turning point" than getting an Asperger's diagnosis for now I was treated more as a "survivor" than a "mistake." For the first time in my entire life, I am being treated as a "whole person" with "dignity and respect" by medical and mental health professionals.

It took all these years to become officially diagnosed because the professionals were secretly afraid of the whole "refrigerator mother controversy," this is because by the time I came around in the 1980s, "psychoanalytic approaches" were being discouraged for the treatment of autism spectrum disorders instead opting for "more behavioral approaches." Now for the first time in decades--- psychoanalysis is being revisited--- because it turns-out that not only do autists such as myself have emotions and an inner life like everyone else, God made our nervous system in such a way that we psychologically heal from anxiety, depression and bad experiences through getting it "off our chests"--- I cannot "psychologically bury" myself, I do not know how.

True--- there *is not* a valid foundation for the "refrigerator mother" principle, "that autism is the result of bad mothering," but there is no reason to believe that humans with autism can also get traumatized, be abused and suffer and develop PTSD as a secondary disorder--- as a result, a condition which also needs to be treated alongside "cognitive behavior therapy." In fact, it is my "hard-won" experience that "cognitive behavioral therapy" is actually dangerous, if underlying trauma and PTSD issues are not acknowledged and addressed. In my case, it led to increased anxiety and depression, suicidal thoughts, elevated aggression, sleep disruption even "psychological destabilization."

The other book on "Toxic Churches" was also very helpful; giving me a criterion for what characterizes a "Toxic Church." I came to the conclusion after reading this book that many of the Churches which I have been dealing with including the Roman Catholic Churches, qualify as "Toxic Churches" and I have been "spiritually abused" greatly by them.

### *Putting the World Together*

Autistic animal scientist Temple Grandin describes my spiritual task of needing to "put the world together,"

> Animals and autistic people are splitters. They see the differences between things more than the similarities. In practice this means that animals do not generalize very well. (Normal people often over-generalize, of course). That's why you have to be so careful when you're socializing an animal to socialize him to many different animals and people… What's different is that the generalizations animals and autistic people make are almost always narrower and more specific than the generalizations non autistic people make.[23]

God told me when I was working on my thesis that one of my spiritual tasks being a person with Asperger, in life, was to be able to "put-the-world-together." The reasons cannot be understated: To make sense of reality, to make meaning of the world, to be able to transfer from one situation to another, to make relevant generalizations, to understand the "big-picture" and to be morally coherent and consistent in your lifestyle choices and political commitments.

More tangibly, this issue came out at several different times in my life:

In Freshman Biology in undergraduate we had to do this lab exercise to learn the process of classifying organisms. It involved a variety of different paper clips. As a "splitter" like Grandin mentioned, I came-up with numerous categories for different taxoms of paper clips. The professor was only looking for two categories. She mentioned "That is very typical of bird people. Ornithologists need to be splitters." I wanted to become an Ornithologist at the time. As Grandin pointed-out, it has more due to the fact that I am a person with Asperger. I saw many different categories, while the professor only saw two. As I will demonstrate later on in this treatise, that my alternative way of classifying still has merit for understanding reality. It is just a different framework for classifying reality.

When I took "Animals and Ethics" in undergraduate, I was very outspoken against hunting and advocated a "Reverence for Life," yet I still ate meat. My professor pointed-out to me that I cannot really have a "Reverence for Life" and still eat meat. So I became a lacto-ova vegetarian, in part to be more morally and political consistent. I am still a vegetarian, even tell this day.

Finally, it came-out in my earlier book, *Creation Unveiled*. One of the consistent critiques of my book was its "unevenness." I would have "very good insights," amongst materials which were "rambling, "off topic," or "just poorly written." Also, I could not write *Creation Unveiled* as a coherent narrative or logical argument. I wrote many different chapters at different times and then pieced it together, into a treatise. You might notice these things, if you read *Creation Unveiled*. This is because; I had not yet "put the world together," when I wrote *Creation Unveiled*.

While in my later books such as *Christian Environmental Studies* (Amazon, 2008 2012) and *Have Mercy on Me, an Ecological Sinner* (Amazon, 2012) I was praised for my "coherence" even my "parallel structure" (the logical flow of my paper). This is because God used the writing of *Christian Environmental Studies* my master thesis and later---*Have Mercy on me, an Ecological Sinner* as an opportunity for me to "put the world together." For the purposes of my thesis--- my major professor Mark Heim wanted *Christian Environmental Studies* to be framed systematically into a coherent argument, the minimalist standard for it to be called academic—in his opinion. More recently, Heim who has stayed on in my life in a mentoring capacity encouraged me to take it a step further in *Have Mercy on me, an Ecological Sinner* and encouraged me to make my writing more accessible for a wider audience by adding a personal, creative dimension to my academic writing.

When I defended my thesis, Heim affirmed that my "putting the world together" was not only helpful for myself and my project, but also helpful for neurotypicals too. Heim is a systematic theologian. A systematic theologian is a theologian who organizes and brings coherence to theological concepts, ideas and themes, in other words, "puts the world together" into a coherent "cosmic scheme." As a systematic theologian, Heim most likely saw great beauty and elegance in how I "put together things which have never been put to together before" in a "meaningful manor."

Although what I thought I was doing something quite basic, Heim claims that no one has "put together" what I "put together" before. This is because Western, Enlightenment culture is marked by its compartmentalization and fragmentation of knowledge through forcing people to specialize into increasingly narrow fields of expertise very early in life, an "assembly line," "banking" approach to education, completely divorced from everyday life even one's own humanity, the whole "mechanistic mindset."

So, when a person with Asperger's like myself is able to make "relevant generalizations," the end result is a new systematic theology, still a "narrower generalization" than a neurotypical, but still a cogent "generalization" and a coherent systematic theology which actually makes sense, for it is grounded in reality.

This is what Roman Catholic sociologist Peter Berger calls a "sacred canopy,"

> Every human society, however legitimized, must maintain its solidarity in the face of chaos. Religious legitimated solidarity brings this fundamental sociological fact into sharper focus. The world of sacred order, by virtue of being an ongoing human production, is ongoing confronted with the disordered forces of human existence in time.[24]

In my case being a person with Asperger, I had to take on this task as an individual, on myself, being estranged from culture and religion and as a result not stabilized by a particular cultural or religious narrative. Aspie primatologist Dawn-Prince Huges writes, "Like all human and other persons [animals], we are not only part of things but whole already. As whole cultures within one, we have much to sing about."[25] That describes my reality being a person on the spectrum; my inner life is a distinct, self-sustaining "culture-of-one" to use Prince-Hughes words. That is the only culture-which I say that I am authentically a part of--- "rooted in."

As a result, I have needed to create my own legitimizing narratives, taken from other existing legitimizing narratives. Translated into my own personal context. This includes creating my own "sacred canopy." Any existing "sacred canopy" cannot encompass all of my reality, all my experiences, all my beliefs and values. Judaism cannot. Christianity cannot. Environmentalism cannot. Animal rights cannot. The sciences cannot. Only, my Asperger identity can unify all these disparate elements. All these disparate cultures. Autism is my unifying theory. It encompasses my Jewish upbringing, my Christian conversion, my environmental and animal rights commitments, my progressive politics and my scientific orientation. But, "putting it all together" was like putting together a 5000 pierce jigsaw puzzle.

As Dawn-Prince Huges points-out, that it is equally true that neurotypicals also have a "culture-of-one,"[26] but I will contend that because of the strong sense of belonging many neurotypicals experience to a particular community or culture, they are not as "in-touch" with their own unique inner identity as a person like myself, being on the spectrum. Maybe this is why many great geniuses come from the "margins" of society and culture? They are not as indoctrinated by cultural norms/taboos. They are not as "socially produced" as the rest of the population, so new ideas and creativity can emerge.

Part of my autistic personality is that I tend to "perseverate." When I was I child I used to draw everything from stoplights to maps, to airplanes to furnaces. Once I entered college, I used to write out pretend courses of study, such as made-up majors and minors, because of my fascination with courses of study, lists of courses, course catalogs and the like. I even helped lobby a particular dean, with another student, to have an Environmental Studies major at my undergraduate university. And, many years later, an Environmental Issues major became a reality. One of my environmental studies professor even said that by getting the deans talking about the already proposed environmental studies major, played a significant role in expediting the major in environmental studies becoming a reality. When only professors were discussing it, it remained in the perpetual talk stage.

In my "perseverations," I eventually settled down on one made-up program. A Master of Arts Program in Christian Environmental Studies. I went beyond lists of courses, this time, to writing syllabuses with course objectives, reading lists and assignments. I also began to share it with other people: friends, mentors and the like. They were impressed with what they saw.

Then I began to want to put this program into practice as my life dream. Spending my leisure time, refining the syllabuses. Even reading the books, I would read and purchase the books I would assign my students, creating a companion syllabus, even writing my own lectures. I even submitted my proposal of wanting to create an educational module to the Master of Arts Program in Research, at Andover Newton Theological School. I was accepted. My advisor (Mark Heim) who was my committee said that the fact that I was already working on a project already set me apart from other applicants, although this program had the option of continuing a project already began elsewhere.

My project was approved as my Thesis topic, the title of the program was changed from a Master of Divinity in Environmental Studies and I was required to move away from the project being logistics oriented to being more academic orientation with the concession to have two chapters deal with logistics. The rest would be to outline, a systematic theology of the environment, which would undergird the program, based on the core courses in the program.

Also, during my stay at Andover Newton, I improved the syllabuses, particularly the reading lists where I learned about resources I would not have learned about otherwise. I "beefed-up" sections, particularly sections which dealt with various theological and spiritual issues, which I just "slopped" together with what I knew at the time, without much formalized training in academic theology.

Now I was able to know what the important works in the field were and was able to integrate them effectively into my program. I was also introduced to important resources in ecotheology--- both primary and secondary sources which I also incorporated into my program as I continued to work through the books on my reading list, which I created.

I even was able to present my program at an academic conference on ecotheology at Harvard Divinity School, sponsored by the Boston Theological Institute. I even won the prize as the best submitted paper; I won one-hundred dollars.

My own graduate coursework at Andover Newton was preparation to write my thesis---on this topic. In fact, some of the chapters in *Christian Environmental Studies* (Amazon.com, 2012) started as term papers in various courses I took in graduate school.

During my stay in theological school, it was also recommended that I take some education courses, in preparation for putting my program into practice--- which I did. I was able to take my two education courses with a very inspiring professor and unlike the stereotype of education classes; they were very stimulating and engaging. I had many opportunities to share my idea and receive constructive and affirming feedback.

When it came time to defend my thesis, my thesis committee was very impressed and I received an "A" on it, with a recommendation that I could seek a doctorate of education; one of my committee professors recommended his own school, Columba Teacher's College. As well as making me aware of questions and resources I was not aware of before. So unlike other people including many neurotypicals, my defense was actually a positive experience.

I went onto to publish my findings on Amazon.com, Kindle Store, receiving a very positive review from Mark Heim, my former thesis advisor. More recently, I updated and expanded my project to also include over five years of "real world" experience.

Because I embraced, honored and listened to my autistic identity in conversation with the constructive criticism of a professor and other people, I now have developed my own "sacred canopy" which I can use. Whenever I am confused, need validation, affirmation or help with my thinking. I now have my own legitimizing narrative. Even if the program never becomes a reality. No matter what the future holds on the actualizing of this program---- it was not a wasted exercise. And, it did not land me an institution; I got a Master thesis and a book out of it. Getting to this point, being able to use the knowledge and wisdom of my "savant world," I would need to "translate" and make "accessible" to neurotypicals, for them to hear me and to embrace me.

### *Becoming a Soul Survivor*

Methodist Pastor and African-American author Carlyle Steward writes,

> As one of my theology professors observed, any people having to think twice about being in the world are perhaps far more adept at adapting, transcending, and transforming the world because they have appropriated numerous ways of seeing it. Generally speaking, they tend to be more resourceful and creating in the way they see and shape reality. African Americans have had to be creative just to survive. This survival has been aided by their ability to adapt to a variety of conditions.

> African American spirituality has provided black people with the freedom and capacity to use this twoness ["double consciousness"] for positive adaptation and spiritual cohesion. The twoness has not always led to psychological disintegration for black people but has also provided a kind of creative edge over their adversaries, which is often ignored. The ability to appropriate the implements and survival elements of the larger Anglo culture, to look at the world and life situations through a variety of lenses, is the result of a spirituality that implore black people to cultivate creativity as a creative response to external reality.

> Freedom is thus actualized in the capacity to the range or vacillate between alternative forms of consciousness and models of being for survival. This means accommodation or revolution, adaption or cooperation, humanization or radicalization. Because black people have been conditioned to view the world through their own as well as the white man's eyes, they themselves in some respect acquired more fluency and dexterity in actualizing themselves in society.

The doubleness has not inevitably led to a limitation of possibilities but the establishment of alternative modes of being that have facilitated black survival…[27]

All of Stewart's principles about African-Americans developing a "double consciousness" (having two sets of belief systems, your oppressor's and your own) to cope with their oppression apply to me being a person living with Asperger in a neurotypical society. As a person living with Asperger's in neurotypical society, I have appropriated significant aspects of neurotypical culture as a tool for my own personal survival and in the process developed my own unique hermeneutic of existence (interpretive lens for looking at the world). As a person living with Asperger, in neurotypical society, I have attempted, to various levels of success, to take the best of neurotypical society, while leaving the rest behind. As a person living with Asperger, in neurotypical society, the medium where I have epitomized my "culture of one" best is through the medium of writing.

Prince-Hughes writes, "Thus, writing was my salvation. I have said in the past, and I have since heard it repeated by other autistic people, that written English is my first language and spoken English is my second."[28]

As a person living with Asperger, in neurotypical society, I have been formed by neurotypical society and individual neurotypicals and neurotypical institutions have been formed by me. As a person living with Asperger, in neurotypical society, I also struggle with much ambivalence and confusion over my identity. I struggle with much self-doubt. This is because I have internalized the consciousness of neurotypicals (what neurotypicals believe about myself, other human beings with disabilities, other neurodiverse humans, as well as the nature of the Universe and human beings place in it). To the detriment of my own unique consciousness, being a human being on the autism spectrum.

As a person living with Asperger, in neurotypical society, I have also been bombarded with the message that my way of "being-in-the-world" even who I am and what I am are "inferior" to non-disabled, neurotypicals. Whether it is "autism awareness" adds on television or radio, whether being seen as a curiosity on documentaries, a psychopath on mysteries, or worthy to be experimented upon in animal rights literature. Whether in church, in philosophy books, where the predominate images of "autism" in neurotypical society is the popular 1980s movie the "Rain Man." This, combined with my so-called treatment growing-up, definitely has resulted in making me feel "other" and "inferior."

As a person with Asperger, living in neurotypical society, yet, by "thinking twice" about my "being-in-the-world" has made me more "resilient," giving me an "indomitable spirit." I have survived much disappointment, disillusionment, betrayal, setbacks and cruelty, without my "spirit being broken." Without giving-up, where I am continuing to work towards my goals and dreams. I have not "sold-out" my core identity. My core beliefs! My core values! My convictions! My faith! My soul!

This is because I have the power to deconstruct (to use science and reason to question my society). To see things for what they are, to know that there are other "ways of doing things" which are equally, if not more valid, to know what is in my best interest and what is not and to seek-out allies, for I trust my feelings, my perceptions---they have never been wrong. Sometimes unrealistic, sometimes they have the potential to unleash much havoc on my life, they have never been totally wrong.

Finally, as a person living with Asperger, in neurotypical society, I am able to vacillate, navigate, work through difficult situations and survive---- physically, spirituality and even professionally and relationally in many situations.

Even though developing a "double-consciousness" was a "double edge sword," "a mixed-blessing," causing much liberation and success in my life, while at the time causing me to internalize much shame and humiliation, it ultimately was worthwhile and an absolutely necessary task I needed to engage in for my spiritual development, my own "Soul's Journey Into God."

In addition to embracing my autistic identity, I also needed to embrace the reality of neurotypical society. And, respond to the reality that I am a person with autism, living in a neurotypical society. A society which experiences the world very differently than I do. A world which has very different standards, very different norms and taboos, a world with very different beliefs and values, then myself. If I wanted to meet my goals, my dreams, to live out my value-system, I would at a certain level, need to adapt to them. Just so I could survive in a neurotypical society.

Developing a "double consciousness" allows me to do what I needed to do to survive in a hostile, unsympathetic neurotypical society. It allows me to make the best of neurotypical society. It allows me to translate the best of neurotypical society into my own autistic context. It allows me to preserve my unique autistic identity and to honor my autistic self. In other words, it gives me the best of all worlds.

Also, a "double consciousness" gave me a way to explain my unique autistic consciousness to neurotypicals, in ways in which they can hear me, understand it and embrace it.

Finally, I have developed the art of translating, translating my autistic reality into a neurotypical context. Not always by choice though. For example, I spent most of my thesis in graduate school, working backwards, trying to justify the legitimacy and philosophical underpinnings, behind a Master of Arts program which was very "savant" in origins. In other words, translate a savant doddle into an academic argument.

Still, all this adapting and translating did take its toll on my unique consciousness and way of being in the world. And, while not condemning the "double consciousness," the psychological and spiritual "side-effects" and "shadow side" needed to be dealt with.

### *Developing a Second Naiveté*

Christian feminist ecotheologian Sallie McFague writes,

> In childhood we often experience closeness with others-human, animal, and plant life-with a kind of "world-openness," a deep pleasure in exploring the world for its own sake. The first naiveté is an unself-conscious interest in nature, a wide-eyed curiosity about it, as well as identification with it. It is not a state in which we cannot return, such as romantics and deep ecologists wish we might. Rather, our task is to attempt the second naiveté, a return to connection with others that recognizes distance and respects differences…

Nature writers, who combine information and empathy, respect for particular worlds of plants and animals studied with loving attention, illustrate how the model can be extended.

How can we move from the first to the second naiveté, from the child's innocence, innate delight in other life forms to a nuanced, educated, and responsible love of nature? ...[29]

Moving from the first to second naiveté has special complications in my situation---- being an environmentalist on the autism spectrum. I got one of my first breaks with the environmental movement with the Rachel Carson Council, Inc. One of things, they noticed right away about me was my gift for having a "childlike sense of wonder" toward the Natural World. That was one of things they really saw promise in my first book, *Rachel Carson in Carteret County, North Carolina: A Journey to the Edge of the Sea* (1997) allowing adults and families who read this work, to experience a child's perspective on appreciating the Natural World, in the child's own words.

One has to understand the Carson tradition. Rachel Carson was a big advocate of adults cultivating a "sense of wonder" in children in her classic work: *The Sense of Wonder* (Harper Reprint, 1998). My writing was a perfect example, which exemplified and embodied and put into practice this principle, being a kind of "poster child" for the organization. I received much praise and support from the organization for my project. They published and legally copyrighted my book. It sold over two hundred copies, was used as a curriculum in a Northern Virginia School, made an official publication of the organization. I was named the Rachel Carson Council, Inc. "Junior Scholar." They organized book signings for me; I had the opportunity to meet associates of Rachel Carson herself; I even was given the opportunity to stay in Rachel Carson's summer home in Maine. Where I was able to set-up my microscope at the same place where Rachel Carson wrote her most famous environmental treatise, *Silent Spring*.

In other words, while other Maryland students for their high school community service were doing boring, grunt work, like cleaning bathroom at community centers, I was getting my requirement met by vacationing at the beach. This was a wonderful, life changing opportunity. But it was also only "fifteen minutes of fame."

As I got older, my unique "childlike sense of wonder" began to disparate. My strong feelings of "ecstasy" which I felt almost every time I went out in the Nature, where Rachel Carson said "a child's world is fresh and new and beautiful, full of wonder and excitement"[30] were beginning to wan and dry-up. This was being replaced by more rational knowledge of the Natural World.

The year after I did my research for *Rachel Carson in Carteret County, North Carolina*, I took Honors Biology and Earth Science at my local high school. Here, I began to develop more of a foundation in the natural sciences--- both biological and physical. When I went the next summer to Maine, to research and write a sequel, visiting the places which were important to Rachel Carson in Maine including her famous summer cottage, my sponsor, the Executive Director of the Council, felt that my strong and vibrant "childlike sense of wonder" was not as strong in this volume. Instead there was much more factual information about the Natural World. She was even worried that the more scientific training I would receive--- that my "sense of wonder" would begin to wan or dissipate. As I got older and my "sense of wonder" began to wan even further, it even began to impact my relationship with other people. I even lost two long-term friends, in part, over this issue.

Also, at this time, I was beginning to get new experiences in the Natural World. Not all of them- did I like. I *was not* feeling the strong sense of ecstasy in the Natural World, which I used to experience so strongly and forcefully, when I was younger. No matter how hard I tried to generate it, it just would not happen. I would find my "sense of wonder" strongest when experiencing some of Nature's simplest of elements, but would not feel it at all, when I went to famous, world renowned natural areas. I used to "beat myself up" terribly--- for this. For many years, even till this day, I would "slip-up" and find myself doing this, all over again. God explained to me many years later what I was experiencing was a "Dark Night" in my relationship with the Natural World, liken to a "Dark Night of the Soul" but effecting my relationship with the Natural World only, not impacting my relationship with God or my faith or the like.

Finally, I was even getting more interested in "more-than-straight-scientific-approaches" to studying and experiencing the Natural World. Where a scientific approach to environmentalism was other peoples hope and even my own hope of what I would pursue professionally. In other words, my vocation and calling was beginning to change. Instead of becoming just a straight scientist, I was beginning to show more of an interest in an interdisciplinary approach to environmentalism.

I discovered during this period, the Christian environmental movement. I did a project my senior year on ecopsychology. I took three years of ceramics in high school---- where I expressed my love of the Natural World, artistically through clay and other mediums. I was also getting into animal rights activism, speaking out against "hunting for population control" in my local community. With the later, I ran into conflicts with the environmental movement.

Once, I got to college. This issue exploded. For starters, I learned that my "sense of wonder" was not the only correct way to experience the Natural World, or even a valid one. I met environmentalists who *did not* like Rachel Carson and *did not* think she went "far enough." This made it difficult at times--- to experiencing my "sense of wonder" in Nature, in peace, without being tormented.

This was coupled by the fact that I was not that good at the natural sciences. I was okay, competent, but not enough to get a degree in Biology. This is mainly because of the rigid neurotypical constraints of how science is taught. There were several unique issues that I was experiencing being a Biology student on the autism spectrum.

I could not "compartmentalize" very well. I could not separate my phenomenology, my commitments, my agenda and my project, even my enjoyment of the subject, from the tasks I had to perform being a student of science. Mainly "being objective," "disinterested" and "focused on the material" "at-hand," the whole "mechanistic mindset."

I could not conform to the paradigms of the sciences very well either. I had a fundamentally different experience of "raw sense data" than the other students and faculty members. This was particularly manifested in animal behavior science, where I saw many more "human-like" qualities in nonhuman animals, than what many of the professors were willing to acknowledge.

As a result, I was accused of "anthropomorphism," "putting human-like characteristics on nonhuman animals" which was considered a "scientific fallacy" in those days.

I could not confirm to the virulent and very blatant "speciesism" (bigotry toward nonhuman animals) and almost "death possession" with killing nonhuman beings, which seemed to permeate the biology culture at the time. My sensitivity to the Nonhuman World made dissection a "moral dilemma"--- I could not even be in the same room when "vivisection" (dissecting live animals) was going on. Animal rights even animal welfare was invalidated, trivialized and belittled at every "turn." The biology department made it very difficult for animal rights sympathetic students, like myself, to get through the program, mainly they did not give dissection and vivisection exemptions. Most certainly, I could not condone "hunting for population control" as a legitimate wildlife management tool for dealing with animal overpopulation and invasive species problems. Also, many of the students and faculty members were avid hunters and the "hidden curriculum" was very "shallow" indeed. Biology seemed more like the study of death than "the study of life." This was not why I went into Biology--- to torture animals and dominate the Natural World.

Also, I could not do mathematics very well. This was a major issue when I tried to take chemistry. It was more about doing mindless manipulations than appreciating the subject, or even learning the concepts and principles, the required chemistry courses made almost no connections to biology or ecology. Most of the applications were made to petrochemicals and pesticide application. Two anti-ecological industries!

As a result, my relationship with the Natural World was changing. It was no-longer marked by intense experiences of euphoria even ecstasy, but it was beginning to be marked by a plethora of emotional, aesthetic, intellectual, spiritual even religious experiences. Not all these utilized my positive emotions or experiences. I would have everything from "dark nights" to being "overawed." Vacillating between feelings of guilt to feelings of being cheated. Accusing myself of everything from being anti-Nature to squandering once-in-a-lifetime experiences. Once I arrived in theological school, my experiences where more reminiscent of Annie Dillard than Rachel Carson.

Upon a recent vacation to Glacier National Park, I could identify with the Europeans who used to cover their faces when crossing the Alps, so not to be exposed to the temptation of the sensual world. Not because I saw wilderness as evil, but because it was "too good." So good, I could not take its beauty. I could not possibly take it in, savor it, internalize it, enough and have the one correct emotion when experiencing Nature, euphoria. Not only did I experience "dark nights" but I was prone to "get overawed."

"Overawed" (Isaiah 2: 19, NRSV-Catholic Edition) was a word used to describe the Israeli Lights retreating to the caves, to escape the power of the Lord, in the Book of Isaiah. For as mere mortals, they could not take it. When I first encountered this phrase in the Bible one recent Lent, this described exactly what I was experiencing in the Natural World. I was not being anti-Nature, I was "overawed," over-stimulated. Overwhelmed by the beauty, the wonder and the amazement of the Natural World. I was actually overwhelmed by it. Pressured to fully take advantage of it. Not to squander the experience. Guilty if I could not look into it. But, I could not look into it. It was like looking into the sun. The very Face of God. Touching the Mountain of the Lord, where one touch and you are a goner. So, I often headed for the caves, like the ancient Israeli Lights.

God first began to tackle this issue head-on--- when I arrived in theological school. When I was in New Mexico, God pointed-out that I was going through a "Dark Night of Nature." A kind of "dry period" in my relationship with the Natural World, where I could not capture the wonder and the ecstasy of the Natural World--- like I did when I was in child. No matter how beautiful or magnificent the scenery was.

Later on, when we (God and I) studied Ronald Rolheiser book *The Holy Longing: the Search for a Christian Spirituality* (New York: Doubleday, 1999) for a class in graduate school, I learned from Rolheiser the phrase "addiction to experience." It was revealed to me by my Lord, that I was becoming "addicted to experiences." And, one Lent year--- I *was not* to censor my emotions and my feelings, but instead I was to "get in touch with" my emotions and feelings.

I received the most help and guidance on this issue, when I read Sallie McFague's book, *Super, Natural Christians*. Here with God's help, I came across the concept of the Second Naïveté. Her contrast between the First Naiveté and the Second Naiveté described exactly what I felt as a child and what I was being called into. That it was okay, even natural that I was losing my "childlike sense of wonder" and that there was still hope for preserving my spiritual gift of having a "sense of wonder" at-all, which Rachel Carson hoped every child would be able to have throughout life, to deal with "the boredom and disenchantments of later years."[31]

It just needed formation and maturing, as God pointed-out to me. All was not lost. I was to let go of the need to rely on euphoric experiences in the Natural World and instead embrace my new found knowledge and respect for the Natural World. Saint Francis in Heaven added a third category, which he called "tastes." Being a connoisseur of the beauty and wonder of Nature. A category which would encompass the aesthetic experiences, even moments of ecstasy, I still continue to experience in the Natural World, even till this day.

Rachel Carson nurtured me in "the fertile soil," "a childlike sense of wonder" where the "seeds that would later produce knowledge and wisdom" could be sown.[32] Now, that I had "fertile soil," my Lord like the famous Biblical parable indicated, I was ready to nurture my "seeds" of knowledge, respect and good tastes, preventing my "fertile soil" from eroding away to worry and shame. With the end, relieving me of this unnecessary guilt, worry and shame. That I no longer have to feel like a woman, who is losing her beauty as she is getting older, but embracing her oldness as a sign of wisdom.

Before I was this "cute" savant who felt a "childlike sense of wonder" in Nature, now I am moving in the direction of a "manly" elder who instills adult like knowledge, respect and good tastes onto other people, sensitizing them to the Nonhuman World, the glory of God's Creation, while preserving my spiritual charism in the process from "the boredom and disenchantments of later life."

This is what the world and the environmental movement needs right now, as much, if not more, than a "cute" savant who feels ecstasy in Nature. Environmental ethicist J. Baird Callicott writes,

> To sum up my historical review, Western appreciation of natural beauty is recent and derivative from art. The prevailing natural aesthetic, therefore is not autonomous; it does not flow naturally from nature itself; it is not directly oriented to nature on nature's own

terms; nor is it well informed by the ecological and evolutionary revolutions. It is superficial and narcissistic. In a word, it is trivial.

Naturally occurring scenic or picturesque "landscapes" are regarded, like the art they imitate, to be precious cultural resources and are stored, accordingly, in "museums" (the national parks) or private "collections" (the "landscaped" estates of the wealthy). They are visited and admired by patrons just like the originals deposited in the actual museums of urban centers. Nonsceinic, nonpictursque nonlandscapes are aesthetic nonresources and thus become available for less exulted uses. While land must be used, it is well within our means to save, restore, and aesthetically manage representative nonscenic, nonpictursque nonlandscapes-swamps and bogs, dunes, scrub, prairie bottoms, flats, deserts, and so on as aesthetic amenities-just as we preserve intact representative scenic ones.[33]

So in essence, my "childlike sense of wonder" purified by a sense of knowledge, respect and good tastes is the Daniel Salomon, that the world and the movement needs, just as much as the Daniel Salomon who is a "cute" savant who is childlike and pure, if not more. The new Daniel, the adult Daniel and only the adult Daniel, can address the limitations of certain aesthetic experiences, in the West, head-on. This is because; the new Daniel which is emerging, understands the ecological importance and significance of "swamps and bogs, dunes, scrub, prairie bottoms, flats, deserts," not just something to get "high" on. And, can articulate this rationally. The new Daniel, the adult Daniel and only the adult Daniel, can make moral decisions about how to respect "swamps and bogs, dunes, scrub, prairie bottoms, flats, deserts…"

This is because the new Daniel understands environmental ethics and philosophy, the dignity of all life, moral decision making, knows both the science and political economic issues involved and most importantly, can listen to and discern the Will of God. Finally, only the new emerging Daniel, can truly recognize Beauty in Nature, like a connoisseur of fine wine, in "swamps and bogs, dunes, scrub, prairie bottoms, flats, deserts…" because the new Daniel has seen much in God's Creation, over the years and can be intelligent about what he considers to be "aesthetically pleasing" and now has a "sacred canopy" which informs him that all of God's Creation is sacred, holy and good. All of God's Creation is worthy to be respected and protected.

As a result of my Second Naiveté, I was able to work toward restoring a "wild area" with tremendous biodiversity and miraculous ecological fitness near where I lived for two years called

Deer Ridge. I attempted to transform Deer Ridge from being viewed by my neighbors as a "local garbage dump" to viewing Deer Ridge as "a community resource" through cleaning-up litter and garbage, ecologically surveying the property, successfully getting the local state park to come down and delineate the boundaries of a rare naturally occurring freshwater non-tidal marsh, even collaborating with a community leader to lobby my city to step-up their management of this genuine "commons" and a former environmental studies professor from college, Dr. Joan Maloof made a special trip from Salisbury on the Eastern Shore of Maryland to visit Deer Ridge and is currently considering Deer Ridge as a "community forest" in her non-profit organization which she founded called Old-Growth Forest Network (www.oldgrowthforest.net).

In other words, I am able to use my knowledge base, sense of respect even my aesthetic tastes toward a sustainable end--- transforming wonder into passion, beauty into love and ecstasy into peace.

This is what my journey has all been leading-up--- embracing a manly, adult Christian faith, as a servant, lover and friend of my Lord becoming a Man of God on the autism spectrum within the context of all life.

### Meeting God Face-to-Face: My "Life in the Spirit"

Saint Paul the Apostle writes,

And we know that all things work together for good to those who love God, to those who are called according to His purpose. (Romans 8: 28)

In the end, as a person with Asperger, my life and my faith, did work together for good. My belief in the existence of God did bear fruit. I have survived and prevailed in the end.

Although not as dramatic as a Propensity Gospel testimonial, where you pray for a stomach ache to go away and it magically goes away. Or, you pray for your dream wife, house or job. And, you get it all in spades. All these wonderful things did not happen to me once I accepted Jesus Christ into my life. All these amazing things just did not happen to me. In fact, I have suffered greatly on account of my faith.

My future is still uncertain. I am currently living off social security disability, a housing voucher and food stamps. I am currently still under-employed. I am unmarried and do not have anyone serious in my life at this time, or at least in the foreseeable future. Like Paul, I write to you "in chains." I have not lived "happily ever after" with Jesus.

I still struggle with chronic worrying. I am still haunted by ghosts from my past. I am often lonely and depressed.

Yet, everything has worked together for good in my life. Still!

Finally--- I had my first "intense positive experience" this last year at a local Presbyterian Church in the bioregion of my birth between my middle school and my high school. A church where "open and affirming" also includes disability and neurodiversity, where I was treated with "dignity and respect," where I too "am welcome at the table," where I was treated as a Beloved Child of Christ and where my spiritual charism as an Aspie was actually welcome, where this Church met many of my personal needs for safety, comfort, formation and relationality. I received much love, grace and fairness, an "intense corrective experience" with a faith community, in the process.

Most importantly, this church was strong in _**both** social justice **and** sound doctrine._ A rare combination in today's politically polarized climate, actively addressing the disconnect between the ethical-moral imperative for the Christian Church to address "the problems of the world" through community service, dialogue and political activism and the psychological-pastoral necessesity for the Christian Church to "minister to the sick" through prayer, sound Christian doctrine and good pastoral care, in other words, balancing "the global" with "the local."

Also, in the last year, I "banded together" with other disability survivors, after I was invited to be on a moderated panel discussion on "Animals and Disability: Building Collaborations" at the annual 2012 _**Society for Disability Studies**_ (SDS) conference in Denver, Colorado.

The panel was organized by disability animal activist Sunaura Taylor who is a professional photographer and graduate of University of California-Berkley, who is also a vegan and uses photography to document animal atrocities. Taylor also happens to have a physical disability. Taylor invited me to give a brief presentation and field questions based on my 2010 Journal of Critical Animal Studies (JCAS) article "From marginal cases to linked oppressions: Reframing the conflict between the Autistic Pride and Animal Rights movements," after an expensive correspondence.

Taylor also invited two feminist scholars, Mel Chen and Deanna Adams, to be on the panel discussion.

Adams acknowledged my traumatic history through deconstructing the practice of "behavior modification" in the treatment of autism, in animal experimentation, in handling and domesticating farm and companion animals and in overly invasive conservation management practices condemning "behavior modification" as "suppressive practices." Mel Chen, also an Asian-American, acknowledged the parallels between my own autistic tendency "to personify inanimate objects" and the organic cosmologies of traditional Nature-based societies around the world, which do likewise.

Chen even acknowledged that disabled and neurodiverse humans were in fact swept-up into the whole Western colonial project of "world domination" during the Enlightenment of the last five hundred years. That "colonialism" and "culturecide" were in fact the "real reasons" for creating "mental hospitals" in Western nations. That "special education" really is instilling a "spirit of passivity," "learned helplessness," "superficiality," even "individualism" and "consumerism" into our disabled and neurodiverse children and youth. The Western establishment really does see "disability" and "mental illness" as apolitical, private, individualistic matters of "pity," "paternalism," "psychological adjustment," "assimilation" and "segregationist charity." She even acknowledged that privileged non-disabled, neurotypical white women really are in a position of dominance, privilege and oppression over underprivileged disabled and neurodiverse men and women.

She even demonstrated that the "root metaphor" for "embodiment" in many vegetarian and ecological lifestyle campaigns is under the "spells" of both the perfectionist standard of Western beauty "the privileged white male" and the "sin-disability connection." These two unconscious narratives married to ecological or vegetarian aesthetics equates "disabled bodies" with "consumerism" and "athletic bodies" with "moral purity."

All these "cutting edge" findings are just confirming my worst suspicions about my oppression as a neurodiverse human. "Breaking the silence" on disability oppression has began. "It's happening!" We are beginning to become organized. We are beginning to fight back!
I am now a member of Society for Disability Studies (SDS), a professional society for disability professionals and academics of all types from all different types of disabilities, both physical and invisible.

I am currently networking with other academics, professionals and activists in the disability community to "break the silence" on neurotypicalism and abelism.

I am becoming a part of an emerging disability political community which is collaborating with the various ecological, animal rights and social justice movements to address the disconnections between the disability movements and the other progressive movements with the goal of working together toward a "common goal"---"a better world."

In fact, as we speak, I am on the "ground floor" of an emerging "animals and disability" group, our panel--- being the nucleus of a possible disability animal rights movement.

I am now free to devote my entire life to God and worship Him without fear. Serving and loving my Lord and His beloved Son, the Lord Jesus Christ, All-Creation, my best friend. I am able to live the life I have always wanted to live along. Free to do whatever I want and God wants. Pursue the projects, I have always dreamt of exploring. Write the books, which I have dreamt of writing. Living out authentically my convictions. My faith, even live a monastic life with Saint Francis and His Brothers in Heaven and with All Creation, taking "cool water" from whoever would "give me a cup of cool water," until the Franciscans are "ready for my ideas." I have not given-up!

I have finally won my poverty!

God has developed a way to live Franciscan holy poverty which makes sense in the twenty-first century---- becoming a "canvasser," a modern-day Franciscan-like "beggar" who goes "from door to door" asking people to give money to an organization dedicated to a "worthy cause," usually addressing a problem not being addressing by society. That is for the time-being. And, my memories of past oppressions are beginning to fade.

I hope one day to work my way out of social security and subsidized housing, when and if, I am able. I also hope one day to move to a smaller town environment, with easy access to wilderness areas and a nourishing political community such as Portland, Oregon.

In fact, that is exactly what I did. As of May of 2013, I have relocated cross-country to Portland, Oregon, to become more connected to the various planetary movements. I am now a Portlander!

Now because I have had an "intense positive experience" with both a political community and a faith community in the last year, I now feel more empowered to try new communal opportunities out in Oregon.

I also have not given-up on my dream of implementing my Master of Arts Program, in Christian Environmental Studies, making my "dream a reality."

Then my strangest dream re-appeared when I was on a celebratory vacation with my parents in Estes Park, Colorado after the stunning success of my panel discussion and conference.

I also saw in Estes Park, at the end of my journey from "Compassion Fatigue," many years later, on a vacation celebrating my full-recovery from "Compassion Fatigue" and my re-integration into the movement--- the same monastery on an arid promontory which I saw in my dream many years ago and which I saw in real-life on an arid New Mexican hillside.

This time it was the ruins of an abandoned house perched on-top-of a colossal red-rock outcropping above the quant alpine village of Estes Park. A house and landscape even more similar to my dreams, than even what I saw in New Mexico, shortly after I had that archetypical, pilgrimage dream that one night in theological school. The similarities were so strikingly similar, they were uncanny.

My father was the one who drove me to this house. Driving through this house---we went through a suburban neighborhood---very similar to the mid-twentieth century houses in downtown Rockville, my hometown. In fact, the place where my father dropped me off was like my dream; I had to walk through a city park and wild desert-scape, to get to the stone monastery on top of the hill, which fits the pilgrimage archetype, of a person going on a difficult, intense, internally reflective journey to a holy site, an intense struggle, followed by a blessed release. The vacuum cleaner in my dream was my father driving a rental car in real life. I have heard that dreams can scramble the message and the relevant information, so interpreting a dream, is like working through a puzzle or unscrambling a code.

It turns-out that the place my father dropped me off was also a city park. A public park owned by a private Nature conservatory which protects both the abandoned ruins of the house and the surrounding red-rock country, a rugged, semi-arid prairie-scape of red-rock badlands, Ponderosa Pine groves, rare grasslands and even a small stream and marsh.

It also turns-out that this place is also a local pilgrimage site. This area is a memorial garden for Enos Mills, the founder of Rocky Mountain National Park, a preservationist, outdoorsman and naturalist of the early twentieth century. He was also a Christian; he was a very devout Quaker. A secular pilgrimage site!

I even approached the monastery aka stone house from the same angle as in my dreams. I walked along a path through an arid landscape. I began my journey along a pleasant stream and bucolic marsh. In my dreams-it was a landscaped shrub-bed around a small lake. In both my dream and in real-life, the landscape begins to become more and more wild. And, more and more arid!

Visiting this place was eerie and peaceful at the same time.

I encountered tame wild animals like in the Peaceable Kingdom in Isaiah 11.

I was approached by tame ground squirrels, a family of pygmy nuthatches and a couple of dickcissels and a pair of mountain bluebirds who followed me all the way up the hill like the bluebird guide in the classic fairytale "The Bluebird." I saw two majestic Golden Eagles fly through the magnificent glacier-carved valley of Estes Park, hovering above Estes Lake, soaring through snow-caps peaks and red-rock mountains, flying with the sublime majesty of the Wooing Eagles in the Book of Revelations who were prophesized some two thousand years ago to fly across the earthly sky warning of prophetic doom and the hope of ultimate redemption, signaling the coming of both the Apocalypse and the Messianic Age.

Most uncanny of all, was a bird from my own bioregion of the Piedmont Plateau, back east, the American robin. When I arrived at the house, it was just like in my dreams. It was on an arid landscape, on a promontory overlooking a vast landscape.

In real-life, through the ruins of a stone house, I could see a magnificent, panoramic view of all of Estes Park, surrounded by rocky and red-rock mountains on all sides, with Estes Lake and Longs Peak in the distant backdrop. And, yes, in-real life, the view was greener than the surrounding grasslands. A landscape marked by furs, spruces and snow-capped mountains. Yes, there were two path ways, the first path was a main metal platform where visitors are allowed to enter this house and a stone stairway, part of the original house, but closed-off to visitors. I recognized this place from my dreams!

Yes, I felt happy there! In fact, the happiest I felt on the entire vacation! Yes, my father called me on my cell phone in the middle of my spiritual experience! And, yes there was a diner below the stone house, in the town below! And, yes, there were encampments below!

It turns-out that a man, over a hundred years ago, built his dream house on this promontory, but it burnt-down in an unfortunate fire. The same building which appeared as an encampment below was the man's rebuilt house, made to look like a Swedish shallot, to reflect the local character of the region, a whimsical red-and-white log cabin. He built his shallot below the stone house.

No--- I did not have an argument with my parents there. In fact, my parents liked this area so much that they went on my same journey. Where my father even took many pictures of the stone house and all the surrounding views, my parents were in awe at my tastes, finding a spectacular place that most visitors overlook, but even more intrigued by my supernatural, paranormal experiences.

In fact, right across the street was the Stanley Hotel, the hotel which inspired popular horror film author Stephen King to write his modern classic, "The Shinning," a story which involved a mother, a father, a little boy and a haunted hotel during an intense blizzard one winter in the Colorado Rockies. In fact, in looking at my father's photographs, I discovered that the Stanley Hotel had a whole wildlife sculpture garden, with different types of wild animals, in diorama-like displays, like in my dream.

My story had a much happier, more wholesome, life-affirming ending---however. Not only did we all get out alive and in good spirits, having an intensively positive experience, but God revealed that the meaning of my dream is that "I will find happiness wherever the artificial and the natural are one." In other words, anyplace where there is balance between Nature and Culture and God and Nature. A Blessed Trinity!

This now completes my spiritual autobiography being a person with Asperger. This is my life story being a person living with Asperger up to this point.

Now--- the rest of this treatise will delineate, systemize and organize the various elements of my contextual, liberation theology.

## Chapter Two-Method of Theological Reflection: My Autistic Hermeneutic

### *Hyperspecific Reasoning*

Autistic animal behavior scientist Temple Grandin describes hyperspecific reasoning in peoples with autism,

> Animals and autistic people are splitters. They see the differences between things more than the similarities. In practice this means that animals do not generalize very well. (Normal people often over-generalize, of course)…
> …It's not that animals and autistic don't generalize at all. Obviously they do. What's different is that the generalizations animals and autistic people make are almost always narrower and more specific than the generalizations non autistic people make."[34]

Hyperspecific reasoning is the ability to see the uniqueness of each situation, event, idea, or location. That everything is in fact different. Nothing is homogenized or "the same." This is in stark contrast to the overgeneralized, homogenized thinking which thinks in terms of the universality of situations, events, ideas and locations. Of course, as Grandin pointed out and as I have demonstrated earlier, a certain amount of generalization is necessary to survive in the world. If not, everything would be utter and total chaos. One would not even be able to take care of oneself, lest get anything done. In fact, one could not know which foods are edible and which ones are not. That an apple is edible, but a deadly nightshade is not.

What happens with many neurotypicals (non-autistic humans) is that they over-generalize and subsequently need the correction of the hyperspecific reasoning found in autistic humans and nonhuman animals. Neurotypicals tends to assume reality to be universal and homogenized. In other words, "everything is the same." This is especially true in theology circles. Two very fashionable ideas--- one in more leftist Christian circles and the other in more conservative Christian circles, both fall into this trap.

Some neurotypical, liberal-progressive Christians oftentimes contend that all the religions of the world are "*the same*." Not only are Jews and Muslins worshipping the same God, as Christians, but even Buddhists, Hindu's and various indigenous peoples are all worshiping the same God. Both according to this line of argument are connecting to a "sense of the divine." This is fallacious thinking, according to the autistic mind, for this is an "over-generalization." It assumes a fundamental continuity in theology and spirituality which simply is not there. Arhahamic religions worship One personal God who made Heaven and Earth, while in Buddhism; the question of God is not even an important question. It can even be further nuanced between Judaism, Christianity and Islam.

That is why as an autistic theologian, in my other works; I could not endorse "***deep ecumenicalism***" or "***religious synergism***" such as that of people like Joseph Campbell, Thomas Berry or Mathew Fox. My theological differences were undergirded by my autistic intuition that "deep ecumenicalism" "over-generalizes" and assumes that Buddhists and Christians are all worshiping the same God, which could be farther from the truth.

This was not to mention my autistic hermeneutical mindset, to think of other differences---- psychological, anthropological and even ecological. As a result, my hyperspecific reasoning has been able to recover a unique, constructive, Christian ecological and animal rights vision as expressed in my previous works.

Yet, I am willing to make some generalizations about world religions---mainly, all Christian denominations worship the same God, even though they provide different models for doing so. That even Jewish people and Muslins worship the same God, even certain non-Western religions such as many Native American religions, although there are some subtle and not so subtle differences between the Jewish, Christian and Muslim conceptions of God. I am even willing to concede that there might be a continuum of religious experience, that some religious can even access the One, True God more so than others or differently, but *not* that they are fundamentally "the same." Or, even worshiping the same God deep down--- cultural parallels (e.g., Europe, Middle East, India and China in the Middle Ages) are different than religious parallels (e.g., Christianity, Islam, Hinduism and Buddhism). I recognize and see the uniqueness of Christianity too clearly as a Christian on the autism spectrum, such as the "Ten Commandments" which commands that "You shall have no other gods before me" (Exodus 20: 3). To do so, would be to commit idolatry. Also, I do not contend that each and every religion "under the sun" is equally valid either. Some of the notions are valid, other have notions I see as problematic. As an Aspie, I cannot be a "cultural relativist." I cannot make such a generalization about the scope of truth.

I do contend however just because each World Religion is "different" and Christianity is "unique," that *does not* mean that every religion "under the sun" is necessarily "inferior" either, I see each World Religion as completely "different" and "unique." Even religions I "disagree" with--- that *does not* mean I judge the people who believe in such religions as "bad people" or that I believe "there're going to hell." No one agrees on everything, this is just plain unrealistic in such a pluralistic, diverse world. Each world religion, including Christianity has strengths and weaknesses. I look at the World Religion scene like one would evaluate an intellectual idea or political opinion--- analytically and critically with a certain sense of respect for people who might disagree with you. In other words, I am more *pluralistic* than *synergistic*.

Neither can I condone the **neoclassical notion of natural law** either, the more **conservative counterpart**, a popular approach in many Catholic fundamentalist circles. That there is "a universal language of truth," "grounded in human reason," derived from God, consistent with certain Christian doctrines, which can be understood and accepted "by all cultures and religions of the world," "without employing distinctively Christian language." Once again, this is an over-generalization, which I have become increasingly sensitive to in recent times.

Natural law *does not* take into consideration, idiosyncratic differences in cultures, religions and time-periods. It *does not* take seriously enough different contexts and assumes that certain attributes of Christianity and Christian language "are the same," the world-over, for all time.

Even something like "it is a sin to commit murder" *is not* "universal." It is my experience that the probation to commit murder *is not* universal. Just look to cannibalistic societies (e.g., several societies in the South Pacific), whole periods in European history which engaged in regular human sacrifices (e.g., sacrificing little boys to the pagan god---Pan") and even in our country--- even though murder might be against the law--- America still allows American soldiers to kill enemy combatants, America still has the death penalty and gives murderers all kinds of "golden parachutes" and "legal loop holes" from abortion to sports hunting. Seeing "killing" *as* "murder" is far from universality accepted.

In fact, most non-Arhahamic religions *do not* have prohibitions against murder, for most World Religions have very different views on the questions on life and death--- seeing the boundaries of life and death on a continuum--- having a "non-dualistic view of good and evil." Meaning killing is more acceptable---- for death is understood as just a different "state of being" for "All is One"--- the "opened root" archetype.[35]

In fact, prohibitions against "killing" are one of the things which make Western monotheistic religions such as Judaism, Christianity and Islam--- "unique."

This is compounded by the reality that not every value or moral principle, applies in every context. In some situations, a particular moral principle requires a certain response to be moral, but that the same certain moral response in a different situation would be immoral. In other words, context mediates moral precepts. "Pragmatic experiences" requires a certain moral response. To put it in plain English--- "there are exceptions to the rules!" "Exceptions to the rules" must be made in extenuating circumstances. If not, the "law" becomes "death" (Romans 7: 4-6) according to both Lord Jesus Christ and Saint Paul the Apostle. Read your Bible! Such an ethical-moral framework *is not* relativism, but is quite Biblical.

Although granted--- that there are absolute moral norms such as the Ten Commandments --- a particular situation might demand a certain moral situation to be implemented in a certain manor out of a "spirit" of compassion and clemency. Although "the natural law tradition" *does* recognize "context"---the place where one acts morally--- such as a relationship, "it does not go far enough." It *does not* recognize that contextualizing even ignoring certain absolute moral precepts is "the right thing to do" in certain situations, something to be fully embraced on "a clean conscience." Not something, just too merely tolerate. In other words, the natural law tradition *does not* fully embrace "pragmatic experience," "ordinary people solving ordinary problems." So is relatively "useless" in the "real world"---as a practical ethic which can offer concrete moral guidance.

Also, there are serious difficulties with "the isogesis" of certain Scripture verses such as assuming that certain passages in the Bible signify the theme of "natural law." When, really they are talking about something else all together. The over-generalized imagination of those who adhere to natural law *do not* take into consideration that Mosaic Law, in the Jewish tradition is different than Roman Catholic cannon law. Mainly, that in the Jewish tradition "the law" is fiercely debated from the "bottom-up" on what it means and how "ought it be" interpreted, while in the Roman Catholic cannon law, "the law" is "cast in stone" from the top-down, given by the Magisterium with specific instructions on what it means and how it "ought to be" interpreted. No debate! No questioning! Where in Judaism, even the Ten Commandments themselves are up for debate and questioning. For example, in the modern Jewish landscape, the Sabbath commandment in particular is hotly contested between Reform and Conservative Jews and Orthodox Jews, with Reform and Conservative Jews arguing that we are living in the twenty-first century, so a strict observance of the Sabbath is not necessary.

Even Papal exegesis's misses this essential historical-critical detail, for they over-generalize and "project" the Roman Catholic tradition onto Judaism. I was able to see this clearly in my studies, for I *do not* take for granted that the Old Testament times is exactly the same context, both historical and culturally, as post-Trent, Roman Catholic history. Coupled with growing-up in a Jewish context, I was able to see difference, separation and distinctiveness, clearly, where the natural law tradition sees only perfect continuity.

I have noticed that natural law also confuses the mind and the heart, when engaging scriptural exegesis, assuming that your "light" is your "mind" not realizing that your "guiding light" might be your heart, your soul, your conscience, your "gut-level feelings," you could even be hearing the Voice of God (the Holy Spirit).

Finally, "natural law" assumes that everyone is like the Greeks. That all peoples---regardless of what culture, religion or time-period; what gender, class or education level; or what disability, theory of mind or phenomenology is fundamentally "the same." Using "natural law" as the standard of what is a common language for "truth-telling" across all of humanity, derived from a very specific cultural, religious, historical, sexual, class, intellectual and charismatic context. In other words, a very specific social location! And, this very particular social location is used as "the gold standard" for "naming" all peoples, if not all humanity and even human nature itself. Naming a plethora of peoples in the process and annihilating their uniqueness and experiences in the process, not recognizing that there is more than one correct "ways of doing things," that there are more than one valid way to "be human." In otherwords, projecting the norms of the Hellenistic philosophical elite filtered through late-Medieval scholasticism, to all humanity, for all times, assuming that this is the way, all humanity and human nature is like, in all places, times and conditions.

For these reasons, I work more out of a *Divine command ethical-moral framework* than a *natural law ethical-moral framework*---because I contend there needs to be balance, integration, even consistency between our highest moral ideals and our everyday pragmatic realities to live an ethical, moral life at-all, in such an imperfect world---so the "Ought" can truly become "The Way Things of Are." So we can "get started" working toward the world we long for---"right now."

We can only accomplish this through respecting the unique contributions of the Holy Bible and the Christian tradition, through having a personal relationship with the Living God, where we will receive direct, "unmediated" ethical-moral guidance from the Creator, Sustainer and Redeemer of the Entire Universe and through engaging "the real world," "the world-around-us."

So in essence, "***hyperspecific reasoning***," ***recognizing the uniqueness in all things*** is the ***first pillar in developing an autistic hermeneutic***, a critical, interpretive lens for studying religious documents and the world-around, from a particular perspective. A framework, which I use as an autistic theologian, part of my doing theology "in pictures," which can also be adopted and cultivated by neurotypicals, just as certain male neurotypical theologians are now sensitive to be concerned about certain women's issues (e.g., gender inclusive language for human beings) and employing more feminine, less patrarchical, ways of thinking about the world (e.g., being non-dualistic).

### *"Thinking-in-Pictures"*:

Temple Grandin describes her concept of "thinking-in-pictures,"

> When I say I'm a visual thinker I don't mean just that I'm good at making architectural drawings and designs, or that I can design my cattle-restraining systems in my head. I actually think in pictures. During my *thinking* process I have no words in my head at all, just pictures…[36]

"Thinking-in-pictures" as a Christian theologian on the spectrum, like Temple Grandin, has been a "mixed blessing" in my career. I was asked to leave a doctoral program, with a strong scholastic emphasis, which meant absolutely thinking in words. And, thinking in words the first go around. It was not enough to get a fragment of an idea and then fill it in. It had to be coherent, consistent, all the way through, from beginning to end. As a result, among other issues, I was not able to make the very high grades, required to stay in the program. Yet, on the other hand, I got a Master thesis topic and a third published book, out of my thinking in pictures. As mentioned before, my idea came to me through "preservations" on course schedules and schemes.

Just as Grandin studied animal behavior in pictures, I have engaged in theological reflection in pictures. It is a way of engaging in theological reflection which I will contend as equally valid and a way of doing theology which the theology academic establishment must take more seriously than they do now---as is beginning to happen, such as Christian Theologian Sallie McFague's "metaphorical theology."

As Grandin eloquently pointed out, "thinking-in-pictures" *does not* mean that I as am person with Asperger am the best architect in town. Although some of you might. What "thinking-in-pictures" means is manipulating abstract ideas through metaphoric images, in other words, "thinking-in-pictures" means "thinking in metaphors" and "speaking in parables." It challenges certain fashionable ideas in the humanities, that language is a prerequisite for consciousness. Thinking-in-pictures is very Humian in nature, referring to enlightenment philosopher David Hume; human knowledge is gained through "sense impressions" versus "abstract logic."

That is how I engage in theological reflection: "sense impressions" versus "abstract logic."

As a result, like a Medievalist, I am very dependent on liturgical art, signs and sacraments, pilgrimage and hagiography to get much of my theological insights. Even God's Creation provides me with theological data. I see a field of flowers and I am reminded "that Solomon in all his glory is not arrayed like one of these." I see a flock of crows and I am reminded "that the birds of the air neither sow nor reap, but their Heavenly Father, feeds them." I see a family in the mustard family and I am remaindered "to have a mustard seed of faith, to tell the mulberry tree, with my mustard seed of faith to be uprooted and go into the sea."

I even was able to comprehend the Holy Trinity through studying Nature. I saw flowers that had many members, yet were all one flower. I saw the three leaflets of clover, yet were all one leaf. I notice that the human being----is mind, body and soul. Most profound of them all, God pointed-out that the Holy Trinity is like a closed-looped ecosystem. God wanted me to think of His Creation as Trinitarian, made of distinct persons, yet part of an integrated whole. Once I started to understand the Trinity in these terms, it began to make more sense to me. It did not sound like an "off-the-wall" conceptualization of God, but a Model of God, very much grounded in the Natural World. Even through complex. Yet, the Natural World is extremely complex, too.

When I did my reading component for my theology coursework in graduate school, God had me do what we call "Spiritual Laboratories" which was an attempt to make my theological studies more empirical, experimental and experiential. We started doing Spiritual Laboratories formally two-thirds way through undergraduate, for other academic subjects. It really enlivened my learning and made it more interesting and stimulating. Basically, a Spiritual Laboratory are a set of questions developed before reading a text or doing a particular project or writing a paper and I answer them as I read through the text or complete the required work. Some of the questions are more reflective, others more experiential. This was a system where I could work through issues and discover new truth.

Also, fieldtrips were essential to my learning. In America, our educational system is very cerebral, meaning mostly lecture, readings and papers. This is particularly so in the humanities, and especially in theological studies. Since, high school, I needed to go on fieldtrips, to bring-to-life, what I was studying. For example, when I read *Hunchback of Notre Dame* for an English class, my mother drove me to the National Cathedral, in Washington D.C. and we went up to the bell tower, to read a passage from this great classic. We made countless fieldtrips when I completed Honors U.S. History in high school to everywhere from historical gristmills, to living history museums, to an Underground Railroad Tour of my home county. I was really blessed, for almost all the major historical sites in American History, were within driving distance of my house. But, most communities have historical places of interest, including a local historical society. So, resources are available where-ever you live, to do something similar.

Later on, once I arrived at college, I continued this tradition with my Lord. For example, when I did my independent study in "Christian Environmental History" one of the exercises we did was visit churches and other religious institutions in the Washington Area, to study their landscape architecture. It was real revealing!

We used to also take long bicycle rides in the country, to bring alive my science studies. Studying the local ecology, which was very diverse and interesting, on the Eastern Shore of Maryland. When I studied Plant Systematics, we used the campus which was a recognized arboretum, as a living laboratory to learn the plants, both in English and Latin names, for my exams. The plant families and their subsequent Latin names began to make more sense, once I had the opportunity to visit the National Arboretum, in Washington D.C. Even, in graduate school, we kept alive this tradition of going on fieldtrips, too, visiting art museums, monasteries and friaries, going on mini-pilgrimages and going to guest lectures and conferences, in the Boston area.

Fieldtrips were supplemented with other observational and experiential learning opportunities, through the years. When I studied *Great Expectations* in high school, my mother made a blacksmith dinner for me with period dishes which she got out of a period cookbook. My father's old tour guide of Notre Dame Cathedral in Paris, France was very useful when I read the *Hunchback of Notre Dame.* And, when I read Homer's *Odyssey,* an atlas of the Mediterranean Sea was very useful. I would also make visual representations of concepts I learned in my various high school science courses, in ceramics class, to help learn abstract science concepts. I made a coaster set with the stages of mitoses, the process of cell division. I was even able to understand a difficult concept in mathematics, when my math tutor led me out into her backyard and we were able to identify examples of this concept, manifested in the Natural World.

Once, I went to college, God provided me with other important visuals. When I was to take Chemistry, asking the "so what" question, God led me around campus and showed me how chemistry is manifested in "the world-around-me." Too bad, being "turned onto" the subject, was not enough to pass the class. Instead of exploring the relevancy of chemistry to me, they wanted me to engage in mindless manipulations of equations. They could care less whether I understood the concepts or principles or made it relevant to my studies, interests and passions.

In graduate school, We took advantage of religious art on campus, such as everytime I studied Francis of Assisi in my Franciscan Studies course; I had a three-dimensional portrait of Francis nearby. Onetime, we were reading a chapter in Bonaventure about Francis and God had me dress-up like Francis and then as I was reading about Francis overcoming conquering his fear of people with leprosy, when I became conscious of my surroundings, I was touching a fire extinguisher. Growing-up, I absolutely dreaded fire drills in elementary school. Subconsciously, I was conquering my own age old fear.

I particularly liked and did very well in my Spirituality courses, for they had more room for "thinking-in-pictures" than more academic theology courses. They had many opportunities to engage and experiment around with different spiritual exercises and disciplines; they provided a fair amount of the books and other materials with pictures and images and I had opportunities to do things like go on "mini-pilgrimages," visit local churches, study artwork and overall be more creative with my thinking and expressing myself. I even would get assignments like describe using the metaphor of weather, one's mood for the last week. These assignments really resonated with my thinking.

My study pilgrimage to the Franciscan Holy Sites of Italy, with Franciscan Pilgrimages, even more so. Here for example, we would do, as officially part of the pilgrimage; such things as a ritual reenactment of Saint Clare's escape from the world, retracing her very steps or renew our Franciscan commitments at the very same hermitage, Fonto Colombo, where Francis wrote his

Later Rule of Life. Pilgrimage is a good discipline for me-for every step, every action, every choice, every vista, takes on symbolic meaning, for a pilgrimage "at-heart" is "an internally reflective journey."

Also, "thinking-in-pictures" allowed me to access other's "theory of mind" and cultivate a sense of empathy. When I read *Our Town* in high school, I had to play Howie Newson; the milkman in Grover's Corner for a school assignment through giving a speech from his point-of-view. I became very attached to this character and I wore bibbed overalls for many years' afterword. To mimic him, by wearing his clothes! Many years later, I did the same with Saint Francis of Assisi; I purchased on-line a medieval outfit, which resembled Francis's penance clothing. I even wore it around as everyday clothing, as well as wearing it, to events like the Maryland Renaissance festival.

In addition to wearing another man's clothes, literally "walking in his shoes," when I do my fasting--- I would often fast in such a way that would get me in touch with what different monks and friars would feel in past time-periods. One time, I fasted on one-meal a day for a Lent, to see what it was like to function on only one meal a day, like Saint Francis and his early friars did. Other times, I would skip breakfast during a lent period; to get in touch with it was like to be a Benedictine monk, what his stomach would feel like, during the Middle Ages. One time when I studied Cardinal Newman, I only ate bread and water for breakfast, in ritual reenactment of Cardinal Newman's conversion fast at Littlemore, when he made the decision to leave the Anglican Church and enter the Roman Catholic Church. When I first read Bonaventure's biography of Saint Francis, I spent much energy trying to imagine what Francis's body, would feel like, while engaging in his severe asceticism such as his long fasts and the like.

Whether it was wearing another man's clothes, eating another man's diet or reenacting another women's life, all of these are examples of how I came to the same theological truths as a neurotypical. I just go about it differently, "thinking in pictures," doing theological reflection in pictures.

"Thinking in pictures" is my ***second pillar of an autistic hermeneutic for doing theology: using metaphor and images to understand abstract concepts***, whether in literature, theology or life. "Thinking in pictures" allows a person on the spectrum, like myself, to access complex, theological concepts and principles and hold my own with neurotypical religious and theologians. "Thinking in pictures" gives me the "theory of mind" for understanding the Concept of God through giving me concrete "analogies of being."

### *Detailed Oriented:*

Grandin describes how peoples on the spectrum are detailed oriented,

> Normal human beings are abstractified in their sensory perceptions as well as their thoughts. That's the big difference between animals and people, and also between autistic people and non-autistic people. Animals and autistic people don't see their ideas of things; they see the actual things themselves. We see the details that make up the world, while normal people blur all those details together into their general concept of the world…When an animal or an autistic person is seeing the real world instead of his idea of the world that mean's he is seeing detail to know about the way animals perceive the world; animals see details people don't see. They are totally detail-oriented.[37]

As a theologian on the autism spectrum I "bring to the table" my detailed-oriented view of the world, seeing the world more concretely, with all its complexities and diversity, versus a more abstractified "concept of the world." This asset is particularly important in ecotheology and science-faith dialogue discussions. This is because much of the literature on ecotheology and science theology is abstractified into a singular "concept of the world." The complexities and diversity of ecological perspectives are oftentimes reduced to nebulous, amorphous, concepts such as "interdependency" or "sustainability," an oversimplification, which does not take into consideration both the complexity and diversity of ecological thought throughout environmental history. Even the terms "ecosystem" or "ecology" themselves, signify an abstraction of the world. Confusing thinking holistically about the Natural World, with just simplifying the world into an abstract concept of the world, which all the world's denizens must conform too. Not realizing that "the real world" is more complex.

True--- "interdependency" and "sustainability" are important ecological values, as are the terms "ecosystem" and "ecology," but so is "non-anthropocentrism," so is "intrinsic value," so is "natural selection." Three ecological values which oftentimes get neglected or misunderstood in these oversimplified concepts of the world. Then there is the animal rights/animal welfare perspective which consistently gets ignored or dismissed out of hand, by ecotheologians, without a fair hearing. Ecological holism *is not* the only way to "think green."

I had to bring this issue out in *Christian Environmental Studies* (USA: Create Space Independent Publishing Platform, 2012). There is only one thing and one thing only, which unifies the environmental movement. A commitment to do ones part to save the planet and a commitment to create a more ecologically viable society.

To call oneself an environmentalist, one *does not* need to embrace certain scientific or economic dogmas; one *does not* need to embrace certain political strategies or even certain alternative spiritualities like Native American spirituality or Wicca. You can still be a Young Earth Creationist and still call one an environmentalist because you still see the world as God's Creation and believe that human beings have a responsibility to be good stewards of it.

One can still be a free-market libertarian and still call oneself an environmentalist, for they see the environment as a legitimate and important issue, but contend that planetary issues cannot be effectively addressed through an inefficient government bureaucracy.

One can even be an individualist and call oneself an environmentalist, seeing the value in each animal life, honoring each living being, viewing each life as sacred, honoring and respecting the rights of all animals, as much as our own individual lives. These are known as ecological individualists or animal rights/welfare people. My environmental ethic fits most closely with ecological individualism.

Then there is the issue of the concrete reality of God's Creation, which is very seldom addressed in ecotheological or science and religion literature. It is almost always talked about in abstraction, in generality---almost always an indoor activity. For example, in the neurotypical ecotheology and science theology fields, the spiritual and theological significance of Creation at-large is discussed, such as the Universe being made by God. But, very rarely is "meaning-making" made from specific elements in Nature, such as the spiritual and theological significance of the lemon thyme which died in my balcony herb garden or the Canada geese which I saw at a local national wildlife refuge.

Even "place-based" Christian Ecotheologies are only beginning to appear in the literature. This of course is changing as it is gaining momentum. And, certain figures in the movement are becoming aware of this. Yet, if the Natural World is "liken to a book," as some in the movement have suggested, the Book of Nature still reads like a book report than an exegesis. Each stanza, each period, or comma, *is not* carefully studied, dissected and analyzed by a theologian. While, large parts of Earth let alone the Universe beyond, *are not* theologically mapped and subsequently sanctified.

Creation, as a lived reality *is not* homogonous by any stretch of the imagination. There are countless bioregions, species which have not even been discovered by science, let alone being theologically reflected upon, not to even mention the vastness of outer space. All of this remaining a theological mystery, in terms of tying to understand its significance. Much of it challenging what a general Christian sacred canopy of God's Creation can explain: avian siblicide, incest of endemic species, extinction of entire species, even entire evolutionary lineages.

Even the question of animal intelligence in nonhuman animals *has not* been addressed thoughtfully, theologically. What does it mean for a Judeo-Christian view of the uniqueness of human beings, in a world, where humans *are not* the only rational, conscious animals, *are not* the only species with language, culture, who lives in a *polis*, even make tools, where humans are living in a world with other creatures who have emotions, can feel pain, even suffer? Where even such cherished "uniqueness spotting" such as morality even religious capacities *is not* as certain as it was before?

We now know that the elements which lead to later moral development first emerged in nonhuman primates, in Central Africa, not with Greek philosophers in Ancient Greece. And, morality emerged out of pragmatic experience, not abstract rationality. There is even some evidence, that even the capacity to have religious experience is not uniquely human, it is been established that some nonhuman primates have symbolic rituals, and can even engage in rudimentary meditation. Having religious self-understandings liken to animalism.

In many ways, theology is the final frontier of science. And, meaning making, the final frontier of the Universe. Despite all the factual knowledge accumulated by science, in the last several hundred years, recognizing that much factual knowledge still remains to be discovered by science, the various research programs in systematic theology have yet to theologically account for a mere fraction of the major scientific discoveries of the late-twentieth century in the molecular biology, ecology, geography, chemistry, behavioral, cognitive and environmental science fields. Science theology has succeeded in grasping and integrating the major scientific discoveries of the mid-twentieth century like evolutionary biology, physical medicine, computer science, information systems, astronomy and quantum physics, however, although there is still much science-faith dialogue to be done in human evolution.

Finally, in science theology, there is the whole difficulty of using philosophy as "a bridge" between science and theology. Philosophy, far from being an epistemological Switzerland, which can allow "common ground" for science and religion discourse, philosophy, is really an intellectual vortex with its own paradigms, norms, taboos and controversies. So instead of dialogue being advanced on the relationship between science, theology and religion, it is lost in a vacuum of philosophical discourse where both science and religion get equally short-changed and instead the focus becomes philosophy. As a result, very little in science theology involves a direct encounter with science and Nature. Almost none of it involves the use of empirical, experiments and direct meaning-making of the Universe, from scientific data. Working along the side of scientists, reading meaning into freshly, uncover scientific data. Or, even the scientist engaging in theological reflection as he or she unearths factual data, even having the theologian informing the questions being investigated, being able to intelligently and thoughtfully critique the scientist's work.

An Asperger theologian like myself, who is detailed oriented, can help-out these worthwhile research programs in that a detailed-oriented autistic hermeneutic can:

- Nuisance and diversify the picture of environmental thought, for ecotheologians and science theologians. Interpreting the complexity and diversity of the movement.

- Flesh-out the Doctrine of Creation, for both ecotheologians and science theologians. Connect the Doctrine of Creation with its concrete manifestation in lived reality. In other words, break-down the divide between the Doctrine of Creation, "an abstract concept of the world," and "the real world" of real-life birds, trees, flowers, rivers and places. In other words, create an exegesis of the Book of Nature.

- Study, experiment on and experience directly, the Natural World, theologically, for ecotheologians and science theologians alike. In other words, use scientific data to create theological meaning. Use science as nothing less than a tool for theologians. Science in service of theology. Used to verify religious claims.

These are the three main contributions, a detail-oriented autistic hermeneutic, can make to the discussion in Christianity on ecotheology and science and religion. Nuance and diversify the synthesizing of ecological and scientific thought. Flesh-out the Doctrine of Creation. Put together science and religion, more effectively. And, as a result, advance these important "cutting edge" fields in academic theology.

For an example of what a detailed-oriented hermeneutic looks like in practice, I onetime walked into a forest with my Lord growing-up and God pointed-out a mushroom. He explained that I was like that mushroom, living in the debris of the forest floor, yet rising above the death and decay of the forest, to become something beautiful, since than we have codified mushrooms as our symbol for the Resurrection.

On that same foray, I went out into a mountain laurel heath with my Lord and We discovered a stream, with a main torrent and a maundering oxbow with hardly any water in it. God explained that the later, the meandering oxbow, was "the narrow gate" (Mathew 7: 13-14) "the way, the truth, and life" (John 14: 6), the other, "wide and the way easy, that leads to destruction and those who enter by it are many" (Mathew 7: 13-14).

More recently, my senior year of college, when I completed Wetland Ecology, when I visited different wetland types at each different wetland type, I felt different emotions. I visited a freshwater tidal wetland and it was right after Nineleven and I felt much healing and this was most likely the wetland type that Baby Moses was stashed in, so I came to the conclusion that freshwater tidal wetlands are places of refuge.

When we visited a brackish marsh on a fieldtrip, I had an entirely different emotional experience. It was mosquito invested and we had to wade through stands of this plant called black needlerush which had an extremely sharp point at the tip of its stem which "I swore" felted like the "stinging swords" which protected people from entering the Garden of Eden. Also, there is some archeological evidence that the Garden of Eden is in a place in Southern Iraq which is one of the largest wetlands in the world, so I put two and two together and came to the conclusion that the Garden of Eden was not a tropical dry forest but a brackish marsh. And, the stinging swords were a plant like black needlerush. Or, maybe even the mosquitoes.

Some of the real masters of detailed-oriented thinking are some of the great naturalists, John Muir, Henry David Thoreau, Aldo Leopold, Annie Dillard, Rachel Carson, Jane Goodall, John James Audubon, E.O. Wilson and Enos Mills. Many that I contend were proberly on the autism spectrum.

For Muir, every detail of the entire American Western landscape was literally animated with religious significance. Related faithfully back to the Judeo-Christian sacred canopy. For Thoreau, although not as religious as Muir, still- every act, every walk, every experience, a pilgrimage and a retreat with spiritual significance and self-reflective revelation.

Leopold, incredibly sensitive to subtle seasonable changes in his Sand County environment, he knew when the first species of wildflower came-up in the spring. A wildflower most people ignore. Dismiss as a garden weed. He picked-up on "January Thaw," an incredible subtlety in Nature.

Annie Dillard sat still at Tinker Creek, a suburban Virginia stream, visiting faithfully for an entire year, trying to understand its significance. Rachel Carson described in some of her lesser known books, the Natural World in great detail as a great scientist and naturalist must, but with the literary prose of an artist.

Even, our Biblical tradition, gives us a place to begin--- to have a more detailed view of "the world-around-us." In Job 38-42, when God explains His vision and purpose for All Creation, God gave Job a series of questions, describing the religious significance of a plethora of Creatures. Psalm 104--- describes in remarkable depth the Israeli bioregion. The parables and sayings of our Lord Jesus Christ use the Details of Nature to Praise God. In addition, to the metaphor of Creation, which the Bible provides, the Bible also provides many wonderful naturalistic insights, becoming the basis of a more detailed-view of Creation. Even the Genesis Creation account *is not* an abstract conceptualization of Nature. The creation of each taxom is described in fantastic detail. The plants and animals of the Bible can also be cataloged and translated to appropriate bioregions using the phyla-genetic methodology of academic biology (a scientific map of how exactly all life is genetically related to one another within the context of the process of evolutionary history, where scientists often use the metaphor "The Tree of Life," such as finding a family member of a plant or animal species of the Bible in your own bioregion).

The Christian tradition also provides many resources for more detailed-oriented thinking about the Natural World. Francis in Heaven revealed to me that Saint Bonaventure, also a Franciscan, in his essay "A Soul's Journey into God," in his chapter on Creation, provides a framework for finding God in Nature, when religious symbolism, imagery and typologies are not readily apparent in Nature.

Examples of Christian symbols readily available in wild Nature include arrangements of hay shaped like crosses, "the birds of the air" or "the flowers of the field." Other examples of Christian symbols embodied into the Natural World include consecrated Christian sacred spaces, like a place where a Christian saint onetime preformed a miracle.

Yet many times, hay *does not* always fall in the shape of a cross, some days are slow birdwatching days and outside in the middle of a cold winter there is not a flower to be found. Most bioregions of the world are not consecrated as a Christian sacred space, for a saint never set foot there, nor is there an historical connection to Biblical Times in any of the bioregions of the Americas.

Meaning in Saint Bonaventure's method of theological reflection and prayer, Judeo-Christian meaning-making is accomplished through finding vestiges of God's "wisdom, power, and goodness" [something of God] in the various characteristics or properties of each of God's creatures.

Saint Anthony of Padua, another Franciscan, when he preached his sermon "to the fish of the sea," related the category of fish to the Biblical and Christian traditions, to sanctify "the fish" and explain to us, the theological and symbolic significance of "all the fish of the sea."

Saint Francis of Assisi himself was a master of being detailed-oriented in his theological reflection--- making specific Christian theological associations to everything he encountered in God's Creation. Certain places, he liked, because of the disproportionate amount of celestial beings which visited there. Other places he considered especially holy and only let his best friars enter. One spit rock formation at La Verna, where Francis received the Stigmata, God revealed to Francis as the rock which was split in two, when our Lord Jesus Christ was crucified. Francis was also reminded of Our Lord Jesus Christ whenever he saw an animal which he felt most closely resembled Christ, such as a lamb or a goat, for example. He attached special significance to the lark, a native bird to his bioregion. Even after Francis's death, Assisi was dubbed the New Jerusalem and the spot of Francis's burial, went from being the "Hill of Hell" because criminals were executed there to the "Hill of Heaven" once Francis was buried there.

Then there is the Bestiary tradition of the Middle Ages, where the divine significance of a specific creature is described and cataloged. Although their interpretations of animal behavior were often crude, they can easily be updated using the knowledge of modern science and ethology.

In more recent times, in the nineteenth century, in response to the scientific revolution, natural theologians would write essays like "The Theology of Insects" and the like.

Today Cathleen Norris has documented Benedictine Monks creating theological and spiritual meaning from their Dakota landscape--- monks and nuns who live in the Dakotas, integrating their stories, identities and even their European Christian traditions into the landscape.

I *am not* the first to purpose an experimental approach to theology; The late Sir John Templeton also independently came to the same conclusion and wrote a book about it. Even back in colonial times, Reverent Hoar, the president of Harvard University, wanted chemistry labs and greenhouses for his seminary students.

So, a modern-day theologian on the autism spectrum, like myself can pick-up where these previous programs left off, using the resources of scripture and tradition as a place to begin, to develop a more detail-oriented ecotheology and science theology, which is more nuanced, developed, integrated and analytical than current science-faith discourse.

In otherwords, take ecotheology and science theology to its logical conclusion. So therefore, being detail-oriented is the ***third pillar to my autistic hermeneutic***, ***seeing the complexity and diversity of the world-around-us***, whether in Nature or History, ***instead of reducing the world to a singular set of oversimplified concepts***.

### *Extreme Perception*:

Grandin describes "extreme perception,"

> …Normal people can't have extreme perception the way normal animals can, because hyper-specificity and extreme perception go together… I'm calling this ability the hidden figure talent, based on some research findings in autism.[38]

In other words, extreme perception is the ability to find something hidden. A small songbird hidden in a dense cedar tree, an interesting light brown mushroom camouflaged on the dark forest floor. These are all examples of extreme perception or what Grandin calls the "hidden figure talent." According to Grandin, extreme perception and hyperspecificality go together, although the precise relationship Grandin is unsure of it--- what she does know that "it exists" and "it works." In other words, the "extreme perception" abilities of many people on the autism spectrum, is a very real phenomena.

One thing Grandin is clear about is that peoples on the spectrum have a special gift for "extreme perception," the ability to find hidden things, which neurotypicals miss. For example, my mother is always commenting when we go out on a hike in Nature that I am able to point-out birds or other things in Nature, which she misses.

The "hidden figure talent" helps me in my faith and in theological studies, in that I am able to see hypocrisies and problems, which other neurotypical Christians seem to miss. Recover quotes and passages, from texts, which people who have worked with them for years have missed. Uncover insights which no one else is even able to think of. My extreme perception helps me in a variety of theological tasks whether it is hermeneutically retrieval, exegetical work, careful listening or critical engagement with texts or lectures.

All of these, I can attribute to my "hidden figure talent," my ability to see things other people miss, and to see these things clearly, like glaring neon signs. Where to neurotypicals, they do not see a problem or issue to be concerned about, where I see nothing but outrage and injustice. This is because neurotypicals see "Peace, Peace,' when there is no peace." (Jeremiah 6: 14). I see evil and injustice, where no one else does or before anyone else does or begins to notice.

For example, when Nineleven happened, I *was not* shocked, maybe at the magnitude, but I could sense that something like this was coming. My extreme perception combined with my formation as an environmentalist, I could see the destructive tendencies of globalization so clearly. While Bush's approval ratings were the highest in American history and everyone was waving the American flag at every turn, I could see clearly what was going on. The War on Terrorism was being used as an excuse for the government to take away our civil liberalities. I was "scared to death!"

Before the War in Iraq even started, I was against it, for I knew that getting rid of Saddam Hussein would leave a "power vacuum" in the region, leading to much chaos and destruction. That is because the possibility that Saddam Hussein had weapons of mass destructions was the precise reason why we must not go in there and "cross him." It was not worth provoking Saddam Hussein "setting off" in retaliation--- even one atomic bomb, for our fragile planet cannot risk the discharge of even one of these nuclear devices. Even though it played out differently, the end result was overwhelmingly negative. Still this conflict is not solved.

Of course, I am not the only one in "the left" who saw "the writing on the wall" (Daniel 5: 5; 5:13). Many others, in the know, did, but my "extreme perception" helped me find the "hidden figure" whether it was a "power vacuum" filled with a terrible dictator, the damage done by a globalized political economy going array or the "signs of the times" (Mathew 16:3). The "writing on the wall" and "the signs of the times" *are not* always obvious to neurotypicals, for I often go into meetings and everyone is excited, for they are all in agreement of the same breakthrough, really just another fashionable idea, yet I leave, feeling far from "on the same page."

For example, onetime local environmental activists were invited to meet with an environmentally sympathetic county councilman; everyone was in almost unanimous agreement, that the only way that one can get environmental change in our county is to "appeal to people's pocketbooks" as a reason why they need to protect the environment. That people only do what is in their economic self-interest and are not swayed by moral or other higher arguments. I on the other hand, saw sprawl and overdevelopment as in fact, clearly a moral issue. Where I both contended and believed, that one can and must appeal to people's higher natures. I was a fledging Christian at the time and I spoke before the audience about the fact that I am a Christian and one veteran in the movement omitted, "that they are stealing from our children's future." So an entire group of intelligent people convinced themselves to one way of looking at a problem or situation, yet I with my "hidden figure talent" came to a completely different conclusion.

I of course, was vindicated many years later, when the recent oil crisis started to happen and despite phenomenal spikes in oil prices, people would get-up on the local news and say they absolutely plan to still keep driving their SUVs. Appealing to people's "enlightened self-interest" simply does not lead to necessary environmental changes. With the oil crisis escalating follow Nineleven, at the *2008* Republican National Convention, one of the slogans was, "Drill, Baby, Drill!" using the oil crisis as an excuse for both drilling in the Arctic National Wildlife Refuge and Offshore, both extremely ecologically destructive practices and policies.

Now many people want to exploit nonrenewable natural resources even more than ever, because they want to reduce dependence on Middle East oil making every square inch of land and ocean usable. Even, with the Democrats, the talk is still "quick technological fixes" such as alternative energy, some of them more ecologically friendly, than others, for example---"clean" coal, fracking, offshore oil drilling and building a new pipeline are hardly green solutions. Very little talk in the public square of lifestyle change, such as a better, more effective public transportation system, more pedestrian friendly streets, more bike lanes and bike paths, carpooling, or god fid, anything which would involve collective responsibility. Even well loved technological "magic bullets" such as solar, wind and "smart grids" all have ecological "side effects" and "shadow sides."

I saw even in the late 1990s, when realism was a fashionable idea in environmental circles that this idea was misguided and would not "bear fruit" (John 15). I perceived the conflicting reality of the still very serious planetary crisis and the problem was not being addressed. There was still the "nagging question" of "is this sustainable?" In fact, over a decade later---this answer has still not been completely resolved, where global climate change, the worldwide loss of biodiversity, nuclear war even human overpopulation remain very real threats to human and planetary survival.

Yet, on the other hand, ecological consciousness is at an all time high, where appealing to the spiritual ideals of ecological hope and political empowerment are more important than ever to help motivate ordinary citizens to direct action and personal responsibility, so individual, concerned citizens *do not* succumb to despair and inertia and end-up doing nothing at-all, when they could be doing something---such as making personal ecological lifestyle choices and engaging in grassroots environmental activism in their communities.

The environmental movement has made significant headway into organized religion and conservatives in recent years. Mainly, not by appealing to peoples pocketbooks, an environmentalist would lose almost every time, but by appealing to people's religious faith, to people's conscience, to people's sense of empathy and concern and sense of responsibility. This has gotten the environmental movement much farther than enlighten self-interest.

Yet, my "extreme perception" is also telling me that there are serious problems with this approach too, despite the cynical, nihilistic consensus in the Christian environmental movement. The human psyche cannot physically sustain a not stop barrage of moralistic pontification by a hypocritical, privileged clergy class with strong colonialist roots, who are insularly "out-of-touch" with the laity, who put good, ordinary people on a diet of guilt and shame, by a social institution which ordinary people depend on for comfort and grace (disproportionately people with disabilities or those who suffering from chronic illnesses and their family members). The end result of using guilt and shame to motivate the people is "Compassion Fatigue," followed, by the laity and even some of the clergy leaving the Christian Church completely in droves.

From a neurodiversity perspective, this is because the mind is a body a too! Meaning the brain is an embodied, flesh-and-blood organ, a member of the human body system, the nervous system, meaning that feeding and caring for the mind is a "material well-being" issue. Meaning psychological realities are just as real realities as any other biophysical reality. Meaning respecting a person's feelings is non-negotiable, from an embodiment perspective, to remain a morally consistent position. By not doing so, according to Grandin, you trigger a person's "fear-rage system." To get a person to change their behaviors, according to Grandin, we need to appeal to a person's "play-seeking system." As Christian environmentalists, we want to appeal to the "play-seeking systems" of North American Christians, not their "fear-rage systems." In other words, positively versus negativity motivate them.[39]

In fact, one of the goals of the Christian environmental movement is to save community in America. Yet, in addressing the decline of community in America, they are further undermining community in America through dislocating, destabilizing, dividing even destroying many healthy, functional, life-giving, authentic--- multicultural, human scale, place-based communities across the country through insisting on a specific ideology, a specific organization, a certain rigidity and a tremendous amount of "group-think," competitiveness even downright exclusivity and cliquishness, turning "nurturing communities" into politically polarized "viper pits," in the process.

For example, assuming that everyone in North America is this "selfish consumer" leaves very little room for "the disability experience." Mainly---most Americans with Disabilities *are not* getting what we need in terms of health care, housing, employment and love. While, the main thing preventing Americans with Disabilities from doing more on the environment and social justice is that Americans with Disabilities are systematically discriminated against by organized religion and by the progressive movements, coupled with an ecological-animal rights ideology which *is not* only inaccessible to peoples with disabilities, it is even hostile even cruel and downright heartless toward our plight, such as "the argument from marginal cases (AMC) in animal rights and "collective autism" in environmentalism.

For example, when I attended the Society for Disability Studies (SDS) conference this last year in 2012, I went to a workshop called "Activism from the Intersections: Occupying Wall Street, Occupying Ourselves." The panel was made-up of a group of about five disability political activists (Sharon Wascher, Aimi Hamraie, Seema Bahl, Gordon Sasaki and Margaret Price) who told their own personal stories of participating in the "a disability delegation" at "Occupy Wall street," part of a growing anti-capitalist, anti-globalization, highly radical-revolutionary, mostly grassroots movement made up of ordinary, concerned citizens in America which is specifically targeting the Corporate Class (the top 1% socioeconomic bracket, such as our business, political, military and religious leaders). Not only did they have to "stand naked" before "the powers that be," they also had to deal with activist-organizers in their own movement who *did not* want "a mental illness" presence, some members were from the neurodiversity community, for "it would hurt the image of the movement." This is the type of garbage Americans with Disabilities have to deal with by people who claim to be liberal-progressive.

I can give other examples. The most important thing to know is that peoples on the spectrum have an extraordinary gift for "extreme perception." The ability to see things, other people miss, liken to the prophets of Ancient Israel, peoples on the spectrum can be very helpful to discern "the signs of the times" (Mathew 16:3), if you are willing to listen to us.

In other words, people on the spectrum, because of our "*hidden figure talent*" have the ability to discern and discern extremely effectively, a gift which can be utilized by the Body of Christ and various social movements, a gift which must be "carefully listened to," a gift which is the *fourth pillar of an autistic hermeneutic*.

It is important to realize that when I am talking about the spiritual gifts of autism, *I am not implying a supernatural psychic power*, which leads to humans on the autism spectrum being "used" and "manipulated" by misguided neurotypicals, "being put on a pedestal, just to be torn down." What I am talking about is *the spiritual strengths of autism, a biophysical phenomena grounded in biophysical reality---* mainly applying our unique way of perceiving the world, based on our own unique nervous systems, to a spiritual, religious, theological context.

### *Concrete Analysis*:

Grandin writes,

> [Non-autistic] people stop seeing the details that make up the big picture and see only the big picture instead. That's what your [vermis does] for you: [it] give the big picture. Animals see all the tiny details that go into the big picture.[40]

In otherwords, according to Grandin, I as a person on the spectrum am more concrete than a neurotypical, in how I feel emotions, analyze problems or engage the "world-around-me." Neurotypicals see the "big picture," I see the many "little pictures" which "go into the big picture." For example, I feel "confusion" versus "having successfully identifying mixed feelings;" identify with a "specific issue" versus a "vague notion," or bond with an individual animal, plant or biotic community versus the planet or Universe as a whole, although, I always love a good holistic analysis, any day.

A good example in my theological work is my work with Franciscan Studies. Much Franciscan environmentalism seems to reduce Francis's relationship with Animals and the Earth, to a vague notion of interdependency or interconnectiveness. That is how Saint Francis's relationships with Animals and the Earth are translated into today's context, according to such scholars. These scholars contend that what you can get out of studying Francis's relationship with Animals and the Earth is an appreciation of the interconnectiveness and interdependency of human beings to all life. But, when I studied the documents, I saw something else.

When I first read the legend of Saint Francis "taming the very fierce wolf of Gubbio," I *did not* see it as a story about "interdependency" or "the human shadow side," but a story about wildlife-human conflicts and their resolution, non-lethally, nonviolently and non-invasively. In other words, it was all about "interspecies communications."

When I visited San Domino, God had me explore the landscape around the Christian Church where Francis was inspired to write "The Canticle of All Creatures" outside his hometown of Assisi, Italy. We recovered many of the elements in the surrounding landscape, "Sir Brother Sun," "Sister Moon and Stars," "Brother Wind," "Sister Water" and "Sister Mother Earth."

We discovered that San Domino was in the middle of an open field, a place drenched with warm Italian sun. A place where Francis could watch the moon, rise and set each night throughout the year, also an excellent place to go-out stargazing under a dark Medieval sky.

Since, San Domino rested halfway down into the valley below from the City of Assisi which sat on a hill; Francis could watch Brother Wind "bring forth all kinds of weather" from Mount Saberio above the city to the plains below San Domino. From sublime storms to balmy afternoons, Francis of Assisi, saw and felt it all. Sister Water was a small spring below the convent of the Poor Clares (Francis of Assisi turned San Domino into a convent for Saint Clare's Poor Ladies).

The surrounding bucolic landscape was a land of olive orchards, wildflowers and wild herbs. There was also a wetland below San Domino in Francis's day, also home to many edible and medicinal plants. The wetland, was most likely a riparian forest coupled with a freshwater marsh like the one in Deer Ridge, which also explains the presence of mice which tormented the Man of God when he was trying to write the "Canticle of All Creatures", his "swan song," the meaning and purpose of his life, outside in a makeshift lento-like hut, when he was going blind and dying of a mysterious terminal illness, a wetland which has now been drained after Saint Francis's death in the thirteenth century. A wetland who although tormented the Man of God with disease carrying mice, also blessed the hungry Man of God with nutritious food, the thirsty Man of God with a "stream of life-giving water" and the frail, sickly, disabled Man of God with "healing herbs" to use Saint Francis's exact words. Not to mention, providing the Man of God, sanctuary from his persecutors and habitat and home for his beloved swallows and larks.

Saint Francis of Assisi, the Christian Patron Saint of Animals and Ecology, who was not at all judgmental or resentful of his cell in the swamp, whose inclination was to see the good in all God's works, coupled with his picturesque yet sublime, severe yet fecund San Damiano, his "healing space," the historical-critical context of his "Canticle of All Creatures," testifies to why Saint Francis of Assisi in his Canticle, perceived the Natural World to be more like a benevolent mother than "red tooth and claw" wildness, "Sister Mother Earth" to use Saint Francis's exact words, even calling each of his physical ailments a "sister" to his other brothers, at the end of his life, even calling Death in his Canticle, "Sister Death."

In other words, when Saint Francis is talking about the "sun, the moon and the stars" in his "Canticle" he *is not* just talking about "the elements" universally or as metaphors for "common human experiences," he is also talking about a very specific place, Francis's beloved San Domino in Thirteenth Century Italy.

So as the above demonstrates, my concrete thinking can break new ground in theological scholarship. Generate new theological information, allowing me to make a valuable contribution to even already "glutted" fields in theology. This is because most theological scholarship, regardless of the theological discipline, is almost all "big picture." Even scholarship which is very specialized and technical, is responding to a larger program, with preconceived assumptions, such as theologians writing about a particular passage in Saint Thomas within the Roman Catholic Tradition.

On the other hand, I *did not* set-out to "prove" that "The Canticle of All Creatures" was inspired by a particular place, I stumbled upon it. Although at some point I wanted to use the hagiography of the saints, to recover a wildlife management model for "reasoning with" versus "eradicating nuisance wild animals," I did not know in advance, everything which I was to discover. I discovered novelty, because I had an encounter with the "little picture," often overlooked by the "big picture" projects of academic theologians.

Being "little picture" oriented has also informed my views on the conflict between environmentalism and animal rights. I lean towards being an individualist versus a holist, for the lives of individual organisms or places, [for me] is what is the most concrete, what is the most real, what I can relate to and empathize with. In otherwords, what comes most naturally to me, is relating to individual birds or individual forests, not ecological concepts such as integrity or health, ecological processes such as natural selection, or environmental issues such as pollution or global climate change. I need a "face" put on "the environment."

That is why I am not willing to sacrifice the lives of individual organisms for the ecological whole; the ecological whole is an abstract concept, something that does not really exist in the real world---but an oversimplified model describing the complex web of interactions and relationships among individual beings. Or, whose existence is debatable, such as the debate between evolutionary biology ("red tooth and claw" individual organisms and species competing against one another for survival within the context of natural selection) and ecological biology ("mutual aid" individual organisms and species working together toward mutual survival within the context of natural selection).

Or, a little bit of both, like I believe, I contend with evolutionary biologists that individual organisms and species not ecosystems or the planet-- to use secular animal ethicist Tom Regan's words---are "subjects-of-a-life" and I contend with ecological biologists that the Natural World is more peaceful, harmonious and relational than many "hardened" Darwinists are willing to concede. I agree with both Christian ecotheologian Sallie McFague that the theological meaning of the Theory of Evolution is "non-anthropocentrism" not "human domination" and with Christian animal theologian Stephen Webb that the Theory of Evolution does not "disprove" the

Existence of God or refutes Christianity, just introduces new theodyssey questions about natural evil, including calling into question---basing environmental ethics on scientific principles (e.g., ecological holism) and applying scientific principles to the human sphere (e.g., Social Darwinism).

Instead, ethics and morality needs to be based on humanistic ethical-moral frameworks such as philosophy or theology. I contend that these same humanistic ethical-moral frameworks need to be applied to human relationships with Animals and the Earth, such as what animal rights ethicists have done with Emanuel Kant ("moral duties to animals") and what environmental ethicists have done with John Locke ("exists for its own sake").[41]

This is because both individual sentient animals and ecosystem integrity needs to be respected and protected. The various nervous systems of the world, human and animal alike, might be a "subjects-of-a-life," but to take away our social and physical environments, our habitat and home and our love ones is tantamount to "cutting us off" from our "source of healing and empowerment."

Meaning in this model, habitat destruction is in-fact an animal rights issue, because to take away an animal's habitat (ancestral physical environment) such as putting once "free range" animals into isolating and alienating "factory farms" is to take away an animal's happiness, comfort, safety and belonging, even freedom, liberation and self-determination, causing these captive animals, much pain, suffering, fear and want and all around misery and futility, in the process.

This model also contends that it is cruel and inhumane, for the sake of the last Passenger pigeon on Earth, to let that poor bird die a lonely death in a zoo (apart from members of its own species). Individual animals also need their home and their species boundaries' respected and protected.

For these reasons, I also appreciate the value of saving particular places--- a particular forest, a particular wetland versus just protecting samples of particular habitats or sacrificing certain pierces of land to save more desirable pierces of land somewhere else. For example, Deer Ridge, the wild area near where I lived which I have befriended, I am trying to respect and protect by cleaning-up litter, ecologically surveying the land, monitoring water quality and ecosystem health and collaborating with a local community activist to change neighborhood attitudes and behaviors towards this place from seeing Deer Ridge as a "garbage dump" to seeing Deer Ridge as a "community resource" which can be enjoyed and cherished by all. Becoming Deer Ridge's guardian, protector from harm, in the process.

In fact, for many years, I *could not* weed a garden, for I was concerned about the lives of "the weeds," for I valued "the weed's" life. One time, in Freshman Biology in college, I did not want to kill an ameba which I was looking at under the microscope, for I did not want to take its life. This was because I believed that in some mysterious way a dandelion and an ameba was a person, a distinct entity with its own mind (it's own intelligence, dandelions and amebas both have a genetic code, a unique order and "will to live"), its own soul (God's Holy Spirit is in them) and its own body (dandelions and amebas are both biologically alive).

I even value the Life of the Earth, even the Universe, for I see the Universe as nothing less than Christ, "The Body of God." So my objection to the Cosmic Christ is similar to the African-American, Womanist objection, "White Women's Christ, Black Woman's Jesus," that depersonalizing God *is not* desirable for oppressed minorities who depend on a personal relationship with God to access the tradition at-all, as our primary "source of healing and empowerment." Such a view *does not* deny Embodiment or the Incarnation, just insists that a personal relationship with God is non-negotiable for oppressed minorities.

As a neurodiverse human I take this a step further, "Neurotypical Man's Cosmic Christ, Autistic Man's Cosmic Jesus" making the case that a personal relationship with the Natural World is also a non-negotiable for neurodiverse humans, for us to be able to engage the planetary agenda at all, for directly engaging Animals and the Earth plays into our ecological strengths (such as Temple Grandin, Dawn Prince-Huges, Jim Sin Clare and myself) while making "human-human community" a prerequisite for engaging the Natural World, plays into our disability and makes the planetary agenda inaccessible.

In my case, I have much deeper seeded issues with other human beings and community than I do with Animals and the Earth. While, neurodiverse activists such as Grandin and Prince-Hughes found tremendous healing in their relationship with other human beings through reaching-out to the Natural World.

In other words, according to autistic community organizers Melanie Yergeau, Mark Romoser, Emily Titan and Carl Peterson who lead a discussion at the 2012 Society for Disability Studies (SDS) conference in Denver entitled "Yes, Autistic Community Exists and No, It's Not a Metaphor" argued that it's not that we cannot "do community"--- "it's just that we do it differently" because we learn differently and have a fundamentally different way of "being-in-the-world." Much of it has to do with "distance," "inclusion" and "reasonable accommodations."

Most importantly, as a neurodiverse man, that is how I experience the world, I experience the world as a person who I can have a personal relationship with, *I have more an "I-Thou" than an "I-it" relationship with the Earth*. Or, as Saint Anthony in Heaven says, "The Earth is the closest thing you have to a childhood friend, the only place where you have ever felt safe in your entire life, this is the reason why when you travel to a strange land [such as when I returned to the Pacific Northwest in the last couple of years] why you are not in awe, for you are more greeting this place like a long lost friend." Anthony contends that "the Earth is your best friend."

Of course, I have become more nuanced in recent times. I do on occasion pull out a weed, which is affecting my planted plants. Over time, as a student of the environment, I have developed a greater appreciation for ecological concepts, processes, and issues and with God's help, becoming more what We call the Ecological Trinitarian position versus ecological individualistic or ecologically holistic--- trying to balance individual rights with communal needs, recognizing the value of both individual persons and the system or community at-large, even going so far, to make a distinction between taking a plant's life (plants lack a nervous system) from taking an animal or human life (capacity for sentience and consciousness), in certain situations, *basing environmental and animal ethics more on social justice than science or philosophy.* Making ethical decisions based on "needs" versus "inherit worth," *a more conflict resolution approach.*

I might "go off the deep end," "excuse the pun," with my concrete analysis, neurotypicals *do not* pay enough attention to the concrete. For example, neurotypical wildlife managers play around with population dynamics with a confidence that borders on hubris. Where in reality, the concrete does matter. Whether it is the suffering of individual sentient animals eradicated for population control, the woodlot sacrificed for a greater ecological good and all the organisms dependent on this woodlot as habitat and home and all the humans dependent upon the woodlot for pleasure and sanity. Individual organisms and biotic communities do matter. They signify something. I as a person on the spectrum am acutely aware of this reality.

Finally, it's worth mentioning the difference between "concrete analysis" and "being detailed-oriented" in the building of my model, although the differences are subtle and could be disputed as existing at all. They are worthy of being differentiated and given separate sections.

Being "detail-oriented" is appreciating the intricately diverse and complex nature of the "world-around-us," while "concrete analysis" is focusing on the "little picture," as the primary level of analysis. In other words, according to this model, being "detailed-oriented" means understanding "the parts" in relation to "the whole," while "concrete analysis" means focusing on "the parts" themselves on their own terms, in other words, the Democratic Party's popular slogan "putting people first!"

*Parts are not parts of a whole machine! Parts are whole persons who interpenetrate the whole Trinity of Life! We are all people within the God-head! We are nothing less than whole persons within the Holy Trinity! God's Offspring! The Great Overflowing Fountain of God's Goodness!*

This is the ***fifth pillar of an autistic hermeneutic***, concrete analysis, ***respecting the "little picture."***

## Sensitivity to Surroundings

Temple Grandin writes,

> …Animals and autistic people don't have to be paying attention to something in order to see it. Things like giggly chains op out at us; they *grab* our attention whether we want them to or not.[42]

As a person on the autism spectrum, I physically cannot "tune-out" external stimuli in my environment; that's how I encounter novelty, discovering new knowledge and experiences in the process. Such "non-ordinary states of consciousness" challenges certain notions of human consciousness, which have been "hocked" within the last decade or so by neo-dualistic philosophers (those who reject modern brain science) and some Roman Catholic theologians during the Pope John Paul II and Pope Benedict period in Vatican history, such as some of today's Thomist theologians (those who subscribe to the theological vision of Saint Thomas of Aquinas). Such, an altered state of consciousness also gives a window into what nonhuman animal consciousness might be like, from the animal's "point of view," also testifying that there is not a singular, universal, human nature, after all. But, a multiplicity of human natures, which exist on a continuum, with all other living and non-living beings in the Created order.

In otherwords, not all states of consciousness are fundamentally the same. With the most radical contentions being, a serious challenge to the ontological (foundational) logic behind Western hierarchies such as the Aristotelian "Great Chain of Being" or more recently, Peter Singer's "Marginal Case Argument" which implicitly assumes that the most rational (translation---most neurotypical animals--- mainly neurotypical human beings) animals are entitled to the most moral consideration. While the less rational, more irrational beings, are worthy to be dominated by the more rational beings, delineated based on degrees of rationality--- landowners/slaves, men/women, women/disability, humans/animals, animals/plants, plants/minerals. A view which is ultimately classist, sexist, abelist even speciesist, bigoted toward nonhuman animals, an approach which is completely hierarchical and dualistic, even anti-democratic, which assumes that human beings are at the center of and superior to everything else in the Universe, making it also fundamentally anthropocentric and misanthropic too, despite today's apologists celebrating humanity and animalkind.

This is because the method of philosophic reflection itself is fundamentally classist, sexist, abelist and speciesist---it leaves very little room for social justice, anti-oppression, ecological and animal rights perspectives. Mainly such a method necessitates linking "reason, consciousness and moral consideration."

Grandin offers us a deconstruction of the philosophic method which insists on the linkage between "reason, consciousness and moral consideration" which has plagued Western civilization in the form of anthropocentrism/speciesism, androcentrism/patriarchy, racism/classism and neurotypicalism/abelism. Very much in the utilitarian spirit of Enlightenment moral philosopher Jeremy Batham, Grandin refutes the Western notion that consciousness which springs from a rational nature is the basis for giving individuals and groups duties and rights, by arguing that sentience, which allows one to feel pain and suffer and to fear, does not spring from a rational nature or the vermis of the brain, but from ones mammalian brain, one's animality, one's animal side.

In fact, humans with autism and nonhuman animals might be in one respect----be more conscious at the primary level (awareness of one's environment/being alive) than beings with well developed secondary consciousness (ability to reflect on ones experiences of the environment and being alive) who might have less active primary consciousness.[43]

For example, neurotypical beings might be able to write philosophical arguments, record history, and build great civilizations, but might see less bird species when birdwatching, see fewer species of plants on a wildflower walk, miss a beautiful sunset or a full moon in the sky, or even be less emotionally "in-touch" with their own feelings and other's sufferings, being less emotionally responsive to living, feeling less pleasure and enjoyment, being more like "walking dead people," mere "drones." Neurotypical beings might also have shorter memories and weaker senses than autistic beings.

This is why I experience disconnect with much of today's environmental and Christian environmental writing, for not only are non-disabled, privileged neurotypicals in North America "the target audience," they are all "geared-up" to convince you to "become an environmentalist," spending an ordinate amount of time and energy getting you to just "pay attention." Not only am I already convinced, but *"attention epistemology" is my native intelligence. I already do this--- this is my autistic strength! I have been doing this since early childhood! I am an attention specialist!*

Subsequently, jumbling up Aristotelian hierarchy in the process, for what is "higher" and what is "lower," what is "more" or "less conscious," becomes "less clear-cut."

"The playing field" for determining value and moral consideration is subsequently "leveled." It can no longer be determined on mere rational capacities alone. "The rug has been pulled from underneath." This is how it works.

John Perry, author of *Knowledge, Possibility, and Consciousness*, addresses this particular neo-dualist argument, a philosophical, neo-scholastic rejection of the scientific notion that consciousness is grounded in the brain, known as the subcategory "Knowledge Argument" which Perry states as,

> In his original article, Nagel more or less formulates an argument that has come to be known as "the knowledge argument." Frank Jackson develops it is in a series of articles. In "What Mary Didn't Know" (Jackson 1997), on which I will focus, he considers a person, Mary, who is trapped in a black and white room. There she learns, "everything there is to know about the physical nature of the world…she knows all the physical facts. It seems, however, that Mary does not know all there is to know. For when she is let out of the black and white room…It seems, however, that Mary does not know all there is to know. For when she is let out of the black and white room…she will learn what it is like to see something red."[44]

Since Mary knows all the physical facts and then learns something new, there are more facts than physical facts, so "physicalism" (the mind is grounded in the brain) is false. That's the knowledge argument.

In otherwords, novelty is preconceived of in the brain by "the rational animal" (aka human beings) so Mary can gain what is known by animal behavior scientists as insight learning.

Mary can interpret and understand the significance of something she has never seen before such as a red tomato or red fire hydrant, because her brain can learn and understand new impute, according to "the knowledge argument."

Grandin challenges this notion, because neurotypicals seldom encounter novelty, even when surrounding by it, for they do not recognize it when they see it, or Mary, who is obviously a neurotypical, would never leave her black and white world, even when she enters worlds filled with reds, yellows, blues and oranges. This is because one needs exposure and awareness of novelty, to be aware that it even exists. It is not anticipated in the vermis, but experienced in the mammalian brain, the member of the brain, most utilized by animals and peoples on the spectrum. Who by the way, most likely have strongly developed "primary consciousness."

It is contended by one prominent animal behavior scientist, Donald Griffin--- that knowing you are alive, coupled with awareness of other members of your own species and the world-around, comes from your "the primary consciousness" not your "the secondary consciousness." A type of consciousness Donald Griffin contends exists at some level in almost all animals from mammals to invertebrates, but most pronounced in humans, mammals and birds.

This means that humans on the spectrum, like myself are fully conscious, but just have a different type of consciousness than neurotypicals. I, as a human on the spectrum, have a well-developed "primary consciousness" which gives me an intense awareness of my surroundings and being alive, but an underdeveloped "secondary consciousness," reflecting on my surroundings and reflecting on being alive, which is the other way around with neurotypicals, but neurotypicals still have a "primary consciousness," just like I still have a "secondary consciousness." It's just that autistic human and nonhuman animal consciousness is more grounded in a profound awareness of our surroundings and being alive. Or, to be most precise, I need to engage my surroundings (social, physical and built environments) and my subjective sides (emotions, desires, sensuality, creativity, spirituality and intuition) to abstractly reflect on myself and "the world-around-me," "analytical engagement with concrete reality."

When Griffin was alive and wrote his treatise on animal intelligence, the jury was still out on whether or not nonhuman animals could have "insight learning," it is now been confirmed that African grey parrots are able to engage in "insight learning," abstract thinking, a precursor to also having the capacity to "Believe in God." In fact, I never cease to be amazed at the abstract learning abilities in my parakeet companions, also in the parrot family.

I too have abstract learning abilities, if not I could not have written this paper.

However the pluralities of types of consciousness are manifested, one thing remains clear, consciousness of one's environment and one's existence is not grounded in vermus reasoning (abstraction). Consciousness is in fact grounded in emotion, feeling, responding, reacting, experiencing. Something, clearly peoples with autism and nonhuman animals experience, profoundly and intensely.

Subsequently, vermus rationality is not a necessary precondition for consciousness, the same type of consciousness (sentience) which is argued by some to be the most necessary and relevant criteria for determining moral consideration and rights, "sentience" versus "rationality." Sentience is the capacity to feel pain, suffer and fear which many animal rights philosophers consider the real reason for giving moral consideration to nonhuman animals, for animals can also feel pain, suffer and fear.

*Vermus rationality* (conceptualism) is not a sufficient criterion for making moral choices for a strong vermus does not affect one's ability to ensure oppression and subsequently *becomes as arbitrary and capricious as skin color. Out of this conceptualistic mindset flow all racism, classism, sexism, abelism and speciesism! Hierarchical thinking leads to a hierarchical society! Self-deluded thinking leads to a self-deluded society! Stereotyped thinking leads to stereotyping!*

So in other words, Mary the neurotypical would have trouble recognizing red, even if she was surrounded by a room full of red. She sees most naturally in black and white. While a person with autism or a nonhuman sees in vivid color. Both serve invaluable functions to human survival, productivity and civilization-building as a human species. The same with nonhuman animals--- these capacities help animals to "struggle to exist," these differences make one neither superior nor inferior and must not be used as a criteria for determining dominance in human society or in relation to nonhuman beings. *It is the judgment about the relationship between "rational capacities and moral standing" which is inherently invalid and fallacious because "reason, consciousness and the capacity to suffer," "do not go together."*

So *sensitivity to surroundings*, grounded in our mammalian brain, *allows peoples on the spectrum to feel pain suffer and fear and be acutely aware of our surroundings and aliveness* is the *sixth pillar of my autistic hermeneutic.*

An autistic hermeneutic must take into consideration and utilize our acute awareness of our surroundings, allowing us for example in a religious context, to identify novelty in religious texts, which a more experienced neurotypical theologian might miss, because he or she is steeped in an interpretation biased by tradition and official church teachings and dogmas, such as has it has been in the Roman Catholic Church to date. Sometimes even by the theologian's own self-serving projections, their neurotypical reality, imposed upon the text. Creating "intentional blindness" of the text, seeing what he or she expects to see. Missing a possibility valid, possibly prophetic interpretation which contradicts, even challenges the validity of official church teachings and dogmas and the subsequent interpretations.

Peoples on the spectrum expose hermeneutic biases and systemic heresies because we do not have a preconceived notion of what we will find.

**Animality**:

Temple Grandin writes,

> When your [vermis is] down, you have your animal brain to fall back on. That's exactly what happens, too. The animal brain is the default position for people. That's why animals seem so much like people in so many ways; they are like people. And people are like animals; especially when their [vermis] [works differently]. I think that's also the reasons for the special connections autistic people like me have to animals. We use our animal brains more than [non-autistic] people do, because we have to. We don't have a choice… The price [non-autistic] human beings pay for having such [a] big, fat [vermis] is that [non-autistic] people become oblivious in a way animals and autistic people aren't.[45]

In otherwords, humans on the autism spectrum reply more on our "animality," "[our] mammalian brain," than neurotypicals, the same member of the brain relied on by most mammals such as gorillas and whales.

The brains of birds were created differently, with their higher level functions being performed in a completely different member of their brain, which has led to much confusion in the scientific and lay communities over the years about bird intelligence.

I am willing to speculate that an Aspie like myself has a brain organized very similarity to a bird, which may explain my deep personal identification and connection to birds, as well as being able to successfully engage in interspecies communications with them.

For example, I have been able to effective communicate with my parakeet companions, a Canada goose named Wounded Healer when I was in college when I volunteered at the Salisbury Zoo (see, *Creation Unveiled:* Xulon Press, 2003 2010) and with the goldfinches, purple finches, mourning doves and dark eyed juncos which frequented my bird feeder, as well as with a family of grackles, two different crows from two different species, a wren and a flock of wild geese in my neighborhood, while I lived in my outer suburb home in the Piedmont Plateau, the bioregion of my birth. I even silently and nonverbally communicated with the Great Horned and Barred Owls who nested in Deer Ridge this last year, to a point, where I could continue my clean-up of Deer Ridge without disturbing the nesting owls, owls by nature are sensitive to human disturbance. I did stay-out of the immediate areas where they were nesting however.

On my recent vacation to the Colorado Rockies and Red Rock Plateau in the summer of 2012 after my presentation at Society for Disability Studies in Denver, I was able to communicate with a broad-tailed hummingbird, a Lazuli bunting and two mountain bluebirds.

All my life, wherever I have traveled, I have also had this ability whenever I encounter a flock of Canada geese, to be able to "hook-up" with wild Canada geese flocks and walk with the geese through grassy lawns. I also have an unusual gate (connected to my condition) which can easily be mistaken for the waddling of a web-footed goose. So I am accepted into a wild Canada goose flock easily, without incident. In fact, one time when I was in Boston I got into a conversation with another human and it came time for the flock to move, the Canada goose in the back of the flock, turned his head over to me, wondering why I was not moving with the rest of the flock.

I am able to speak bird language and birds are able to speak autism, because I "think like a bird" and "birds think like me." We communicate using rituals, gestures and repetition. We both need "contact calls" (affirmations), "triumphant displays" (celebration), to talk about our feelings (conversation), to be "calmed down" when we are afraid (comfort) and protection from overstimulation when making a major transition ("blinding") to function and communicate our needs. Birds are my "kindred spirits." Canada Geese are my "guiding spirits."

Supplying a reason why an Aspie such as myself, can do much of the same higher level functions as a neurotypical, such as abstract thinking--- I compensate using a different member of my brain, much like birds do. Because I am able to perform these same functions by compensating using my mammalian brain, it is just that when I do these things including certain intellectual, social even religious functions, I just need intense emotional energy to perform these functions.

That is why I cannot separate emotion from being able to perform the task and motivation is tantamount, motivation is not periphery. So being motivated is no small "role of religion" in my life, despite what some conservative theologians might use as an argument against liberal theology and ecotheology. I need an influence in my life which addresses my motivations and motivates me positively and constructively toward productive contribution to society.

The jury still remains out on the full intellectual and emotional capacities of reptiles, amphibians, fish and invertebrates; there is reason to contend, just like birds and mammals, their full capacities have been underestimated, having not been fully studied. Or, fully understood how they can perform these tasks and the neurological basis for these subsequent behaviors.

What is clear to Grandin, is because I am on the spectrum, I have the same "theory of mind" as other nonhuman animals. I, with formation, such as scientific training, developing naturalistic skills and direct exposure to animal-life, can reconstruct what an animal is thinking or feeling, or communicating, from the animal's own point-of-view, as Grandin has successfully demonstrated in her treatise. Our insights and ideas are invaluable to answering the philosophical question, "If a lion could speak what would he say?"

The answer is simple, ask an autist. An autist will give an insight into what a lion is thinking, feeling or saying. As well as the types of thoughts, feelings and messages a lion is most likely to send-out. Explaining how a lion's mind works and does not work. It gives one a framework for translating an animal's inner life into a way a human can understand.

Like with any spiritual gift, it needs formation, for an autist to be able to use his or her gift of being able to understand nonhuman animals.

He or she will need to engage in some type of scientific training where he or she will learn how to think scientifically and gain scientific knowledge about animals. A scientific training which also involves fieldwork including observing nonhuman animals in wild and captive settings and the equipment needed for such endeavors--- such as binoculars, spotting scope, field guides and field journal. Scientific training which in addition, involves direct involvement with animals, such as the opportunity to observe the animals for long-periods, to be able to interact with and relate to them.

In otherwords, a human on the spectrum like myself to access this gift, I would need to gain scientific knowledge of animals for background information so I can situate my insights into a scientific context, be able to explain my insights scientifically and verify my truth-claims using scientific methodologies.

A person on the spectrum like myself, to access this gift, needs more than book knowledge. I would need to see how animal behavior is manifested in "the real world," such as in captive settings to observe animals "close-up" and study their basic behaviors. Captive settings are particularly helpful for studying animal intelligence. Wild settings are also important, to see how animals behave in natural, wild settings, without human intervention. Semi-wild settings are also helpful too, such as duck ponds and birdfeeders, to see how animals behave in natural, wild settings, with some human interference and some human impacts. This is also a good environment to study animal intelligence, as well as an opportunity to study wild animals "up-close."

Finally, I as a person on the spectrum to access my gift, need more than book or observational knowledge, I would also need to have the experience of being in a relationship with an animal or animals, so to develop not only a bond with an animal or animals (developing love and respect for animal life, in the process), but also so I can interact with an animal or animals, to discover different types of animal behaviors, with the result being, getting in touch with the inner life and the ways of a particular animal or group of animals.

Also, as I mentioned above, I most likely do most of my higher level thinking in my mammalian brain, meaning there is a strong connection between "emotion and learning," so an animal cannot be an abstraction, but something I have to have an encounter with and develop an affinity for.

An affinity helps me learn to care about the animal or animals, to love, to respect, to show reverence toward them, to value their life and most importantly, to empathize with them.

Also, I need the "anthropocentric" knowledge of neurotypical natural sciences, to check excessive tendencies to "anthropomorphize," "putting human-like characteristics on nonhuman animals," so I can have a realistic view of what an animal is actually capable of and is actually doing (animal behavior). Also, a profound understanding of Darwinian evolutionary theory is also necessary, so to have a scientifically grounded framework for understanding animal motivations plausibly. So my insights do not just get reduced to mere poetic musing. Finally, a certain sense of "objectivity" is necessary, not for the purpose of remaining detached, disinterested or becoming callous, but to remain intellectually honest, to observe and record evidence, which might be contrary to what I am trying to verify, in otherwords, to be a "good scholar."

Spirituality, religion and theological reflection "fits into this" by A) providing me with a "conversion experience," B) an "Idea of Nature," C) a tradition for "meaning-making," and D) a methodology for engaging in a hermeneutic feedback cycle. I will explain each of these four.

The thing which separates a person with autism who uses their gift like Grandin and a person on the spectrum who becomes a computer tech, boils down to a "conversion experience" where the autist "falls in-love" with a particular animal or all of animalkind itself. Then, decides that is what he or she wants to do with our life or make a part of our life.

In my case, this involves some sort of exposure to animalkind, whether it is a primary (saw the animal live) or secondary encounter (learned about the animal) and in my case it was not just one, but many, over my life. As, God put it to me, this is my "first love" and I am to go back to my first love, as an antidote against disillusionments with movements, groups and research programs. This conversion experience, I will contend is fundamentally spiritual or religious in nature because it allows a transformation in the person to occur.

Second, just as science provides essential formation for the autist interspecies communicator, so is religion, just as essential. Religion, broadly conceived, including philosophy, spirituality, literature and the arts, provides an Idea of Nature, a sacred canopy, about the ultimate significance of animal life and subsequently gives me an ethical-moral framework for valuing the life of animalkind. Answering the questions, why do individual animals and animalkind as a whole have value? How does one value the life of both individual animals and different species of animals? What are the ethical and moral duties to individual animals, different species of animals and the whole animal kingdom collectively and the matrix of relationships and habitats which sustains their lives?

An "Idea of Nature" can serve as a kind of validation of the autist's experiences and the validity of his or her endeavors. That he or she is not crazy! That what he or she is contending is true, particularly when scientific evidence remains inconclusive or the scientific community skeptical. It can also serve as a motivator for the autist pursuing and continuing with his or her work. It can make his or her work with animals more meaningful, important, more interesting, significant and fulfilling even more enjoyable. It can help give the autist a strong "sense of self," a healthy self-esteem, even dignity.

An "Idea of Nature" can also help the autist interspecies communicator receive and give oneself affirmation and discover good role-models in a particular tradition's history. An "Idea of Nature" can also help the autist to form his or her beliefs and values, helping the autist to gain a coherent worldview, helping "to put the world together" and see "the bigger picture." Finally, an Idea of Nature can check, Obsessive Compulsive Symptoms (OCD) or excessive perfectionism, which will destabilize the autist's mental health, preventing him or her from accessing his or her "cognitive strengths," also helping to check excessive, negative emotions, possibly even having the animal or animals, he or she is working with "pick-up on it" and react negatively.

Third, it is not enough to just have a mere amorphous Idea of Nature; one needs the foundation of a particular religious or spiritual tradition. In my case, it is Christianity.

A particular tradition provides the autist with a system for meaning-making. Meaning-making, can be defined as asking the question: what is the significance of animal life? This system for meaning making helps makes the autist's Idea of Nature, concrete and tangible. Otherwise, an amorphous, nebulous Idea of Nature just becomes another set of abstract conceptualizations, which the autist cannot relate to. This is possibly why some on the spectrum, identify themselves as atheists, for when religion or spirituality is reduced to mere presuppositions or principles, religion becomes inaccessible to the concrete-minded autist.

Religion or spirituality must be made concrete and tangible to a person on the spectrum, for that person to be able to assent to religious belief. Only, a concrete and tangible religious tradition with a personal mysticism versus an impersonal mysticism, a mysticism where one can relate to the object of their worship, in a manor liken to a personal relationship, can an autist's religious faith emerge.

This can only be accomplished within the context of a particular tradition, such as Christianity or Hinduism. Some vague New Age or Unitarian Universalist spirituality, where the religion is organized around principles versus deities, goes against the autist's nature.

I know in my case, I absolutely need the experience of a personal relationship with God, as a Christian. Impersonal doctrines, without direct experience of God, are not enough to sustain my faith. That is why a particular tradition for meaning-making versus a vague spirituality, is so essential. It makes my Idea of Nature, concrete and tangible, even visible and touchable.

I will not be surprised that peoples on the spectrum, which are more mathematical, are the same too, just that they would relate to their mathematical schemes as persons not abstractions like the Ancient Greek Mathematician Pythagoras.

Finally, the role of theology in an autist's formation as an interspecies communicator is to provide a hermeneutic feedback cycle. Let me unpack this!

A hermeneutic feedback cycle is a technical concept in academic theology which states that there is a "push-and-pull" or "dialectic" or "mediation" between a particular religious tradition and a person or group's "social location."

A religious tradition is a particular religion's doctrines and practices, as well as a person or group's social location. A social location is what a person's station in society is, such as their socioeconomic status. This station can be affected by a variety of factors such as race, class, gender, sexual orientation or disability. Just, to name a few!

What a hermeneutic feedback cycle does is illustrates that where one stands in a particular society, effects how one interprets the religious tradition. For example, a nineteenth century cotton plantation owner in antebellum Georgia will look at certain passages about slavery in the Bible differently than a twenty-first century African-American small business owner in a post-racial, multicultural neighborhood in Washington D.C. For example, our plantation owner will see slavery as compatible with Christian living, while our African-American small business owner will see slavery as diametrically opposed to Christianity.

Of course, there are theologies "out there" which argue the other way around. That one's tradition must inform one's social location, such as creating social order. In otherwords, such theologies start theological reflection from tradition versus social location.

As a person on the spectrum, my social location being an Aspie male, deeply informs my social location and subsequently my interpretation of the texts. So, a hermeneutic feedback cycle provides a framework for an autist to bring our unique perspectives being an autist into conversation with our specific religious tradition, which we have converted to and vice versa.

In otherwords, an autist's insights into animal nature will also inform how we make our religious tradition meaningful, relevant, useful and accessible, as much as a religious tradition helping to formulate our Idea of Nature and insights into animal nature.

The reason I know all this is because--- this was my path!

Being in-touch with my animality, combined with scientific, ethical and spiritual formation, has allowed me to both gain and sustain my primary insight into animal nature that "animals are smarter than we think!"[46]

This is the crux of my insight into animal nature.

It is the set of assumptions I work out of, when I study, experience, interact with, relate to and making meaning from animal life. It is my axiom, my paradigm, my ontological foundation, my "relative absolute."

This is the *seventh pillar of my autistic hermeneutic*, that *the autist's inherent animality combined with scientific, ethical and spiritual formation, gives the autist both a unique and a realistic insight into animal nature*, subsequently giving a forceful affirmation that nonhuman animals are intelligent, rational, sentient, language-bearing beings.

### Functional Holism:

Aspie primatologist Dawn Prince-Hughes describes the gorillas she befriended and profoundly identified with,

> They didn't have to narrow their vision and cut the world apart. To look closely would have kept them from seeing and choked off the moving and breathing parts of the world, making it flat-worth little. And so we spent the first day, looking without looking, understanding without speaking. Writing poetry in our living, and reading it like weaving.[47]

Prince-Hughes who sees the world more holistically, "big picture," versus Grandin, who sees the world more "little picture," hyperspecifically, might seem like a contradiction in our model. It is not! Remembering that with any group, each person is a completely unique individual, no two people are alike, I am going to make the case that Grandin's hyperspecificality and Prince-Hughes's holism are complementary models. Both are completely true in the mind of an autist.

Using myself as a case study, I both see the details of the world--- hyperspecifically, with extreme perception (Grandin) and I am profoundly sensitive to my surroundings (Prince-Hughes). This means I cannot think about one thing, without thinking about the other. This is where hyperspecifically ("little picture") and holism ("big picture") intersect.

For example, my resource room teacher in high school, oftentimes said when we were talking about something social and then all of sudden, I was talking about philosophy, which she found very confusing and annoying. What was really going on is that I could not look at a discussion about social or independence skills, without looking at its philosophical implications. Because I could not "tune out" other subjects or topics from my mind, for I was making philosophic connections, along with the topic at hand, which was social skills. I physically and neurologically could not "tune out" philosophical thoughts--- I saw too clearly how philosophical thoughts relate intricately to social or independence skills. That far from a discussion being just about social skills or independence skills which had nothing to do with philosophy, I saw it as having everything to do with philosophy. Mainly, that certain discussions of social or independence skills using a strict medical model, fundamentally contradicts certain philosophical concepts or values, using a critical social theory model, which insists that "social skills" are both culturally relative and morally and politically problematic in our culture.

For example, the planetary crisis tells a very different story about what is "normal." In fact, from a planetary perspective, much of what is considered stereotyped neurotypical behaviors such as superficiality, deception and cliquishness are considered "abnormal" even "anti-social" to the rest of the biosphere and to oppressed minorities around the world, who feel oppressed by Western consumerism and subscribe to what they believe is a more authentic, communitarian, life-affirming way of life. Where superficiality, deception and cliquishness are not seen as "the way the world works!" or "that's life!" but as the noxious vices they are, while spiritual depth, honesty and hospitality are respected as moral virtues.

I also ran into this same thing when I studied Biology at the University. For a while, I would always read Job 38-42 before studying my biology homework or studying for a test. God tutored me in all my science classes. I was also always looking at the religious and theological implications of what I was studying in biology, trying to figure-out "what it all means."

For example, one time when I was studying the flatworm with my Lord, I learned that the flatworm "only sees light and darkness," God pointed-out, "that all a creature would need to function in a spiritual Universe is to be able to know the difference between light and darkness."

God also helped me work through "the instinct" issue, "that certain animal behaviors function on instinct." He recommended that I "not look at instinct as a pejorative statement about animal nature, but instead see instinct in animals as behaviors which were created by God."

We also understood "genomes" (gene sequences) to be "a sacred text" for they possess all the knowledge and wisdom necessary for creating living organisms, in otherwords, a type of Divine Logos, a sacred pattern, created from God's own body (Christ), embodied into all living creatures, the archetypal "Tree of Life" mentioned in the Bible, the true nervous system of the Earth *not* human beings, connected to the very "Mind of God." This is because genes are the embodiment of the Plutonic Ideals ("ideal types" "chair-ness," "human-ness," "bird-ness," "plant-ness") forming all the evolutionary chaos of life into coherent classes of beings. In other words, this "thought experiment" helped me to better appreciate and respect genomes as an integral member of God's Creation, enlivening and enriching my studies in the process through creating a "sense of wonder" (amazement at what is) and a "reverence for life" (respecting all life).

I have always been interested in the theological implications of different scientific discoveries, from animal intelligence to natural selection, because my inclination *is not* to compartmentalize "the world-around-me."

In fact, as a personal Nature mystic, I *do not* even want to compartmentalize the world into disciplines and dualisms, even if I could. As a personal Nature mystic, I *do not* want to dull my emotions, desires and the sensual "world-around-me." I *do not* want to become dispassionate, disinterested or even detached.

As a personal Nature mystic, I want to integrate the various academic disciplines and various human endeavors into a coherent "cosmic scheme." I want to be passionate, interested and attached. I *do not* see my emotions, desires and sensuality as my enemy. I see attachment as part of my humanity which connects me to the Entire Universe even to God.

Once, I went to theological school, it was the opposite. I brought my scientific background to my theological studies. I used my scientific training, to question everything from the doctrines of transubstantiation (the belief that the Eucharist is the literal "body and blood" of Jesus Christ) to the doctrine of "humans as the rational animals." It also was not all; deconstructive either, some doctrines were forcefully affirmed because of my scientific background, such as the Doctrine of the Holy Trinity.

For example, I came to believe in the Trinity, when I considered the Natural World. The Natural World is a closed-looped system, made up of many distinct persons who are "interrelated, interconnected and interdependent," yet are members of a unified whole. So, is the Holy Trinity! The Holy Trinity is a closed-looped system, with three distinct persons who have interpenetrated each other, forming a unified whole. In otherwords, I discovered my God is a "closed-looped ecosystem." My Lord is an ecosystem. God is an ecosystem.

This is a Model of God, which is both ecologically friendly and animal friendly. This is a Model of God which both models natural, ecological processes and systems, yet, preserves the individual personhood of each and every creature, oftentimes lost in certain ecological holistic models which *do not* take into consideration the theory of evolution (the role of chaos, history and individual survival), animal behavior science (the role of animal intelligence, human evolution and embodied neurology), animal rights (animal ethics, animal issues and biocentric individualism) and place (landscape, local community and specific places).

The ethical implications of this cannot be understated. This has the potential to do nothing less than solve the individualism versus holism debate between environmentalists and animal rights/animal welfare people, once and for all, because one would not sacrifice the Son for the Father or the Father for the Son, to preserve the Trinity. Sacrifice in this sense means complete elimination or obliteration, not Christ dying for the Father, than only to be resurrected from the dead. Where you "pull out" of the Doctrine of the Holy Trinity a certain ethical-moral framework which contends that you *cannot* sacrifice an individual animal for ecosystem integrity, which is the position of ecological holism. Yet in Trinitarian ethics, ecosystem integrity matters, unlike what some animal ethicists contend against.

In an Ecological Trinitarian ethical-moral framework which is neither holistic nor individualistic, both individual animals and ecosystems matter and the need to balance individual persons with a community or system, when managing a biotic community is tantamount, such as balancing the individual rights of nuisance animals with the health of the entire ecosystem, weighting both preserving individuals and ecosystems equally. Liken to The Son self-sacrificing to the Father and the Father than resurrecting the Son from the Dead.

Practically, this could look like in a wildlife management situation as still addressing nuisance animal problems, but doing so in a manner which is only non-lethal, non-invasive and nonviolent, such as "reasoning with" versus "eradicating nuisance animals" through "interspecies communications." See my book, *Human-Animal Reconciliation: Franciscan Faith-Based Interspecies Communications and Its Implications for Wildlife Management* (Amazon, Kindle Edition, 2008) which is available at Amazon.com, Kindle Store, for more information on my proposal.

This model can also apply to the whole individualism versus communitarianism debate too, which is currently permeating through today's religious and political landscape. Even though individualism has caused all sorts of problems in our society, granted, that *does not* mean, that individuals on the other hand need to be sacrificed "for the greater good." Individual rights and values must be honored and affirmed and must not be lost in an overly corrective "militant communitarianism."

Militant communitarianism *is not* desirable for nonhuman animals and humans with disabilities. The minority absolutely needs to be protected and honored too, which also includes other minority groups in North America.

Neither is "eco-fascism," such as the Eastern totalitarianism of China, desirable either, for animals, humans with disabilities, other oppressed minorities, even for specific biotic communities such as suburban woodlots and particular watersheds, sacrificing individual rights-holders for "a common good."

One cannot ignore the fact that the individual is where suffering is experienced, because the individual has a nervous system which makes suffering conscious, whether the individual is a human being or an animal such as a Canada goose or a White-tailed Deer.

One must also recognize that the survival of individuals, whether human, animal, vegetable, mineral are dependent on both a community (the relationship between beings, such as human-animal, human-human and human-Earth relationships) and a physical environment (the sum total of living and nonliving beings including animals, plants and microorganisms and the natural elements including light, water, land and air). That altruism and concern for others is in fact virtuous. Compassion and altruism are good qualities to develop in an individual person. They lead to "moral living" and "right relationships."

The above is an example of a functional holism, which is how I, as an Aspie "put the world together."

There has been much publicity in certain circles including ecological and religious circles about the importance of "holistic thinking" and "holistic living," the belief and contention that human beings in the West, in modern times have become "compartmentalized," whole academic disciplines, even whole social institutions have become "compartmentalized."

This is causing all kinds of ecological and sociocultural, even spiritual problems. This is what makes science, unethical, medicine, invasive, technology, destructive and people, spiritually famished. This is what limits religious behavior to Sunday morning and make pastoral care, otherworldly. This is why science goes ahead and does something, just because they can. While, religious formulates doctrines and teachings oblivious of scientific discoveries or psychological wisdom. This is why we have all these false dualisms: mind/body, emotion/spirit, science/faith, faith/reason, psychology/religion, masculine/feminine, reductionism/structural analysis, theory/practice, learning/life, work/leisure, action/contemplation and liberal/conservative, just to name a few.

In other words, ecological holism challenges the whole "mechanistic mindset" and offers the "organic mindset" of premodernity, which is still present in many Nature-based societies around the world---a worldview marked by interdisciplinary integration, the physical embodiment of the soul, belief in the interconnectiveness of all life and a call for more community in modern, Western industrial society.

Ecological holists contend that we have become a very dualistic, compartmentalized society. We are "paying a very heavy price" in our souls, in our health and in our environment, for such a posture. Even our progression of knowledge, is effected in no small way. Our humanity has been compromised. Even religion has been compromised, relegated to "the sidelines" and "to the fringes" of human society and activity, with the holist's remedy to exclusive dualism and compartmentalization--- develop a more holistic worldview and become a more holistic society. Seeing and living under the "big picture," "putting the world together," seeing how things relate to one another, as part of an integrated whole.

This means, instead of the Natural World being picked apart and dissected apart in a laboratory, it needs to be studied systemically in the field. This means that knowledge needs to be acquired through interdisciplinary studies across academic disciplines, even across whole sectors of academia, such as the arts and sciences and through interdisciplinary dialogue, collaboration, even integration. Interdisciplinary degrees, such as environmental studies, woman/gender studies and disability studies need to be offered at colleges and universities. They need to be more than multidisciplinary; a certain amount of conscious integration needs to occur, as part of the program. It is okay to come-up with a "Theory of Everything!" Ecumenical and interreligious dialogue is necessary. Science and Religion dialogue an absolute must. A liberal arts education tantamount!

Holism needs also to occur outside the Ivory Tower, too. Bureaucracies need to be integrated and collaborate. Medicine must deal with "the whole person" within the context of a person's physical, social and built environments, not just treat diseases and injuries. Being open, to non drug or surgery related treatments, as well as "non-invasive" natural treatments from traditional societies. Money must be weighed with other values. Business and pleasure must somehow interpenetrate one another. One's religious faith, personal spirituality and value system must permeate through one's entire life. Secular knowledge must be incorporated into religious schemes and vice versa.

Yet, despite much talk and some action on this front, neurotypical society has largely failed to bring about a more holistic, less compartmentalized, less dualistic society. Why is this, so?

The first reason is that holistic thinking quickly degenerates in the neurotypical mind, into an oversimplified "abstract concept of the world," divorced from the complexities of reality. So a cosmology, worldview or sacred canopy, oftentimes provides an inadequate framework for knowing or understanding the world. Second, this means, that it cannot become "functional," in other words, be used in "the real world." It is too difficult to live. To put into practice, to implement, to apply, even to act upon. Or, if it is acted upon, the results are absolutely disastrous.

This is what might have happened with certain great ideologies during the Enlightenment such as Marx, Freud, Hegel, Smith, or Hobbes. They did not take into consideration "exceptions to the rules," "pragmatic experience," or realities which just did not fit their ideology. They "threw the baby out with the bath water." They let go of wisdom that might have been useful, if not essential to their cause and they did so at their own peril.

Marx and the Communists which came after him, for example, did not take into consideration that although one of the dangers of organized religion is being the "opium of the masses," that does not mean that all forms of organized religion had to be, or are, or could be, or even "ought to be," seen as "opium." Or, that "banning religion" is the solution either.

For example, certain forms of Christianity emphasize getting "in-touch" with your sufferings over trying to "appease them" or "fix them" such as the Christian existentialism of the mid-Twentieth century, "black coffee for the masses," empathizing "sober thinking" over "positive feeling." Other forms of Christianity, such as the liberation theology movement of the late-twentieth century used organized religion as a "catalyst for social change" on behalf of the oppressed versus "social cohesion of a hierarchy of inequality." Even certain ways the Bible, even God Himself can be understood, can be conducive to a communist or social revolution, such as understanding the God of the Israel Lights, as a Revolutionary God, a God who stands-up to your oppressors and liberates you from slavery and other forms of oppression, then proceeds to help you build a new, more just society like in Ancient Israel, such as the contextual theology of the African-American tradition.

Little could the early Marxists and Communists anticipate, that it was the Christian Church which would be instrumental in keeping alive Marx, such as different liberation theologies, contextual theologies and social justice initiatives and would be the most outspoken in the twenty-first century, against corporate capitalism and its subsequent injustices against the oppressed and the planet. This is just one of the many problems with Communism and why it ultimately failed.

We are now in a current economic crisis, seeing a similar failure of Adam Smith. Not only has capitalism caused all kinds of problems for the Natural World and ordinary people, it collapsed essentially under its own weight, like the Soviet Union, for the system ultimately did not work in "the real world." There were "salient variables," "unintended consequences" and "corruptions to the system." Leading to system collapse!!! Capitalism like communism just plane did not work as a viable economic system.

So in essence, even though neurotypical society finds holistic analysis satisfying, neurotypical society is resistant to holistic thinking and living, because neurotypicals tend to become abstractified in their thinking about the "big picture" and subsequent cannot "put into practice" their ideologies, coherently or consistently, because of the discrepancies between their abstract conceptualizations of the world ("in their heads") and lived, embodied, concrete reality ("pragmatic experiences").

A person on the autism spectrum, like Dawn-Prince Hughes, is inoculated against compartmentalized, dualistic thinking for three reasons:

- First, the way we perceive the world, is less abstractified and more concrete. Meaning we are more "in-tune" with what is really "out there" than a neurotypical. We see the world, more the way the world really is. We still have a definite "social location," "self-interests," and a "filter" for "editing and splicing" the "raw, sense data" of "the world-around-us," for "there is no such thing as a naked eye," but we do see the world, more clearly than neurotypicals, however, for we "live in reality."
- Second, this means, we can develop a cosmology, worldview or sacred canopy which is more "in-line" with reality, than a neurotypical. Meaning we can make our holism, "functional." Put it into practice!
- Third and finally, we also see clearly the relationship between hyperspecifically ("the uniqueness of the individual," "the little picture," "the details") and holism ("the connections between seemingly unrelated topics," "the big picture," "the cosmos").

In other words, as a neurodiverse human, I *do not* completely erase "the individual," "the details," "the edges," when studying a system, holistically. Nor, do I ignore "the system" or "the common good," when looking at individuals.

As a human on the autism spectrum---I have developed a "functional cosmology" which I "live out of," "under" and "by." "A functional cosmology" which takes into consideration and respects--- concrete, embodied, lived, complexified, non-homogenized, experienced reality, which has liberated me from compartmentalization, homogenization and dualism, for I take into consideration both "the individual person" and "the system" at-large.

This is the ***eighth pillar of an autistic hermeneutic***, ***functional holistic thinking and living***.

**From the Outside:**

In the photographic essay *Souls: beneath and beyond Autism*, author of the written portion, Sharon Rosenbloom, writes:

> People with autism do not live by the rules of the world they were born into. It is from this reality that we stand in awe at what profound lessons, each are capable of teaching. They see a reality our larger picture of life does not allow us to view. The absence of social programming, cultural conditioning, and all that prejudices everything we taste, touch and see gives people with autism the closest thing to God's eyes we have here on Earth.[48]

This means that from an ecological and social justice perspective, autistic humans, such as myself, *are not* as corrupted by –isms, like racism, sexism and homophobia, as the rest of the populace. I *was not* born into this world, with an innate awareness of race, gender, species and other "socially produced," "culturally constructed," distinctions. If left to my own devices, I am virtually racially colorblind. I am innately accepting of all peoples and creatures.

For example, when I experience estrangement from a particular class of beings, I have an innate desire to get reconciled with them. This goes for other human beings too.

For example, in early childhood, when my parents had me meet a reprehensive from a social agency, he asked whether I would feel comfortable working with an African-American, it never occurred to me before it was "pointed-out," that this was an issue. Growing-up I had no problems, having a crush on an African-American girl, having peer friends or acquaintances, which were African-American or from other races and ethnicities. Even in college, I had no problem, attending the African-American fellowship and even attending an African-American church, one Sunday. I have been in African-American homes before, growing-up.

Most dramatically, I follow a man, outside my ethnicity, nationality, culture and social class, Saint Francis of Assisi. A Medieval Italian knight, son of a wealthy merchant.

On the ecological front, I used to be tremendously fearful of yellow jackets, a type of wasp which hangs around picnic areas and garbage cans and is quite aggressive and I had a couple of nasty run-ins with them including getting stung. So one day after school, I had this mysterious desire to want to use my autistic "stemming," to try and overcome my fear of yellow-jackets. I learned many years later that this type of an experience is connected to the Divine Child masculine archetype, a boy's desire for "right relationships" with All Creation. In manhood, this archetype is manifested as idealism and passion.[49]

Even through, I suffer from serious anxiety, phobias of spiders and snakes are largely absent from my extensive repertoire of fears. In fact, I have found both spiders and snakes to be absolutely fascinating, even beautiful. I became certified when I volunteered at the Salisbury Zoo to handle constrictor snakes such as boas and pythons. Growing-up, I used to observe spiders for long-periods of time and still do, even tell this day. In fact, just this last summer I was mesmerized by a giant wolf spider building an intricate web in a gazebo near where I live before my very eyes. This is because I view "spiders and snakes" as "just another one of God's creatures."

This same phenomenon is also at work with my inherent self-understandings about gender, class, and age. I almost went to a women's college, whose graduate program was co-ed, for graduate school, for I liked the program and found it "life affirming." I have many plutonic friendships with women over the years, including married women. There is even a part of me, which finds intelligent and professional women, fascinating.

The same can be said with class too. I used to love reading stories about "poor people," such as *Great Expectations* and *Grapes of Wrath*. I go to "unschooled people" for guidance and advice. Finding I can learn much from their "common sense," their non-judgmental, accepting, spontaneous way of life, their hospitality and solicitude.

I also *do not* have an inherent, innate propensity to only associate with generational peers. Even during my teen years, most of my friends were older adults. Subsequently, I circumvented or at-least delayed adolescent rebellion.

Sexual orientation is a more complicated issue-for two reasons.

- First, becoming a Christian was a relatively late development for me and I was originally introduced by the evangelical church, which was very against homosexuality, so I was under the false impression that you have to be against homosexuality to consider yourself an orthodox Christian.
- Second, I resented the liberal-progressive Christian push to legitimize homosexuality in the Church, mainly in regard to the whole "language about power" issue, such as insistence on homosexuality being the most urgent issue in the twenty-first century (like the treat of planetary annihilation mattered) and working out of a banking-propaganda-anti-dialogical education model which used intimidating pontifications and rigid, anti-democratic ultimatums in an attempt to address homophobia in the Christian Church. I would have much more benefited from a more diplomatic, informative, conservational and I would dare say theological approach to addressing of this issue where scriptural, doctrinal and critical social theory evidence would be produced in favor of homosexuality, while balance and attentiveness to other social justice and pastoral issues continued to be addressed such as disability and the planetary crisis, not the least of

which the Christian Church actually being about "Worshiping God"(Philippians 3:3) and following the Biblical imperative for "Church Unity" (Ephesians 4: 1-14, 1 Peter 8-9)."[50]

With God and Francis's help, I have resolved this issue on both fronts.

First, God had me look at Romans, one of the books in the Bible, which is used to argue that "homosexuality is a sin." What I discovered was surprising and shocking. This passage by Christians has been distorted, taking out of context. Based upon reading this passage, I discovered that the evidence that "homosexuality is a sin" was inconclusive. It seemed to be that Saint Paul was more against "lustful" homosexual relationships (such as "going from partner to partner") *versus* homosexuality forestay (such as "gay marriage"). So Paul was really against "lust" *versus* "love" in romantic relationships--- homosexual and heterosexual alike, he **was not** opposed to loved-based homosexual relationships such as "partnerships."

Remember Paul lived in a time period and in a culture where men had physically intimate "friendships" with each other. It was not uncommon for men in Paul's world (Ancient Turkey) to hug each other, kiss each other, manhandle each other even have sex with one another as a form of male bonding. In fact, in Paul's world, bisexuality was the norm. A man had both his wife and his male friend. And, in Paul's world, homosexuality *was not* always fraternal comradely, in classical times according to friendship research, this was a period where friendship was also the strategy to "get ahead" in the Roman Empire, "the networkers" of those days. So it was not that men were *only* having sexual relations with one another "out of love," but also out of political and economic utility, objectifying "lust." This particular historical situation was what Paul was addressing in this passage. No more, no less!

Also, another interpretation indicates that this passage could be interpreted as of all things, as an anti-war passage.

So, I learned from God that there is no conclusive evidence that there is not anything inherently wrong with homosexuality from a Biblical perspective.

Also, Saint Francis in Heaven has helped me "warm up" to this idea too, for I took a course in graduate school on "friendship" at Harvard Divinity School and there I learned about the classical friendship tradition of Ancient Greece, where men had very intimate friendships which oftentimes took on a sexual dimension, too, where I learned that homosexual sex was seen as a form of male bonding. Francis in Heaven claimed that this model for male friendship survived into his time-period through the tradition of chivalry in Medieval Courtly Society.

From Francis's perspective, the Medieval Church was okay with this. They did not consider "homosexuality as a sin." In fact, Francis in Heaven claimed that in his order, friars having sex with other friars within the fraternity was considered acceptable and not a violation of their "vows of celibacy." Sort of like the Anita Community, a nineteenth century Christian utopian society, basing their "way of life" on "living like the Angels in Heaven" where one was allowed to have sex with any member in the community, but a member could not have sex with anyone outside the community, in otherwords, a "group marriage." The Anita's were also leaders in the abolition, pacifism and Christian anarchist movements of the nineteenth century and they founded the Anita refrigerator company which still exists tell this day.

Francis in Heaven does not consider himself, "gay;" but considers himself as engaging in "male friendship." He does not understand why this has "divided-up" the Christian Church so much.

Yet, I remain against the "open expression of sexuality," including "open homosexuality," for I fundamentally believe that one's sexuality is a private, personal, intimate matter. It must not be a public or political issue. This goes for heterosexuals, too.

Heterosexuals when they "get married" *must not* "cut-off" their single, same gendered relationships, nor must heterosexual weddings be made as big a deal as they are today. The Christian Church's focus *cannot* be mere "family values." A nuclear family-centric approach to Christianity *excludes* un-married, single, celibate Christians such as myself, divorced Christians or Christians who have found love through other unconventional venues such as homosexuality, which is just as good of a relationship as "a relationship between a man *and* woman, in holy matrimony." These diverse expressions of love are not only, ***not sinful***, but are in fact, ***virtuous***.

Prophetic challenges to the excesses of individualism, consumerism and middle class morality in the United States.[51]

So, as I have demonstrated, that at-least one man on the autism spectrum *does not* have a natural propensity toward bigotry whether it is racism, sexism or homophobia or ageism, classism or speciesism. This is because people such as myself *are not* as conditioned into accepting these harmful and oppressive ---isms as neurotypicals are, mainly we are not as immersed in or even as sympathetic to the status quo of the conventional American society as many non-disabled, neurotypicals are. In otherwords, peoples on the spectrum are not as racist, sexist, classist, speciesist, anthropocentric, ageist or homophobic as the rest of the population.

I contend that neurotypicalism undergirds all these other ---isms. That neurotypicalism is intricately related and linked to these other ---isms, too. That other oppressed minority groups need to be in solidarity with the neurodiversity struggle, for abelism and neurotypicalism are fundamentally linked to almost every other oppression. Not the least of which, anyone can be autistic, anyone can have a learning disability and anyone can struggle with mental illness issues, regardless of our race, class, ethnicity, gender, sexual orientation even species. Yes, even species. Elephants can develop Post Traumatic Stress Disorder (PTSD), parrots can develop Obsessive Compulsive Disorder (OCD) and almost all nonhuman animals can develop "stereotyped" autistic behaviors in captivity such as animals in "old school" bar and concrete zoos and aquariums and neglected pets.

For example, racism really *is not* about skin color. Racism is really about excluding, targeting, bullying, dominating and all-around scapegoating other human beings who are not like yourself (neurotypicalism) and insisting that the world be all "geared-up" for white Northern European people and white Northern European values (abelism).

Sexism is really not about gender roles. Sexism is about privileging masculine virtues such as "abstract reason" over more feminine virtues such as "embodied relationality" (neurotypicalism) and insisting that the world needs to be all "geared-up" to celebrate masculine virtues and degrade more feminine virtues (abelism).

Classism *is not* about economic inequality. Classism is about a hierarchy of abilities, valuing some abilities, such as those who work with their "heads" over those who work with their "hands" (neurotypicalism) and insisting that the world be all "geared up" to reward those who work with their "heads" and shame those who work with their "bodies" (abelism).

The same can also be said for ageism, speciesism, homophobia even transgender. This is not the valuing of certain bodies over others as some like Christian theologian Sallie McFague has offered, as I have shown you, *but bigotry is really about valuing certain minds over others*. In other words, *anybody who deviates from the neurotypical identity* (*a certain personality, mindset, consciousness and skill set*) in anyway, whether we are other human beings with physical disabilities, women, African-Americans or Native Americans, those from lower socioeconomic classes, those on the homosexual spectrum, children, youth, senior citizens or members of other species are likely to also be targeted and oppressed by neurotypicalism and abelism.

Even white men who dare question their neurotypical identity like what happened with the men's movements and self-help movements of the 1980s and 1990s were also subjected to the same type of oppression by neurotypicalism and abelism that I experience. Such stances cost many of these men, their marriages, their families and even their careers as they sought a more compassionate, authentic, life-affirming lifestyle.

This is why American neurotypicals continue to find immigrants from Latin America, Southern Europe, Eastern Europe and The Middle East, a threat to their identity (they have a more passionate personality which leads to political radicalism). This is why American Middle Class neurotypicals do not want to give money to homeless panhandlers, not because they do not believe that the body on the street does not deserve to be fed, under the spell of neurotypicalism, they assume aka "blame the victim" that the man on the street is an alcoholic or the woman on the stress is a drug addict (a little "mentally ill" aka does not have the neurotypical consciousness of trusting the system and believing in the status quo).

This is why the First Nation struggle is increasing becoming a worldwide phenomenon, with groups of people around the world, even people in Europe and the Middle East seeking First Nations status. In the Middle East, everyone from Jews to Palestinians is seeking First Nation status. Already the Bedouins and Druze (two nomadic tribes) are enjoying First Nation status in Israel. While in Europe---The Scottish and The Welch are seeking independence from Great Briton as we speak, while the Irish have sought independence for now almost two centuries, in other words, the Celtic culture is slowly being revitalized, reversing centuries of genocide and culturecide. Also, an increasing number of Latino cultures are also contending First Nation status too. And, the Gypsies are not far behind in revitalizing their culture and history. Could this be that the whole neurotypical mindset---the whole Hellenistic-Enlightenment project—is not working?

I would say---absolutely yes! *This is because the neurotypical identity really does not exist! It only exists in the heads of the philosophers of Ancient Greece! It is their perfectionist ideals! In a sense, all our "skill sets" do not "measure up" to Hellenistic standards! In a sense, these standards do not include any of us!* This is why neurotypical children when given "reasonable accommodations" also do better in school.

*The Solution:* **We Need New Standards!!! We Need To Socially, Culturally, Politically and Economically Change How We Think!!! It Turns-Out That Negative Thinking Is Also "Socially Produced"!** Of course, we would be negative when we spend our whole lives trying to "measure-up" to a standard which we can never meet, a standard which does not even exist, a standard which is not at-all "life affirming."

*The autistic identity provides an alternative standard:* _A standard marked by an authentic personality, coupled with a humane consciousness, a holistic mindset, with an attention to details and certain sensitivities to the world around_. Everyone, whether we are autistic or neurotypical, mentally or physically challenged, all need to cultivate the autistic virtues of passion, honesty, compassion, empathy, solicitude, thoughtfulness and curiosity about the world-around-us and in us.

In reality, all of these ---isms are about an inability for people to deal with other peoples and creatures which are not like themselves, expecting all these "others" to conform to their whims and wishes, in the process. This is what neurotypicalism is at-heart, expecting everyone else to conform to the reality of peoples with a fully developed vermis. To make other people live their lives by your expectations! Believing that your ideals are better than everyone else's! That your way is the only correct way of doing things! Oppressing anyone else who is not "in lock-step," whether we are neurodiverse humans, humans with physical disabilities, African-Americans, women, the poor, homosexuals, or nonhuman animals or even Nature. It all comes back to an expectation that one only wants to associate with peoples and creatures which are like themselves. This is because; each of these groups has characteristics, which makes us non-neurotypical. Such bigoted behavior from a neurodiversity perspective is the true "anti-social behavior" because neurotypical bigots want to control everyone and everything in their environment. Bigots of all types are the truly "selfish," "self-absorbed," "narcissistic" people of this world *not* peoples on the autism spectrum, for they are the ones lacking compassion and empathy for other people. A case of classic projection!

This is the ***ninth pillar of an autistic hermeneutic***, because peoples on the spectrum are less "socially produced" and "culturally conditioned" then the larger population, ***we are less indoctrinated into certain harmful ---isms and can provide a powerful example to neurotypicals of what racial, sexual, economic, generational and ecological equality looks like in reality***.

### Linked Oppressions

Christian ecotheologian Steven-Bouma Predinger describes "linked oppressions" as a potential option for motivating people to be environmental,

> One might call the fourth argument [in his typology of environmentalism] "poor and oppressed unite" since it posits a link between various forms of oppression. It is more commonly called the ecojustice argument, since it is grounded in an appeal to justice...

> This argument, as many have increasingly recognized, is persuasive and important. For example, there is a growing body of empirical evidence for the existence of environmental racism. There are positive correlations, and, many argue, a causal linked

between the location of toxic waste sites and the residences of people of color. Given that sexism and racism and the exploitation of the earth are connected, concern for one should entail concern for the others. The ecology movement and the various movements for human liberation, which have for too long been separate and at times antagonistic projects, must see themselves as allies in a common quest. There is, happily, growing recognition of this fact.[52]

So in essence, a "linked oppressions model" helps two competing groups of oppressed people, be in solidarity against one another, fighting a common cause of resistance, against their oppressor. Recognizing that they have both a shared plight and a shared oppressor. That they must not fight among themselves. That is counterproductive.

There are currently two existing variations of the ecojustice linked oppressions model- *ecofeminism* and *environmental racism*.

*Ecofemism*, coming out of the radical feminist movement, argues that there is a correlation between how women are treated and how nonhuman animals and the Earth are treated by our patrarchical-male dominated society.

*Environmental racism* is the concept that African-Americans and other minority communities are more likely to bear environmental costs, such as having toxic waste dumps in their community, over and against the privileged majority, whites.

I am going to propose a *third variation* of the link oppression or ecojustice model. 1) There is a positive correlation between how human beings on the autism spectrum are treated by neurotypical society and how neurotypical society has a whole, treats nonhuman animals and the Earth. 2) That the causes of neurodiversity, disability justice, animal liberation and ecological activism are intricately linked, interdependent on one another. 3) They share a common "root cause," neurotypicalism, judging any person who has a different brain type than you as "other" and "inferior." Whether that person is on the autism spectrum, is dyslectic or has Attention Hyperactive Deficit Disorder (AHDD), struggles with a mental illness such as bipolar, Post Traumatic Stress Disorder (PTSD), Obsessive Compulsive Disorder (OCD) or is blind or deaf, or is transgender, or just different for any reason. Anyone who judges another one of God's

Creatures who has a different brain type to be "other" and "inferior" is guilty of bigotry. This also includes anthropocentrism (bigotry toward the Natural World) and speciesism (bigotry toward animals). In otherwords, bigotry toward anyone for any reason, not just racism, sexism or homophobia is fundamentally oppressive and unjust, in this model.

Neurotypicalism I contend is bigotry because neurotypicalism expects those with different nervous systems to conform to the whims and wishes of the dominant nervous system of society, the nervous system which is most in-line with the Greek ideal of intellectual perfection, an unrealistic, unattainable standard which also blatantly excludes neurodiversity, physical disability, mental illness, women and the economic poor, as well as Animals and the Earth and is not desirable for human beings who come from a non-Western ethnicity and culture such as the various First Nations around the world, Latinos, Africans and African-Americans and Asians, in other words, most of the human race and beyond.

This insular philosophical framework from antiquity is both legitimized and accomplished through establishing certain norms and taboos, a system of social etiquette, which is strictly if not violently enforced, to bring all these non-neurotypical persons into neurotypical reign and to perpetuate a dysfunctional, unjust status quo, at all costs.

More recently, some religious fundamentalists and some postmodern philosophers through the "neo-dualistic" argument under the guise of deconstruction (process of refuting an argument) are calling into question the credibility of the scientific method and the subsequent credibility of scientific discoveries---including modern brain science which insists that psychological phenomena is both embodied and mortal, including autism and mental illness. Philosophers and theologians are accomplishing this through revitalizing Hellenistic conceptualism (aka neurotypicalism), insisting that academic philosophy (reason and metaphysics) provides an alternative, even a substitute for modern science (empirical testing and data), an approach which seems immune to scientific criticism, "the facts," even "common sense," in the process, perpetuating, even revitalizing, a philosophical narrative and methodology which is inherently inaccessible even hostile to nonhuman animals, neurodiversity and humans with disabilities.

When non-neurotypical beings such as human beings on the autism spectrum, nonhuman animals and Nature, do not conform to the whims and wishes of neurotypical society, neurotypical society starts to "interfere with, censor, and control,"[53] any and all, understandings or behaviors which do not conform to neurotypical standards or desires, putting the "burden of proof," all the responsibility, on the shoulders of those who dare to question these destructive beliefs. Making what is "normal" the "ought." When what is considered "normal" by a given society in reality might not be even be desirable or maybe even is morally evil. ***This is an ideology which a mounting number of Disability Studies Scholars are calling normalcy (what is morally right is what is "normal" in a society at any given time).[54]***

In other words, three good slogans to remember this ethical-moral framework by are "Keeping up with the Jones," "meeting social obligations" and "everybody is doing this." The classic "bandwagon" logical fallacy! If taken to its logical conclusion, if "drug dealing" is "normal" than neurodiverse humans "should" also become "drug dealers."

This hyperbole shows the fallacy of trying to make people like me "normal." Such an approach leaves very little room for critical thinking, social change and ethical reflection. Such an approach is so absolutist, it become relativism even amoral in "the real world."

In addition, to autistic neurology being supported by factual reality, conclusive scientific evidence and pragmatic experience, I will demonstrate that my linked oppressions model is very useful for solving a very specific conflict--- mainly the conflict between ecology, animal rights disability justice and autistic pride. A conflict manifested in certain religious, ethical and public policy debates.

Establishing an autist-animal-Nature connection subsequently has the power to break down another powerful false dualism and false choice, to choose between preserving human dignity at all costs and giving the nonhuman world significant moral consideration. This is a false choice to *choose between* Princeton University animal rights philosophy professor's Peter Singer's "Argument from Marginal Cases" (AMC) *or* Pope John Paul II's "Dignity of Man" argument, "lock stock and barrel." This is the problem and inadequacy of each of these two paradigms.

At one extreme, you have animal liberationist Peter Singer's version of the "Argument from Marginal Cases" (AMC) which contends that it is not speciesist to entertain the notion that it is preferable to experiment on those who have mental disabilities, those in comas and infants under a year, in certain situations over certain species of nonhuman animals such as birds and mammals. This is because Singer contends that these nonhuman animals have a stronger capacity to suffer, to engage in recipical relationships and are ultimately more rational and subsequently have more morally valuable lives than those who are severely mentally disabled, those in comas and infants under a year old.

"The Argument from Marginal Cases" (AMC) is extremely misguided at best. This is a toxic and untrue narrative for humans on the autism spectrum and other humans with disabilities. A narrative neurodiverse humans and members of disability communities must forcefully, reject. "The Argument from Marginal Cases" negates both our intrinsic value as human beings, as well as the productive contributions humans on the spectrum and other disabilities can, do and could make to society, if given a chance.

Yet, the other extreme is just as destructive and must also be rejected by autists and other peoples with disabilities, with as much gusto. The "Dignity of Man Argument" hocked by people like Pope John Paul II. An argument that the unique value of human beings must be preserved "at all costs," to prevent such practices as abortion and euthanasia. An argument which maybe has helped in no small way, to create the conditions for someone like a Peter Singer to argue for animal liberation, using "The Argument from Marginal Cases" to deconstruct an insular, uncritical humanism.

This is because an insular, fundamentally dogmatic contention that humans are superior to all other creatures and that the boundaries between humans and nonhuman beings must be "iron clad," regardless of what evidence comes their way (mainly in the form of scientific data, logical contradictions in philosophical arguments and the recovery of pro-animal teachings in a particular religious tradition) forces animal rights academics in the Critical Animal Studies field like Singer (a philosophy professor at Princeton University) to take such a position, in an attempt to deconstruct speciesism and effectuate animal liberation.

"The Dignity of Man" position is absolutely resistant to anything which contradicts or threatens to challenge the fundamental uniqueness and specialness of human beings. This is true, whether it is new discoveries in animal behavior science which have the potential to shake Western assumptions about the uniqueness of human beings to the core through making the case that humans *are not* the only conscious, sentiment, intelligent, language-bearing beings which exist in our world. That the lines between species are very "blurry" indeed, calling for animals to be given more moral consideration, than previously human society has felt justified in giving.

*It is important to point-out*, however, that the Christian mystical traditions (e.g., the Franciscan, Celtic and Desert Father traditions) and the Holy Bible (e.g., Hebrew Bible), as well as the emerging Christian animal rights movement does account for animal intelligence and sentience, however.

Whether it is claims by deep ecologists (a more radical splinter of the environmental movement: many deep ecologists are now academic philosophers, historians, psychologists and literary analysts who teach courses in Environmental Studies at prestigious universities), who argue that a fundamentally "anthropocentric anthropology" (beliefs about human nature and the place of human beings in the cosmos) is one of the root causes of the planetary crisis. An anthropology which both A) insists that human beings are at the center of and superior to everyone else in the Universe and B) insists that human beings can do whatever they want to the Natural World.

In other words, humans in our "species chauvinism" are doing nothing less than destroying the very planet which human beings are dependent upon for our own physical survival.

Not to mention, the deep ecology, environmental ethics imperative that the Natural World *was not* created for human beings, but "exists for its own sake." In other words, the Natural World has value outside its usefulness to human beings. The Natural World has intrinsic value! Rocks, waterways even whole entire ecosystems *do not* need to defend their right to exist; they "exist for their own sake."

*It is also important to point-out* that the intrinsic value position is compatible with sound Christian doctrine (e.g., the Doctrine of the Incarnation "the world is God's body") and with the radical theocentrism of the Hebrew Bible which insists that A) God created the world for His own sake (Genesis 1-2), B) God cares for "the wastelands" not fit for human habitation (Job 38-42) and C) "the Earth is the Lord's" (Psalms and Prophets).

It's just that the Judeo-Christian tradition takes the deep ecology argument two steps further.

- Humans are dependent upon the Earth for more than our mere material needs (economic, materialistic, survivalist values). Humans are also dependent upon the Earth to meet some of our emotional, sensual and social needs too (aesthetic, spiritual, relational values).
- Human beings have a place in Nature too! Human beings have a functional ecological niche, a legitimate role to play in sustaining Life on Earth; mainly helping "the evolutionary weak" to "survive and reproduce" to preserve genetic diversity, ensuring species survival through creating the ecological fitness of biodiversity. In other words, human beings are part of the ecology. This is what I call *Messianic Ecological Anthropology*; that A) the basically good nature of human beings (Imago Dei) has been corrupted by Original Sin (the fallen, brokenness of the world) and B) that the ecological job of human beings is to "cancel-out," "balance-out," even neutralize the "red tooth and claw" of natural selection (Dominion and Subdue). A position which I contend *is not* weak anthropocentrism (protecting the environment for human beings) *but* weak ecocentric (that human beings also "exist for their own sake," human beings are called to "participate in" the Natural World and human beings are essential to sustaining All Life on Earth).

In other words, **we are not "the rational animal," we are "the animal's animal."** Where in this model, human beings *might not be* the "crown of creation," but human beings *are* the "keystone species" for all life.

A position about the uniqueness of human beings which although ecologically counter-cultural, I contend is both relevant and credible to discussions about Animals and the Earth and is consistent with postmodern, animal behavior science and more persuasive to secular audiences than defending "humans as the rational animals," at all costs.

Messianic ecological anthropology is an ecology which also includes human beings and provides an original, unique scientific paradigm (a non-scientific hypothesis for asking scientific questions) for both studying scientifically A) the relationship between artificial ecosystems and natural ecosystems at the scientific ecology level (functional level) versus at-the environmental science level (dysfunctional level) and B) integrates scientific ecological-evolutionary principles with "the values of society," through intensifying animal intelligence and mutualistic evolution, with the goal of working towards an ecological cconomic model for living more sustainability, justly and nonviolently on this Earth which appeals to our highest religious and moral beliefs, our religious and moral "self-interests," such as our desire to "make a difference" (moral self-interest) and "honoring ancestors" (religious self-interest).

In other words, I am arguing that we need a model and a strategy which finds synthesis, from the thesis and antithesis of the "Dignity of Man Argument" and "The Argument from Marginal Case." Both extremes are mutually harmful and counterproductive. Both positions are fundamentally inadequate. Yet, both positions are salvageable and ontologically true. It is just that these three disparate causes need to reframe their positions, ideas and communication strategies, to mutually account for each other's truth claims.

This is because the "Argument from Marginal Cases" is fundamentally oppressive to humans with autism and other disabilities, while the "Dignity of Man Argument" is fundamentally oppressive to Animals and the Earth.

Both positions are fundamentally inadequate, because "The Argument from Marginal Cases" keeps intact certain speciesist assumptions and traditions (speciesist residue) as it tries to deconstruct them, such as the primacy of vernal reasoning (conceptualism) found in some Hellenistic, Enlightenment and postmodern philosophies. While, "The Dignity of Man Argument" fundamentally bypasses the very people whose humanity needs to be preserved at all costs, mainly humans on the spectrum and other peoples with disabilities. Such as excluding peoples with mental disabilities from Roman Catholic religious orders, even from mass and first communion.

Yet, these two positions are fundamentally true. There is something inherently sacred about all human life. Yet, it is equally true that there is something also inherently sacred, of value, about all nonhuman life, animals, plants even nonliving beings such as rocks and waters. So in essence, what needs to be preserved at all costs is the dignity of all life, both human and nonhuman, as well as both the evolutionarily strong and weak, in both human and nonhuman societies, alike. This means that P.E.T.A. must stop coming-out with statements saying that "drinking milk causes autism," as evident in one of their recent campaign.

Autistic bloggers must stop attacking the ontological foundations of animal rights and animal welfare and start developing personal relationships with live animals and getting informed about animal issues and the various arguments for animal rights or welfare. Part of this means getting information and experiences "off line," for much of the information on animals "on-line" and in "mass media" is propaganda.

I agree with Christian animal rights theologian Reverend Andrew Linzey at Oxford University in England, that there is no substitute for reading academic books on animals. I agree with Linzey that "animal rights" does not do well in "SoundBits," that you *do* need to know all the hydraulics (all the philosophical, ethical, practical and rhetorical details) that goes into formulating an argument for/or against animal rights.

I also agree with Linzey that you also need to understand the political economy of human-animal relationships, that governments and multi-national corporations have a very strong economic incentive to defend animal experimentation, factory farms, eradication even sports hunting, at-all costs, "follow the money!"

In other words, what we as concerned neurodiverse members of the human species need is a "behind the scenes" tour of the animal rights debate, to access the sociosymbolic life of the animal movements.

I would go two steps farther and argue that 1) anthropocentrism and speciesism is "clear and present danger" to the neurodiversity community and disability cultures and communities everywhere, because anthropocentrism and speciesism as well as institutional animal cruelty contains abelist, neurocentric, objectifying even eugenics residue (mainly abstract, hierarchical, stereotyped, rigid thinking, the mind-body dualism, mechanistic cosmology, capitalism even behaviorism and scapegoating).

For example, *the same scientific speciesism* (normal, animal behavior science) works out of the *same behaviorist-medical model* "behavioral analysis" which does not respect our feelings, denies our empathy and inner life, even our humanity, treats us a "means to an end" and "dopes us up" on medications experimented on innocent animals, *the vivisection-medical-industrial complex.*

For example, *the same religious anthropocentrism* (Roman Catholic fundamentalism) *not only does not include us, but is very paternalistic even disparaging to disability and neurodiversity.*

Meaning that disability and autistic pride groups need to be careful when aligning themselves with the pharmaceutical industry (such as some in the autistic pride movement supporting "Big Pharma" and being in solidarity with the government study that mercury does not cause autistic symptoms) as well as with an un-critical humanism such as pre-Vatican II Catholicism.

Meaning there is also no substitute for idealism and integrity either.

2) That neurodiverse humans need to develop personal relationships with live animals, in other words, develop our own relationships with animals, so we can develop commitments to animal liberation independent of Peter Singer or PETA which is strong enough to survive adversity, persecution, betrayal, disillusionment, abandonment even "Compassion Fatigue." It is a completely realistic expectation that with any worthwhile cause---you will experience adversity, persecution, betrayal, disillusionment, abandonment even Compassion Fatigue at some point in your activist career, the animal movement is "no expectation." It is also realistic that in any movement, you can expect at-least some unfortunate, misguided actions, by certain individuals and organizations.

A personal relationship with animals will affirm that animalkind and animal rights are not the same animal, animals and animal issues have value apart from the follies of the human beings who speak on their behalf. Just go outside and get to know an animal! You will see!

Also, if you have an animal companion or a guide dog, this is the role of your animal companion. Your animal companion will offer you unmediated; concrete guidance "right from the horses' mouth" that all animals are intelligent, sentient and have "inherit worth," as well teaching you what your animal companion needs socially and emotionally.

For example, my new parakeet Brother Spirit has taught me that he has no difficulty understanding my audible speech, even my God-talk when I do my parakeet Eucharist with them, which they look forward to every day, where celebrating the Eucharist becomes a kind of "non-material treat." Brother Spirit has also taught me that he does not like it when I work on my computer at night for the glare keeps him up at night (also the dim from some of my lights disturbs them too, as well as the new bright light street lamps) or when I watch overly violent television, which gets him all worked-up about predators.

I know that many animal activists have serious concerns about pets, companion animals and guide dogs and many people in the disability communities are getting "flack" on this issue alone, as we speak, so I am offering Christian animal rights as an "alternative" to animal abolition or animal welfare.

The Christian animal rights tradition (see above) insists that not only must animals be liberated from all cruelties whether they are a dog neglected by his owner, hens in a factory farm or deer yearlings targeted by sports hunters and eradicators through developing "creative solutions" to human-animal conflicts such as "interspecies communications" and "interest-based conflict resolution" such as Saint Francis of Assisi "taming the very fierce Wolf of Gubbio."

The Christian animal rights tradition also insists that healing the human-animal bond is possible through human-animal reconciliation--- developing nonviolent, non-exploitive, mutualistic relationships between humans and animals like the "Peaceable Kingdom" in Isaiah II, creating a multi-species society which values all life, creating a sustainable Western culture in the process.

This can be accomplished through an ascetic diet (becoming vegetarian), empathizing with the plight of animals (witnessing a concrete act of animal cruelty in your community), approaching animals in a spirit of peace (interspecies communications), showing "ridiculous bravery" to save an animal's life (altruism) and through the grace of the Holy Spirit ("expecting miracles").

In other words, from a Christian perspective, *"animal abolition"* is *"right relationships."*

Animal abolition from a Christian perspective means ecological nonviolence, human-animal reconciliation, even developing mutualistic human-animal relationships, in other words, a "Reverence for Life."

Meaning that it is okay to have a companion animal, it's just that in this model, that giving your animal companion everything your animal needs (such as a proper diet, enough clean water, a sanitary environment, a larger enough enclosure, protection from the elements, gentle handling, rest and veterinary care) and some of what the animal wants (such as loving attention, access to members of the animal's own species, other animal species, toys and other behavioral enrichments and a tranquil environment) *needs to be your first animal rights commitment.*

Once your animal learns to trust you (the animal is getting everything the animal needs and some of what your animal wants in life) and you are developing a more positive, life-affirming relationship with your animal (No cruelty! No neglect!), than the animal just might give you deeper moral and spiritual guidance.

In otherwords, in this "thought experiment," I am getting my people to not "through the baby out with the bathwater," in other words, reject the entire cause even animals themselves, just because they do not approve of everything PETA or Peter Singer does. I do not support or condone everything PETA or Singer believes or does either.

This does not mean that I dismiss the whole cause or even PETA. This is because I know that PETA, even Singer have done some very positive things for animalkind too (my best friends), which are not offensive to the autistic community. Such as naming speciesism and challenging institutionally cruel practices like factory farms and sports hunting.

I even feel indebted to the animal movement, for the good they have done in advancing animal rights discourse. Even though much of my career is "clean-up" after "their mistakes," but I at-least I have "mistakes" to "clean-up after," in other words, there is already a precedent for the notion of animal rights. There is already an intellectual, ethical-moral, even a political-legal-scientific argument already "on the table." There is already a movement which I can collaborate with. There are practices which I can celebrate--- like becoming a vegetarian. But most importantly, I have my own relationship with animalkind, outside of the animal movements, which can "stand on its own," for this reason alone, I am a life-long committed animal activist and vegetarian.

So in essence, the issue needs to be radically reframed. Neurodiverse humans are not a "*stumbling block*" to animal liberation; we are in fact "*an asset*" to the cause. Neurodiverse humans need not see PETA or other animal liberationists as the enemy either, for we are fallible, limited human animals, trying to do the best we can, in a very difficult situation.

Instead, ***it is neurotypical society*** *"at-large,"* not every last individual neurotypical; people are all individuals, ***which is the problem***.

For example, it is important to realize, that humans with developmental disabilities do not own the factory farms and slaughter houses. It is just good strategy to target the real "power holders" such as Frankin D. Perdue and company and McDonalds and company, extremely wealthy and powerful, neurotypically run and operated, multi-national companies *not* Temple Grandin (one of the only celebratory role-models for peoples with autism and an "inside" reformer, addressing the most egregious institutional cruelties in agribusiness, putting "absolute limits" on what factory farmers can and cannot do to animals).

I personally believe however that factory farming *does* need to be completely abolished (or at-least "downsized" to small family farms like in the olden day) and everyone (at-least in the West and especially Christians) need to work towards a more lacto-ova vegetarian diet (no meat, fish or seafood) and egg laying hens and milk producing cows need to truly become "cage free" (not less dense pens) living on verdant green pastures like in the olden days.

It is important to realize that humans with developmental disabilities are not the ones, who set bag limits for hunting each year. In fact, as an Aspie I am morally opposed to all forms of hunting: sports hunting, eradication, fishing even ethical hunting (especially among Western consumers).

Nor are peoples with development disabilities the ones who experiment on animals.

Peoples on the spectrum are the ones who care about and are in solidarity with nonhuman animals when no one else cares, doing work no one else wants to do in society.

I personally as an Aspie, am a lacto-ova vegetarian, I do not meat, fish or seafood; I have been a vegetarian for fourteen years. I am also an animal activist--- in the past I have publically testified at public meetings against hunting for population control in my own bioregion, as well as urban sprawl and habitat destruction. I am involved in both the Christian animal rights movement and the emerging disability animal rights movement. I have written extensive in my books and other published articles about the animal struggle. I also do not attend circuses, rodeos or bullfights, I do not visit inhumane zoos or aquariums and I feed wild birds. I pray for the animal movements and protect wildlife habitat. I also engage in interspecies communications, I follow the animal intelligence debate and I continue to research and develop nonlethal and nonviolent ways of relating to animalkind and resolving wildlife-human conflicts. I even have taken courses in animal behavior science and animal ethics, even animal theology at the undergraduate and graduate levels. I am a Christian who actually believes animals have immortal souls!

I am not alone either, Temple Grandin although "not going as far" as I would like, too animal welfare, not enough animal rights, I am more of an abolitionist---I do not believe that factory farms, hunting and animal euthanasia have redeeming value, I believe that dissection and vivisection needs to be phased-out and that our anthropocentric, speciesist society does need to be radically changed through cultural critique, lifestyle change and political activism.

Grandin however has made substantial "in roads" in regulating the treatment of animals in agribusiness, has given us more radical activists necessary information about the industry and its problems and has made important discoveries in animal intelligence and sentience which definitively have ethical-moral implications, such as protecting animals from fear and overstimulation which also leads to animal pain, suffering even death.

Going further than Grandin, primatologist Dawn Prince-Hughes has become a world renowned expect on gorillas and animal identity who reached out to a community of captive gorillas at a local zoo during a very serious personal crisis. Only to witness how poorly the gorillas were being treated by ignorant visitors, seeing in their own suffering and oppression, her own suffering and oppression, being a person with Asperger's. She identified with the plight of these gorillas so deeply that she sat in solidarity with them the rest of that day.

That day was a "turning point" in her life; she left her life as an exotic dancer and went on to work at that zoo as a paid employee. There she was accepted into the gorilla community, where the gorillas gave her direct, "unmediated" guidance in "true" Nature-based tradition, which lead not only to a better scientific understanding of gorilla intelligence, individuality, behavior and sociability—a major scientific discovery in its own right. Prince-Hughes also received much personal healing for her own traumas and sufferings as a neurodiverse human, she even got new insights about the meaning of community through observing and participating in the communal life of her gorillas which brought about healing in her relationships with other human beings too.

From zoo employee and guardian of a troop of gorillas, Prince-Hughes went back to school, graduated from college, from there went to graduate school where she got a Ph.D., becoming an adjunct professor and advocate for gorilla conservation and welfare where she had the opportunity to collaborate with Jane Goodall (mother of postmodern ethology and world renowned expert on chimpanzees, animal intelligence, animal welfare and conservation education).

Prince-Hughes was also able to find her own autistic political community (a group of Aspie "like minds" which she could collaborate with) and she is now in a long-term, committed lesbian relationship with a neurotypical woman where the two women were able to birth a child, which Prince-Hughes is currently helping to raise.

Jim Sin Clair (founder of Au-treat) has gone the farthest of us all, from an animal abolitionist perspective, *he is a vegan.*

My point is that autists like Grandin, Prince-Hughes, Sin Clair and myself are living relatively sustainably with the Earth. We live relatively simple, austere lifestyles. We have a strong ecological conscience and sensibility. We are a voice which must be heard. We are a population which is indispensable to the neurotypically dominated environmental and animal movements.

I contend that all human beings with disabilities can contribute much to the environmental and animal movements and develop these movements in new ways.

It is also important to realize, that one's allies on the autism spectrum, cannot be taken for granted either. Aspie humans to become environmentalists and animal rights people need scientific, ethical and spiritual formation, for our ecological and animal libratory sensibilities to form and to circumvent us from retreating back into becoming "computer techies," perpetuating the status quo and the planetary crisis.

Also, it is important to realize, that only some of us on the autism spectrum have the propensity to become environmentally and animal libratory, being what God calls "ecological savants" or "animal liberation savants."

Yet we "ecological savants" and "animal liberation savants," once we receive scientific, ethical and spiritual formation, can surpass neurotypical environmentalists and animal rights people. So, therefore supporting and affirming autistic environmentalists and animal activists like myself is even more vitally important.

For example, if autist animal welfare consultant Temple Grandin received more support from the movement, she might not be working with slaughterhouses, but instead be working towards their abolition. It is just that her personal history and the opportunities given to her, resulted in her career and vocation, progressing in such a manor, that animal rights people find so disturbing, being for welfare instead of rights.

Despite Grandin's "lack of purity" on the subject, it is important to realize that it is neurotypical society which owns and manages the slaughterhouses and factory farms. It is neurotypical society which orders animal experimentation. It is neurotypical society which sets the bag limits on how many animals can be murdered each year. It is neurotypical society which is the reluctant followers of environmentalism and animal rights. It is neurotypical society which is the most resistant, even insular, to non-anthropocentric and non-speciesist views and ways of living in the world.

It is neurotypical society, which is unsustainable. Fundamentally ecological harmful. Ecologically soulless. It is time that neurotypical society "reasonably accommodates" autists and nonhuman beings, even the whole Earth. Neurotypical environmentalists and animal rights people must learn from and be in solidarity with the neurodiversity and other disability communities. Although not ecologically perfect, we, autists are among the ecologically saved.

Now that I have established that "pitting" human, animal and ecosystem rights against each other, "is not working," through establishing that A) humans on the autism spectrum *are not* causing the planetary crisis or institutional animal cruelty, it is neurotypical society, collectively, as a whole, which is the "root cause" of both the planetary crisis and institutional animal cruelty. That B) the oppression *is* in-fact linked between Audists, Animals and Nature, for we are all non-neurotypical beings, meaning we do not have a fully developed vermis.

Yet, C) despite non-neurotypicals such as myself not having a fully developed vermis, specified to precise neurotypical standards, it is important to realize that a fully developed vermis, does not make neurotypicals superior to everyone else. I have demonstrated that the autistic mind has its own gifts and virtues. Yet, D) neurotypicals believe that their fully developed vermis makes them superior and worthy of the conquest of all others who do not conform or "measure up."

I have already talked about the former (A-C), now I am going to "flesh-out" (D) how the collective, unconscious *__narrative of neurotypicalism__* (aka Hellenistic conceptualism) impacts how individual neurotypical humans treat non-neurotypical beings such as myself and the planet. I am going to demonstrate how this oppressive dynamic "plays out" in the "real world," building a profile of the harmful "shadow side" of neurotypical society and how neurotypicalism impacts human-human, human-animal and human-Earth relationships, perpetuating bigotry, the status quo and the planetary crisis, in the process. A narrative once individual neurotypicals become aware of--- can than make a conscious decision, to accept, reject or modify. In other words, making conscious, unconscious narratives helps activists and critics to *__effectuate cultural change__* in both our own personal lives and in our communities, in the process, making the world a better a place, for ourselves and others.

*__The first chapter in the neurotypical narrative__* sees animals, the Earth and neurodiverse humans as "periphery" or "tack-on issues" on neurotypical anti-oppression, social justice agendas. Meaning we are all considered by neurotypical society to be the "undeserving poor," getting in the way of "the real poor," defined exclusively in either economic terms ("the poor") or racial, ethnic or sexual terms ("racism, sexism and homophobia"). Making neurological minorities "neither fish nor fowl," through such overgeneralized dualisms as "rich and poor," "white and black," "men and women" and so forth. Are we rich or poor? Are we all whites? Are we all men?

This was also University of Missouri Women' Studies Professor Sharon Welch's whole objection to Boomer feminism in North America. Many feminist leaders in North America have not yet accepted the reality that they "won," that white, middle class Boomer women in North America are now fully "liberated," enjoying tenured level professorships and directorships, even high offices in positions of authority in government and industry, meaning women in this situation need to make the transition from "social critic" to "servant leader," meaning "watching their language about power." As well as exploring the various ways that white women too are privileged, oppressors (such as answering the Womanist objection that white women oppress and exclude women of color) but without going back to "self-hatred" and "self-denial" such as the mistake that someone like feminist theologian Sallie McFague made.

Welch contends that all women are entitled to "equal rights" and "equal participation" in all aspects of a democratic society from politics to religion. All women are entitled to "self-determination" on all issues which effect women directly such as "equal pay for equal work," childcare and reproductive rights. All women are free to address the most important moral and political issues of our time through scholarship and activism. All women in this model are even entitled to a "healthy self-esteem," "self-care," "self-love" even "happiness and joy" as any man is allowed in a democracy.

Feminists in this model just need to compromise on their need to "control the outcomes" of their political actions on behalf of the planet, be open to the possibility that they are not the only group who has suffered from oppression, that not "everyone has to be the same," that they do not have "all the answers" and that their issue is not "the only issue." In other words, Welch is calling Boomer women back to feminism being about women's rights (no more, no less) not a "magic bullet" for all the problems of the world or a call for men to "just go away." She is calling Boomer feminists to "get back on track" with "equal rights."

Yet, some neurotypicals "lumps me in" with "privileged white males" claiming that I have all this racial, ethnic and gender privilege which I do not have or enjoy, where such privileged, non-disabled, neurotypicals use this as an "excuse" for not giving me what I need, not treating me with "dignity and respect," even using "playing the victim" as a manipulation tactic to "get there way." In other words, using "victim" as justification for scapegoating me for problems which are "not my fault" and are "not my responsibility" such as all the very bad "privileged white males" "out there," instead of taking personal responsibility for their feelings of powerlessness and sense of injustice and confronting those issue directly through going after the real "power holders," our industry, government and religious leaders ("The Corporate Class," "The Top 1 %").

Then there are other neurotypicals, when they acknowledge our struggle for justice at all, it is framed oftentimes as a "tack-on issue," appealing to neurotypical political self-interests. This is true, whether in the form of "feel good" paternalistic, "segregationist charity" for humans on the spectrum, which is more about appeasing a privileged person's "liberal guilt," making non-disabled, privileged neurotypicals "feel good" about themselves for showing "pity" and performing "acts of charity" than truly "doing something nice" for another fellow human being. Where such a privileged "do-gooder" has no intention of treating us as equals.

In an animal rights context, this is manifested in the apolitical "modest reform" culture of the animal welfare movement. In an ecological, planetary context---the enlighten self-interest argument ("if you breath, thank a tree" argument), the environmental justice argument ("the what's in it for my species" argument) and the environmental education argument ("there're just ignorant!" argument).

*What I need as a full human being with autism instead is A) to be treated as a spiritual equal and B) be given "reasonable accommodations" based on my disability. While animals need "social justice" not "humane treatment" and the Earth deserves nothing less than giving the planetary crisis, the attention and respect it deserves.*

*The second chapter in the neurotypical narrative* sees Animals, Autists and Nature as "expendable" to neurotypical society. Meaning if an Animal, Autist or the Natural World gets in the way of the agenda of neurotypical society, we are sacrificed to "the common good" of neurotypical society. I could be intimidated out of a "public place" based on a clique of neurotypicals who cannot deal with people who are "not like themselves." An animal could be murdered because a neurotypical landowner does not want Canada geese "pooping" on their golf course. While, a forest could be "clear-cut" because a city planner resents there being land not being "used" by other human beings and gets developers to build luxury townhouses over a mature hardwood forest to "grow" the local economy. This is because the neurotypical mindset divides the world up into "likes" and "others," seeing anyone else who is not like themselves as not only "other" and "inferior" but even worthy "to be conquered." Such a mindset is fundamentally imperialistic!

*The autistic mindset (with origins in Biblical and Medieval Europe and in Nature-based societies around the world) on the other hand, sees Animals, Nature and other human beings not like us, as formidable equals worthy of respect! Such a mindset is fundamentally life-affirming!*

*The third chapter in the neurotypical narrative* is that neurotypical society likes to patronize and dominate Animals, Autists and Nature. Meaning neurotypical society looks down upon Animals, Autists and the Natural World. Neurotypical society does not treat any of us as equals. For example, a domestic dog is seen as "cute" and "made obedient." An autist is treated like a little child, even as a full adult. I have personally experienced this in my own life-journey. The Natural World is treated "like art" and is made "safely wild" but not allowed to "unleash her full fury." Some illustrative examples include damming mighty rivers such as the Columbia River in Oregon and the Colorado River in Arizona. Other examples include suppressing forest fires in National Parks, draining wetlands and eradicating wild wolves and bears on Western ranches. Such a mindset is fundamentally oppressive!

*The Nature-based, autistic mindset, on the other hand, which respects all life, is fundamentally libratory toward Animals and the Earth!*

*The fourth chapter of the neurotypical narrative* is that neurotypical society expects Animals, Autists and Nature to conform to neurotypical sentiments, standards set "by and for" neurotypical society which benefits the most, those who have a strong neurotypical personality, such as "shallow extroverts."

Animals are expected to *not* be a nuance. Canada geese are *not* to "poop" on neurotypical golf courses. White tail deer *are not* to eat neurotypical azaleas. Wolves, bears and bison *are not* to wonder onto neurotypical ranches.

Autists are expected to become "normal" aka "shallow extroverts." A "shallow extrovert" is a person who is completely "outward" socially, who "toes the party line," easily "fits in" to the conventions of neurotypical society, does not think "too deeply," does not "question authority" and is a militant "status quo affirmer" who "defends the values of society," at all costs. A "shallow extrovert" is the "gold standard" that all neurodiverse humans must strive toward. A "shallow extrovert" is the primary "role model" in special education--- historically speaking.

The Natural World is expected to "be useful" to privileged neurotypicals, where the Natural World is understood solely in economic, utilitarian terms like a tree is "so many boards of feet" and "worth X amount of money." The neurotypical narrative also does not "account" for non-neurotypical "uses" of the Earth, which are non-economic by nature, such as many Native Americans seeing a tree as a "house of worship," Biblical Jews seeing a tree "as pleasing to look at," Medieval Christians seeing a tree "as a religious symbol" and an Aspie like myself seeing a tree "as a person." Such a mindset is very ecologically shallow indeed!

***The Nature-based, autistic mindset, on the other hand, by nature, "goes deeper"!***

***The fifth chapter in the neurotypical narrative*** is that neurotypical society is to punish any and all Animals, Autists and Natural Beings who do not conform to neurotypical standards. Difficult animals are "put to sleep" (animal euthanasia). Autistic humans, such as myself, were subjected to dangerous psychotropic medications and violent behavior modification interventions growing-up in the 1980s and 1990s (I am 33-years old as of writing this book), leaving behind post-traumatic emotional scars and economic disadvantage in adulthood. While, open war is declared on Nature.

***The autistic, Nature-based mindset on the other hand, empathizes with the plight of animalkind and longs to live in peace and harmony with the Natural World!***

***The Sixth Chapter in the Neurotypical Narrative*** enables neurotypical society at-large to subconsciously, oppress Animals, Autists and Nature by "throwing" us into situations, where we are incapable of properly defending ourselves or even properly handling ourselves. This causes us to perform poorly at best and at worst; such situations provoke aggression, even violence. This then leads neurotypical society to feel justified in oppressing us more. We feel "set-up" for violence and failure in much the same way the men's movement claims white men are violently socialized to compete, dominate and oppress "in the name of" "meeting societal obligations." Only for the men who are "the losers" in such sexually explicit competitions to be "left behind" as "broken men," only to be humiliated and scapegoated for all "the problems of the world" such as what happened with the disgraced veterans of the Vietnam War.

For example, a pet chimpanzee who was being neglected and poorly treated in a small New England town became violent, even homicidal, leaving the compassionate police officer no choice, but to "shoot-down" the chimpanzee in "self-defense," to protect himself and other members of the community, giving this compassionate police officer such a serious case of PTSD (Post Traumatic Stress Disorder) that this officer had to "give-up" police work, all together. This terrible tragedy could have been prevented if the chimpanzee was not given alcohol.

In fact, it is illegal to keep any primate as a pet under any circumstances (unless you have a special license). All primates mean all primates: chimpanzees, gorillas, baboons, orangutans, monkeys and lemurs. All nonhuman primates are highly endangered, undomesticated, wild animals who need specialized handling and a specialized environment to be treated properly. Only a trained specialist such as a trained zoo employee or a trained primatologist has any business keeping a primate in capacity. This chimpanzee was being used as an actor in commercial advertizing.

I as an autist have been denied support which would help me to succeed, in the past and when I did not do well, despite much effort, institutions really "clamped down" on me and severely punished me.

With Nature, because of the complacency in American society about global climate change, when a terrible hurricane hits, it is almost always blamed on El Niño. In fact, I watched a documentary, one-year before Hurricane Katrina "warning" that the levies in New Orleans needed to be "dismantled" in case of a major hurricane, that it was a "ticking time bomb" for disaster. In fact, only one year later, Hurricane Katrina came, "broke" all the levies and completely devastated the entire region with a hurricane disaster "un-heard of," even on hurricane coast, displacing millions of Americans in the process. Another preventable disaster!

*The Nature-based, autistic mindset on the other hand is rooting for animal liberation and is in solidarity with the planetary struggle!*

**The Seventh Chapter in the Neurotypical Narrative** is that neurotypical society feels justified in violating the rights of Animals, Autists and Nature with impunity; because neurotypical society conceptualizes Animals, Autists and Nature to be cognitively inferior to the neurotypical human and subsequently believes that non-neurotypical beings such as myself cannot handle these rights. For example, Animals are seen as "irrational beings" (Hellenism) and "complicated machines" (Enlightenment) and therefore neurotypicals feel they can do anything they want to nonhuman animals, while being in the moral clear. An autistic human such as myself is given "segregationist charity" versus "human rights," for we are seen as "strange curiosities," which "do not have an inner life," not the "emancipated adults" and "moral agents" that we are, who are "just different." Nature is just seen as mere material, "matter in motion," "stuff," "a thing" to be devoured and consumed by the neurotypical mind.

*The autistic, Nature-based mindset on the other hand, sees and treats animals as "rational beings" and "moral agents" and sees and treats the Earth as a miraculous "living organism" filled with much beauty and wonder, which we can have a personal "I-Thou" eco-kinship relationship with. We see and treat Animals and the Earth as sacred!*

*The eighth chapter in the neurotypical narrative* gets neurotypical society to look down on Animals, Autists and Nature's ways of knowing and being, privileging neurotypical ways of knowing and being, over non-neurotypical ways of knowing and being. Animals are seen as "dumb" and "inferior." Autists are seen as "idiot savants." Non-animal life is not given much standing at all, hence the "mind-body dualism."

**The autistic Nature-based mindset on the other hand, respects and carefully listens to the different ways of knowing among the various animal and plant societies, even neurotypical human society. The autistic way is the way of "compassionate curiosity"!**

**The ninth chapter of the neurotypical narrative** makes neurotypical society suspicious of intelligent behavior in Animals, Autists and Nature. Perceived intelligent behavior in Animals is dismissed as "being anthropomorphic" (projecting human-like characteristics onto nonhuman animals). Perceived intelligent behavior in Autists has historically been dismissed "as unbelievable." Perceived intelligent behavior in Nature such as "plant intelligence," "Gaia theory," or "intelligent design" is dismissed "as fringe."

*The autistic Nature-based mindset on the other hand is willing to give Animals and the Earth the "benefit of the doubt."*

*The tenth chapter of the neurotypical narrative* makes neurotypical society suspicious of the special relationship Autists such as myself have with Animals and Nature, which serves as a prophetic witness against the anthropocentrism and speciesism which dominates Western culture. For example, growing up, I have been bullied repeatability, because of my views on Animals and Nature. In Boy Scouts, the kids used to tease me about my interest in birdwatching. Even today, I still feel intimidated on this front. This has gotten better as environmentalism and animal rights is becoming a more acceptable and respectable position in many aspects of neurotypical society from politics to religion. This is because people like Temple Grandin, Dawn Prince-Hughes and Jim Sin Clair and myself have broken completely out of anthropocentrism and speciesism before it became "the in thing" to "go green" becoming "early adaptors" in the process, where we are still available to further the environmental and animal rights cause.

I contend that Temple Grandin has broken completely out of anthropocentrism and speciesism. Grandin's major problem is that she has not broken-out of psychological reductionism ("it's your own fault!") and mechanistic cosmology ("machine" metaphors). The same "hard luck" "modest reformer" mentality which Grandin applies to animals in factory farms, Grandin also applies morally consistently to herself and other human beings on the autism spectrum. Grandin not only sees the lives of factory farm animals as "expendable," but Grandin also sees the lives of other neurodiverse humans as "expendable" such as referring to "discrimination situations" as an "autistic being ruined." Grandin even see's her own life as "expendable," such as Grandin "blaming herself" for "her own problems."

If Grandin was to radicalize, she would need to "crackle into" the sociological narrative ("we are all socially produced!") and into organic cosmology ("embodiment" metaphors).

Having said this, neurotypical environmentalists and animal rights people are still struggling to empathize with Animals and the Earth because of the neurotypical bias toward post-animal vermal reasoning which thinks outside one's animal-based, ancestral mammalian, reptilian brains.

*Neurodiverse humans and Nature-based societies around the world on the other hand are "in-touch with" our animality and have used our human mind to structure and channel our animality toward a more rational, non-exploitive and I would dare say, a more civilized relationship with Animals and the Earth. In other words, we have developed a mature animality, pulling morality, spirituality, relationality even knowledge and culture "out-of" structuring and channeling our animality. There is nothing primitive or base about animality!*

*The eleventh chapter of the neurotypical narrative* bullies Animals, Autists and Nature whenever we engage in our natural God-created behaviors. Animals are bullied through sports hunting, recreational fishing, bullfighting, rodeos and circuses. Even in middle school, high school and even undergraduate level when a dissection or vivisection is involved, I have personally witnessed bullying behavior such as malicious teasing, sarcastic humor, belittlement, trivializing, ignorance, sadistic torture, even "targeting" compassionate students.

Neurodiverse humans are mercilessly bullied in school and even into adulthood, it does not let up. I know in my case, I can easily become "a target" based on my disability and get repeatedly revictimized such as when I engage in my natural behaviors being an autist, even when I pray silently, enjoy Nature even cleaning-up a stream can attract unwanted attention.

In Nature, rivers are damned, wetlands are drained, pesticides are poured on "weeds," bugs are squashed in anger, just because they exist and get in the way of neurotypical "progress" or are just plain "annoying." Even a vacant woodlot or meadow becomes the "personal project" of the local developers because they resent that God-forbid that there is land "out there" that is not being "fully utilized" to "grow" the human economy. A forest and a meadow cannot just "exist for its own sake" in neurotypical society.

*The autistic, Nature-based mindset on the other hand, respects the "rights to exist" for all individual animals, plant species and ecosystems. We see in the bullying of innocent Animals and the Earth our own bullying and suffering. Grandin understands first-hand how painful "being made scared" really is and has devoted her entire life to significantly reduce fear in the lives of factory farm animals, even when she was unable to change their situation. Prince-Hughes when she witnessed a tribe of gorillas being bullied by ignorant zoo visitors saw something of her own childhood bullying situation and stood in solidarity with the gorillas. Later to become their ally, their advocate, even their liberator! I saw a positive correlation between my own belittlement at the hands of medical professionals and exclusion by religious leaders and the belittlement of animal intelligence by scientists and excluding animals from religious life by theologians, that I have made it my lifework to defend the notion that "animals have immortal souls!"*

As I have demonstrated in the above profile, ***neurotypicals also have behavior problems***, which negatively impact other people, when the entire Earth community beyond human beings and the middle class is taken into moral consideration.

So in essence, this is the *tenth pillar of an autistic hermeneutic. A) There is a positive correlation among the systematic bullying of neurodiverse humans, institutionally cruel practices toward animals and excessive human interference in the Natural World. B) There is a positive correlation among neurodiverse behaviors, human-animal reconciliation and ecological sustainability. C) The various neurodiversity, disability justice, ecological and animal movements must unite against a common oppressor, the neurotypical narrative and have a truce among ourselves and not get in each other's way.*[55]

**Balance versus Hierarchy:**

Cognitive scientists George Lakoff and Mark Johnson describe balance versus hierarchy in their work, *Metaphors We Live By*,

> Not all cultures give priority we [Western] do to up-down orientation. There are cultures where balance or centrality plays a much more important role than it does in our [Western] culture.[56]

In other words, Western culture uses hierarchical metaphors, or what Lakoff and Johnson calls "Orientation Metaphors," using the metaphors of "higher" and "lower," or "up" and "down," to describe everything from consciousness, health, control, quantity to future events, status, goodness and virtue. According to Lakoff, not all cultures take this for granted, such as certain Asian cultures. These cultures empathize instead the metaphor of balance or centrality to describe reality. In otherwords, in such cultures concepts *are not* looked at dualistically, "either/or," "more important/less important," but instead these cultures, look at reality, as "both/and," "equally important." So truth is attained not so much, when a hierarchy is attained, but instead when "a balance" or "dialectic" is achieved between two or more, opposing ideas. I would argue that autistic culture is also a culture, where balance is more important than hierarchy.[57]

For example, in Dawn-Prince Hughes *Songs of the Gorilla Nation*, Dawn-Prince-Hughes writes about the role of balance in her thinking,

> At this point in my life [when she was a child] it was the symmetry of the mechanical that I liked. Things were made to fit together in ways that always made sense, in never-failing patterns that had purpose. Machines were both reliable and aesthetic, the perfect blend of function and form. Looking back, I understand that I had a very developed aesthetic sense and was constantly framing the world around me with borders informed by purpose and balance…[58]

Later on in Prince-Hughes's classic autobiography, Prince-Huges describes how she reconciled opposing forces in the ape advocacy movement,

> Though one might optimistically believe that ape advocates would, necessarily, see eye to eye, those of us who have spent years promoting welfare of apes, whether captive or wild, know that it is not easy. People who feel passionately about the animal nations find that they are often strongly bound up in one particular mean of solving the complex problems we face. Since the ape advocates I meet all have noble intentions, I have been

inclined to believe that all of them are essentially right and have invaluable parts to play toward the peaceful resolution of these violent times. I try very hard to synthesize the strategies I come upon; when I can't, I remind myself that the dynamic tension resulting from irreconcilable approaches is the very place where new creations emerge-not necessarily through human effort, but perhaps something more creative.[59]

So in essence, Prince-Hughes instead of becoming polarized into either an "animal welfare" or "animal rights" camp sees truth and good intentions in both approaches while at the same time, being open, to some type of integration. When irreconcilable differences come-up, she is a "possibility thinker," having faith that a "creative resolution," still to be defined, can be formed. A possible reason for why autists tend to think more in balance than hierarchy is that our intense emotions are inclined toward simple "black and white" feelings. We tend to gravitate towards balance, for balance provides us with peace and satisfaction, as well as safety and stability. So, balanced answers are inherently more satisfying to us than dualistic answers. Hierarchical, dualistic answers fundamentally leave us wanting and unsatisfied.

Neurotypicals on the other hand, with a fully developed vermis, tend to structure truth using a hierarchical, dualistic even binary logic, for that is what the vermis does. The vermis reasons, organizes, systemizes, categorizes, in otherwords "puts the world together" and creates order out of the world, for the neurotypical. Yet, this same hierarchical, dualistic thinking is at the root of many cultural and ecological problems and prevents debates from being resolved, or resolved, in a way, which makes sense, or is ethically responsible.

To use as a case study, to demonstrate how an autist like myself, works through an issue, using balance versus hierarchy, I am going to use as an example, how I worked through the God versus Nature dualism, using one of feminist ecotheologian Sallie McFague's latest book, *A New Climate For Theology: God, The World And Global Warming* (Minneapolis: Fortress Press, 2007) which I talked extensively about in my last book *Have Mercy On Me, An Ecological Sinner* (Amazon.com, 2012) in conversation with ecofeminist, ecopsychologist Chellis Glendinning's book *My Name Is Chellis & I'm in Recovery from Western Civilization* (Boston: Shambhala, 1994 2005) as a "complementary model."

God wanted me to read Sallie McFague's latest book, *A New Climate for Theology: God, the World and Global Warming* (Fortress Press, 2007), to help work through questions of theodyssey and despair, related to the whole issue of "global climate change." God turned me to McFague because many books on "global climate change" mainly only addressed the questions of "global warming" from a science, policy, economics and ethics perspective. God felt that she went further and addressed some of the deeper, faith questions I have been wrestling with about "global warming."

So we ordered a copy of it from Amazon.com, as part of my birthday present and worked through the issue. We even tested out her ideas in "the real world."

Some of the answers which came out of reading her book to my theodyssey questions about "global climate change" in relation to the whole question of "despair" are as follows:

- I *need not* fall into despair but *instead* turn that energy into "taking action" on behalf of the planet.

- I *need not* focus my intention on asking--- why? Why would God allow people to destroy the planet? *Instead* I needed to focus my attention on the question of--- where? Where do I live? So I can turn my attention to accepting the reality of global climate change and begin to work toward a solution.

- I *need* to realize that "living green" is a good start but *not sufficient*, because I cannot save the world, all on my own, I need the help of other people, meaning I *need* to get more involved in the political, even the economic process. To help transform the system, to make it easier to "live green."

- *Another way* of looking at "global warming" is that of a "cautionary tale," to what degree I am interdependent on the planet and other people. That although God might not be able to stop every bad thing which might happen to the planet, to realize that God is ultimately "in-charge." In other words, God is the "Ruler of the Universe." Meaning God is working through the Healing Power of Christ and the Holy Spirit, toward the redemption of our world. A healing process which involves combining human effort and planetary resilience. In other words, God is not causing "global warming," human beings are engaging in certain destructive behaviors which are causing "global climate change."

- Despite human "unworthiness" and "free will" issues involved, the same God who "made and loves" this world will also be the same God who will "keep it." That whatever happens to this world also happens to God. My job *is* to "keep hope alive."

I will "get there" by doing the following things:

- I am to preserve my "wild spaces"---the members of myself which do not fit into American society (Neurodiverse). Offer a neurodiversity critique of society (too abelist). Use my neurodiverse virtues toward helping to create a better world (my species inclusive, organic mindset).

- I am to be attentive to mine and others "material well being" versus just "consumer demand." "Material well being" according to McFague includes food, water, shelter, clothing, health care, education, love, family and transportation, as well as art, poetry and music, even "enjoyable work and peace and well being among all creatures." For my situation having an invisible disability, I add physical, emotional and spiritual safety, mental health care, dental care, holistic medicine, a comforting religious faith, access to wild Nature, participatory democracy, artistic and academic freedom, individuality, non-material rewards, leisure time and to be treated with "dignity and respect." I subtract meat-eating and unlimited child-wearing as "material" needs. I contend that meat-eating and having more than three children are unsustainable luxuries that not everyone enjoys. I refine transportation as access to reliable, affordable, safe, sanitary and accessible public transportation options which are not overcrowded and are hospitable environments. I *am not* wedded to automobiles! I am also not wedded to single standing housing either! I am a single, celibate man. I am content to rent an apartment without a roommate in a safe neighborhood, with easy access to wild Nature.

- I am to "hang in there," persevere tell the end. I am to remember, that I *do not* have to save the world or even myself, "that saving is God's business" and my business is to "do what I can." In other words, cultivate the virtue of "radical patience." Defined as "longsuffering."

- Finally, I am to transform my urban ecological sensitivities (wanting to preserve urban wilderness areas) into an urban ecotheology which means: 1) To recognize that "second natures" such as buildings, chairs, parking lots and city parks ("Brother Fire") are ultimately derived from "first natures" (wilderness) for our artificial built environment comes from natural materials found in pristine wilderness areas. Buildings come from trees, stones, soil, oil and water. Chairs come from precious metals. Parking lots come from the fossilized remains of prehistoric wilderness areas. City Parks are the ruins of once vast, unbroken forests and plains. In other words, "Nature encompasses the City." 2) To embrace "the place where I was placed," that God placed me in the twenty-first century for a reason and that reason is good, I *am not* a twenty-first century medieval misfit. Although, I contend that I can archetypically visit the Middle Ages whenever I want, for medieval peoples are my "historical ancestors" and the middle ages is one of my "healing spaces." 3) That although Saint Francis will always be an intricate part of my life, trying to replicate exactly what Saint Francis did, in the twenty-first century, has only led to despair and inadequately in my life and instead I am to focus on fulfilling my own destiny of becoming "a saint in my own right." 4) That I need to move beyond my grieving the loss of Tower Oak and other wild areas in the city which I have faithfully tried to preserve, which has caused me to become "forgetful," retreating into "consumerism," and instead seek to preserve the cities themselves through "welcoming the [wilderness] into the city" (heal and preserve urban wilderness areas and other open spaces, take care of plants and wildlife, make God's world beautiful again and see the wild in the urbane) and work to make cities more livable (make cities safer, more friendly, hospitable, accessible and beautiful).

- Yet, to make McFague's urban ecotheology more "functional" and "accessible," because of my situation, I need to live in a city not bent on growth, consumption and homogenization. A city where there is enough "critical mass" of environmental-types to support and complement my ecological work. A city with many entrenched ecological institutions. A city which respects "nature, community and place." A city which "celebrates diversity." A city which is "open and affirming" to disability and neurodiversity. A city which is reasonably safe and shows hospitality to strangers. A city where I can be part of a nourishing political community. A city which is a grassroots, participatory democracy. A city filled with natural beauty. A city where the ecological lifestyle is made accessible and truly includes everyone. I have found such a city when I visited Portland, Oregon two summers ago. That is why as much as I love the Piedmont Plateau and feel indebted to the Piedmont for giving me my ecological identity, I needed to relocate using my Section 8-Voucher to Portland, Oregon so I can live-out my Christian urban ecotheology.

- My *most interesting breakthrough* in reading McFague is that the metaphor of Creation, which was integral to my Christian ecotheology, was in crisis too, my first "anomaly," being how I spiritually reacted to global climate change. I was seeing God as too external to Nature through "the Doctrine of Creation," Since God made the Universe, the Universe therefore is sacred. Instead, I needed to see God as more embodied in the Universe through "the Doctrine of the Incarnation." Basing my Christian ecotheology more on The Incarnation than Creation. The Incarnation ("The Cosmic Christ") is the Christian belief that "God is all reality" and that the Universe is nothing less than "God's body" symbolized by the Birth, Death and Resurrection of Jesus Christ ("The Physical Manifestation of God"). Divine Transcendence is than addressed through contending that A) in God "we live, move and have our being" (Acts 17: 18) using metaphors for God-world relationships like womb, fountain, home or matrix to describe our relationship to God. B) That the Holy Spirit is the Transcendence in Nature, all the non-economic, non-materialistic, non-scientific--- spiritual, aesthetic, moral and relational properties of the Universe including peace, justice, love and order. I contend that such an approach is not pantheism for Incarnationalists *do not* worship the pagan god Pan and preserve key Christian monotheistic categories used to describe the theological meaning of the Universe. I contend that such an approach is methodologically pantheistic however in that Incarnationalists see "the world around us," naturalistic phenomena even everyday life as fodder for revelation and theological reflection.

- I even agree that the Incarnation is sound Christian doctrine because such an approach militantly rejects the Gnostic heresy--- that the material world is evil. This means that the fundamentalist Christian belief "that the world is just going to blow-up anyway with the Second Coming, so why take care it" is in the Gnostic heresy, while sound Christian doctrinc contends that the material world is sacred, holy and good. True idolatry according to Holy Scripture and sound Christian doctrine is to "give the name 'gods' to the work of human hands" (Wisdom 13: 10) either by limiting the language about God (limiting God to a disembodied spirit "spiritualism") or through turning our technologies "into a god" (marrying technology to ideology "technological optimism").

- The *implications* of using this model for addressing global climate change cannot be understated and why the Incarnation is a better model than Creation. The Creation model insists that God is contingent (Creation was something God did not need to create), while the Incarnation model insists that God is imminent (Creation is the natural overflowing of God's goodness). Meaning, God cannot and will not, "just sit back" and let planetary annihilation, just happen. Creation means too much to God! In the Incarnation model, God is a very vulnerable God, whose Own Body is affected by global climate change. In other words, God is not only the Creator of the Universe; God is also the Sustainer of the Universe, actively involved in all aspects of Life on Earth including working toward an ecological resolution to global climate change. Meaning the Kingdom of God is not a "dead letter."

- This model *also* makes the Idea of God all of a sudden scientific, for now you can touch, taste, smell, hear and even see God. Yet, be affirmed at the sametime through Judeo-Christian meaning making, that the Meaning of the Universe is that the Universe is "very good." In other words, the Entire Universe is universally beautiful. That there is a certain order to the Universe which makes our world inhabitable, intelligible, livable, even a hospitable place to live.

- As a neurodiverse human, this has the spinoff, in a number of other areas in my life, too: All of sudden, mundane activities like health, hygiene, cleaning-up my apartment, even personal finances become faith even ecological matters. It has implications for my celibacy commitment in that now I can See My Love, God. I can physically connect to Him, in romantic intimacy, like a man and a woman. God, My Love, is made visible, even touchable, to me. The Incarnation holds together my twin-devotions of God and Nature, in perfect balance. Even more so than Creation. The Incarnation gives me "common ground" for explaining my Christian ecological message to secular audiences. The Incarnation helps explain my spiritual experiences in the Natural World.

- I do need to *improvise* on the Incarnation model based on my own "embodied experiences." As a neurodiverse human and oppressed minority in the Christian Church, I do need my own personal relationship with God outside "official church channels." I do need safety and solitude and I do need concrete images and metaphors to make religion accessible to me at all. As a life-long committed environmental activist, I do need grace and hope, I do need pleasure and rewards, I do need to be able to take care of my physical and mental health and I need to be able to have time to think, pray, even play and I need to be to connected with my "sources of healing and empowerment" so I can live my "life of good works" at all.

- So I am *offering* the Doctrine of the Holy Trinity as a complementary model to the Incarnation in an age of planetary crisis. The Trinity is equipped to address the weaknesses of the Incarnation--- such as respecting the identities and integrity of individual persons (including individual nonhuman animals), acknowledging the details of the Universe (including specific places), addressing the ecological activist's need for hope, grace, safety, patience, solitude, self-care and critical distance (including questioning authority) even providing an ethical-moral framework for evaluating "limits to freedom" claims (including separating "inherent worth" from "moral contracts," "wants" from "needs," the proper place of the "common good" even the conflict resolution of competing moral claims). This is because the Holy Trinity integrates all the dualisms---mind and body (imminence and transcendence), body and soul (person and substance), individual and community (persons and relationships), the parts and the whole (the gods and the One God), order and chaos (eternal and dynamic) even Heaven and Earth (The Spirit World and the Material World). The Holy Trinity then allows you to "pull-out" Green Esctotology (Christian beliefs about the future of Life on Earth), Cosmic Grace (Christian beliefs about the redemption of this world) even Christian Spirituality (A personal relationship with the Living God).

The above "thought experiment" is just one example, where I came to the truth, through "balance versus hierarchy." Instead of making a false choice between Worshiping God or Honoring the Earth, which many people in the Christian and secular environmental movements, have forced me to make. I find myself assenting, coming to believe in a doctrine which encompasses the best of both worlds, God and Nature. Instead of assigning ranks on a hierarchy, the importance of God over Nature, I see God and Nature as equally important. I even make McFague's model even more balanced than McFague already very balanced model. Remember, McFague, is still a neurotypical.

So to make-up for the inadequacy of her model, I incorporated into her model--- the legitimate role of the individual, the animal rights/animal welfare perspective, passive contemplation and solitude, my personal relationship with God, men's studies, the afterlife and Trinitarianism. In other words, I did as Prince-Hughes did, with the "ape protection movement," took everything which I believed was true in this model and integrated this truth into other models for Christian ecotheology, which I believe are also equally valid.

Having said this, it is also important to realize, that there are some legitimate dualisms and hierarchies, which must be preserved at all costs. I want to spend a minute talking about these.
An essential part of a balanced perspective is recognizing that there are legitimate dualisms "out there," in otherwords, accepting the Christian critique of relativism, that saying "there are no absolutes is an absolute."

For example, such dualistic, hierarchies as "good/evil," "right/wrong," "better/worse," "ought/is" and "monotheism/non-monotheism," must be preserved at all costs. This is so there can be some standards for ethics and morality. Not falling into extreme moral or cultural relativism, where anything is morally or culturally "fare game," literally and figuratively.

I do contend and believe, that despite there being much moral and cultural ambiguity, there are some absolute moral and doctrinal standards, which *are not* open for discussion.

For example, a debate about whether cannibalism, genocide, murder or cheating, "is right or wrong," *must not be* open for discussion. On the cultural end, having intellectual debates such as did the Holocaust really happen *must not happen, either*. Some truth-values *must never be* sacrificed, whether for the appeasement of certain groups of people or to account for different cultural norms/taboos or to support certain agendas or goals. Let me talk about each necessary dualistic hierarchy, on its own terms.

For example, blurring the categories of "good and evil," as some New Agers and neo-pagans, have attempted to do, is both dangerous and confusing, for such a framework can become a virtual incubator for oppressive, violent, destructive and perverse thinking and acting, for things that were once considered "evil," all of a sudden becoming okay and acceptable. This is unfair to the most vulnerable in society. We need to preserve the categories of "good and evil," at all costs.

Having said this---it is both legitimate and justified to question some of things which are labeled as "evil," such as mental illness, when a so-called evil act has been tremendously overstated for political reasons such as "terrorism," when the word "evil" is used an as intimidation tactic to coerce other people into behaving a certain way such as the Roman Catholic Church's condemnation of abortion and homosexuality. It is also both legitimate and justified to severely question the practice of scapegoating other groups of people as being "evil" such as enemy combatants, terrorists, criminals and some peoples with mental illnesses. It is even legitimate and justified to question the category of Satan, in this model. Yes, in this model, to deny the fundamentally categories of "good" and "evil" is morally perverse and must be avoided at all costs.

Another dualism which must be preserved at all costs is the categories of "right" and "wrong." Even though most situations fall under the category of ethics, "gray areas" where it is not clear, what is right or wrong, in a given situation, as well as the complexity of the appropriation of punishments and consequences. It is important to realize, that in certain situations, there is definitely a clear-cut, "right" and "wrong." For example, cold-blooded, premeditated murder, is always wrong. There is no justification for committing cold-blood, premeditated, murder. Yet, how a murderer is dealt with by society, is open for fierce discussion and debate, particularly in terms of the appropriation of a punishment.

Also, the dualism of "better/worse" must also be preserved at all costs; ethical decisions must always aim for the "better" than the "worst." In addition, in recent years, the dualism between "ought/is" is slowly being deconstructed, which is particularly disturbing, for the way the world "is" might not be the way the world "ought to be." This is a particularly important dualism to preserve in discussions about economics and ecology, as well among other critical issues. Yet, there is a place for "radical acceptance." That we need to accept "the reality they are dealing with" so pain does not lead to suffering and we can focus our energies on what we can control. Such as accepting the reality that invisible disability, global climate change and animal sentience are real phenomena. Yet, there is an implicit "ought" in "radical acceptance," mainly that suffering *is not* desirable and focusing ones energy on things one cannot control, is counterproductive and a waste of time, such as actually including and reasonably accommodating our fellow human beings with non-physical disabilities instead of discriminating against us and just being all around rigid and insular. The same with the planetary crisis, actually working towards a sustainable solution to climate change instead of just sitting around debating climate change. Actually researching and developing practical humane alternatives to factory farming, animal experimentation and eradication, instead of trying to rebut robust scientific and other rational arguments for animal welfare and animal rights.

Finally, as a Christian, I contend that the dualistic hierarchy, between monotheistic and non-monotheistic religions, must be preserved at all costs. Paganism and certain Eastern religions are not worshipping the same God as we do, as Christians, Jews or Muslims, nor are all religions equally valid, in terms of truth-value. Cultural relativism whitewashes over the reality of objective truth. Masking forms of oppression in these other religions and cultures, which does not and must not be occurring. Religions and cultures must not be able to hide behind morally reprehensible actions and practices, just because it is "part of their culture." This does not mean that the practioners of these other world religions are terrible human beings or that they will not get "salvation" or "eternal life," but that certain doctrines in these religions, might not be objectively true or even desirable.

This does not negate the role of partial truths in these religions and cultures, though, or, the value of dialoguing with people in these separate cultures or religions or treating them and even their belief systems with "dignity and respect," such as not destroying their temples, nor always imposing the Gospel on them, in all social situations. Or, a recognition and appreciation, that different non-Abrahamic cultures and religions, might have valid anthropologies, moral codes or even a praise-worthy spirituality. It is just that we *do not* need to agree with a person's religion or culture, to love and respect that person. It is just that the uniqueness of monotheistic religions, needs to be preserved at all costs and be used as the "gold standard" in infrachurch circles (within Christian communities) for what is right and true, mediated by different cultural, historical, generational and identity contexts and realities.

So in essence, the autist knows he or she has discovered the truth, when he or she has attained a balance of competing ideas versus a hierarchy of importance. Recognizing that a certain amount of hierarchy is necessary to have a just humanity, an autist like myself or Dawn Prince-Hughes, and I would argue also Temple Grandin, "errors on the side" of "balance versus hierarchy," when searching for the truth or making moral decisions. This is the ***eleventh pillar of an autistic hermeneutic, balance versus hierarchy***.

## Rule-based versus Legalism

Saint Paul writes in Hebrews 8 about the problem of religious legalism and the promise of religious freedom within the context of Ancient Israel and an emerging Christian religion,

> This is the covenant that I will make with the house of Israel after those days, says the Lord: I will put my law in their minds, and write them on their hearts, and I will be their God, and they shall be my people….In speaking of "a new covenant," has made the first one obsolete. And what is obsolete and growing old will soon disappear. (Hebrews 8: 1-10; 13)

Apostle Paul, who popularized the newly emerging Christian religion to the Gentiles (the non-Jews) makes the case that although the first covenant was also from God; Christ brings a new and better covenant. Paul argued for a new covenant based on the Life Death and Resurrection of Jesus Christ, which is less legalistic and more virtuous, lifting the heavy religious burdens of the rigorous Jewish laws, to make the Christian faith more accessible to newly converted Christians, freeing the Christian convert to live under a "state of grace." Freeing the new Christian believer from "fear-based" religion and empowering the Christian believer to more positively "hunger and thirst for righteousness" (Mathew 5:6). This is the main difference between Judaism and Christianity and also between more liberal-progressive forms of Christianity and more fundamentalist-conservative forms of Christianity. The later is seething with anger, leading to shame and fear. The former is overflowing with love, leading to healing and joy.

Progressive Christianity, unique from almost all traditional world religions, including certain sects within Christendom, empathizes that "love and grace" are more important than "obligations and guilt," yet progressive Christians are just as committed to their religious faith, as more fundamentalist and traditional religious. It is just, that Christian progressives have a fundamentally different theological and religious vision than more fundamentalist religious.

A certain theological vision, grounded in a belief in a Loving God, a God who helps people with their problems, loves them unconditionally and works toward social justice for all the oppressed. A subsequent devotion to a belief in such a God, leads Progressive Christians to model such love in their attitudes and actions, through performing loving, empathetic acts towards those who are most vulnerable and oppressed by society. A life of good works! Taking up the cause of the poor and the oppressed, being in solidarity with all who suffer unjustly, subsequently forms the basis of the Progressive Christian's moral code.

Liberal-Progressive Christianity also believes in a Mysterious God. A religious sensibility which is sensitive to historical zeitgeists, sociocultural contexts, psychological insights, multicultural realities, scientific discoveries and anti-oppression, yet without the tendency toward assimilation, which has plagued Reformed and Conservative Judaism. Progressive Christians remains firmly and distinctively Christian. At their best and most mature, Progressive Christians believe that "though we live in the world, we do not wage war as the world does" (2 Corinthians 10:3).

Although I was brought into the Christian Church with more "fundamentalist-conservative" sensibilities, I migrated more towards "the religious left" of the Christian spectrum, for liberal-progressive Christianity squares more with my experience with and subsequent Model of God, which names the God I know, experience and love. As well as believe in.

I am atheistic to a "harsh and punishing god." The only God I believe in is a God who is radically loving and radically good. This is the God whom I worship, choose to associate with, am in relationship with and is most real to me. This is the God of the Progressive Christian.

Yet, as I have approached different Progressive Christian communities over the years, I have encountered some unique challenges, because of my Jewish upbringing, identity and sentiments and because I am a person on the autism spectrum. One such issue is that I have been accused of being a "legalist" more than once, because I tended to be "rule-based" in my thinking, believing and acting. Certainly my Jewish background certainly plays no small role in my tendency to error on the side of "legalism," but what I believe plays a much bigger role is my autistic sensibility toward what is more "rule-based," one of the characteristics of an autistic personality. So, I want to "clear the air" on this issue.

First, I want to define what being "rule-based" means and how it is different than "legalism.

Being "rule-based" means following a certain format for learning, growing and living, making being and doing more systematic and concrete, subsequently making living one's ideals, easier. In other words, being "rule-based" means, thinking and acting, in a systematic, ritualized, orderly manner. This is different than "being legalistic" for being "rule-based" does not have a certain implicit religious guilt or fear of punishment in it, rather being "rule-based" is the strategy I use as an autist for achieving a desired goal.

In fact, in my "rule-based" thinking and acting, there is an implicit, sense of grace, even non-judgementalism. If I fail to meet the very high standards I have set-out for myself. I know implicitly that "bad things are not going to happen to me" and that "God is not going to punish me." I secretly recognize deep down that I do not have to follow the rules perfectly in a religious or ethical context. It is just that Progressive Christianity has made me more conscious of this, "brining it above board," making the implicit, explicit. Helping me to become more flexible in my thinking!

This is one of the roles neurotypicals play in my life and has corrected some of my tendencies towards "religious legalism," in the past.

Although, because of my "rule-based" thinking, I might have a propensity toward legalism, neurotypical Christianity, particularly Progressive Christianity does not take seriously enough, "rule-based" approaches to thinking, believing and behaving.

Two of the reasons why Progressive Christians have not been as effective as Fundamentalist Christians are two-fold, according to cognitive scientist and progressive activist George Lakoff. In one of Lakeoff's more recent books: *Don't think of an Elephant: Know What Your Believe and Frame the Debate, an Essential Guide for Progressives* (Chelsea Green Publishing, 2005 2011) Lakeoff writes, "First, Progressive Christians are not as well organized as Fundamentalist Christians. Second, progressive theologians do not do a good enough job articulately what they actually believe."

Both these difficulties can be helped by the autist mind. This is because, the "rule-based" autist mind can help neurotypical Progressive Christians, systematize their thinking, believing and acting, by helping the neurotypical Progressive Christian become more coherent, clear and cogent in his or her thinking, believing and acting, through being more "rule-based." In otherwords, help Progressive Christian theologians and religious to know exactly "what they believe and frame the debate," something Lakoff contends is necessary for the success of all progressives.[60]

This is the *twelfth and final pillar of the autistic hermeneutic*: *thinking more systematically and less nonjudgementally*.

### Conclusion

I have demonstrated in the above *twelve pillars of an autistic hermeneutic*, *that autism is more than a mere disability*, *autism is an alternative phenomenology*, *autism is not a mere weakness*, *but also a strength*, a gift, even a charism.

Despite the cynical consensus about the nature of autism by powerful neurotypical leaders from Peter Singer to Pope John Paul II, peoples on the autism spectrum do have something valuable to contribute to both humanity and the planet. We can and already do, contribute to society and the planet, in the process, providing a prophetic challenge to the neurotypical projects and paradigms which are also harmful to humanity and the planet. Neurodiversity and other disability perspectives absolutely must be heard and listened too, alongside other silenced voices in our society. This is because neurodiversity and other disabilities voices can even help in no small way to address and even ameliorate many of the problems of the world.

Also, I have demonstrated that *autism and neurotypicalism are more than just different ways of perceiving the world*; *autism and neurotypicalism are worldviews*. These worldviews are "unconscious narratives" which have ramifications far beyond the private worlds of individuals on the spectrum, their families and caregivers and the "hyperspecific" politics of autistic-neurotypical relationships.

***There is still the lingering question that "the status quo," the current standard for "what is normal" is perpetuating the planetary crisis and is an imminent threat to both human and planetary survival. That "normal" and "functional" are not the same thing! That neurotypical social etiquette toward Animals and the Earth and other minority groups around the world is "anti-social" and not at all "necessary" for human survival!***

In other words, both neurodiverse and neurotypical human beings alike have our own attitudes, beliefs, values and behaviors/actions which I would contend are the necessary elements for forming a worldview. Where our attitudes, beliefs, values and behaviors/actions definitely impacts how we treat other people and the planet. Our worldviews impact everything from race relations to ecological debates, even our theological reflection.

Subsequently, ***the autistic and neurotypical worldviews must be critiqued like any other worldview in a postmodern age***. With ***the autistic worldview*** making the case that the ***neurotypical worldview*** (privileging vermal reasoning over other forms of reasoning *like* autistic visual reasoning) ***is a fundamentally inadequate worldview***. The unchallenged neurotypical worldview is fundamentally harmful not only to the increasing numbers of human beings on the autism spectrum, other neurodiverse humans, humans with physical disabilities and our love ones, the neurotypical worldview is also harmful to Animals and the Earth, First Nations and other oppressed minority groups, women and ultimately to neurotypicals themselves.

Neurotypicalism is the reason why men in our society are "violently socialized" to become "lonely warriors and desperate lovers" through bullying and intimidation in our educational system, where we are also not allowed to express our emotions and weaknesses, nor are we allowed to pursue our dreams, leaving us as "broken men" in the aftermath. In other words, men in a neurotypical society are not allowed to have natural, "human reactions."

195

Neurotypicalism is also the reason why women in our society are still suffering from the oppressive symptoms of patriarchy even in a society where women are allowed "to do anything." No matter how many women, we put in positions of authority, power and responsibility. No matter how many women athletes we send to the Olympics and how many women soldiers we send into battle. This is because our society is based on certain neurotypical paradigms which also do not include women. Mainly, despite our "celebration of womanhood" in our society, women are still expected to use a certain highly hyperspecific Greco-Enlightenment ideal for intellectual perfection which does even exist in reality, yet this archaic, ethnocentric standard is also imposed on the everyday private and professional lives of women professionals turning today's women also into "lonely warriors and desperate lovers."

All this oppression and injustice is occurring because when we defend Greco-Enlightenment ideals at all costs whether it is "the linguistic turn in philosophy in the twentieth century," Thomistic Aristotelianism in Catholic fundamentalist circles or market-based economics, we are basing our philosophy, religion even political economy on an extinct civilization which collapsed largely impart because Ancient Greece exhausted all its natural resources according to many environmental historians such as Donald Hughes.

In fact, Hughes has documented that Ancient Greece did such an excellent job defoliating their temperate woodlands that when one visits Ancient Greece today, the Greek countryside is a stark, barren wasteland from when Ancient Greeks "clear-cut" giant Cedars of Lebanon to build ships thousands of years ago.

In fact, I witnessed this personally when I flew over the mythic Aegean Sea on my way to my sister's wedding in Israel. The same enchanted, life-filled islands I knew first from Homer's famous epic poem *The Odyssey*. Where thousands of years ago, Homer through the lens of Greek mythology described exotic island paradises in the Mediterranean Sea overflowing with biodiversity which boggles the human imagination. Now in the twenty-first century, is nothing but barren lifeless deserts, more barren than the stark Judean Desert I was later to explore, just like Hughes documented in his classic work in environmental history.

It is no wonder that during the Enlightenment, when Hellenism was being systematically recovered, revitalized, updated and implemented by philosophers, scientists, economists and social theorists of all kinds that this "set in motion" a series of historical events which eventually led-up to the planetary crisis. This is because we are basing our civilization on an extinct civilization which was unable to live sustainably with the Earth.

This section of this treatise is a ***clarion call for neurotypical society to "turn" towards the autistic worldview***. Which is at heart, compensating, utilizing other sources of knowledge and wisdom, other than relying strictly on our vermis in our brain, to study, experience, interact with, relate to and make meaning from the world-around. Leading neurotypical society to value and respect these other faculties in non-neurotypical humans and nonhuman beings, as well as women, the poor and other human minorities.

In otherwords, this is ***a call for neurotypicals to "turn" away from the philosophical conceptualism of the Ancient Greeks***, which is marked by internally generated logic, which by nature is consistent, coherent, conceptually hierarchical, binary, dualistic, abstract, simplified, generalized, homogenized and artificially compartmentalized, developed devoid of experiential reality.

***Instead calling neurotypicals to "turn" to the visual reasoning of Medievalists***, which instead is defined by experiential wisdom, which is grounded in hyperspecificality, is in-pictures, detailed oriented, with extreme perception, concrete, non-dualistic, functionally holistic, balanced and rule-based.

Now that I have formulated up to this point, my spiritual autobiography and my theological anthropology, revealing how I think and reason as a full human being on the autism spectrum.

In the next section I will reveal the various pillars of my personal spirituality, being a Christian on the autism spectrum. In otherwords, how I understand and practice my religion. To this we turn, in the next section.

**Chapter Three-My Religious Experiences: My Theological Authorities Being a Person with Asperger**

## Pillar One: Hearing the Voice of God---The Foundation of My Faith

Brother Lawrence, a seventeenth century Carmelite monk who was a monastery cook and great mystic writes about the legitimacy of ordinary religious claiming to be able to hear the Voice of God,

Anyone is capable of a very close and intimate dialogue with God.[61]

My dialogue with God is the foundation of all my religious faith. It is why I believe! It is what has kept me going in my faith, despite years of disillusionment with the Church. Without my dialogue with God, I would not have a Christian faith. Without my dialogue with God, I might not even believe in God. Doctrine is not strong enough! Tradition is not strong enough! Even, faith community is not strong enough! That is because, doctrine is too abstract, tradition is too alien to my upbringing and cultural identity and faith community, historically has been too weak, although this is beginning to change, in my life. What has proven itself to be concrete, familiar and mighty strong, over the years is my personal relationship with the Living, Loving God, through the direct communication with God's audible voice.

I *am not* hearing voices, for three different psychiatrists are absolutely convinced that I *do not* have schizophrenia. As three different licensed mainstream psychiatrists have remarked, my "Conversations with God" *is not* schizophrenic because I *do not* have any of the other symptoms, such as radical changes in my behavior and they believe that it has been going on for quite some time now. One of these psychiatrists was an expert in mental illness and contends that I *did not* show any of the "flags" for someone with schizophrenia and that religious experience, like everything else in my life, would most likely be more concrete, being a person on the autism spectrum.

Proberly the greatest evidence that I *do not* have schizophrenia is that through all these years of seeing doctors and professionals monitoring my physical and mental health, "like a hawk," I have never been diagnosed with schizophrenia.

I have never been diagnosed with schizophrenia, nor will I most likely ever be.

This is compounded by the reality that most if not all the things which God tells me to do *is not* "anti-social" or "violent." In other words, I am *not* "a threat to myself and others."

Even my mother, which was at first was highly skeptical has embraced this reality. While my father, the physicist, recognizes that there are still many mysteries in this world which science *does not* completely understand. He now believes me too!

It is also important to note that it is my perception that psychology and even psychiatry is slowly moving away from the Freudian position that "religious experience is a neurosis" and instead is moving in the direction of respecting the role that spirituality and religion plays in a patient's "healing and empowerment." Not judging a patient's religious beliefs and choices, supporting the patient's religious lives and decisions, even involving the patient's religious life in their psychological treatment, only intervening in a patient's religious life, if it is "harmful to themselves or others." This is a major "in-road" the spirituality movement has made for modern-day mystics!

In light of all this, it is safe to say, that my "Conversations with God" *cannot* be dismissed so easily. They most certainly cannot be dismissed, responsibility on psychiatric or psychological grounds. Then, what about on religious grounds?

One of the arguments which are often used to question my "Conversations with God" by other Christians is the "Discernment of Spirits" argument. How do you know it is really from God?

My Lord has helped me refute this argument by rebutting that trying to make everything God tells me "square with scripture" goes against the "spirit of faith," "a complete trust in God" and leads into a relationship grounded in perpetual doubt and suspicion. This belief has done nothing but wreck havoc on my relationship with God and my faith, causing me "to doubt." This "knee-jerk" reaction has caused me to stumble!

There is also an implicit arrogance in this concern---that "the witness of community" is inherently more reliable than "direct revelation from God." Like the Crusades, the Spanish Inquisitions, the burning of Saint Joan of Arc, the forced conversions of Native Americans and the Holocaust ever happened.

My personal experiences testifies and history bears me out, that there are many personal and political examples of Satan coming "like an angel in white lights" in the form of fleshy human beings and their so-called faith communities. Just look to the Crusades, the Spanish Inquisitions, and Constantine's Cross, the genocide of the Native Americans and Nazi, Germany for historical examples.

Just look to the Roman Catholic Church's sex abuse scandals in Boston, Ireland, Alaska and Wisconsin and the subsequent "stand offs" between the Roman Catholic Magisterium in Rome and the Catholic laity and American nuns for a more contemporary example. By the way, in the most recent Alaskan sex abuse scandal, pedophilic male priests targeted Native American children and in Wisconsin, pedophilic Catholic priests targeted Deaf children, only for the Magisterium to "cover-up" all this reprehensible sexual abuse with all their "spin and propaganda." All the Magisterium is doing by targeting nuns is targeting the very Christians in North America who are the most committed to social justice; the very people on the "frontlines" working to eradicate poverty and social inequality, once and for all.

Even the Cruxifixation of Jesus Christ himself happened partially because the religious in Jesus's day poignantly misjudged Jesus's religious testimony.

Religious community has proved time and time again to be just as an unreliable witness as an individual's private, direct revelation from God. If not more!!!

Groups are automatically more violent than individuals by nature because groups are "socially produced" by nature. Individuals can only do so much damage. The damage done collectively by groups is virtually infinite. Just look to the planetary crisis! Just look to the nuclear treat!

So a certain "proof-texting" combined with "official approval" *is not* a necessary prerequisite to trust my testimony---"that God talks to me." In fact, a person's personal revelation can even check an out-of-line and out-of-control, toxic faith community. Being, nothing less than prophetic, in the truest sense of the word!

Then, what about the objection on theological grounds? That it is inherently arrogant to say God told me this and to act and tell others do accordingly. In other words, arguing against "Divine command ethic." Divine Command Ethics is an ethical-moral framework where ethical decisions are based on Divine Revelation. The theological objection makes Divine Command Ethics inherently invalid and suspect. For example, one professor I had in theological school told me, "If I take seriously that God talks to you, than I have to take seriously that God talks to Ben Laden seriously too."

This argument is indefensible and shows a profound inability to "Discern Spirits" in the truest sense of the word. It also lacks all nuance and even "common sense." It makes no distinctions. It is a virtual "straw man argument." A logical fallacy!

Here are some more nuanced and reliable people than Ben Laden that give testimony that having "Conversations with God" is both a valid spiritual discipline and a legitimate moral guide, subsequently being reliable spiritual, theological even ethical testimony.

The great twentieth century theologian and missionary Frank Laubach writes about this matter:

> How infinitely richer this direct first hand grasping of God Himself is, than the old method which I used and recommended for years, the reading of endless devotional books. Almost it seems to me now that the very Bible cannot be read as a substitute for meeting God face to face.[62]

While more recently, Jan Johnson in her book, *Enjoying the Presence of God: Discovering Intimacy with God in the Daily Rhythms of Life* writes:

Friendship with God is not only possible, but it is God's will…

Johnson continues,

When God becomes a constant companion, every corner of life is occupied by the sense of God's presence. There's so much to say to God and to listen to God about that it's no longer boring to wait for an appointment. Even filling the gas tank of a car presents possibilities for conversation with God.[63]

Neale Walsh, author of the popular series, *Conversations with God: an uncommon dialogue*, who has a very similar relationship with God to me, writes about the validity of his mystical experiences, which is worth quoting in its entirety:

…You proberly think (or have been taught) *that's not possible*. One can talk to God, sure, but not *with* God. I mean, God is not going to *talk back*, right? At least not in the form of a regular, everyday kind of conversation!

That's what I thought, too. Then this book happened to me. And I meant that literally. This book was not written *by* me, it happened to me. And in your reading of it, it will happen to you, *for we are all led to the truth for which we are ready.*

My life would probably be much easier if I had kept all of this quiet. Yet that wasn't the reason it happened to me. And whatever inconveniences the book may cause me (such as being called a blasphemer, a fraud, a hypocrite for not having lived these truths in the past, or-perhaps worse-a holy man), it is not possible for me to stop the process now. Nor do I wish to. I have had chances to step away from this whole thing, and I haven't taken them. I've decided to stick with what my instincts are telling me, rather than what much of the world will tell me, about the material here.

These instincts say this book is not nonsense, the overworking of a frustrated spiritual imagination, or simply the self-justification of a man seeking vindication from a life misled. Oh, I thought of all of those things-every one of them. So I gave this material to a few people to read while it was still in manuscript form. They were moved. And they cried. And they laughed for joy and the humor in it. And their lives, they said, changed. They were transfixed. They were empowered. Many said they were transformed…

You can say that this book is "God's latest word on things," although some people might have a little trouble with that, particularly if they think that God stopped talking 2,000 years ago or that, if God *has* continued communicating, it's been only with holy men, medicine woman, or someone who has been mediating for 30 years, or good for 20, or at least half decent for 10 (none of which includes me).

The truth is, God talks to everybody. The good and the bad. The saint and the scoundrel. And certainly all of us in between…

Shortly after this material began happening to me, I knew that I was talking with God. Directly, personally. Irrefutably. And God was responding to my questions in direct proportion to my ability to comprehend. That is, I was being answered in ways, and with language, that God knew I would understand. This accounts for much of the colloquial style of the writing and occasional references to material I'd gathered from other sources and prior experiences in my life. I know now that everything that has ever come to me in my life *has come to me from God*, and it was now being drawn together, pulled together, in a magnificent, complete response to *every question I ever had.*[64]

As the above passage demonstrates, a belief that God talks to you is a perfectly reasonable and valid position, it *does not* make your arrogant or insane. Also, the validity and plausibility that God talks to people like me, can also be backed-up with extensive Scriptural support, too. Let me trace this theme throughout the Bible, with a few highlighted verses:

- "… Now therefore, if you obey my [God's] voice and keep my covenant, you shall be my treasured possession one of the peoples…" (Exodus 19: 3-6).
- "…Has any people ever heard the voice of God speaking out of a fire, as you have heard, and live?…From heaven he made you hear his voice to discipline you. On earth he showed you his great fire, while you heard his words coming out of the fire." (Deuteronomy 4: 32-36).
- "… All your children shall be taught by the LORD, and great shall be the prosperity of your children. In righteousness you shall be established; you shall be far from oppression, for you shall not fear; and from terror, it shall not come near you." (Isaiah 54: 11-14).
- "… I will ask the Father, and he will give you another Advocate, to be with you forever. This is the Spirit of truth, which the world cannot receive, because it neither sees him nor knows him. You know him, because he abides with you, and he will be in you. I will not leave you orphaned; I am coming to you. In a little while the world will no longer see me, but you will see me; because I live, you also will live. On that day you will know that I am in the Father, and you in me, and I in you…" … "I have said these things to you while I am still with you. But the Advocate, the Holy Spirit, whom the Father will send in my name, will teach you everything, and remind you of all that I have said to you… (John 16-31).
- Therefore whoever rejects this rejects not human authority but God, who also gives his Holy Spirit to you. Now concerning love of the brothers and sisters, you do not need to have anyone write to you, for you yourselves have been taught by God to love one another… (1 Thessalonians 4: 8-10).
- Therefore, as the Holy Spirit says, 'Today if you hear his voice, do not harden your hearts as in rebellion, as on the day of testing in the wilderness, where your

ancestors put me to the test, through they had seen my works for forty years…' (Hebrews 3: 7-15).
- "And they shall not teach one another or say to each other, 'Know the Lord' for they shall all know me, from the least of them to the greatest…" (Hebrews 8: 11-12).
- "Listen! I am standing at the door, knocking; if you hear my voice and open the door, I will come in to you and eat with you, and you with me... Let anyone who has an ear listen to what the Spirit is saying to the churches" (Revelations 3: 20-22).

So, scriptural revelation not only affirms that it is both possible and legitimate to have Conversations with God, but in fact it is both desirable and virtuous and even a necessary, non-negotiable, part of a believer's faith-life. To deny this possibility, would be to do nothing less than fall into a type of Gnosticism, a major Christian heresy, which not only "sees the material world as evil," but also believes that only a select elite group of people can access God, "through certain mystery codes." A certain perverted Protestant, Calvinist sentiment which uses Scripture as a mediator, to gain access to Divine Revelation, falls into such a trap.

It is not Biblical nor is it theological correct, to argue that all of God's revelation is contained within Genesis and Revelations in Holy Scripture. Although Scripture is the infallible Word of God, God's Holy Spirit cannot be confined to Holy Scripture. What the Holy Spirit says in the twenty-first century is also the infallible Word of God. The Living God is very much alive today and continues to be at work in both Nature and History. God is still talking and revealing Himself to humans and nonhumans alike.

Those of us who "have ears" "must listen" (Revelations 3: 20-22). Those who *do not* must make it a priority, to do so. As in Laubach's contention, reading endless devotionals, even Scripture, although illuminating, healing and edifying is an insufficient substitute for "meeting God face-to-face."

Granted, that different people experience God differently, based on their cultural identity or neurological composition or a variety of other factors. All these are valid and legitimate encounters with the Holy Spirit and ultimately with God Himself.

For example, some neurotypicals experience God through "synchronistic experiences" and come to actually See God at work in their everyday life, like my mother. Or, See God in the beauty of All Creation, like my father. Having common ground with such saints as Saint Anthony of Padua (Franciscan) and Saint Teresa of Avilla (Carmelite).

Other neurotypicals encounter God directly through The Sacraments, encountering God's Holy Spirit indwelling in religious rituals and observances such as my Aunt Frances, my sister Rachel and my Franciscan mentor, Sister Helen--- becoming a "Beautiful Trail" from "womb to grave," having "common ground" with such saints as Saint Clare of Assisi (Franciscan), Saint Benedict (Benedictine) and John Calvin (Protestant).

Other neurotypicals such as my friend Maria and my late mentor Dr. Phil Bosserman rely on certain feelings and certain thoughts to Experience God. Having "common ground" with Saint Igneous of Loyola (Jesuit), Saint Augustine of Hippo (Augustinian) and Cardinal Henry Newman (Roman Catholic convert), as well as many of the early environmental saints like Thoreau, Muir and Enos Mills.

Still, other neurotypicals even tell this day rely on signs, miracles, dreams and wonders like ecopsychologist Chellis Glendenning and the late-environmentalist Rachel Carson. Having "common ground" with Saint Francis of Assisi (Franciscan), Saint Mother Ann Seton (American's First Natural Born Saint and native to my own bioregion), Saint Bernadette of Lourdes (lay Catholic saint) and many of the Celtic Saints like Saint Kevin, Saint Cuthbert, Saint Bede, Saint Benno and Saint Brendon.

These neurotypical approaches are all valid, for the mystical tradition testifies to the breath and diversity of different mystical charisms for experiencing the Living God. It is just that your "point of contact" with the Living God must be experienced personally outside of socially constructed doctrines, traditions, faith communities and other official channels. In other words, even though your "private revelations" must be "private," that *does not* mean that your "private revelations" are apolitical. The "personal is political!" This means your "private revelations" do have political implications.

I also recognize the reality that other neurotypical believers might have a different Model of God. A Model of God is a way of conceptualizing God using a series of metaphors. For example, the Holy Trinity is a Model of God. A way of visualizing both the Mysteries of God and the seemingly contradictory dipolar natures of God. Where one might use metaphors like "personal relationships," "same-self," "the web of life," or "Father, Son and Holy Spirit."

This is because other believers are also having valid mystical experiences too, even if they see or hear God as a women, an African-American man, as a gender neutral Spirit or even as a physically disabled man in a wheelchair, which is different than myself.

I personally experience God in the masculine, as a Jewish male, as an avian Spirit who hovers over me, who is on the autism spectrum (imminence). I also personally experience God in the feminist (a champion of women), as a woman of color (the Sabbath Queen), as a humanoid-like Spirit which has befriended me (an intelligence), even as a neurotypical caregiver (an advocate) (transcendence). That is how I know that not all my thoughts *are not* my thoughts and not all my ways are God's ways. That is why I am basing my autistic liberation on the Holy Trinity as my primary Model of God or "root metaphor." Out of the Holy Trinity, I "pull-out" a personal mysticism, a public theology and an ecospirituality.

I even believe people that have personal relationships with their Guardian Angel, different Saints in Heaven or have encountered the Blessed Virgin Mary are also having valid mystical experiences too.

The most important thing to remember is the essentialness of engaging in some type of personal relationship with the Living God through the Holy Spirit which involves some type of a dialogue with and responsiveness from God and not relying excessively on the impersonality of one's tradition, religious doctrines or even faith community, as one's sole and only source of religious or spiritual experience.

Having said this, there is definitely a role and place for doctrine, tradition and community. I need doctrine to meet my need for safety as a survivor and a person living with an incurable disability through offering a certain set of standards which protects me against spiritual abuse. I need tradition to give me a sense of stability in my life. I need community for comfort.

To re-frame the "discernment of the spirits" arguments, tradition, doctrine and community can lie too and also needs to be discerned through the Holy Spirit.

Concerns for social justice or the environment arc *not* mutually exclusive with such a personal relationship with the Living God, either. For example, oftentimes it is my experience that God will be my "source, strength and strategy" for best using my energies toward Saving Earth. The God, who talks to me, also cares as much as I do, if not more, about His Creation. In fact, He is zealous about it, even too me. So, engaging in "Conversations with God" has led to me becoming a better activist and even more involved in the world, then if I was left to my own "will-power." In fact, the God who talks to me, singlehandedly, got me through my bought of "Compassion Fatigue" and brought me back into the planetary struggle. God alone, encouraged me not to "give-up too soon" and to "try again" despite everything.

Most certainly, a personal relationship with the Living God in my case *did not* cause me to retreat from the world, as some modern-day theologians have cynically contended and concluded. Quite the opposite, God has given me the strength and guidance to "live more sanely and sustainably on this Earth."[65] A "source of healing and empowerment" many technology survivors and neurodiverse humans such as myself enjoy, according to ecopsychologist Chellis Glendinning. Because we have the power to have "non-ordinary states of consciousness," becoming what Glendinning calls "Wounded Healers" in the process.[66]

Yet, how can my "religious experiences" as a modern day mystic be deliberated in the academic milieu where theological discourse occurs? Can the "mysteries of autism" help decode the cryptic language of Christian mysticism? Can such mystical religious experiences even be rationally defended through modern science?

According to career counselor and artist herself, Carol Lloyd contends that the appropriate venue for modern day mysticism is neither academia nor is it in the employment sector nor is it even faith community or do mystics belong in insane asylums either, but the appropriate venue for mystics in our society is in the art world. Lloyd contends that mystics are really artists who create certain types of experiences. Mystics create experiences, as painters paint paintings and writers write books. This is why mystics are so often misunderstood, historically and even today. Mystics by our very nature *do not* follow the "law of non-contradiction" for we *are not* philosophers or ideologues, nor do mystics follow the "scientific method" for mystics *are not* scientists or technocrats, we are artists, we broker in raw creativity. We create things. We create art.

In fact, Lloyd also contends this is the also the reason why mystics also are notorious for not being "pigeonholed" into a particular religious tradition, such as why Saint Francis of Assisi could not just disappear into a monastery to become a good Cistercian monk or why Saint Igneous of Loyola could not just be another Franciscan penitent or a very traditional Roman Catholic clergyman like Thomas Merton had this need to dialogue with Buddhism or why a good Jewish boy like myself has this almost instinctual, nagging intense longing to take the vows of holy orders in a Franciscan order, which never goes away, no matter how much I am discouraged.

According to Lloyd, most mystics have actually invented their own religious faith, like an inventor coming up with a new invention, to solve a practical problem in their life. This means mystics are struggling to create something completely new through taking energy from all the existing spiritual and religious traditions available to them, in their time and place. In other words, mystics improvise on existing traditions.

Lloyd also gives us mystics the knowledge that society "at the end of the day" actually likes our ideas, but still expects us to meet the same societal obligations as everyone else. Lloyd encourages us to use our mysticism itself, to solve our professional predicaments through envisioning a single solution to all our career problems through identifying all the different types of energies we need and want in our lives and where we can find these different combinations of energies.

Saint Francis of Assisi's solution was "Lady Poverty," where he no longer let himself be intimated by threats of starvation, want or persecution, filly embraced his hunger, his thirst, his homelessness, his nakedness and his unprotected body exposed to harsh natural elements, "all the principalities and powers of the world" and other forms of adversity like his various disabilities and illness. Yet, he was free to stand in solidarity with the Crucified Christ and worship and serve and fight for the Lord, "all the days of his life," which was his dream, free from "life draining" societal expectations, obligations and influences.

My solution is Portland, Oregon, a place "where the artificial and natural are one" and I have the possibility to experience comradely, belonging and the freedom to be openly eccentric, for the first time in my life, where I would be in a more conducive environment to live out my convictions and fulfill my destiny, in a "land of hope," a "land of opportunity," a place with a future, my Promised Land, my New Jerusalem. A healing venue! Portland will give me the cultural identity my soul so longs for!

Most importantly, Lloyd advises modern-day mystics not to waste another minute trying to be normal.[67]

This means for an Aspie like me to accept and embrace that I have been presupposed to a more mystical spiritual and religious faith because according to neurotheological research, a person such as myself who has suffered a serious trauma to my nervous system, can have "religious experiences," where we feel like it is God who talks to us, this is because our neurological tissue structure has been fundamentally changed, meaning we channel spiritual and religious stimuli differently. This is further intensified as a person on the autism spectrum, where I have a propensity to "personify intimate objects," making my ascent to a Deity religion with a personal mysticism like Christianity possible, where I experience God and other Spirits as people who I can have a personal relationship with. Both Dawn Prince-Hughes and Temple Grandin have also reported similar experiences.[68]

Remembering that just because it is psychological, does not mean, it is not real, anymore than "myth means lie!" Psychological phenomenon is biophysical phenomena grounded in biophysical reality which is enveloped by biophysical realities which is manifested in our conscious brains through immaterial metaphors, images, ideas and dreams (spirituality, religion, theology, philosophy, literature, creativity, the arts and aesthetics). Our mind most likely uses immaterial metaphors to describe neurological realities, because neurological realities are invisible to our senses, yet we know they exist, we feel their existence, every moment of every day of our lives.

My "non-ordinary states of consciousness" as an autistic human definitely sheds scientific light on the historical plausibility of the deep mystical experiences of the great prophets and saints reported throughout the Jewish and Christian traditions. Mainly, many of the great Jewish and Christian mystics throughout history were most likely on the autism spectrum. They most certainly *did not* "enjoy good physical and mental health."

To the great mystics of the various world religions, the Divine *was not* an abstract ideology which you could defend or refute like an argument for/against abortion or gun control or more/less government. No, the Divine, was conceived of in both monotheistic and polytheistic religions alike, even in non-theistic philosophies of life as something very concrete, real and tangible. Something to experience, participate in, even relate to. This was true, whether a mystic believed in God or many gods/goddesses or just believed in the virtues, some sort of a higher good or ideal, or respect for country or culture, or a particular community or place or even the phenomena itself. Whether you were a nature mystic or a political mystic or a religious mystic, religious experience was never just a set of principles nor was it just merely a series of root mechanical religious rituals, it was always about seeking integration between your highest ideals and your most mundane, everyday realities, it was always about putting theory into practice. An ancestral trait shared with autistic humans throughout the world today in the twenty-first century, who also gravitate toward "analytical engagement with concrete reality."

Jewish and Christian mystics take this a step further. We not only make the Divine concrete, tangible and real through participatory experiences and embodied relationships. We also make our experiences and relationship to the Divine---personal, living, transcendental and accessible.

We attribute human-like or animal-like attributes to Divinity, naming the Divine as God, claiming to have a personal, intimate, one-on-one, recipical relationship with the Divine and the Divine with us, grounded in love and reason. We also claim that God is immortal, meaning God lives forever, meaning God *did not* just create the world and clock-out (deism) nor did God just die in childbirth in creation (paganism) nor was God just revealed to our ancestors ("Pagoda Worship" to use Henry David Thoreau's exact words[69]), no, God also speaks to us in the twenty-first century, to our decedents in the twenty-second century and even to those in the centuries after. God *is not* only in the past; God is also in the present, even in the future.

We also claim a transcendental God; a God who is a "higher power," a moral agent and historical actor, who exists outside of humanity, yet who gives humanity "wisdom, power and goodness." This is because we believe God is the Creator, Sustainer and Redeemer of the Entire Universe. We believe in a created, sustained and redeemable Cosmos. We believe in a God who is good, fair, just and righteousness. A Loving God! A Mysterious God! We believe God made this world good.

We even believe that God's love is made accessible to all through "God's Only Begotten Son" (Nicean Creed), the Lord Jesus Christ, the Physical Manifestation of God, embodied into a fallen, broken world marked by destruction, suffering, futility and injustice.

Such a personal mystical vision has "common ground" with the autistic propensity to "personify inanimate objects."

In other words, our autistic psychological and neurological propensity to gravitate toward the personal and the concrete can definitely give academic theologians, historians and religious studies scholars a fresh understanding of the psychological and neurological mindset of our mystical ancestors, to better understand where they were coming from and to authenticate and contextualize the plausibility of their mystical experiences as a real phenomenon. Such as Western mystics using personifications as metaphors or models for describing deeper truths or realities which defy logic or reason like emotions, desires, longings or intuitions or contradictory, chaotic, novel, unexpected, surprising, life-changing or instinctual realities, or even the sub-conscious mind, natural inclinations or wild experiences, as Franciscan gender theologian and modern day friar and mystic himself, Richard Roar hypothesized.[70]

So, now that I have established the validity of my relationship with God, through direct communication, psychologically, religiously, theologically, scripturally, ethically even scientifically, I am now going to proceed with specifics, about my personal devotion to hearing the Voice of God, which is the heart and soul, of my Christian faith and what has held it together, all these years.

The *crux* of God's role in my life through direction communication is being *my Teacher* or *Rabbi*. God has played an integral role in my education and learning by tutoring me in all my courses.

My former Christian education professor in graduate school Bob Pazmino in his book *God Our Teacher: Theological Basics in Christian Education* (Baker Academic, 2001) outlined five ways God is our teacher from a Biblical, doctrinal perspective: "God for Us," "God despite Us," "God with Us," "God through Us" and "God beyond Us."

God is for me through God being committed to my education and growth.

God loves me despite my doubts and skepticism though God remaining committed to my education, growth and who I am as a person.

God is with me through God always being solicitous in my education and growth, permeating through all aspects of my learning.

God works through me, so other people will be moved by the Holy Spirit and be edified.

God is beyond me through being involved in my education, learning and growth in ways that I cannot even imagine or understand such as working through other people, the Natural World, ancestors and certain "synchronistic experiences."

Using Pazmino's educational module as a guide, I have the following "teacher-student" relationship with my Lord.

God speaks to me through the Holy Spirit which is the Promised Tutor.

God is always solicitous, caring, compassionate, empathetic, patient, merciful, gracious, committed and present in our relationship.

God does not have any power over my grades.

God is not coercive in His teaching and in our relationship; instead He uses love, grace and persuasion.

God allows me to question His relationship and the knowledge and wisdom which He teaches me. God accepts my doubts and questions graciously and maturely, never abandoning me or judging me about any of these concerns.

God is one of my most important relationships in life. God is the closest friend that I had ever had and according to God, relationship issues in our relationship may be one of the deepest and most profound issues that I will ever struggle with, for these issues impact my ability to make meaning.

Using Pazmino's framework, this is "the role" my Lord plays in my education and lifework:

God educates me in accordance with the Holy Scripture, Christ and His Kingdom.

God prepares me to do His work in the world.

God fosters integration, internalization, empowerment, self-formation, self-purification, self-reflection, meaning-making, growth, discernment, experimental learning and relevancy.

God helps me to realize my full potential in life.

God fosters a more meaningful relationship with Him.

Even though I came to the above conclusions while I was still in theological school, now that I have graduated from theological school and I am currently not in school, yet "God the Teacher," still remains at the heart of our relationship and interactions with one another. That is because being a Rabbi is God's personality. I think of God teaching me in a manor very similar to Jesus teaching His disciples, when He was on Earth in human form. I feel it in God's voice.

Since graduating theological school, in 2006, God's role in my life has only complexified. God is not only my Teacher, which has historically been His role in my life. God has now become my Employer too. Increasingly God is becoming my Lover, even Spouse and Partner.

So, God is my Father, Creator, Teacher, Boss, Lover, Spouse, Friend and Savior. In other words, God is my Godfather.

I am begotten by God. God is my Father and Creator.
I am saved by God. God is my Friend and Savior.
I am taught by God. God is my Teacher and Mentor.
I now work for God. God is my King and Master.
I confide in God. God is my Confessor and Judge.
I make love to God. God is my Lover and Partner.
I am even in love with God. God is my Bridegroom.

I resonate with Saint Francis of Assisi when he prayed all night at Bernardo's House, his first follower, saying over and over again, "My God, My All!"

As a mystic, none of these above Models of God can even begin to capture the fullness of God's relationship with me and who God is.

For example, I experience God as a father-figure, yet as a non-patrarchical father-figure which respects women. More like the Jewish ideal of fatherhood which Jesus was familiar with in the first century where a father is a more benevolent, gender egalitarian figure lovingly referred to in Jewish culture, even tell this say as "Papa" or "Abba."[71]

More like the fatherhood in many animal societies, where fathers fulfill many of the same functions of mothers, such as raising the children in emperor penguin society (the males do the "lion share" of the child care) and even child-bearing (males share the burden of pregnancy and child-birth in many egg laying societies) in many bird, fish and frog societies. In fact, the male seahorse even has his own womb.[72]

Yet, even through this relationship has been an absolute blessing in my life and I *would not* give it up for the world, I have suffered from much doubt in my relationship with God.

Yet, God has persevered through all of this, remaining "compassionate and gracious, slow to anger, abounding in love" (Psalm 103:8) and I know deep down that I *am not* in any danger of losing Him. In fact, when I completed Mark Heim's (my mentor's) course on Systematic Theology in theological school, God gave me the following framework to go back-to, when I am struggling with my faith. This is to be my framework whenever "Problem of God" issues come-up on my "Soul's Journey into God."

One of the major breakthroughs, I made on understanding the principles and processes of God, based on the study of official church teaching is that I must allow God to be God's self and not force-fit God or His nature, capacities or behaviors into human paradigms, metaphors or models of God. These thoughts like "God lied to me" or "God is totally incompetent" and all sorts of other blasphemous thoughts I have experienced and hate, occur not because God was literally doing these things to me or that God was literally these things or that my revelation from God was false, imagined or projected, but that my paradigm of God was in crisis, not God Himself. God was not meeting these human imposed expectations of God-self. That my own personal encounters and experiences with the Living God through transpersonal communication and contemplating "the Divine substance" found in All Creation is the most reliable way of knowing

God's nature, capacities and behaviors, not prescribed "sets-of-suppositions." Not that these "sets-of-suppositions" are invalid, many are very valid, but that they must be discerned in light of my experiences with the Living God, not the other way around.

Some of my other breakthroughs, which I made in terms of understanding God's principles and processes include breakthroughs from Oduyoye, Cobb and Moltmann.

From reading Mercy Oduyoye, a womanist and African liberation theologian, work entitled *Hearing and Knowing: Theological Reflections on Christianity in Africa,*[73] I learned that:

- "Without God, nothing holds together-nothing has any meaning."
- My God, the Christian God "is not the Impassable God of Greek philosophy. God is affected and is not immune to mutability. In fact, God is plainly vulnerable."
- "We make a mess of our world when we ignore God's voice and misuse both the natural order and our human companions in the process of seeking our interests, the Earth is the Lord's, not ours, and hence there is a limit to how far we can bend it to suit ourselves."
- "Our refusal to observe limits is the outcome of the yearning to be independent of God. To be totally dependent on God, we have to have absolute trust in God."
- "Cynicism in our relationship with God cannot make for a healthy human community. Our community with God depends on our complete trust in God. We experience a chaotic world of human creation, ecological disruption, and the absence of Peace-the groaning of the whole Creation. By magic, science, and technology we claim the right to use and misuse the Earth, assuming that it is humanity that is in-charge here. When the human beings (a-theistic) is in charge instead of people(s) growing into communities, a hierarchical system of domination exists, blame is apportioned where situations are the creation of communal irresponsibility, and the desire for community is blatantly exploited."
- "Jesus had a unique way of looking at the world. He spoke and lived a life that declared that the only reality in this world is God. He taught that all our attempts at securing ourselves, our self-concern are basically atheistic."

This author affirmed much of my "key insights" that God revealed to me, making me feel like I can trust God just a little-bit more.

Some of the breakthroughs, in my understanding God's principles and processes in John Cobb and Ray Griffin's book *Process Theology: an Introductory Exposition*[74] include the following:

- Personal experiences are valid determiners of the truth.

- Process thought (a research program in academic theology which tries to integrate scientific knowledge with philosophical reasoning and theological meaning-making using the shared metaphor of "emergence") *is not* in conflict with the Judeo-Christian understanding of God, because the Bible portrays God as active in and responsive to the historical process, which was one of my initial concerns about Process Theology.

- Enjoyment is more complex than mere pleasure, meaning that I can enjoy a thing in Nature, an event, a place or an experience without having to feel pleasure, but I am enjoying an experience by the mere fact that I am participating in the event, experience or place, for enjoyment means "actualization-of-self," to act upon others, to share in a wider community, being an experiencing subject. In fact, it is a logical impossibility to lack enjoyment, for it is impossible to merely exist apart from responding to or participating in "the world-around-us."

- I am interdependent on God.

- God influences me by "interpenetrating" me, that is why when I hear God's voice, I do not hear the voice externally like an auditory hallucination, but it sounds like a voice inside my head, for something transcendent has interpenetrated my being, but I also interpenetrate God when God's thoughts become my thoughts.

- God created me for the purposes of achieving freedom, autonomy, self-determination and self-expression of creativity, meaning God initially created me, but allowed me to partially create myself through "free-will," environmental factors and making the choice to let God into my life, to help form my sovereign identity. So in essence, a Creature is something made by God, but has a sovereign identity apart from God.

- One of the reasons, why God often gives me many drafts when communicating information to me, often rewrites documents He has revealed to me, sometimes changes His story or position or reveals things that might be contrary or in addition to scripture or tradition is not because God is inconsistent or that God is not prepared to help me with my work or I am hearing an "unclean spirit." What is going on is that God in preparing assignments for me often has a data-base of possibilities and God's task is to determine, which of these possibilities is the most viable for me, in addition to the fact that God is forming order in my life and in the cosmos through process, over a period of time, for God's Divine Logos is in flux versus the conventional understanding of the Divine Logos being "steady-state."

- Freedom and free-agency including the freedom to doubt God or question His character or judgment is a gift from God and whenever I doubt or do not believe, I must thank God for giving me this freedom for I would not have it otherwise if God did not give me those powers, mainly freedom.

- God uses His power persuasively versus coercively, yet God's power is the most effective power in the cosmos.

- Doubting God is a higher level of spiritual development.

- God must not be constricted by ideas about God, for paradigms can become limiting.

- God does not have to be absolute to be perfect, for God is "perfect in love."

- God has a dipolar nature, a nature which influences the world and a nature which is being influenced by the world.

- Since future events are no-longer determinable so that even perfect knowledge cannot know the future and God does not wholly control the world, so therefore, any divine creative influence must be persuasive not coercive. God seeks to persuade each occasion toward that possibility, but God cannot control the finite occasion's self-actualization. This does not make God less perfect, but more perfect, for God has rejected domination, for our God, the Christian God, by nature, is neither a domineering nor controlling God, but a God who is "perfect in love" and to be "perfect in love" requires one not to control or dominate the other.

- God wants all His Creatures to enjoy their life; God is more than just a Cosmic Moralist.

- God does not know the results of what He created, so therefore the act of Creation is an adventure for our God.

- God is both the source of order and novelty, but they are "means to an end, not ends in themselves."

- "God own life is an adventure," for the novel enjoyments that are promoted among the creatures are more than mere experiences, these enjoyable experiences provide inspiration for God's own enjoyment. When you enjoy something, you bring God pleasure and enjoyment.

- God's life is also an adventure in the sense of being at risk, since God will feel the discord as well as the beautiful experiences involved in the finite actualizations.

The major breakthroughs in my understanding God's principles and processes from Jurgen Moltmann,[75]

- God is not entirely free when God can do and leave undone what He likes; He is entirely free when He is entirely Himself. In His creative activity He is wholly and entirely Himself. This means that ecologically that extinction and other things which endanger the gene pool of different species and thwart the future evolution of life on Earth is denying God to be God-self and causing God discomfort.

- Creation is God's destiny. This means that by destroying Creation you are robbing God of His destiny.

- Creation is the physical manifestation of God's glory. This means that by the act of destroying Creation, you are taking "honor and glory" away from our God.

So therefore, God wants me to go back to these principles whenever I feel doubt about Him. This is because the Holy Spirit's whole job is to reconcile me with God's Self.

This is *my first authority being an Aspie Christian*, the *Primacy of the Holy Spirit* and *a special devotion to the Voice of God* which is *the foundation of my Christian faith*.[76]

### The Bible as the Experiential Word of God:

Saint Francis of Assisi describes his method for reading Holy Scripture,

> "Brother, I was likewise tempted to have books. But, in order to know God's will about this, I took the book, where the Lord's Gospels are written, and prayed to the Lord to deign to show it to me at the first opening of the book. After my prayer was opened of the

holy Gospel this verse of holy Gospel came to me: *To you it is given to know the mystery of the kingdom of God, but to the others all things are treated in parables."*

And he said: "There are many who willingly climb to the heights of knowledge; that person be blessed who renounces it for the love of God."[77]

It can be implied from Saint Francis, that one does not need to be an erudite scholar or have attained a certain proficiency in certain ancient languages, to be able to read Holy Scripture and make a meaningful, valid, cogent interpretation of it. Reading too many books about Holy Scripture can both insolate and inoculate one against the power of the Holy Bible. All one needs to do is open the Bible up and read the Bible with an open heart and an open mind and be willing to be transformed and convicted by God's Wisdom.

Too much reading of commentaries on Holy Scripture can prevent one from having a simple and pure encounter with God's Word, liken to what our saint was able to do. Instead one gets bogged down with the historical-critical method and scrupulous language study, attempting to find the story behind the story, developing a "hermeneutic of suspicion," no longer seeing Holy Scripture as the infallible Word of God, but instead as a fallible, human, culturally manufactured document, which only an elite group of erudite scholars can read and interpret and determine its full significance, leading to a kind of elitism, which cuts Holy Scripture off from the oppressed, the uneducated, the laity and those of us who have a learning disability which makes learning a foreign language difficult.

Too much academic study of the Bible makes Holy Scripture inaccessible to the ordinary person and not at all desirable for neurodiverse humans such as myself, who are all too often "cut-off" from such elitist, non-disabled, neurologically chauvinistic discussions about how the Bible "ought to be" interpreted.

Such an ability privileged interpretation of the Bible by non-disabled, neurotypical Biblical scholars leads into a type of cultural relativism, because the Bible is interpreted through a non-disabled, neurotypical lens, where the Bible is seen by an elite group of non-disabled, neurotypical scholars as just another "myth" or "tradition" and everything within and outside the tradition is "put on the same plane," whether or not it is Biblical or even just or right.

In other words, I am asking the postmodern identity politics question: Who is to determine what the correct interpretation of the Bible is? Who gets the final say on whether or not a particular interpretation is oppressive or benign? Whose historical context are we talking about? Whose language are we talking about?

Tragically, what has happened in many forms of Roman Catholicism and mainline Protestantism, both liberal and conservative alike, liberal Catholics and Protestants with the historical-critical method and conservative Catholics and Protestants with academic philosophy and foreign language study is that non-disabled, neurotypical, white, upper-middle class, Westerners are getting the final say in how Holy Scripture is being interpreted in both academic and pastoral contexts, while only more recently welcoming a few white women and a few token minorities into the Scripture interpretation clique, leading to much religious hypocrisy in the process.

Yet, a more confessional reading of Holy Scripture, reading the Bible as the Word of God has been dismissed "out of hand" by Bible experts as mere Biblical literalism at best and at worst, religious fundamentalism.

The historical-critical method, combined with extensive language study has been dubbed by the academy as the one and only correct way to interpret Holy Scripture. Putting the interpretation of Scripture into the hands of a certain intellectual elite, this approach has been strongly criticized by countless liberation theologians as only representing the spectrum of the ruling classes, instead of the full diversity of the people.

I would also add that even educated, intelligent people such as myself, I am on the autism spectrum and have a learning disability which make learning a foreign language difficult are also excluded, for we cannot always master a foreign language, meaning we cannot comment critically on what specific passages in the Holy Bible mean in Hebrew or Greek, meaning that my group's voice by default is systematically excluded from being factored into Scripture Interpretation and Official Church Teaching by Biblical scholars and Church leaders. This makes our religion's Sacred Texts inaccessible and unintelligible to our particular situation and context and our everyday, mundane lives. Such a neurologically elitist methodology makes Biblical religious language "irrelevant" and "exclusive" even "harmful" to our neurodiverse brothers and sisters.

Yet, at a deeper level, adding all these layers of meaning to verbal language, such as trying to make meaning from word origins or needing to hear a word in Ancient Greek is not how I interpret and understand the authority of Holy Scripture as a Christian on the autism spectrum. The historical-critical approach is inconsistent with my own, personal, embodied, experiential, concrete, lived encounters with Holy Scripture--- completely "unmediated" by non-disabled, neurotypical experts.

Know when I am talking about reading the Bible "unmediated" I am not talking about reading the Bible brutally "literally." I get that the Bible in my society has been taken out of its historical, rhetorical and literary context. I get that the Bible was written in a particular period in history (the historical-critical argument). That certain passages in the Bible were part of a larger meta-narrative (the narrative theology argument) and that the Bible does in fact employ certain literary devices such as mythic poetry, metaphors and historical allusions (the Bible as literature argument).

Yet, we can read the Bible devotionally without reading it literally. In other words, we can go to the Holy Gospel for guidance about animal rights, but we do not need to eat everything Jesus ate. We can accept that the Bible is recording actual historical events from an eyewitness perspective, but we can also use all the allegories, metaphors and allusions employed when recording these historical events to make sense of our twenty-first century world.

I also get that there is no such thing as a "naked eye." All of us bring our social location and neurological sensibilities to the reading of the Bible. In other words, I get that all of us are biased. That having "subjective experiences" are an integral part of what it means to be alive. Subjectivity is also what makes our lives meaningful, enjoyable and worth living. Subjectivity is definitely a behavior created by God. Subjectivity is definitely a gift from God. Yet, that does not mean we cannot also develop methods for reading the Bible more objectively, like scientists are trained. Scientific eyes are not necessarily "naked eyes." Scientists are human beings too!

Instead scientists are trained when doing science to be aware of their biases and to separate their biases from the data they are collecting.

My major problem with the historical-critical method, both conservative and progressive variants alike is that the historical-critical method is too abstract and too confusing for my autistic sentiment which gravitates towards balance and the concrete. In other words, the historical-critical method leaves me spiritually lost and confused.

Instead, based on my spiritual experiences, I see Holy Scripture as the experiential Word of God. When I open-up Holy Scripture, I see it as speaking infallible truth. Truth that speaks directly to my life, my world, my times! I see what I read in Holy Scripture as good. Relevant. And, useful. I find what I read in Holy Scripture to be prophetic and convicting. I experience the Holy Scripture as coming from the same Lord which talks to me.

I also contend that scholars who are overly negative about Holy Scripture have greatly overstated their case. I find as a Christian environmentalist, the Bible to be very ecologically and animal friendly, as well as friendly to different oppressed groups of people. Most of the ecological and animal cruelty problems with the Bible is not what is actually in the Bible, but how the Bible is being interpreted, to justify an anthropocentric, speciesist society.

Granted, that certain interpretations of Holy Scripture are very problematic, to say the least, but that is what they are, fallible, human, culturally manufactured interpretations.

My autistic hermeneutic allows me to make a distinction between commentaries even translations of Holy Scripture and Holy Scripture, itself, which I see as the infallible Word of God. Despite weakness of certain translations, through some miraculous and mysterious power, which I do not totally understand, some of its infallibility shines through.

I also make a strong distinction between a confessional interpretation of Holy Scripture, where one reads Holy Scripture with an open mind and an open heart, accepting it on faith, as the Word of God and accepting Scripture at face value, proof-texting to support certain preconceived assumptions, without any interpretation or self-examination of cultural conditioning or personal context.

In otherwords, making one's interpretation an isogesis (reading into scripture one's own interpretation), instead of an exegesis (letting Scripture read out its own interpretation). I am arguing for the later, not the former!

I am also open to letting Scripture read and convict me. As well as using the Holy Scripture, to make my case. Working within its confines. And, limits. Accepting it on good faith. Trying to reconcile myself with passages, which I find troubling.

Here are some Spiritual Disciplines, which I have found helpful in my life, which you might benefit from, to experience Holy Scripture as the experiential Word of God.

One discipline, I use is reading Scripture using the Lectio Divina method, opening up Scripture three times randomly, to objectively verify what God's Will is for me liken to the random sampling method in scientific ecology.

Random sampling is when you go out into the field and drop a crate, let's say every ten feet and you record all the biodiversity in that given area. Ecologists use this method to get an accurate, objective mathematical reading of the biodiversity in a given ecosystem. This is because in the scientific ecology field, biodiversity is more than a mere rare bird or a mere old-growth tree, biodiversity is a mathematical formula which is the balance between species richness (number of species) and species mass (number of individuals).

A very Medieval discipline, employed by Medievalists including Saint Francis of Assisi, Lectio Divina takes the power out of the reader, of choosing which scripture verses to focus on. Instead, the Spirit selects the appropriate passages. I have found that many times, I have identified many relevant, convicting, life altering, passages, over the years, along with the variant, discussed below. Even after all these centuries of scientific discoveries, I still have found Lectio Divina a helpful method for verifying God's Will.

Another technique I have used in the past is reading "Battle Psalms." A technique I learned when I attended the Vineyard Church of Cambridge, where I was instructed that if one reads the "Battle Psalms," Psalms who use battle metaphors, these war images must be interpreted spiritually (allegorically) versus nationalistically (literally). In other words, I am engaging in "spiritual warfare" against "spiritual oppression," persecution by evil spirits.

Also, my mother used to read the Bible to me before going to bed, growing-up. I found her reading to be a very smoothing and calming experience, leading to deep peace, beyond understanding.

Another approach which has helped me come to the realization that the Bible is the experiential Word of God is just reading the Bible itself, picking a book or part of a book in the Bible and reading it out-loud to myself. Reading out-loud enlivens my holy longing, my deep desire for more of God, as well as providing me with a self-soothing effect. Reading out-loud harnesses and structures my intense passions, transforming desire and longings into religious zeal. I have had the mystical experience of assuming the voice of the reader, feeling like it was me saying these words or that I was that Biblical persona speaking, even assuming the tone of voice of the text, and that Biblical times were my times and my times were Biblical times. That I was living in Biblical times or that this was speaking to my times. That the society described, was a society, not unlike my own.

I could literally feel the energy, the passion and the zeal of the persona. Because of this, some of the pilgrims on my pilgrimage to Italy said that I have a real gift for reading scripture. More recently, I was invited to read Holy Scripture at a local Presbyterian church in the 2012 Pentecost. Later I was invited back in November of that year to give a homily based on my last book, *Have Mercy on me, an Ecological Sinner* (Create Space Independent Publishing Platform, 2012).

This is because when I read the Bible out-loud, boundaries of time and space, natural and supernatural begin to dissipate, creating a kind of "thin space" where the boundaries of the physical and spiritual, begin to dissolve, into one continuous reality.

Finally, I have written exegesis's of passages in both the Old and New Testament from a cosmological, scientific, ecological, and animal rights perspective. An exegesis is a careful line-by-line analysis of scripture or any religious text. Instead of using exegesis material, I just sit down and write them, with whatever background information I have had at the time, looking-up things if necessary, for the purpose of documentation.

This has helped me work through passages which I have struggled with, as well as praise God with analysis from passages which I absolutely adore. I plan to use them, as lectures, once my Master of Arts Program in Christian Environmental Studies is implemented and people I have shared them with have been sufficiently impressed. In otherwords, these readers see that my interpretations are actually valid, although counter intuitive at times.[78]

When I interpret Scripture academically, I use what God one time called the "ecological-critical method," for God believes that we also need an ecological-critical method to go alone side with the historical-critical method. God and I have found that the historical-critical method is not very useful to the ecological or animal rights cause, for some historical-critical scholars do not recognize two critical paradigms: 1) The continuity of ecology---that environmentalism has deep historical roots, it is not just the latest fad. 2) The role of ecological wisdom--- that historical documents and texts, as well as oral histories and biocultural landscapes, do in fact have something constructive to contribute to contemporary environmental debates.

Historical-critical scholars are very insular about this position, despite much contrary evidence uncovered by environmental historians which both independently corroborates many of the reported miracles and historical events in the Bible and vindicates "the ecological complaint against Christianity."

In otherwords, religious historical-critical scholars unfortunately see environmentalism as a modernist, liberal construct, something that was not addressed by ancient texts or ancient societies, because they are ignorant of the environmental history field because of the Lynne White Debate.

These very strict historical-critical confines makes it almost impossible for the Christian ecotheologian to recover ancient ecological wisdom from sacred texts, oral histories, folklore, biocultural landscapes and material culture. This intimidates the Christian ecotheologian from making the most persuasive argument for the "Greening of Christianity" possible, for Christian ecotheology has been systematically "cut off" from the center of the tradition.

This results in Christian environmentalism being addressed as a "tack on" issue to social justice (stewardship/ecojustice/ecofeminism) or as a militant fringe-heretical movement (creation spirituality/process theology/emergent). Neither approach gives the planetary crisis the attention it deserves.

We need to integrate Christian ecotheology into traditional Christian orthodoxy if Christians are going to take ownership of their ecological responsibilities at all and do so in an authentic manor which does not utterly destroy Christianity completely, in the process.

In otherwords, holding Christian ecotheology to historical-critical standards makes ecological ownership by Christians almost impossible and the texts and traditions virtually inaccessible, to the Christian ecotheologian. For one needs the foundations, blessings and permission of the tradition, to forge a successful, sound and stable ecotheology campaign.

If not, Christian environmentalism would then just be another fashionable idea, imposed upon the tradition, with the Christian Church pushing Christian ecotheology off to the periphery, mistakenly viewed as a "tack-on issue," relegated to the domain of "liberalism." Where the liberal Christian Church than feels justified in needing to import heretical doctrines from other religions and philosophies, to justify the existence and legitimacy of ecotheology, at all. Mistakenly viewing non-Christian sources as the authority on the subject and undermining not only attempts at the "Greening of Christianity," but also Christianity itself.

There is an alternative, which I have outlined in my book, *Christian Environmental Studies: Toward A Graduate Program* (Amazon.com, Kindle Addition, 2008 and revised, expanded and republished in 2012, Create Space Independent Publishing Platform), which I will reiterate here, which can become the basis for what I call the *ecological-critical method*. It involves three pillars, which would help recover ecological themes in the Bible. It can also be utilized for animal rights themes too.

The first pillar of the ecological-critical method is a *"bottom-up," praxis-based* interpretation of Scripture. In other words, an interpretation of scripture which comes from the individual environmentalist's personal views on scripture, with the goal of this interpretation being useful for the oppressed, Nonhuman Animals and the Earth. This is because traditional commentary is either inherently anthropocentric and speciesist or when pro-environment or pro-animal oftentimes become anti-Christian. This means a direct encounter with the Bible is tantamount.

The second pillar of the ecological-critical method, an *ecologically sympathetic* interpretation of Scripture, means working from the premise that the Bible offers something constructive to the ecological or animal rights cause, although not always "party line" to certain environmental or animal rights agendas. In these countercultural areas, the Bible must be given special consideration, for the Bible provides many prophetic views on ecology and animal rights, which must be heard and given a voice in contemporary environmental and animal debates. It is the environmentalist's or animal rights person's friend not foe. The Bible is not the root cause of planetary crisis. The Bible is not the enemy.

The third pillar of the ecological critical-method is a *good faith* interpretation of Scripture. This means the Bible must be read with an open mind and an open heart. When encountering ecologically difficult passages, the environmentalist must try to reconcile environmentalism with the Biblical passage in question. This means giving the most possible, generous read of the Bible. A hermeneutic of suspicion *must not* be employed.

So in essence, the ecological-critical method provides the reader with the ecological context of scripture, which sometimes is trans-historic, even a-historic. Or, written in such a way, that it can be translated for all times. Subsequently all of it, still relevant today! That is the genius I see in Holy Scripture. No other document, in my opinion, can hold such a claim.

This is because the Bible is one of the only ancient historical documents written in the wilderness. In other words, the Bible was written in some of the most arid wilderness areas in the ancient world, by a subsistence-based, nomadic group of people, the Israel Lights, who lived, worked and even slept in wild Nature. A vast desertscape of rugged canyons, desolate streambeds, salty seas and only a very narrow band of temperate woodland along the Mediterranean Sea with open spaces which dwarf many of the open spaces out in the American Southwest which exist, even tell this day. I know, for I stayed a month in Israel when my sister got married.

Having said this, my ecological-critical method does take seriously mounting eco-archeological and environmental historical evidence which can illuminate and contextualize all the environmental themes of the Bible.

For example, there is mounting eco-archeological evidence that the historical Garden of Eden was in present day southern Iraq, one of the largest brackish marshes in the world. Meaning the Garden of Eden was most likely a brackish marsh not the often depicted desert island, tropical dry forest, oasis paradise of art, literature and popular culture.

For example, when environmental historians are not trying to deconstruct the Bible with a hermeneutic of suspicion, there is mounting environmental historical evidence that such cherished Biblical stories as the fall in the Garden of Eden, Cain and Able and the enslavement of the Israeli Lights by the Egyptians were describing a very real historical event, mainly "the ancient environmental crisis," which occurred when the West made the transition from "hunters and gatherers" to "farmers and herders" to "city dwellers."

Then there is the oral history evidence. Ethnographic, psychological and medical studies of all the Nature-based societies of the world, from Native Americans to traditional African tribes which independently corroborates that many of the reported miracles in the Biblical tradition from interspecies communications to visitations by spirits are in fact within the realm of what is possible.

The ecological-critical method is what I "bring to the table," my unique way of experiencing Holy Scripture, as the experiential Word of God; identifying environmental themes in the Bible, in the process.

This is *my second religious authority*, which is integral to my autistic Christian faith, *experiencing the Bible as the Word of God*.

### *Hagiography as Social Story*

Special educator Carol Gray defines her unique method of using the "social story" to teach children on the autism spectrum about social skills,

> Social Stories are flexible teachers of young children. They describe what most of us dismiss as obvious, patiently considering the world through the eyes of a child with an ASD. A Social Story can inform, reassure, instruct, console, support, praise, and correct children with ASD *and* those who work on their behalf. In less than a decade, Social Stories have earned their place in homes and classrooms around the world.[79]

So in essence, a Social Story is the use of simple written narrative and pictorial illustrations to teach a child on the spectrum a particular social skill, such as describing everything from "self-care" to "home" to "going places." It utilizes our "thinking-in-pictures," combined with our "rule-based nature," to make unspoken neurotypical social rules accessible and understandable to us.

Hagiography, the lives of Christian saints told through story and sometimes pictorial illustrations, usually written in the Middle Ages, serves a similar function. Hagiography uses narrative, combined with visual imagery, such as icons, frescos and liturgical art, to teach the believer about their religious tradition.

As a Christian on the spectrum, I have done just this. I have used hagiography, to work through complex existential, faith crises over the years. In otherwords, using the hagiography of the Christian saints to self-actualize (answering fundamental questions of existence such as Who am I? Who are They? What is my place in the Cosmos? What do I do?).

Although people, even people in religious life, such as monks, friars, nuns or priests, oftentimes misunderstand the importance of the use of the centrality of hagiography in my faith-life, trivializing it as mere romantic musing, at best. When in reality, hagiography plays no small role, in helping me to grow more nuanced in my faith.

For example, early on in my faith, like when I was in high school and the first year of college, being an environmentalist and animal rights activist, I struggled terribly with uncontrolled anger, even hatred of human beings, for their miserable treatment of Animals and the Earth. I just wanted to live in a world, without human beings, only Animals and Plants and God. I was outraged by such practices as hunting and development and the like. Humanity's complete insensitivity, if not callousness to this injustice. I was fixated on what human beings were doing wrong to animals and the planet. Almost exclusively! It led to intense despair and anguish.

Then I discovered two vitally important books in my growth and development as a Christian and environmentalist, one was a commentary on the "Lord, Make Me An Instrument Of Your Peace" prayer, attributed to, but not written by Saint Francis of Assisi and second was this book, *Beast and Saints* translated by a woman named Helen Waddell in the 1930s and republished by a modern-day woman named Ester De Waal, within the last couple of decades (see, Pook Press, 2010 addition). The later, was hagiography of the relationships different Christian saints had with nonhuman animals. The book included entries and illustrations from Irish and English Saints, as well as the Desert Fathers. I read both books, while I was volunteering at the Salisbury Zoo, one summer. Reading these two books with my Lord, combined with the Zoo experience, changed my theological anthropology, my beliefs about the human race, human nature and the human condition, forever. I was able to forgive humankind for their ecological sins.

I now began to see that despite the deep estrangement human beings have had with the nonhuman world, dating back to the Fall in the Garden of Eden, that there was the possibility of human beings being able to live right with animalkind. Hence, I with my Lord's helped coined the term, "human-animal reconciliation." I saw through the examples of the Christian saints, combined with my experiences at the Zoo, coupled with reading the "Lord, Make Me An Instrument Of Your Peace" prayer, that it both possible and desirable to repair human-animal relationships and for the vision of the Peaceable Kingdom in Isaiah 11 to be actualized and if not actualized, at least work towards. I came to believe the example of the early Christian saints was just such an attempt. I wanted to make it one of my missions in life, to work towards this goal, with my Lord's help.

Hagiography, combined with my whole zoo experience radically revitalized my faith in humankind. For the first time in my life, I saw the human species as something beautiful, through the veneration of such Christian saints as Saint Cuthbert and Saint Kevin, seeing these saints as the "Earth-creatures," which they were. As part of God's Creation, just like any other animal or plant. Who were Christian men, no less, who had the "mind of an animal" (Daniel 4:16) because they were so gentle and kind, as well as sensitive and simple. The Peaceable Kingdom than became the model of the world I wanted to live in.

Not only did this become a model for forging an ecological pacifism, where human beings could live in nonviolent, just and participatory relationships with nonhuman animals, but I even went further, than what I called "*human-animal reconciliation*." I came to believe that human beings even have a functional ecological-evolutionary niche in the Natural World, what I call "*Messianic ecological anthropology.*"

In my ecological anthropology, human being's ecological niche in the Natural World is to reduce intra and interspecies competition in the nonhuman world, meaning not only did I want to push for peace between humans and animals, but even peace between animals and animals, "where the wolf" truly "will be able to lay down with the lamb" like in Isaiah 11 in the Hebrew Bible. I came to believe that far from animals needing to be protected from human contact, human beings had the capacity to develop non-exploitive, nonviolent, mutualistic, participatory, interpersonal relationships with animalkind.

Such personal, life-affirming relationships with animals could be forged through working towards the eliminating of all lethal consumption of animals (adopting a vegetarian diet, finding humane alternatives to animal experimentation and ending all blood sports like hunting and fishing). Through developing nonlethal, non-invasive, nonviolent wildlife management practices (prioritize your wildlife "battles" along non-anthropocentric, non-speciesist lines, find humane alternatives to eradication when possible and respect animal sentience). Non-exploitive, respectful, personal relationships with animals can be attained through engaging in "interspecies communications," forming a kind of multi-species society, which values all life.

This is my "Dream for the Earth"---that the Peaceable Kingdom is within the realm of possibility, that there can be forgiveness and reconciliation between humans and animals, that the human-animal bond can be healed.

This is just one example of how hagiography has served as a type of social story, for learning about my Christian faith and about life in general. Hagiography has also helped informed my thinking through everything from realizing that different saints and believers had different types of relationships with God, meaning that different Christians experience God differently, to realizing that God can talk to me through other people, to even helping me confront my fear of fire drills.

This is my ***third authority, hagiography used as "social story" to discover theological truths***.

### *Nature as Miracle: My Creation-Centered Spirituality*

Environmental Studies scholar Neil Evernden writes,

> One of the reasons that miracles has largely disappeared from our lives is that we have come to know the world as homogenous and contentious...And if we ever find that nature-as-miracle has found its way into the columns of *Time* magazine, we may begin to wonder whether nature, whatever it may be, is about to slip its leash.[80]

Yet, the Idea of Nature which sees "Nature-as-Miracle," seeing Nature as unpredictable, lives on in the minds of some autists like Temple Grandin, Dawn Prince-Hughes and myself, in other words, the premodern, archetypical "the Enchanted Garden" is "far from dead" in our lives. As you can tell by now, the Natural World plays an integral part of my faith and spirituality. So much so, that I would say that I have a Creation-centered spirituality, a spirituality which still believes in the Judeo-Christian conception of God, but that the nonhuman world plays a central and crucial role in my faith-life. In other words, I have a special religious devotion to the nonhuman world.

Seeing and experiencing "Nature-as-Miracle" is how I experience the Natural World. It is my model! It is my sacred cosmology! As an Aspie, I see and experience the Natural World as the theater of the unexpected, the unpredictable, the unexplained, the chaotic, the surprising and the sublime. Yet as a Christian, I forcefully affirm Nature's inherent goodness and beauty.

Before we proceed any further, let me explain how I define the terms Nature and Miracle.

*Nature*, I see as anything which *was not* created by humans. Nature includes both first and second natures. *First Natures* are the undisturbed, pristine Natures, which predates human penetration and alternations, such as the times of the dinosaurs. *Second Natures* on the other hand are the Natures which post-date human penetration and alternations, such as our twenty-first century reality.

I agree with my Sociology of the Environment Professor in college that most Nature which exists today is Second Nature. Nature which has been penetrated, altered, defined and managed by human beings such as second growth forests, protected parks and multi-use management areas. I one time even saw in a doctor's office a cocktail book on photographs taken from The Voyager spacecraft. One full page photograph was a "touched-up" photograph of the Entire Universe, in two dimensions including all the theoretical oblong boundaries of our Universe and all the zillions of galaxies reduced down to two pages in an overstuffed book. In fact, I would argue that all Nature seen on television, on-line, in calendars and in photographs is Second Natures by nature. There is nothing natural about it!

Yet, I also agree with ecotheologian Sallie McFague that Second Natures come ultimately from First Natures and are still dependent on First Natures, for their existence. McFague quoting from a prominent geographer argues "that even a Twinkie or a Big Mac 'begins with a plant growing in a specific patch of soil…somewhere on earth."[81]

I even go further, agreeing with what my Lord revealed to me, that Second Natures are still ultimately created by God and that they have the potential to become Resurrected Natures when Second Natures are "redeemed" (Leviticus 27: 19-21) enough that they start functioning like First Nature again. The beginnings of the New Heaven and New Earth! Liken to the First Nature process of natural succession, "new life, coming out of old" like fields of native wildflowers rising from the ashes of a devastating forest fire, like hemlocks shooting up after colossal oaks falls, like seabirds colonizing the cooling cone of an underwater volcano erupting out of the sea. Meaning Nature is not dead; the Natural world just has a very bad case of oppression, meaning that Nature already naturally has the power to "regenerate" after great losses. Similar to what prominent Christian environmental ethicist and professor at Colorado State University, Holmes Ralston III, concludes in his article "Does Nature Need to Be Redeemed?" in *Horizons in Biblical Theology* (1994).

Second Natures *are* First Natures! Brother Fire!

God one time explained to me, when I was walking in a hiking trail in a local state park a few years ago that I was in Heaven. That was because I was walking through a maturing, second growth forest. A forest overflowing with pine, poplars, birches, wildflowers and primitive plants, home to squirrels, deer, foxes and migratory songbirds. A forest "redeemed" by the archetypical "Children of God" (Romans 8: 18-20) who both protected the forest from development and allowed the forest to repopulate with new wildlife, literally allowing the land to go from farms to fields to forests. I literally was walking through "the Resurrection of the Body" (Nicean Creed). In other words, even though these "Children of God" *did not* create "Heaven on Earth," they *did* "give Creation back to God." They did stimulate the land's ability to heal.

Ironic, several years after God revealed this to me; I would be living and healing within walking distance of this same state park, finding my own "road to redemption" in this small biological corridor of "healing space."

I believe that living in such a bioregion, has given me such an unusual ecotheology and environmental ethic---*redemption ecology*. This is because most of my exposure to the Natural

World has been through Second Natures or Resurrected Natures; I have had only limited exposure to pristine wilderness areas. So living in a Cruciform Creation, a Nature which is "struggling to become something better," a Nature which is relatively peaceful, allows me to develop such an Idea of Nature.[82]

I literally grew-up in a facsimile of the New Jerusalem, Washington D.C! What is now the District of Columbia was once un-habitable swampland, it mind as well have came down from Heaven with "a river of life-giving water flowing through it," with "trees of life" (Revelations 22: 2) on each side of this river. There are extensive forests, parks and grassy open spaces on both sides of the Potomac River.

The bioregion which I was born into influenced my cosmology and theology, in a manor very similar to how Saint Bonaventure's cosmology and theology was informed by growing up in a small Italian town on top of a mountain, overlooking a vast valley below. Franciscan ecotheologian Ilia Delio, O.S.F. describes in graphic detail how Bonaventure, official biographer of Saint Francis of Assisi and former minister general of the entire order in the fourteenth century and great scholastic theologian was informed by the bioregion of his birth which is worth citing in its entirety,

> Scholars have pointed to a correlation between Bonaventure's thought and his birthplace, Bagnoregio. Situated in the Etruscan country about sixty miles north of Rome and Viterbo and Orvieto, Bagnoregio is perched high on the crest of a spur of land jutting into the Tiber valley. About seven miles to the west lies Lago di Bolsema, a deep blue lake that shines like a jewel in the crater of an extinct volcano. On its eastern slop, this volcano stretches in a plateau, which, after several miles, divides into what appear to be fingers of land separated from each other by deep gorges. Extending towards the Tiber, these fingers break off abruptly into the valley below.
>
> Bagnoregio is built along the thin edge of one of these fingers. Scanning the horizon, the visitor has a breathtaking scene of the vastness of space-deep gorges plunging down on each side, massive cliffs rising across the gorges, directly ahead the steep drop of into the Tiber valley and in the distance lofty mountains in the direction of Todi. This setting easily awakens a sense of joy in nature-of awe at its power and at the same time peace and harmony. Bagnoregio seems to the midpoint of a vast and ordered cosmos, the center of the earth as it were; for it lies on a pinnacle of land rising from the valley, ringed about by a sweeping circular horizon whose outlines are traced by massive mountains.

Although little is known about Bonaventure's early years in Bagnoregio, we can see how this landscape could have shaped his vision. In the sweeping landscape of this unusual place, there is a natural resonance with the distinctive elements of his thought. As the town now stands, it is a powerful symbol of one of the principal metaphors of Bonaventure's theology and spirituality, that is, the symbol of the circle with its circumference and center. God can be thought of as "an intelligible sphere," he wrote, "whose center is everywhere, and whose circumference is nowhere."[83]

So just as Bagnoregio Italy, informed Bonaventure's ideas and metaphors in his writings, growing up thirty minutes from the White House has informed my own ideas and metaphors in my writings, such as my insistent belief that the Peaceable Kingdom is within the realm of plausibility and my insistent using of "peace" metaphors to describe the nature of the Natural World and human being's place in it. The Peaceable Kingdom is not as much of a stretch, as someone who might have lived and grew-up somewhere else. Like out West!

In other words, our ecological autobiography, our relationship to the bioregion of our birth, as in the case of Bonaventure and as in the case of my life and in fact for everyone, our relationship to where we were born, colors our thinking about the world universal, even if it is nothing more than feeling estranged, dislocated and alienated. Our "roots" like it or not, does impact what we believe and what we value and why. We need to be aware of this reality.

For example, it makes perfect sense that Western monotheism emerged into fruitarian in Israel, for Israel is in many ways is a microcosm of All Creation. Located at the nexus of three major continents, Europe, Africa and Asia, Israel, has rivers, mountains, tide pools, coral reefs, sand dunes, inland saltwater seas, deserts, temperate woodlands and tropical savannahs, just to name a few. Birds from as far as Siberia funnel through Israel.

One can find plants like Sodom apples a plant native to tropical Africa natively growing side by side with mosses and ferns from more temperate regions of the world, in Ein Gedi National Park in Southern Israel.

At the Tel Dan National Park in Northern Israel, one will traverse through both flowing streams and lush thickets and vast dry temperate woodlands, all within a very short Nature walk.

It makes sense than that there is a certain oneness which unifies all these disparate realities, all jammed packed into an area the size of New Jersey and that the God of the Entire Universe and His chosen people would naturally reside there. That Israel would be the natural foundation for the New Jerusalem. Israel is almost like God's display garden, a representative sample of all His different Creation-types. Subsequently, it is hard not to have a strong and vibrant Creation-centered spirituality while living in these parts.[84]

Now that I have defined what I understand Nature to be, I will now define what I understand Miracles to be. This is more complicated then appears on the surface, for the theological concept of a miracle does not translate very well into a modern, scientific age. As a result, many Christians have rejected or misunderstood the testimony of miracles, yet I look at traditional Christianity and the miraculous is central and tantamount to our faith and religion. So, there is a part of me, which wants to hold onto the notion of miracle, so more translation work is absolutely necessary, into a twenty-first century, scientific context, if a belief in the existence of miracles is to be preserved. Make any sense and not lead into doubt, disbelief, confusion or worse, a self-mutilating faith, where the modern-day believer blames him or herself for not receiving a miracle or questions God's goodness, such as in the case of the Prosperity Gospel or Calvinistic Predestination.

One way, God has helped translate a belief in miracles into a twenty-first century context, is to understand miracles to be the transcending of natural selection. If people or any other living creature is able to transcend the judgment power of natural selection, then that is an example of a modern-day miracle, according to my Lord. For example, if someone survives terminal cancer, that is a miracle. Or, if someone survives and lives a successful or productive life, despite all the odds, or survives a life-threatening, traumatic experience, these are all examples of modern-day miracles. Whether it is the "Truth and Reconciliation Commission" in South Africa, the fall of Nazi, Germany, the rise of the State of Israel, the collapse of Communism.

Evernden (the environmental studies scholar) also offers me a complementary way of reviving miracles. Evernden contends that the miraculous is integral to the Natural World; it is all the unexpected, unpredictable, unexplained, the chaotic and the sublime in Nature. A belief in miracles is a recognition that Nature is not homogonous and continuous, but is in fact, very diverse and chaotic indeed, it is just that our worldview has changed our understandings of the Natural World. Where, Nature is seen now as more predictable and tamable. In otherwords, instead of Nature being seen as the theater of the miraculous, it is now seen as an object, to be treated like an object. Yet, the nature of reality has remained the same. The "Enchanted Garden" lives!

Nature is still the realm of mystery and magic, as it has always been and will continue to be, until the end of time. This is because in Nature, even in Second Natures, one can still find the unexpected, the unpredictable, the unexplained, the chaotic, and the sublime. Walk a suburban street and you will find "weeds" which manage to exist in the most manicured neighborhoods, which were not placed there "by your wisdom" (Job 38: 26). Human wisdom has not been totally successful at eradicating them. No matter how much chemicals humans, use! God directly put them there!

There is always something of Nature which remains untamable and wild, for one cannot stop God's will to Create. Even, when I onetime grew some hot pepper seeds, even though I grew them in my former downtown apartment, on the eleventh floor in a high rise, in a virtual concrete jungle, with egg cartons and soda bottles, in human prepared soil and gave them filtered water from my water facet, I still had no say, ultimately whether they germinated or not. They did not germinate. I was still dependent on God breathing life into the inert seeds and giving them a body (I Corinthians 15: 37-39), as Apostle Paul was in the first century, when he was inspired to make this naturalistic observation.

Even within the last couple of years a swine flu pandemic has broken-out, putting the entire ultra-civilized world, into frenzy. People have still not totally mastered Nature. It is impossible to totally master Nature, for Nature is nothing less than the Body of God. God by nature is immortal!

Now that I have defined my Idea of Nature and what my beliefs are about Miracles, which I feel are adequately persuasive for a twenty-first century audience, but strongly rooted in the tradition and my phenomenology and experiences being a human on the autism spectrum, let me put these two concepts together.

I see and experience the miraculous as being embodied into and encompassing the whole Cruciform Creation which is "struggling to become something better," the New Heaven and New Earth, the actualization of the Peaceable Kingdom. Sort of like the quote from American poet, Robert Frost, "Miracles not only happen in Nature, they happen all the time."

I did not expect when I woke-up one morning while sleeping over at my mother's house, that I would see a magnificent Rufus-sided Towhee, at our family bird feeder, in full breading plumage. We have never had a Towhee in our backyard before. The areas around our neighborhood have experienced much sprawl, even though our neighborhood has greatly matured in the last decade.

I did not know when I went on a walk around the block that day, in my family's neighborhood that I would get really close to a black-and-white warbler. I have never seen a black-and-white warbler in my family's neighborhood before.

So whether one sees a rarity, like the famous Ross's Gull, a bird native to Siberia, which was cited in Newburyport, Massachusetts a number of decades ago or I seeing unexpected unusual bird sittings in my family's own suburban neighborhood or if one sees a rare astronomical phenomenon, one has just come face-to-face with a modern-day miracle. This is because, the distance between the miraculous and the mundane, the natural and supernatural and the sacred and the profane are not as great as one would initially think. But in fact what might be considered mundane, might in fact be miraculous, what is natural, might have been interpenetrated by the supernatural and what is sacred and what is profane, is a matter of perspective.

We live in a mysterious and amazing Universe and modern science has not taken away from any of this mystery and wonder, but has heightened it, helping us to better understand this mystery, uncovering new mysteries. Even phenomena that has been discovered and explained away by science, has not lost its magic or wonder, either. There is no substitute for seeing a phenomenon in Nature, in person. There is no substitute for direct experience! Even going to a local park can be an adventure, a celebration of abundance, beauty and glory, a "wilderness of sweets" as blind English Christian Nature poet, John Milton, stated in *Paradise Lost.* That is my way of "being in the world" being a human on the autism spectrum.

Liken to a child in a candy store, where my senses are bombarded with all these amazingly beautiful delights. I literally come to life when I am in Nature. My usual dour demeanor and chronic unhappiness living in the city, dissipates before my parents' eyes, as my mother often remarks that I am "like a new person" when I am out in Nature. It does not take a great wilderness area, to have this effect. It can even be a local park or local garden. Even the simplest elements in Nature, can stimulate me in such a manor.

I believe I experience Nature, emotionally, spiritually, and aesthetically in this manor, because I am a person on the spectrum, meaning I experience the world more hyperspecifically, more concretely, in much more detail, with extreme perception, than a neurotypical person. I also believe and contend, this is liken to how Dawn Prince-Hughes and Temple Grandin, sees and experience the nonhuman world, "Nature-as-miracle," although I add a certain layer of Judeo-Christian meaning making, which they do not.

This is ***my fifth authority***, being an autist Christian, ***seeing and experiencing Nature-as-miracle***, embodied into and encompassing, a meaningful, purposeful, divinely infused, beautiful, good Universe. With the later separating myself from certain mechanistic, scientific cosmologies which sees chaos as brutal and meaninglessness, I see chaos as beautiful, good, peaceful even miraculous. I see chaos as nothing less than the Will of God at-work in our world, God appropriating His powers nonviolently and justly in a fallen, broken world. A thistle might be a "thorn" in Eden, but a thistle also has a beautiful flower, a fascinating seedpod and is the favorite food of goldfinches. A view, I contend is consistent with medieval organic cosmology, like that of Saint Bonaventure, mentioned above.

*Experience as Evidence*

Disability liberation theologian Nancy Eisland writes,

> Moments in the method [David Tracy's correlational method] include a de-idealization of scripture, a pragmatic interpretation of experience, a critical theory of emancipation and enlightenment, and a social theory to transform praxis. This [Eisland's] libratory theology of disability includes deliberate recognition of the lived experience of persons with disabilities, a critical analysis of social theory of disability, and of certain aspects of the church's institutional practices and Christian theology, and the proclamation of emancipatory transformation.[85]

My liberation theology project too, has attempted to do something similar, especially applied to the autism spectrum, develop a liberation theology which is formulated based on the lived experiences of persons on the autism spectrum, such as myself. Like Eisland, I provide a critical analysis of social theory about autism, as well as certain aspects of the church's institutional practices and Christian theology, with the goal of proclaiming emancipatory transformation, to peoples on the spectrum, from and in neurotypical society.

This section will make conscious, something which was implicit throughout my entire manuscript, that Jewish and Christian theological claims, must be tested in light of the lived experience of peoples on the autism spectrum and other disabilities, for autists like myself and "cousins" with other disabilities to be able to believe in Judeo-Christianity at all.

In other words, autists and other cousins with disabilities are given permission in this liberation theology, to only believe what is consistent with our lived experiences as non-neurotypicals and what is useful for our healing, liberation and full inclusion and empowerment in neurotypical religious life and the greater society and culture at-large. What I have professed and confessed so far is what I believe as a Christian, within the confines of my lived experiences being an autist, myself. The rest I have had to let go of or am in the process of letting go of.

My experiences being an autist are what I use as the verification process and evidence to test-out, interpret and translate Judeo-Christian theological and religious claims, as well as non-Arhahamic religions. As an Aspie, I need to synchronize, harmonize and integrate my Jewish identity and Christian faith, into my autist reality, for my faith not to be undermined, for it to make any sense or to be authentically and coherently lived out, in my everyday life with integrity. Any other approach to theology or religion leaves me wanting. It becomes compartmentalized, confusing, irrelevant, useless and even hurtful, leading to much unnecessary suffering in my life. Leading to what academic sociologists call "anomie," confusion about what is the right thing to do, in a given situation.

It is either this or nothing at all. This is non-negotiable, for me to have any faith at all. I have tried many times, in a variety of different denominational and communal contexts, to ignore this factor and submit. It plane does not work!

I am not able to continue with this denomination or communal context, such as what happened with Roman Catholicism. No matter how hard I try to work within them. I end-up rebelling and undermining myself. I go into these situations thinking they were going to work and end-up leaving, feeling like an abysmal failure. Devastated and disillusioned in the process.

This is why I had to leave the religion of my birth, Judaism; I could never become a Roman Catholic under the current canonical structure (although the "jury is still out" with the exciting and promising new Pope Francis who promises great reforms in the Roman Catholic Church) and why I can never become a Buddhist.

Modern Judaism does not square with my lived experience of God, who unconditionally loves me by nature and plays down excessive legalism and guilt, which plays into my disability and forces me to psychologically bury myself and all my hopes and dreams. Causing me to suffer and want, making me unhappy and bitter in the process. Such a fear-and-anger based, graceless religion does nothing less than sentence me to a life of low self-esteem and dysfunction. Such a callous religion forces me to be dutiful at all costs, even when it is not in my own best interest, even when such blind duty is at the expense of my own vocation of helping others.

Instead, I need a religion and spirituality which encourages me to build-up my sense of self and pursue my calling and vocation, leaving abusive, dysfunctional and potentially damaging situations and relationships, in the process.

To be honest, why must I have to believe in a religion, which has cursed me, since the day I was born, yet at the sametime demands my unconditional loyalty. Despite much flack from the Jewish community, my lived experiences being an autist have caused me to look elsewhere, for faith, religion and meaning.

That does not mean that I reject that being born a modern Jewish is an integral part of my cultural and religious identity. I feel greatly indebted to modern Judaism, for giving me a certain sentiment, a unique cultural identity, an appreciation for education and learning, a sensitivity to the oppressed and down trodden everywhere, a love for food and life, a vibrant, passionate charism and the ability to question authority, including religious authority. Modern Judaism definitely has giving me a unique perspective which I bring to my Christian faith. It has given me an additional set of spiritual disciplines to work from and not the least of which a special appreciation for and deep devotion to the Hebrew Bible.

I even contend that the Judaism of the Hebrew Bible, the Judaism of the Middle Ages, even some Jewish forms today provides an alternative to all the fear, anger and all around moroseness of today's Judaism. Ancestral Judaism has more in common with today's Christianity which is more love-based and mystery-based, more grace infused, more positive and uplifting.

Jewish grace is even able to do something which Christian grace has not been able to, counter emotional repression with permission to express our full kaleidoscope of God created, human emotions and accepts, non-judgmentally what ordinary people have to do survive in a fallen, broken world.

This is why when going through a traumatic crisis, I find reading the Hebrew Bible more satisfying than the Christian Bible, for I find the Hebrew Bible ultimately less emotionally repressive, less judgmental of people who cannot "virtuously suffer" very well, leaving more room for doubt, skepticism, even complaining, even leaving room to have natural, human reactions to intense suffering and injustice. Most importantly, the Hebrew Bible almost never "blames the victim." In other words, the Hebrew Bible lets a human being be a human being.

In fact, the Jewish religion is the only World Religion which I know which actually has rituals for trauma, such as Passover (remembering the enslavement of the Jewish people in Egypt with connections made to current traumas people face even today) and the Sabbath (a day of rest which cultivates resilience to those of us who have on-going oppression issues).

Yet, the Hebrew Bible does not just take one from a journey from shame to rage, the Hebrew Bible after acknowledging our shame and our rage, eventually takes us into the more positive territories of hope, faithfulness and resilience, even resistance and action.

So yes, I can appreciate that Judaism is the religious and cultural matrix which helped make me who I am; it is where I came from, at least partially. Judaism is my "ancestral soul" which resides in me, a combination of both my genetic history and the cultural transmission of the Jewish tradition handed down to me by my Jewish biological family of origin. For this reason, God has encouraged me to embrace my Jewish roots, yet realizes that I only was able to fully embrace this member of myself, through becoming a Christian.

This is because I came from not only Biblical Israel, I also came from Greece, Spain and Italy (enter Franciscanism), I also came from Lithuania and Latvia (enter Protestantism), I also came from North America (enter post-Judaism), I came from the Piedmont Plateau bioregion, the temperate forests between the mountains and the sea (enter environmentalism and animal rights) and most importantly, I come from the neurodiversity of the "human spirit," a membership and identity which cuts across religious, ethnic and geopolitical lines (enter my "wild space").

In other words, "all or nothing" religion, whether it is Judaism or Roman Catholicism, plane does not work for me.

I ran into this same issue with Roman Catholicism, when I was discerning whether I had a "religious calling" to be a Franciscan friar, because of my special devotion to Saint Francis of Assisi and the Franciscan/Medieval tradition which I so much loved and wanted to become a part of where I thought today's Roman Catholics were the primary guardians and gatekeepers of this tradition. In other words, my interest in Roman Catholicism was a "means to an end." I did however see Roman Catholicism, as a much richer and more rigorous tradition of Christianity than Protestantism. I wanted to be a part of it so badly, to be part of the Roman Catholic world so badly, not because I believed in Roman Catholicism, but I was desperately trying to access Franciscan sociosymbolic life.

Roman Catholicism would also give me a more stable Christian denominational identity however. I still have not declared a denominational identity. Yet, because the Roman Catholic Church hierarchy has become increasingly rigid and insular at the beginning of the twenty-first century as the Roman Catholic Church continues to decline in the Western world, I am not able to become Roman Catholic at this time. Hopefully this will begin to change under Pope Francis with time, which would be an answer to a prayer.

This is because the current Roman Catholic magisterial social teachings and policies (the whole Vatican project) are fundamentally inconsistent with my lived experiences, being a Christian soul on the autism spectrum.

Some teachings just did not square with my beliefs, experiences and vocation, such as certain doctrines which profess a certain uniqueness and superiority of humans over nonhuman animals. Or, others I just found plane hurtful such as "closed communion" (only legally baptized and confirmed Roman Catholics in good standing with the Vatican can take the Eucharist) where I have literally walked out of Masses in tears, for being excluded, on multiple occasions. While still other teachings, I felt justified and rationalized oppression and exclusion, such as "infant baptism," which gives cultural Roman Catholics, a competitive edge over converted believers. Making me feel less than welcome! While, certain mandates for obedience to "church authority," I felt were not in my best interest.

Particularly, since the Magisterium (which has been taken over by a fundamentalist pre-Vatican II sedge) has for the last decade been enforcing this "the party line" even in a person's professional, secular life, such as the ballot box or what trained academic theologians can teach about academic theology in an academic context.

I absolutely need "academic freedom" as a "Thinking Christian," because "original scholarship" and "independent thinking" is how "good scholarship" is done.

I absolutely need to vote my "conscience" in the ballot box as an American citizen in a country with a clear Separation between Church and State, meaning political candidates *are not* Christian candidates. Only being allowed to vote for a militant "pro-life" aka "anti-abortion" political candidate would rule-out almost everyone in the Democratic Party and even moderates in the Republican party, meaning that I would only be allowed to vote for a candidate which might be *also* "anti-peace," "anti-social justice," "anti-disability" and "anti-ecological."

The "seamless garment" model of American liberal-progressive Catholicism argues that for "Pro-Life" to be a morally consistent position, one also needs to be equally against the death penalty, wars, bigotry and poverty. I would also add being against ecological destruction, anthropocentrism and speciesism, institutional animal cruelty, neurotypicalism and abelism and environmental racism, classism, sexism, abelism and anti-Semitism.

Environmental anti-Semitism is solely blaming Arhahamic religions for the planetary crisis, such as Genesis I-III in the Torah (e.g., Lynne White argument); letting other groups "off the hook" like corporate capitalists, amoral scientists and pagan-based dualisms and hierarchies of inequalities. Such a view is unconsciously "taped into" the "Jewish conspiracy" myth which irrationally insists that "the Jews" have taken over the world and are to blame for everything which goes wrong in our world. Such a "lie" was one of the ideological rationalizations for Hitler's Holocaust. A lie which explains the neurotypical left's almost preservative fixation on the Israeli-Palestinian conflict. And, as an Aspie, I thought I was on the obsessive side.

In other words, a "seamless garment" position insists that "Pro-Life" means all life. Not just unborn children, but also scapegoated, oppressed and vulnerable human beings everywhere, Animals and the Earth, anything which can thwart Life from flourishing, even providing for "unwanted children" once we are born, physically, emotionally and relationally.

Yet, my fears of being re-victimized through a devastating excommunication process ran very deep because I have felt like an "outsider" and "other" my whole life, never really "fitting in" into such a neurotypical, abelist society.

Also, as a Christian convert on the autism spectrum, I just found becoming a Roman Catholic plane confusing, having a social impairment, which is one of the trademarks of having an autism diagnosis. I ran into politics, hidden curriculums and people plane not giving me straight answers and getting contradictory answers from liberal versus conservative Catholics, lay versus clergy, educated versus uneducated. It was an absolute vortex! I dealt with so many "bizarre experiences," run-ins, unstable relationships and discouragement, that I did not even make it to RCIA class. It made me feel like a second-class Christian and hurt me very deeply in my faith. Even, the rule that those exploring Catholicism cannot even take the Eucharist at even non-Roman Catholic Churches made it almost impossible for me even to go to RCIA class.

I was already a baptized Christian at this time (believer baptized into the Christian church in theological school) and I already had a deep Christian faith and relationship with God and to go almost a whole year without the Eucharist was unbearable. Just so I can explore the possibility of becoming Roman Catholic. This whole experience really soured me to Roman Catholicism. I have still not recovered.

All I wanted from the Roman Catholic Church was to be viewed and treated as a beloved Child of God, accepted for who I am, what I am, where I was at in my life, with both my history and disagreements, with both my strengths and weakness and to not be persecuted for my beliefs or my disability, but, to be treated respectfully and be fully included in church life. I do not see why that was not too much to ask from a Christian denomination which claims to be Christian.

By the way, some humans with certain environmental, animal rights or vegetarian commitments, have made it has Roman Catholics. More power to them!

It is also important to point-out; they were able to do so, because they were all neurotypical. This is evidence that there is definitely bigotry toward peoples on the autism spectrum and other disabilities in the Roman Catholic Church. There is definitely such a thing as neurotypicalism and that it is just like racism, sexism or homophobia and must be treated in the same accustomed manor by those who claim to be progressive, enlightened and tolerant in "the left."

Since being neurotypical is a privilege, neurotypical environmentalists, animal rights people and vegetarians know how to negotiate the system, a person like myself on the spectrum, was at a tremendous disadvantage.

This does not mean however that there is not a linked oppression between Autists, Animals and Nature in the Roman Catholic Church. This is because the Vatican still has bigoted teachings towards Animals and the Earth, for the same reason, the Roman Catholic establishment still is holding onto the neoclassical belief that the ability to be proficient in "abstract reason" is superior to all other gifts, whether it is "thinking in picture" (autistic ability), "migration intelligence" (animal ability) or "beauty" and "embodiment" (natural ability).

It is important to realize that I am not anti-Catholic. I did not go into life, with an intense hatred of Roman Catholicism; it was cultivated through years of bad experiences and being cut-off and suffering profoundly as a result, like what happened with most young people when they have a genuinely "bad experience."

My love for Medieval Catholicism and Franciscanism has remained virtually unaffected by all this however.

It is just that the current Roman Catholic establishment, which is grounded in nothing, but a certain fundamentalist vision of trying to go back to a mythical past, which never existed and certainly does not exist anymore, is what I am so against. It has made Roman Catholicism virtually inaccessible to me. Because of the current state of the Catholic Church, I have had to go elsewhere for a denominational identity and Christian community.

The reasons for not becoming Buddhist are more complicated, than either Judaism or Catholicism. First, I am not Asian, so I have no direct cultural connection to Far Eastern culture and religion. So, I would have no reason to have an Eastern sentiment.

Yet, I went to a secular college for undergraduate during the height of post-modernity (a cultural movement which started in the 1970s which questions cultural absolutes in both Enlightenment, modernist science and pre-modern traditionalist Western religions, with the goal of deconstructing oppressive cultural narratives which have been used to oppress certain minority groups such as African-Americans, women and homosexuals). Meaning the curriculum at my school and especially in the humanities and environmental studies program was in particular, anti-Christian, among other things.

Also, what was going on as a spinoff of post-modernity, at least at my school, was a virtual revitalization of spirituality. This was not the spirituality of traditional Arhahamic religions. It was instead a generic, "bottom-up" spirituality, a spirituality not tied to institutionalized, organized religion.

This type of spirituality was all of sudden recognized as important in student's lives and education. Strict scientism and rationalism, in otherwords, Classical-Enlightenment thinking, was considered wanting. Yet, Jewish, Christian or Muslim spirituality were not taken seriously as viable alternatives to classical, modernist, enlightenment thinking.

Instead, what was purposed, was the militant advocacy of a bastardized, sanitized, ill-defined Buddhism and Native Americanism, filtered through Western sentimentality which was used as a critique of both Judeo-Christianity and secular Western culture, such as corporate capitalism and extreme scientism. So, being an environmental studies minor, as well as a conflict analysis/dispute resolution minor, I received much pressure to give-up my Christianity and become a Buddhist. I even received pressure from a therapist to become a Buddhist, which I had to fire as a result.

Yet, even as people thought I would be happier being a Buddhist, I saw things in Buddhism which were disturbing, particularly as I looked through, beneath and beyond all the spin and propaganda. At first, I saw it as a conflict between Christianity and secularism, liberalism. God pointed-out recently, that the real reason why I did not want to become a Buddhist was on autist grounds. God asked me, in my attempt to critique Buddhism from a Christian perspective, why did I zero in on things like their teachings on suffering of all things not the fact they were are not Christian?

God answered this rhetorical question, it turned out that in talking to God, that what I was finding so disturbing about Buddhism was not that Buddhism was not Christian, although that was part of it, but that it actually contradicted my experiences being a person on the spectrum.

For example, making a "Sand Mandela," where every grain of sand needed to be painted and than once a beautiful pattern was created, it had to be destroyed, had an uncanny residence to Obsessive Compulsive Disorder (OCD). I was thinking that this would only be fodder for my obsessive thinking. I must have seen this as painfully tedious, playing into my motor disability. Even at a sub-conscious level.

More serious objections were Buddhist views on suffering, such as their axioms "life is suffering" and "life is unfair," which are virtually irreconcilable with my experiences being a person with a disability. Granted, suffering is a large part of the reality, of a fallen, broken world. In addition to the reality, that embracing and enduring suffering can be a sign of one's manhood or holiness. To deny suffering is to deny part of life.

Yet, not "all life is suffering," though. There are also experiences of great hope, joy even pleasure. Life is also beautiful! Life is good!

More importantly, as a person who has suffered greatly in life, succumbing to the axiom "life is suffering" was completely unsatisfying. I needed reduction in suffering in my life and in the "world-around-me." I needed to work towards social justice, for both myself and the planet, even if such suffering cannot totally be eliminated. Succumbing to a vision of reality which just accepts the totality of reality as mere suffering does not do anything to albeit a person's suffering, where passively accepting suffering is tantamount to succumbing to negativity and despair, in my opinion. Letting the world get away with evil and injustice! I found this perspective completely unsatisfying. So I subsequently rejected it.

Also, just accepting that "life is unfair" and then going on with or lack of going with your life, I also found extremely negative and unsatisfying.

This does not mean that countless unfair things have happened in the world, including my own life. But that does not mean, *all* "life is unfair." Such a notion is an overgeneralization. A logical fallacy! I agree with Reverend Dr. Martin Luther King Jr. "that the Universe is bent toward justice," because such an overgeneralization excludes knowledge of nonhuman, spiritual even past and future realities, as well as some cultural realities even today, which are telling a very different story about the existence and possibility of fairness.

For example, some religious traditions teach that there can be method to God's madness. To say that "life is unfair" is to imply that God is unfair. I strongly believe and contend that God is fair, even though it might not be obvious to us mortals that God is a fair God, behind the mystery of the seeming unfairness, brutalities and indignities we experience on a daily basis.

"Life is unfair" as an autist I see as a neurotypical over-generalization. Instead my autist and sociological sentiment leads me to believe instead like Reverend Dr. Martin Luther King Jr. "time is neutral," but it is society "which is not fair."

Most things labeled in a neo-Buddhist sentiment as "unfair" are really societal injustice. Most of these injustices have activist, religious and psychological remedies, which can reduce unfairness and suffering. That human-introduced Original Sin has made our lives and our world so unfair, even unjust. That it is within our power to work towards making a fairer and more just, society and world, for everyone.

Another objection I have to Buddhism is its learning by confusion, as an autist, this way of learning and truth-searching is an absolute nightmare. Many Westerners I have encountered who were strongly into Buddhism (so I am not sure whether this is endemic to the religion or not, or just another perversion), seem to have this need to get to the truth through making things deliberately confusing. Truth-searching to these people is more like a game or puzzle, than something deadly serious. They love to argue. They love to debate. They relish twisted logic and counterintuitive arguments, any-day.

Learning by confusion just makes me feel frustrated and leads to powerless to solve serious problems or make critical decisions about how to live my life or plan my future. In other words, learning by confusion, I find useless and completely ivory tower. As a person living with a disability, I do not have this luxury. I need real working answers. Or, at least resolutions! A place to begin! "Living with the questions" is debilitating to me and certainly not helpful to me getting closer to the truths critical for my salvation. It seems like Buddhism seems like it attracts a certain charism, a charism which is not my spiritual charism. Buddhism is not my spiritual path!

For example, I am a very sensual being. I see desire as fundamentally good; it just needs to be harnessed toward godly desires. I do not believe we need to eradicate all desire and that this is the best response to suffering. I do not believe we need to become an empty shell. Possibly our stomachs!

I believe godly desires can be used for God's glory. I believe desires must be satisfied by pursuing our passions, dreams and destiny. I believe desires makes us human. I cannot live or be where I am today without my godly desires. Eradication of desires goes against my autist nature, being a sensual being.

My mystical path has more in common with the personal mysticism of Judaism, Christianity and Islam, the place-based Nature mysticism of First Nations societies around the world, the sensual mysticism of early environmentalists like Thoreau, Muir, Carson and Mills and the political mysticism of twentieth century activists like Gandhi, Martin Luther King, Simeon Wells and Ellie Wesel. So, I have to look elsewhere for spirituality and a spiritual practice than Buddhism. Having said this, I have found the anti-anxiety practices of Buddhism helpful alongside the anti-depressive practices of Native Americanism, Judeo-Christianity and African spirituality and going to God and Nature directly.

I personally, even among the Eastern religions find some of the more obscure Eastern religion more satisfying than the Buddhist and Hindu "flagships" in the Western world. For example, Jainism unlike the Delhi Lamma (Tibetan Buddhist) are raw foods vegans who believe that taking any life, whether they be human, animal, vegetable or mineral is wrong. Jainism even considers killing microorganisms to be murder. Sheiks are monotheists like Jews, Christians and Muslims who also believe in social justice and cultural change. Zoroaster's, the religion of the Magi who brought Baby Jesus's Christmas gifts not only have the most in common with Western monotheism, they are the Eastern religion most historically likely to have influenced the development of Western monotheistic religions.

I find certain strands of Protestantism and certain individual Roman Catholics, to be more straight shooters. These are the traditions I can assent to and persons I can be in relationship with and these traditions, subsequently squares with my experiences as a person on the spectrum.

This is my *fifth authority* being an autist Christian, *weighting my "pragmatic experience" being a person on the spectrum and a person with a disability, very heavily*, in determining the "truth-value" of various theological, religious or spiritual claims. This is absolutely necessary and justified in my opinion. It is tantamount to a religious sentiment burning bright in my life.

### *Friends and Mentors for the Journey:*

Aristotle writes about "friendships of virtue,"

> ….for when a good person becomes a friend he becomes a good for his friend.[86]

Up to this point in this treatise, we have been critical of Hellenism, the philosophies and cultural sentimentalities of Ancient Greece, which I have established are far from dead in our twenty-first century world. But it is worth noting that Hellenism provides one of the most satisfying models for friendship this world has ever known. This is what is known in postmodern circles as "reconstruction," which is a very fancy way of saying "holding onto the positive."

*Ancient Greece* provides *a model of friendship grounded in solicitude and hospitality*, being totally available to your friend, marked by intimacy, even physical intimacy, close identification with each other's identity and personhood and extensive "shared activity," *versus* the more contemporary model for friendship, what I call the *social science ideal of friendship*, derived from the social science disciplines of psychology and sociology. Which is more *grounded in boundaries and pseudo-community*, meaning friends are scheduled in at the bottom of one's other priorities and commitments and "shared activity" is limited by the modern reality of busyness. Becoming more like a bad therapy session than an intimate relationship which can make you even more lonely, because such a rigid relationship instills a sense of "learned helplessness" and a spirit of "overfunctioning" which can make you dependent on another finite, mortal human being to the point of becoming e-meshed, where you lose your ability to take care of yourself and your ability to develop your own identity to such a point that you no-longer feel like a whole person without clinging to that other person.

This is because a classical friendship is about love, warmth and intimacy, while a modern friendship is about flattery, manipulation and being judgmental, even contempt for one another.

I contend that the classical ideal of friendship is preferable, when classical friendship is appropriately translated into our twenty-first century reality as neurodiverse humans, such as "good boundaries," so as neurodiverse people; we are safe---physically, emotionally and spiritually. The social science ideal, which is etiquette and social skills driven, has hurt me many times over the years. It is been like Job's friends revisited: Judgmental, distant, repressed, tenuous and negative, with little or no "shared activity," making me "touch deprived" in the process. With these types of friendships, I have "to literally walk on eggshells," in other words, "over function and never fell good enough." I cannot be myself!  Or, if I try to be myself, I would be "torn into" through a tacky "social cue." And, such "friends" seem more like a bad therapy session than a meaningful, life-giving friendship. Such an approach to friendship does not respect the dignity of neurodiverse humans. Such an approach is fundamentally hurtful, abusive and disrespectful.

Also, at this point it is worth interjecting that this treatise so far has focused on the problems of communitarianism in the lives of neurodiverse peoples, but community and other people, including neurotypicals play an integral and essential, although somewhat limited role in our lives as neurodiverse peoples. Despite common misconceptions both within and outside the autistic community, humans on the autism spectrum do need relationships, including relationships with other live human beings, even relationships with neurotypicals.

I do not know about you, but I struggle with intense feelings of loneness and at times, I long deeply for intimate human contact. I desperately want meaningful human relationships in my life. Even despite many bad experiences and bad relationships, I still want friendships and other relationships in my life. Despite the false assumption by the Hellenists, peoples with mental illness can have and can keep---mutualistic friendships. I certainly have.

It has not been easy. It has been thwart with much struggle, much trial and error and much disappointment and betrayal. And, of course much hard work! Yet, it has born much fruit.

This is the role friendship and other relationships play in my life, including my faith life.

Friendship and community gives me "support and plausibility structure" in my life and faith life.

I will explain what each of these technical terms means.

*Support* is fairly self-explanatory, friendship and community helps me when I am struggling with my life and faith. Supplementing my relationship with God and what I can achieve or understand on my own, providing me with constructive guidance, affirmation and a healing human touch. Making me feel like I am not alone or crazy, for the way I feel. Realizing that other people have had similar experiences of what I am going through. Being able to both name and contextualize what I am going through, at a particular time. Being soothed and calmed down in the process. My friends can even open up new perspectives and opportunities which can change my life situation in very concrete ways.

"Plausibility structure" is the sacred canopy which enlivens and enriches my personal experiences, helping me to make sense of my experiences by acknowledging them, interpreting them, even validating them. "Plausibility structure" is secondary to the revelation I get from God. Supplementing and complementing my revelations and Conversations with God. Used as a resource, support and standard for measuring and validating the things God reveals to me. I get this through what God reveals to me through my friends and through faith community.

Sometimes it is also just more believable hearing what God reveals to me corroborated, reinforced and fleshed-out through a live, mortal human voice.

I cannot tell you how many answers to prayers I have gotten not through my Conversations with God, but through other people, such as friends or through Sunday morning sermons or homilies. God even told me once, that there is at least one issue which He does not resolve directly, through transpersonal communication, but through a human being, this is so I would be brought into relationship with other people.

This was upon reading the legend of Saint Francis of Assisi where Francis was struggling with an existential crisis which was making him very depressed, about whether or not he must be a hermit or a preacher. So, he asked some of his friars and some of the Poor Clares to pray for him and they all got the same answer, he must go out and preach.

Francis definitely had a direct, personal, relationship with God like I do, but in this context, God choose to answer through other people. "It is not good for man to be alone" Genesis 2 in the Bible teaches us. We autists are no exception!

For some mysterious reason, we need other members of our own species. Maybe it is because, members of our own species, share our own basic "theory of mind," knowing what it is like to be human and have had similar thoughts, emotions, desires and experiences as us. And, we can benefit from their experience. Or as one of John Steinbeck's characters said in *Of Mice and Men*, "that all we need is another guy to be with."

This is ***my eighth authority being an autistic Christian. The role of human beings!*** The role of friendships and community! Other human beings are my "friends and mentors for the journey."

### *My Home in Heaven*

Sarah York, ordained minister and author of *Pilgrim Heart: the Inner Journey Home* writes,

> Home, it turns out, is more in time than it is in space, more in events than in time, more in people than in events, more in our own minds than in other people. Home is ours to create and too long for, to remember and to dream about.[87]

A few years ago, I attended a reception at the Israeli Embassy, in honor of those and their families which are planning to make Ali Ah, Israeli citizenship. My sister was one of those people, planning to make Ali Ah, so to attend graduate school in Israel. One of the things the various guest speakers empathized was that Israel is the homeland of the Jewish people. It is a place where Jewish people from around the world can go and be with their own people, a place where they can belong and be accepted and understood for who they are. In other words, be with people who are like themselves and not feel like their customs are weird, but the norm, what is considered normal.

One of the most moving speakers was a middle age man who told the story when he was in some kind of a meeting and he blurting out, "We need to go to Minion!" Or, something to that effect. Minion is a daily Jewish prayer ritual. Everyone knew exactly what he is talking about; everyone in the business meeting immediately stopped doing what they were doing and went to Minion. He explained that in America, he would have to say that he is not available during such and such time. Not, that everyone needs to be in Minion right now. My heart sunk when I heard all this!

I realized as a person on the autism spectrum, I have never had that privilege. All my life, I have been surrounded with people who were very different than myself. I have not always been even politely tolerated. Oftentimes instead I have become "a target," having to oftentimes "apologize for my existence." "Fighting tooth and nail" to participate or even being left alone.

I wished as a person on the spectrum that I could feel such a deep level of belonging and mutual understanding in my life. Where my stemming and other mannerism are not considered as weird or bizarre or worse, but instead seen as actually normal. Where I can say to a group of people, "We need some time to stem right now" and everyone would know what I am talking about and will all do likewise. In our own "accustomed fashion." Of course!

Instead of myself saying "I need some time to myself." Or, even secretly slipping away, hopefully without notice. Or, only doing it in the privacy of my own apartment. Dreading the discovery of my secret. Dreading attracting unwanted attention.

I wished there was a homeland for me, a homeland for peoples on the spectrum and other peoples with disabilities. Where all our customs would not be considered bizarre. But, normal. Where I would be with my own people! People like myself, peoples with similar experiences, histories and customs. Where I would not feel isolated and alienated from my own kind.

This does not mean, however that I am not willing to accept, care about and be in relationship with those who are not like myself. Many of my closest friends and mentors are not at all like myself, in many ways. Yet, I am still able to accept, love and be in relationship with them. I also need some type of anchoring, with people who are like myself. So I *would not* become less isolated and vulnerable. I need a home. A refuge. A place of safety and security. Where I would be understood and where I would not feel alone in what I was going through. Instead, I would have a community rallying around me, who would support me in my struggles. In other words, what I want is ***self-determination***. Something most oppressed groups long for.

Unlike my Jewish sister who has found it in a tangible space, in a particular location and with a particular community, in a land called Israel, the Promised Land to the Jewish people, "the land of our ancestors." In Israel, Rachel has found acceptance, belonging, safety, love and understanding. I have found my *self-determination* through an intangible time-period, everywhere and nowhere and through a certain mindset, a certain envisioning process, in a promised, prophesized time called the Messianic Age. A time when everyone will live in peace and harmony with one another, where suffering will be no more, where I too will belong and where I will find everything I am looking for. A time "when knowledge of the Lord will cover the Earth, as the water covers the sea" (Isaiah 11: 9) and God will truly be "in-charge." I *have not* given-up hope that I will be there someday, somehow, even if it is not in this lifetime.

I believe the Kingdom of God is in fact a *realistic expectation,* for the Kingdom of God is promised to all Christian believers because it is so reasonable. This is because one *does not* need to be perfect or meet certain standards of physical, intellectual, moral or spiritual perfection, to be part of it. Anyone who "accepts" Jesus Christ as their "Lord and Savior," somehow, someway, in "one's own accustomed fashion" and in light of God's just, righteous and fair judgments, taking into consideration a person's life circumstances and social location, is entitled to it, according to the tenets of the Christian faith. All one needs is a little tiny "mustard seed of faith" (Mathew 17: 20).

In fact, one might even need to let go of perfectionism and expectations in all its forms, to actualize it and be able to live in it. Be part of it. Accepting God for the God He is and accepting that He is both good and loving. Living within God's ordinances, boundaries and limitations. Both ecologically and spiritually. Allowing a new society and new world to emerge. A world without violence, injustice or apathy, but a world instead filled with faith, justice and peace. Yes, there is one catch.

This sense of belonging can only be attained through people who are radically different than each other, banding together in mutual acceptance, safety, love and understanding of one another. This is the Promised Land of the outcast, the oppressed, the marginalized, the poor and the disabled. I also strongly believe that Animals and the Earth are also included. Welcomed there too! This is my Promised Land. My homeland. Promised to me by my Lord! In which my Lord is an integral part of!

Some may say this strong Heavenly Bound, otherworldly, utopian sentiment is ecological harmful, socially irresponsible and psychologically grandiose. Even though there is always the danger that you can become "so Heavenly bound that you are not of any Earthly good." Whether it is neglecting the survival of the Natural World, the materials needs of the oppressed or side-stepping reality. This *has not* always been the case in my situation however.

Knowledge of the Kingdom of Heaven (otherworldly expression) and the Kingdom of God (worldly expression) has enriched my appreciation of this world. It has given me "the sacred pattern," for working to create a better world, in both the human and nonhuman spheres, as well as the relationship between the two, telling me nothing less than "how things ought to be."

That a world riddled with violence, suffering, injustice and destruction *is not* the way things are supposed to be. Have to be. Can be. Or, could be, sometime in the future. Or, were created or intended to be. Knowledge of the "Kingdom of God" and the "Kingdom of Heaven" has helped me both identify and articulate the world I want to live in, empowering myself to work towards it, in my activism and lifework. A world instead marked by nonviolence, healing, justice and the edification of all created beings.

In terms of "psychological grandiosity" or "side-stepping reality," Heaven has already become part of my reality. Indwelling deep within my soul. Permeating throughout my physical body. Expressed in my writings. The seeds of the Kingdom of God are already germinating in my soul, through my relationship with my Lord, my relationship to the Communion of Saints and every celestial being I have come into contact with over the course of my life, embodied into my "at-homeless" in the Natural World. In other words, Heaven is my "sacred reality" for "living more sanely and sustainably on this Earth."

I have attained some level of finding a homeland, where I belong, am accepted, loved and understood for who I am, rallied around and supported in all my struggles and endeavors. Whether it is in my relationship with God and Saint Francis of Assisi and his Medieval "band of brothers" in Heaven, whether it is in the Great Outdoors, whenever I sleep at night, when I contemplate what the future holds in store for me or even when I am home with my parents and family, I, with my Lord's help have been able to create a refuge for myself. A cell. An enclosure. A place to go, when everything else is not working out. When I have nowhere else to go!

For example, when I am with Saint Francis in Heaven, we share as my Lord pointed-out one time, the same interests, passions and fetuses. I have another person like myself, where we can perseverate together and about the same things. I have met my match in Francis, in terms of my enthusiasm in experiencing the joy and glory of the Natural World, mutually enriching and en-livening each other's experiences, being free to experience the Natural World, in my "own accustom fashion," without having to perform or feeling pressured to feel a certain sense of ecstasy. Having someone I can share my experiences with and understand and appreciate what I am experiencing. When I do struggle with negativity in Nature, Francis helps me through it. Being with Francis is as fun as it was for his contemporizes in Medieval times. I can see why after getting to know Francis, why everyone wanted to be in his presence.

I was honored to be in Francis's presence, when God arranged to mediate a transpersonal relationship liken to what I have with my Lord, through auditory voice, with Francis. Now our souls are knit together and Francis can see all the things I see, hear, touch and taste---the world, through my body. Giving Francis, what he calls a "second chance" to be alive. God although reluctant in the beginning, because of the inhibition in our faith against spiritualism, did finally gave into my desire and found a way for the two of us to be together, even conquering the boundaries of time, history and death in the process.

Once I got to know Francis, I learned that he was as enthusiastic about being in my presence, as I being in his. He respected, admired and loved me, just like I did, him. In the process, re-maculating me, giving me a sense of security in my manhood, which society has tried to take away from me, as well as restoring a positive body image of myself, which society has also tried to take away from me too.

In the areas where he is radically different then myself, he has become a source of fascination and intrigue. I love Francis telling all his Italian Medieval stories. We really have bonded through this. His observations and fascination with my twenty-first century, American world, are delightful to watch, observe and listen to. Francis sharing his physical suffering with me has been real male bonding and has helped me cope with my own sufferings and afflictions.

Although mine being more mental and cerebral in nature than his, being more physical and concrete in nature, both the result of being different and not totally fitting into our societies.

Through God and Francis and his Band of Brothers from Heaven, we have become best friends, forming a tight nit family, community, partnership, even if I dare say so, a little makeshift friary. I am never alone or separated from love and acceptance. They even prepare a table before my enemies. I can take them everywhere I go.

This is just one venue where I have created a homeland, a refuge, a place of safety and belonging for myself, in the world.

The goal of my fraternity of spirits is to make me feel more welcomed in this world, through helping to make this Earth a more hospitable place to live, through stabilizing imbalances in the Universe and helping my life to flourish. As God has been telling me for the last few years, the Kingdom of God is being built! The New Jerusalem is coming down from Heaven! Heaven and Earth are becoming one! "The Messiah is among us!" Our promised Messiah is already in our world "like a thief in the night" (I Thessalonians 5:2).

God has shown me several places where the Kingdom of God is beginning to germinate.

God in 2010 (the same year as the tragic Gulf Coast Oil Spill) shepherded me outside to local streams, ponds and vernal pools which were overflowing with chorusing frogs and tadpoles so thick they blacked the beds of streams. We counted at least four species of native frog species to my bioregion: spring peepers, wood frogs, bullfrogs and green frogs. It looked like a scene right out of Captain John Smith's field journal of the Mid-Atlantic region, what the Piedmont might have looked like before colonization. Yes, here we are in 2010 and amphibians have been declining worldwide. A real modern-day miracle!

Since, 2010, I have experienced this phenomena again in 2011 and again in 2012, adding American toads and cricket frogs to the list and this year, the Spring of 2013, adding chorusing frogs and carpenter frogs to the list.

All of this began after the Blizzard of 2010, where the mid-Atlantic region was hit with the most severe blizzard in over a decade, a New England style blizzard which occurred in very late winter, practically at the end of February, where melting snow replenished seasonal vernal pools everywhere in my bioregion just before frog breeding season that one noisy spring.

Vernal pools, the tide pools of the forest, which is really a very fancy, technical term for rain · puddles, are really sensitive ecosystems, critical breeding grounds for frogs, toads, salamanders, newts and even a special freshwater shrimp species and for this reason are classified as wetlands and are protected under the Clean Water Act. This life-giving Blizzard watered God's vernal pools, helping to revitalize declining frogs in the process and was one of God's first direct actions on behalf of the planet in peril! Global healing is happening!

God's second major direct action on behalf of the planet was revealed to me in 2011. God showed me how the water in the streams, rivers, ponds and lakes in my bioregion where clearer then I have ever seen in my entire life. Suburban waterways flowing like clear mountain streams, "sparkling like crystal" (Revelations 22: 11). Here I was in 2011, seeing the beds of the same streams, rivers and lakes I grew-up with, transparent and crystalline for the first time in my entire life, I literally was "knowing the same place for the first time." Growing up, local suburban streams, rivers and lakes were so oblique and muddy with pollution that I could not see anything underwater at all, let alone, the intricate details of massive underwater rock formations which undergirded my local watershed which have remained hidden until now.

Where out of this "Living Water" (John 7: 38) I saw increasing numbers of fish, filling these dying waters with rebirth and new life. I not only saw the usual minnows, sunfish, catfish and bass. I even saw fish species thought to be locally extinct: rainbow trout, even shad. Spawning and breeding too! With water now, so clear, you can now clearly observe our local fish and all their various behaviors, from land, like you were snorkeling through a coral reef in the Caribbean.

Yet, God told me that he cannot take full credit for this second miracle of ecological healing. This healing miracle is literally the fruits of several decades of environmentalists persevering on recycling, storm water management and clean water. Some of the oldest environmental campaigns! Yes, recycling, storm water management and clean water is "shallow ecology." Yet, these same ecological efforts which were primarily for the benefit of human beings, by their very nature, forced the planetary agenda to literally "go deeper," restoring the beauty of the Natural World, helping wildlife to repopulate and giving the various ecological movements, "reason for hope," in the process.

A phenomenon, I saw dramatically repeated in 2012 and now in 2013. This is God's second major direct action on behalf of the planet in peril! [88]

There is much "reason for hope" in my own life too. Whether it is new budding relationships, new opportunities, reconciliation with old ones, Satan and evil are slowly being defeated and God is triumphing victoriously.

This is true, whether it's my new political community, healing in my family, finding Deer Ridge (my new Tower Oaks),[89] new friends, allies and mentors and recently relocating to Portland, Oregon. As well as continuing travel opportunities, having already visited Oregon, The Bahamas and Colorado since I published: *Have Mercy on me, an Ecological Sinner* (Create Space Independent Publishing Platform, 2012).

The Apocalypse and Messianic Age is happening in my life. The boundaries between Heaven and Earth are beginning to dissolve, giving God more opportunities to exercise His will in my life. So God can act in the world, changing my reality and reality itself, creating His "Will on Earth as it is in Heaven," which I contend is "good news" for all Life on Earth.

Yet, this has not been fully attained in my world and in my life yet, but my world and my soul, I believe is moving in the direction of the Messianic Age. It is already beginning. "It's happening!"

This is ***my eighth authority being an autistic Christian***, ***the Peaceable Kingdom***. A magnificent transformation and restoration of a fallen, broken world, which is already beginning to be actualized in my soul and in my world, even in certain expressions of Christian and secular community. In other words, Heaven is my "sacred reality" for "living more sanely and sustainably on this Earth."

### *I am the Acid Test:*

One of the great mid-twentieth century Roman Catholic theologians, also a priest and an early disability advocate Henri Nouwen writes,

> If there is any posture that disturbs a suffering man or woman, it is aloofness. The tragedy of Christian ministry is that many who are in great need, many who seek an attentive ear, a word of support, a forgiving embrace, a firm hand, a tender smile, or even a stuttering confession of inability to do more, often find their ministers distant men who do not want to burn their fingers. They are unable or unwilling to express their feelings of affection, anger, hostility, or sympathy. The paradox indeed is that those who want to be for "everyone" find themselves often unable to be close to anyone. When everyone becomes my "neighbor," it is worth wondering whether anybody can really become my "proximius," [Latin for neighbor] that is, the one who is most close to me…
>
> So long as we define leadership in terms of preventing or establishing precedents, or in terms of being responsible for some kind of abstract, "general good," we have forgotten that no God can save us except a suffering God, and that no man can lead his people except that man who is crushed by its sins. Personal concern means making [the individual] the only one who counts, the one for whom I am willing to forget my many other obligations, my scheduled appointments and long-prepared meetings, not because they are not important but because they loose their urgency in the face of [a suffering person's] agony. Personal concern makes it possible to experience that going after the "lost sheep" is really a service to those who were left alone.[90]

Just as true in our twenty-first century ministry landscape as it was in the 1970s when Nouwen wrote this eloquent insight. In my own Christian faith journey as a human being on the autism spectrum, I also have too many times been at the receiving end of an "aloof minister." I have personally experienced and endured ministers (on both the right and the left) who refuse to give me "an attentive ear, a word of support, a forgiving embrace, a firm hand, a tender smile, or even a stuttering confession of inability to do more" in my "darkest hours" or at my most vulnerable periods in my faith journey. But instead I am apathetically "left" literally "out in the cold." I am left spiritually destitute and in despair, with nowhere to go, left "to fend for myself!"

For example, one time when I was desperately seeking out Franciscan fraternity and a Roman Catholic affiliation, I learned about this Franciscan church which was open to the public in the Boston area, so I enthusiastically visited it during Lent one year, to get the experience of what Franciscan religious life was like and to find ways I can get involved with it. But, instead of this friary church being the welcoming, hospitable and warm place which I envisioned from my studies of the early Franciscans and their beautiful charism, instead I found it to be a very dreary, morose and cold place, indeed.

I first went to the welcoming desk to tell them my interest in Franciscanism and Catholicism. The person at the desk summoned the priest, but the priest said he did not have time to talk to me. Then I went into one of the chapels to listen to the friars perform the "Stations of the Cross"; it was filled mostly with mostly cultural Catholic woman. No liturgy was given; it was assumed that everyone there had already memorized it. They were in absolute tears, weeping at the solemnity of it all. No joy! Just moroseness, religious guilt and legality. I could feel it in the energy, in the negative aura of this place.

After the service, I asked to be welcomed by one of the Franciscan priests and he sent me to the confessor in the confessional. I went in and said that I was new and needed to be welcomed. With all the aloofness in his heart, he said, "I am not here to welcome you; I am here for you to confess your sins." Then, I asked him again, "So if you can't welcome me, can you at least listen to my problems, or is that out of the question, too?" He responded again with more aloofness, "I am not here to listen to your problems, but I am here for you to confess you sins." He then sent me out with a mechanical prayer, honoring the sacrament, which most likely from his perspective was defiled by my messy, but earnest and sincere spiritual curiosity and enthusiasm.

I was so upset by this altercation, that I went out, alone onto the cold and heartless Bostonian streets and cried non-stop for about fifteen minutes. No one came out to comfort me. Only a passing man barked at me to stop crying.

I then ended-up calling my Jewish mother long-distance, collect, from a pay phone for I needed desperately to experience something remotely loving. With my mother's counsel, she recommended that I give it another chance, since I was down there anyway, so I went into a worship service and I did not find it much help either, for it was all about how "we are all miserable sinners." So, I walked-out and called my Jewish mother again and she omitted, "This is why people are leaving the Roman Catholic Church in droves."

I made one final stop, at the welcome desk, to complain and all the guy could come up with, "This is real bad!"

I got more grace from my Jewish mother than this so called Christian Church.

Unfortunately, this is not the only time I have encountered an "aloof minister." The ministers at a United Church of Christ (UCC), Disciples of Christ Church I was a member of for a while, while I was in theological school in Boston, became so obsessed by an "abstract, general good" and needing to be there for "everyone" as Nouwen talked about in his writing, that they lost sight of my very serious pastoral needs being a Christian on the autism spectrum. They had this "abstract, general good" called "mathematical equality" and their strategy for attaining this "mathematical equality" was to give everyone what I called "managed pastoral care" ---giving everyone rationed, equal attention, regardless of the inequality of needs and they did not know how to delegate, so they worked themselves into a position, where almost all responsibilities for all aspects of church life, even what is served at coffee hour fell on their shoulders. When there needed to be a ministry team. This was applied to everyone exactly, equally, except for two notable exceptions. They made a special effort that the needs of woman and gays/lesbians were specially attended too and they were obsessed with recruiting as many new members as possible.

Meaning, if you did not fall into one of these categories, you were cast to the side and your spiritual needs put on "the back burner."

Yet, I was un-Churched at the time and going through a very difficult time in my life, so I needed additional "pastoral care" and "spiritual instruction."

The final example is when I attended an Episcopal Church for a brief period of time. I went to a Celtic Mass, since I am into Celtic Christian spirituality because of its ecological and animal rights connections.

After the service, I talked to the woman priest, with tons of questions and she had a meeting to go to and she abruptly intercepted the conversation and said, "I need to set up a boundary!"

Another time after a religious service, she gathered a whole group of my peers, young adults and went onto the lecture me about "singing to loud" in a very patronizing manor. After that public humiliation in front of my young adult peers, I never went back.

All three are examples, where ministers in an attempt to protect some "abstract, general good" at all costs, such as "community" or "equality" or even protecting their own personal boundaries and space at all costs, ended up causing me to "stumble," hurts, which I have still not recovered from. If my faith was not as strong as it was, I might have given-up on Christianity all together. Instead I kept searching for more "open and affirming" faith communities.

When I am talking about "open and affirming" I am not just talking about gays and lesbians, I am talking about "everyone," which absolutely also includes neurodiverse humans, peoples with physical disabilities, Jewish converts, Generation Xers, nonhuman animals, even the Earth. When churches profess that they "welcome everybody at the table," it needs to be "everybody," no exceptions! Anything else is a contradiction! A logical fallacy! And, is fundamentally oppressive!

I strongly believe that I did not deserve to be treated the way I was, by all three of these faith communities, because I believe in a Loving God, I am atheistic to the "angry, distinct, critical" god of American Christianity. I militantly believe that a Loving God *is* the Historical Christ. I insularly believe that the "angry, distant, critical" god of American Christianity is a different Christ than the Jesus which the Disciples, Apostles, Prophets, Saints and Doctors of the Church, our ancestors, preached, confessed, converted to and followed to the death. I believe American Christianity (on the left and the right) is nothing less than a bunch of militant heretics. I full-hearty agree with my Lord, "If it is not love, it is not from God!" In other words, the anger-and-fear based ideologies of American civil religion are fundamentally Satan-centric and death affirming. American Christianity needs to be fundamentally Christ-centered and life affirming.

My issues could have been dealt with in a more sensitive, loving, empathetic and Christian manor. It did not have to be!

For example, the Franciscan priest could have offered to see me at another time, like after he is finished with his confession responsibilities or had me make an appointment with him at the front desk, to meet with me to talk about my interest and conversion experience. I also should not have been turned toward the confession by the other Franciscan. There was no excess for not offering liturgy, in case a new person, unlettered in the tradition, might come by. Simple things could have been done, to make this place a more inviting and hospitable worship experience for me.

In terms of the UCC-Disciples of Christ Church, they could have given everyone, everything they needed and some of what they wanted, if the two leaders delegated some of their authority to the laity such as forming committees, appointing specialized ministry leaders, using volunteers for ministry and outreach versus just empire building and actually educating the community about homosexuality and domestic violence versus just issuing them ultimatums.

For the Episcopal Church, she had no right to stifle my enthusiasm for praising the Lord and I needed to sing loudly to help internalize the liturgy, just to protect the sentiments of very privileged, wealthy white folk, just because they give tons of money to the church. Such an approach also excludes African-American Christians and mainland African Christians who also insist in praising the Lord loudly with "Amen's!" In fact, such a sentiment not only portrays a certain bias toward normalcy, toward privileging non-disabled, neurotypicals over everyone else, such a worship environment is also fundamentally classist, ethnocentric, even northern Eurocentric, privileging Nordic European cultures like England and Germany over Southern and Eastern European cultures like Spain and Poland.

To stay with that church, I would not be able to Praise God in peace, but be made "self-conscious" of my disability and behaviors every moment I was in that church. Granted, it is possible to Praise God effectively in a softer tone of voice and I have been able to do it, when necessity requires it, but in addition to it being unnatural, I need to speak loudly so I can internalize the words, for according to Temple Grandin, words have little power over an autistic human in terms of transforming my negative emotions to more positive emotions. In otherwords, I need to sing loud, to "self-soothe."[91] This is my way of praying!

In terms of the confrontation, even if this woman pastor absolutely felt justified in comforting me about my singing, she could have at least given me the courtesy of confronting me in private and in confidence, not humiliating me in-front of my peers. There was no excuse for her behavior! As the above demonstrates, these pastoral opportunities could have been handled much better than they were.

What is more important, according to Nouwen, I was their priority, the preverbal "lost sheep" (Luke 15) which our Lord Jesus came to Earth to tend to. "Loving your neighbor" *does not* mean loving starving children in Africa or some other abstraction at the other end of the world, it means loving who is right in your midst, in your vicinity, a real live human being, not an abstract cause. Jesus after commanding his disciples to "love their neighbors" answered the question, "Who is my neighbor?" by pointing to an outcast in His own community not some person at the other end of the world, "The Good Samaritan" (Luke 15: 25-37). The Great Commandment is also "lop-sided" toward "personal relationships," Loving God versus fulfilling religious obligations, loving other people versus loving humanity.

In fact, an argument can be made that the liberal-progressive church of American civil religion have abstractified "humanity" so much, that is has become idolatry, as many animal rights theologians have argued. Such an "uncritical humanism" and idolatrous worshiping of "the human spirit" is also not desirable for Animals and the Natural World, for such an ideology also excludes nonhuman beings. Such a universalized anthropology in fact was the logic behind European colonialism: "paternalism" and "white man's burden." Even as liberal religions purport to talk about "the poor" and "the virtue of charity," "the poor Christ" and "the virtue of charity" have already been defiled even scandalized by such colonialist, imperialistic residue, becoming its own form of escapism, its own form of otherworldliness: "utopianism" and "nationalism."

My situation and needs were just as important, as tending to the "fold." This is because as Nouwen so eloquently put it, the "fold" can benefit from their "shepherd's" temporary absence. This is because apathy is the opposite of love, not anger or hate, so if a pastor or priest or congregation cannot show "personal concern" for someone like me, most likely they are incapable, according Nouwen, of showing "personal concern" to anyone in need. So no-one is really guaranteed love or is completely safe in those churches, even people in those groups which the pastor has a special affinity for. This is because these types of pastors and priests "love humanity, it is human beings which they cannot stand."

As a result, our Lord Jesus Christ has testified at many times in the Holy Gospel, how one treats the "lost sheep" is "the acid test" by which God judges ones fruits as a Christian (Mark 12). Those, according to the Bible, who fail this test, are denied their "eternal life" (Mathew 18: 2-12). I am one such "acid test" (Luke 16: 19-31)! People like me, the outcastes, the marginalized, the meek, weak and so for, are "the acid test" which determines whether a minister or believer is really doing God's work and showing Christian love (Mathew 10:5-8, 11: 4-5) or is even fit for "the Kingdom of God" (Mathew 19: 13-28) at-all.

This is because if "loving your neighbor" means "loving humanity" even Nazis, Soviets, fascist dictators around the world, colonialists, imperialists, even the superrich, claim to "love humanity" and to do what is in best interest of "the greater good."

If "loving your neighbor" means as our Lord has commanded us, means loving whoever the Good Lord chooses to stick in front of us, at any given time, whether it is an annoying and rude next door neighbor, a cockroach infestation, an obnoxious Tea Partying uncle that you cannot stand being around or a human being with a developmental disability who sings too loud in church, all of us "fall short of the Glory of God" (Romans 3: 23).Now the Atonement begins to start to make some sense and give us pause, to be a little less judgmental of those of us with less social privileges.

In other words, we *are not* called to "Save the World," that is our Lord Jesus Christ's job, instead we are called to be the humble "door openers" in the Great Temple of the Lord, to usher in individual souls (humans, animals, vegetables and minerals) and our local bioregion (to bravely and candidly address the ecological, social justice and animal rights issues right in our own local communities). Christians are called to take a hint from the environmental movement's slogan "think globally, act locally!" We "think globally" when we Love God with our whole heart, soul, mind and body. We "act locally" when we Love our Neighbors as Ourselves.

It turns out, our neighbors are our literal neighbors after all. All the people above us, below us, next door to us, in back us and around us, even in us. Our neighbors are all the people around us, our friends and enemies, our families and communities, our ancestors and our descendents, our species and other species, even the bacteria in our own bodies, even the very air we breathe, are our neighbors too. Even the God around us is our neighbor too! The Kingdom of God is a virtual "city of neighborhoods."

This means, God *does not* judge people on how well they treat the people who are personally useful in advancing their own careers or social mobility. Or are sufficiently, like themselves. It is the very people, the minister rejects, ignores, looks down upon, feels threatened by, dismisses as a "situation" which needs to be "handled," that God is most interested in how the pastor, priest or minister responds. If my life is a testimony to this, many have flunked miserably "the acid test."

Not all Christian communities which I have come into contact with have failed "the acid test." These communities can serve as models, as witnesses that I, as an person with Asperger's can be accepted into a community and can even be seen as an asset, with definite gifts which I "bring to the table."

This is ***my ninth authority being an autist Christian***; ***I am an essential, indispensable member of the Body of Christ***. To deny me my rightful place in the Body of Christ is tantamount to denying God Himself. People like me are the ones whom God uses to test an individual's or a community's "true nature." I am the acid test! This is my "theos-right"!

### Freedom of Conscience: The Role of Democracy

Saint Francis of Assisi and his original followers in their Papal Approved Later Rule wrote about exceptions to their vowels to obedience and the primacy of listening to one's own conscience, one's own power of discernment apart from and above any worldly or churchly authority,

> The brothers who are the ministers and servants of other brothers should visit and admonish their brothers and humbly and charitably correct them, not commanding them anything which might be against their conscience and our Rule. On the other hand, the brothers who are subject to them should remember that they have given up their own wills for God. Therefore I strictly command them to obey their ministers in all those things which they have promised the Lord to observe and which are not against [their] conscience and our Rule. And whenever there are brothers who know and realize they cannot observe the Rule spiritually, it is their duty and right to go to the minister for help. The ministers on their part should receive them with great kindness and love and should be so approachable that these brothers can speak and deal with [the ministers] as masters with their servants, for this is the way it should be: The ministers shall be the servants of all the brothers.[92]

So, according to Saint Francis of Assisi, obedience *does not* apply in "matters of conscience" or when his Rule of Life is being perverted. Ministers are not to put brothers in such situations. Brothers are allowed to get help from ministers when struggling with their religious obligations. In other words, a Franciscan Vow of Obedience allows a certain sense of freedom, enough freedom to not be coercive to a brother. Yet, obedience is something Saint Francis of Assisi took very seriously, he was not lax. Writing in his "The Salutation of the Virtues," that:

Holy Obedience destroys every wish of the body of the flesh and binds its mortified body
to obedience of the Spirit and to obedience of one's brother
And [the person who possesses her] is subject and submissive to all persons in the world
and not to man only but even to all beasts and wild animals
So that they may do whatever they want with him
Inasmuch as it has been given to them from above by the Lord.[93]

Francis in his visionary wisdom recognized as both modernity and post-modernity forcefully affirms that unconditional obedience can be highly dangerous, destructive and damaging to both individuals and society at-large. Unconditional obedience can lead to nothing less than Nazi Germany and more recently in a religious context, the Vatican Sex Scandals. As history bears witness, authority figures, even religious authority figures, cannot always or even often be trusted. It cannot be assumed that authority figures have our best interests or even the best interests of the "common good" at heart. This is why in secular schools, students are taught to "Question Any and All Authority" to protect themselves, society and the world from abuse, exploitation, oppression and injustice. This is why one is taught in school to "think critically," "to think for oneself," "to be an independent thinker." To ask questions. To critique, argue and refute. To detect hypocrisies and inconsistencies. To be skeptical and suspicious. To even disobey, if necessary, in the wake of great injustices and tyranny.

This is also why Francis gives his friars permission to disobey their Vow of Obedience in matters related to conscience and contradicting their Rule of Life. Brothers are not required to obey another, if it is against their conscience or against the Franciscan Rule of Life. In those cases, a brother is not obliged to obey, instead following his conscience and the tenets of the Rule. Because our conscience might be prophetic and from the Spirit and our particular monastic order might be a self-serving perversion.

Also, Francis commands his ministers, those who would be in a position to call for a certain sense of obedience, not to put any of his brothers in such an awkward, compromised position. Ministers are not to abuse their power of commending obedience. An example of an abomination of the abuse of power can be found in Bonaventure's official biography of Saint Francis of Assisi, in the legend of one brother using humility to lord over another brother:

Two friars once came from the Terra di Lavoro, the elder of whom had given much scandal to the younger. When they reached the father, he asked the younger friar how his companion had behaved toward him on the way. The friar replied: "Quite well"; but Francis said: "Be careful, brother, not to tell a lie under the pretext of humility. For I know, I know; but wait a little and you will see." The friar was amazed at how he could have known in spirit what had happened at a distance. Now not many days after, the one who had given scandal to his brother left the Order in contempt and went out into the world. He did not ask the father's forgiveness nor accept the discipline of correction as he should. In that single fall, two things shone forth clearly: the equity of the divine judgment and the penetrating power of the spirit of prophecy.[94]

Francis would not tolerance his brothers using their Vow of Obedience to lord over other brothers. Francis was on guard, about this type of perversion of his way of life. Francis would not tolerate the defiling of something which he saw as very precious indeed. He would not tolerate scrupulous obedience or the practicing of this virtue in excess. This is because obedience does not mean "Following Orders" or "Respecting Authority" as it is commonly understood. That is the virtue of excess. Obedience means something entirely different in the tradition. In other words, in our twenty-first century context, "obedience" like "self-mortification" has also become "irrelevant," "exclusive" and "harmful" religious language.

Obedience in the Christian religious life tradition does not mean blindly following the leader nor does it mean preferential treatment for authority figures, in fact, authority figures are under Holy Obedience, too. In fact, obedience is to be followed indiscriminately, without partiality to hierarchical positioning. As in Francis's poem, the virtue of obedience also included obedience to the nonhuman world. This is because obedience was understood as obedience to God's Reign. Both in ones conscience and in the world. Grounded in a strong faith in the Power and Authority of the Living God, obedience can be seen today as the antidote to the vice of domination. Obedience puts dominion in perspective. Subsequently, the imperative for obedience in the Christian tradition must be read with the Dominion imperative in Genesis 1.

Obedience means letting go of the need to control everyone and everything in your environment. Whether they are other people, the outcomes of political campaigns, the direction of organizations, how history is interpreted, how the future is envisioned, even wild animals and wild Nature.

Obedience also means letting go of the need to dominate "the-world-around us," humans and nonhumans alike, through violence and paternalism.

Instead, obedience means recognizing the integrity, dignity and autonomy of all things. Recognizing that God is the only reality which matters. That one cannot do whatever they want to themselves or the world, which is under God's reign. That is what authentic obedience looks like in this day and age.

This view of obedience is consistent with the tradition. This is because obedience is sometimes defined as "carefully listening" by religious people and implicit in Francis's Rule of Life, obedience not only keeps in check human arrogance, through keeping the human "accountable," obedience also sets up a relationship of mutual interdependence.

Obedience understood in this context can be a "tree of life" (Proverbs 15:4) and essential in spiritual development and survival. It can teach one, it can form one; it can help one discern, it can confront one of their destructive tendencies. It can help one "enter through the narrow gate. For wide is the gate and broad is the road that leads to destruction, and many enter through it" (Mathew 7: 13). Obedience is nothing less than the virtue of asking for help. Obedience is also the belief that asking for help is in fact virtuous. Obedience is receiving constructive criticism graciously.

In other words, in this model, the "Vow of Obedience" is not taking a vow to "follow orders" from an elite authoritarian body, but a vow to listen to other people, a vow to be a "good listener." Now we are back in democratic territory, even populist and anarchist territory!

Yet, advice from other people needs to be weighed in your own conscience and with your own Lord, to make sure it is in yours and other's best interests, that it is morally and spiritually cogent. That it has integrity! In other words, there needs to be dialectic between obedience and conscience, even "creative tension." That each keeps the other in check. Obedience keeps in check individual tendencies towards rationalization, while the human conscience keeps in check an organization's tendency toward collective violence.

One way God explained to me to tell the difference between whether an issue is a question of obedience and whether it is a matter of conscience, is to think of the example of boiling water. One might have a more efficient way of boiling water, such as in the microwave, but a minister tells you to boil water on the stove, that is clearly an issue of obedience. Even through one might have a better method for boiling water; one is obligated to comply with the order, since there is not a moral or spiritual issue in question. Even if you feel like you know best. One must still submit. Obedience is ignoring your own judgments in matters of how to boil water, not questions of morality, spirituality or politics. One is a matter of plain insubordination and being overall disagreeable and divisive, with the other, something more important is at stake.

Although some religious would like to think there is no conflict between obedience to the Lord and obedience to the Order, I have found there can be incredible tension. Sometimes there are situations when the Will of God contradicts the will of the community. What one individual believes God is telling is them, might *not* be inherently wrong either. It might be the community which is "in error." To believe anything else would be sociologically naïve.

Community being "in error" is both an historical and sociological fact, communities need to be ever vigilant of this reality and vice versa, the possibly and probability that certain visionary individuals are in the right. So in essence, a private revelation must be taken seriously. As seriously, as collective wisdom. To do otherwise, would be to fall into the "bandwagon fallacy." A logical fallacy! "Something is right, because everyone is doing it." When in reality, something might not be right or true, just because everyone is doing it.

An example in my life, where conscience applies, is my belief that human beings are not the only rational animals in existence, but that nonhuman animals have a certain capacity for rationality (reason). I have thought about this issue, prayed about this issue, worked through this issue, read books about this, taken courses on it, written about it in published writings and held onto this belief for many years, ever since a teenager when I was first exposed to the notion.

Yet, the Roman Catholic Church teaches contrary to this teaching. They hold onto this axiom, "humans are the rational animal." Yet, I contend in my heart and conscience that this *is not* true and I can back up my belief in nonhuman rationality, both rationally and scientifically. This is definitely a "matter of conscience." This is because if I teach "humans are the rational animal," despite my unbelief in this axiom, just to please the Catholic Church hierarchy, I would not only be dishonest, proceeding without integrity, I would be doing a disservice to the animals I so dearly care about and love and want to help improve their lot, so badly.

I cannot just believe as one Roman Catholic I came into contact with one time told me, "you have to believe something you do not believe in." I fundamentally do not believe in this axiom. That is not how I want to live my life. I absolutely refuse to live my life like this. As a Christian and Man of God, the God I know and love, does not make such a demand on me. This is clearly "a matter of conscience," for it involves a spiritual, moral and political issue and is not just being rebellious, but is a weighed, well discerned, judgment about what is true and right. Holding to the contention that "animals are also rational animals" is a conviction with much at stake; it is not a petty or trivial matter. Nothing less than the future of animalkind is at stake. Nor is it something, which warrants and sufficiently justifies unconditionally trust in church teaching. In other words, I believe the mortal church is in the wrong on this issue and I contend that I have permission to resist both passively (believing) and actively (teaching) this church teaching, within the confines of God's Reign.

God's Reign and Church Authority are radically different realities, one is a legitimate objective reality and the other is a human made, socially produced, culturally constructed institution. Humans are fallible and mortal by nature. Even the Pope has to stand before God in judgment. Even the Pope is under God's Reign. Even he is not above God Himself.

It is also worth discussing a framework for obeying one's parents or whoever is or was your legal guardian growing-up in a manner which honors one's own God-given conscience. The commandment, "Honor your father and mother; so that your days may be long in the land that the Lord your God is giving you" (Exodus 20: 12) is sometimes quoted out of context--- to get children to obey their parents or legal guardians. This simplistic theological axiom does not take into consideration several factors which complexity what this commandment really means and means for us as autists in our own unique non-neurotypical context. Using this commandment as leverage to get children to do their parent's will *does not* take into consideration passages in both the Old and New Testament, whose ignorance of these certain passage, intimates children, even adult children, to do the will of their parents, despite what is in their own best interests and what is developmentally appropriate.

These alternative complementary passages takes into consideration such issues as abusive parents, adulthood and in our context, well meaning, but sometimes misguided neurotypical parents, who do not always understand or even respect our autist ways. These alternative scripture passages can liberate us to become more emancipated, dignified and self-confidant adults. These passages will give-us courage to stand-up to our parents, guardians and councilors, who want to "cure" us, "fix" us," even try to make us "normal," in the process, forcing us to carry ourselves with our heads down-low, sentencing us to a life of low self-esteem, shame and phoniness, never realizing our true selves, our true gifts, our true virtues.

The good news is that we do not need to listen to them on all issues, especially on certain personal decisions which only we can make for our own lives, which is our right and only our right, to make. The good news is that we have forceful theological permission to take back our own lives and live the life God intends us to live.

For example, (Genesis 2: 24) affirms that "man leaves his father and his mother and clings to his wife and they become one flesh." This means that according to Genesis, it is only developmentally appropriate and God-ordained, for when a man or a woman matures to a certain point, that they would leave their mother and father and forge new relationships which would carry them throughout adulthood.

In the New Testament, no less than Jesus Christ Himself proclaims in the Holy Gospel, "Whoever comes to me and does not hate father and mother, wife and children, brothers and sisters, yes, and even life itself, cannot be my disciple" (Luke 14: 26). This means there is nothing un-Christian about parting ways with your parents or legal guardians, especially as a full-grown adult and even as a youth, so you become the man or woman, God created and ordained you to be, becoming His disciple, doing much good in the world, with your talents, gifts, virtues and strengths, being nothing less than adopted into your Heavenly family. This means that if you believe God created you autist, you need to embrace it, despite what your parents or councilors want or desire for you, no matter how well meaning or good intentioned, they might be. Despite how much they love and care about you. I can say this because, Jesus our Savior gives us this assurance, "And call no one your father on earth, for you have one Father- the one in heaven" (Mathew 23: 9). This means, "be not afraid" for your Father in Heaven will be your parent, once you leave home. You will not be alone. You will not be left destitute. Instead you will be adopted into a spiritual family of believers, saints and spirits, who also claims God as their one true Father, who only call God and God only, their father.

This does not mean you must disown your biological mother and father, I happen to have very understanding and open-minded parents, who remain at the core of my support system, even into adulthood, even tell this day. I have preserved my relationship with them at all costs!

Some humans on the autism spectrum are not as fortunate. The later is the problem I am addressing in this section, a major societal problem in the neurodiversity community, at-large, collectively and politically. My own parents are not the intended recipients of this message; instead I am trying to address a major controversy in the neurodiversity movements and in the Disability Studies field over the direction of autism research. Does autism research need to focus on a "cure" as many parent groups and some medical professional insist upon or does autism research need to be more focused on "care" and "management" as many Aspies, disability studies scholars and an increasing number of medical professionals are insisting? I am arguing for the later, not the former.

So if you have parents like I do, by all means do not stop loving your biological mother and father. Even if you do not have loving and supportive parents, you can still love and forgive them, for both the women's movement and the men's movement have developed rituals and treatments for healing the parent-child bond (see appendix). In fact, Dawn Prince Hughes, who had a difficult home life, growing up, was able to get healing even reconciliation with her biological parents.

Remembering that no healing tradition promises miracles, that you absolutely must take appropriate safety precautions and when in doubt, absolutely consult a medical professional you trust, for further advice and assistance. Also, remembering that you are the expert on your abuser's power over you, you will automatically have a more realistic assessment of your abuser's power over you than any friend, councilor, self-help book, program or clinician.

By all means, both respect and love, your biological mother and father, but also claim your manhood or womanhood and know you are not obliged to listen to everything they say, if it goes against your conscience. Most importantly, *do not* feel guilty or ashamed for doing this. You *are not* doing anything wrong. You *are not* sinning. You *are not* violating the tenants of the Jewish or Christian religion, if you identify yourself as one. Instead, you *are* part of a proud tradition of saints, prophets and holy men (and women) who have come before you, who have parted ways with their biological parents to be adapted into God's family.

As the above demonstrates, there is definitely dialectic tension between conscience and obedience. Yet at the "end of the day," despite the benefits and virtues of holy obedience, it is one's conscience, which must have the last word. Conscience is fundamentally more important than obedience. This is **my tenth authority being an autist Christian**: "**matter of conscience**."

### *Exorcism as Deconstruction*

Ecotheologian, Sallie McFague writes about the nature and role of metaphor in theology,

> ...could we then dare to let metaphor try its chance, be a detour between nonsense and truth, always aware that it can never be 'true' and certainty not the truth, because it contains a "definite absence," its own death within it...[95]

According to McFague, metaphors occupy the space between the unreal and real, whose function is to provide an approximation of the truth versus actual absolute, objective, truth-claims. Sort of like a model in science, but more versatile. Metaphors and models make reality intelligible, knowable, explainable and understandable. It is a device humans use to make sense of their world. Yet, these metaphors and models *are not* absolute or completely objective, either. As new information is discovered, as new circumstances emerge, the structure, even the nature of these metaphors and models must be changed and sometimes even eliminated, replaced with the cultivation of entirely new metaphors and models. In other words, metaphors can and sometimes must undergo a certain "metaphoric death" as new knowledge and circumstances emerge.

This is one way according to this perspective that new theological discoveries are both possible and made--- putting to death of old metaphors, coupled by the birthing of new metaphors, as new knowledge becomes available and new circumstances emerge. With it being argued by McFague, that metaphors and models is the closest to objective, absolute truth, a human being can humanly comprehend or know. Although recognizing as the slogan of the opening of every X-files episode forcefully affirms, "The truth is out there!" The truth might be "out there," but a human must be humble enough to know how much he or she really *does not* knows about the truth.

In other words, what McFague is arguing for is a type of "critical realism," which argues that there is such a thing as truth, but that humans *might not* know all there is to know about such a truth. So a posture of humility must be taken. This approach recognizes the finitude and limitations of human reason, without degenerating into relativism, a belief and value system, which *does not* recognize the existence of absolute, objective, truth, at all. In the process, McFague's "metaphoric theology" provides an alternative methodology to conceptualism for engaging in philosophical and theological reflection, a methodology which has "common ground" with autistic reasoning, "thinking in pictures."

Autistic hermeneutics might take humanity further in understanding truth and reality, than neurotypical hermeneutics, yet we autists are ultimately *still not* immune to the limitations of human reason, that neurotypicals are oftentimes plagued with. Even Grandin herself recognizes that there is much she still *does not* know about animals.

The same principle also applies to mystical revelation too! God might be talking to me, revealing Him to me, but that *does not* mean that I know everything there is to know about God or His Will or even the full significance of what God is trying to desperately reveal to me. All I know is that I hear a voice which sounds like the Voice of God and that I find it ultimately nourishing and life-giving.

There is no reason why this same approach can also be applied to demonology, too, as it already have been applied to certain positive theologies, such as the Doctrine of God. Such Christian religious images as Satan can also be understand as metaphors, signifying certain very real, even naturalistic, phenomena, existing in our cosmos. For example, there is some anthropological even scientific evidence, such as Girardian theory (anthropological) and neurotheology (scientific) that the person of Satan is signifying a certain part of our brains, which gives us the capacity for certain types of evil, such as "mimetic rivalry and scapegoating" (archaic religion and totalitarianism) and "anger married to ideology" (fundamentalism and liberal religion).

So according to this understanding, Satan is a metaphor (a personification to be exact) for describing and articulating an undergirding reality. Satan is a metaphor given to a particular phenomenon, which is very real, which is nothing less than a truth. Yet, the word Satan is only a human-made, culturally constructed, representation of the real thing, which the term Satan, signifies. In other words, Satan really *does not* exist in reality. Satin is a term, a label, a metaphor, the language used, to describe something in reality. Only reality itself is real, as Gandhi pointed-out onetime, "There is no other god higher than truth."

That is what truth is, reality, with reality including both the material and immaterial states of existence, which can be construed as the One True God, the monotheistic symbol for reality. I contend that the word God *is not* only a metaphor for "all-reality" but also a personification of "all reality."

A personification is figurative language which puts a "human face" on "inanimate objects" to make inanimate objects more concrete, intelligible even sympathetic such as "the sun is smiling on me." Yes, the sun *is not* literally shining on me (metaphoric theology), yet personifying the sun transforms "the sun" from an abstract conceptualization ("the sun") to a more concrete, intelligible manifestation ("Sir Brother Sun"), all of the sudden making the Sun a more sympathetic "historical actor," worthy of acknowledgement and respect, leading one to treat the Sun with more "ecological restraint" when "the sun" is addressed as "Sir Brother Sun" versus just "the sun."

Viewing Nature as a "person" versus a "thing" literally "puts a face" on overwhelming concepts, processes and problems, leading to sympathy, empathy even care. This leads to an individual human being developing a more "I-Thou" eco-kinship relationship with the Earth, where humans start to treat the Earth as sacred, holy and good. It is harder to dismiss a "live person" who you can have a personal relationship with, than an "abstraction with a belly," reducing "climate denial" in the process.

Personification is how most humans make sense of the world and our place in it, from First Nations around the world from mainland Africa to the South Pacific to the Americas, to peoples in Biblical and Medieval times, to many women and most ordinary people and a significant number of us on the autism spectrum. This is why environmentalists and other political activists have found story (such as making movies about the food industry) and reprehensive samples ("wildlife ambassador" programs like saving Bald Eagles from extinction) such a powerful tool for social and cultural change.

Yes, such a tool is anthromorphic, yes, such campaigns are at the "species level," but as a student of environmental history, I also know that the powerful industry interests in John Muir's day went to enormous efforts to prevent President Theodore Roosevelt from visiting Yosemite, for they feared that if the President visited Yosemite with environmental master John Muir as his guide, that Roosevelt might actually "fall in-love" with Yosemite and make Yosemite into a national park, casting industry out of Yosemite forever. Yes, Roosevelt did visit Yosemite with Muir as his guide, yes; Roosevelt absolutely "fell in-love" with the Yosemite wilderness and yes Roosevelt made Yosemite into a major National Park. Yosemite might never have been a National Park, if Roosevelt never visited Yosemite and absolutely "fell in-love" with the place.

If the same can be said for God, there is no reason, why we cannot say the same thing about Satan. This means that Satan is a metaphor for certain aspects of reality, which we sometimes judge and interpret as evil like imbalance, violent impulses, suffering, amorality and destruction. In this model, Satan is the personification of the evil in us (moral and systemic evil) and in our world (natural evil).

You might ask, "so what?" Why is this important in a discussion on autistic liberation theology? For two reasons, *first*, demonology is the unconscious narrative in the Christian tradition, which places the "sin-disability connection" identified by physical disability liberation theologian Nancy Eisland into a neurodiversity context. In fact, a significant number of Christians, even today, in the twenty-first century have this belief that "your negative emotions come from Satan" and "mental illness is demon possession." Making a certain un-Biblical, anti-Catholic stretch that just as you need sound Christian doctrine (orthodoxy) and consistent moral conduct befitting of a Christian (orthopraxy), you also need "right feeling" (orthopathy).

Such a view is unbiblical because many Biblical characters and even God Himself had many very natural human reactions to intense suffering and injustice like rage, sadness, dread even bitterness. Such a view is also anti-Catholic, for such a notion contradicts almost two thousand years of Christian Church History which saw negative human emotions as part of God's Creation used by God to foster healing and change, even wholeness, a position consistent with modern psychology and psychiatry. In other words, "right feeling" *is not* only socially oppressive, "right feeling" is also emotionally repressive. "Right feeling" is both repressive and oppressive.

*Second*, when exorcisms *are not* trying to "get" autism out of us, we as neurodiverse humans can use exorcisms safely and responsibility, with much wisdom and discernment, in certain situations, as a powerful anti-oppression, anti-repression, liberation ritual like how the Haitian people used Afrocentric exorcism rituals from African animalism and African American Christianity to gain their independence from French colonialism and slavery. This is how it can work!

These understandings of metaphorical theology and demonology are important paradigms for understanding the exorcism and its responsible place in my autist Christianity. First, when I exorcize Satan, I *am not* really, literally exorcizing Satan, there is no such thing as Satan. Satan, is a metaphor for something else, which I am really exorcizing. Second, what I am really exorcizing is false beliefs about myself, God, and the world, with my exorcism serving as a type of deconstruction, delegitimizing certain toxic narratives, which historically have been self-destructive to me.

In other words, I am engaging in deconstruction, taking apart neurotypicalism, pierce by pierce, argument by argument, ritualistically, using a Christian religious ritual as holistic psychopharmacology, "calling a spade a spade," using it as a form of resistance and rebellion, forcefully making my stand for truth against lies and betrayals, trying "to break" a sociocultural "spell" of oppressive ideologies, intergenerational cycles of violence, abusive relationships and dysfunctional social institutions.

You might have seen movies like the "Exorcist" and envision that is what an exorcism really is. That is not at all what I do. No levitation, no bizarre rituals or even dangerous demotic visions. Just deep healing and intense empowerment, in other words, exorcism to me is nothing less than a glorified intercessory prayer (Praying to God), although I have had some paranormal experiences, of certain energies being released from my body, as I exorcise my tendency to internalize my abuser, such as all their "guilt and shame."

This still begs the question----is not engaging in exorcism as an autist very dangerous? Tragically, there have been some very unfortunate incidents of autists like myself, being accidently injured even man-slaughtered, while performing exorcism rituals irresponsibility and for the wrong reasons.

This is because misguided and mistaken non-disabled, neurotypical celebrants of this ritual, mistake having an autistic personality as a type of demon procession. In the incident that I am aware of, the child died of suffocation. This is because the form of exorcism which the particular non-disabled, neurotypical, fundamentalist church was using, involved physically attacking a child, which was completely unnecessary, downright dangerous and not at all justified in the form of exorcism, I am advocating. Yet, I completely understand that because of these tragic and unjust "horror stories" why the various neurodiversity movements more specifically and the various disability movements more generally are negative and suspicious of exorcisms, for good reasons.

**No one should ever be allowed to hit you or suffocate you, for any reason! That is abuse!**

**All physical, emotional, economic and sexual abuse is a violation of your fundamental human rights!**

**All physical, emotional, economic and sexual abuse is against the law!**

Yet, I as an autist, need to do something to delegitimize and deconstruct, the harmful messages I have gotten about myself and who I am, so I can develop a sense of personal empowerment and a healthy self-esteem and manger my grief symptoms, my shame and my rage. What more peaceful way to do this, them to attribute these toxic messages to the Devil himself, something which does not even exist in "flesh and blood," "the perfect scapegoat" to appease our "shadow sides," so we can work through all our intense negative feelings and become whole and at peace with ourselves and our world.

In the Christian tradition, the Devil, otherwise known as Satan, is a recognizable symbol of the embodiment and personification of evil. So, as a Christian, I cannot take seriously anything which comes from Satan. My whole being has to reject the teachings of the Evil One, with everything I got. So, exorcist interventions done to neurodiverse humans by certain misguided Christian groups, has it backwards.

*I as an autist am called __not__ to exorcize my autistic identity, but instead as an autist, I am called __to__ exorcize certain negative neurotypical messages, imposed upon my autistic identity and reality.*

*Most importantly, exorcism does not need "forgiveness!"*

*You can "let go," "move on" and "react" nonviolently without needing to "forgive" aka enable your abuse, through being manipulated and entangled.*

In other words, by doing exorcisms, I am engaging in a process of "letting go." I am doing nothing less than renouncing neurotypicalism, reclaiming my autistic self-autonomy and free-agency in the process, liberating myself from within and without, doing something which is within my power to control. Something I need to do, to recover from trauma and victimization, becoming whole and empowered in the process. Mustering-up courage and inner strength to survive and fight injustice and evil in my life and in the world, all without needing "to forgive" aka "cheap grace!"[96]

Judith Herman, a psychiatrist, a foremost authority on PTSD (Post Traumatic Stress Disorder) and author of *Trauma and Recovery: The aftermath of violence---from domestic abuse to political terror* in her seminal work voiced two objections to the use of exorcisms with trauma survivors, which I want to address.[97]

*First*, peoples suffering from Post Traumatic Stress Disorder (PTSD) have been mislabeled as being "demon possessed" historically.

*Second,* peoples suffering from Post Traumatic Stress Disorder (PTSD) often metaphorically liken their desire for recovery to an "exorcism" versus a "race." In otherwords, peoples with PTSD often greatly desire "quick fixes" from their traumatic symptoms and memories, instead of what they really need to have addressed, "root causes," which often involves long-term recovery and integration of traumatic memories and perseverance through life struggles.

As someone who has great respect for Herman's approach, which is both sociologically savvy and psychologically productive, I agree that the issues which she raises are completely legitimate. Yet, I part ways with her, while taking into account her concerns, on the above two points about exorcism.

To answer the first objection, another reason why exorcisms were used historically, to treat those with PTSD, might be because exorcisms were being used as medicine, meaning that in the twenty-first century, exorcism rituals can be recovered and employed today as holistic psychopharmacology, employed in a responsible manner, to go along side other more conventional treatments for this condition, which effects so much of us on the spectrum. In terms of Herman's second objection, exorcism does not necessarily have to be a one-time ritual, although I have received one-time exorcisms in the past, where I have had amazing healing experiences with. I have found that I need to constantly exorcize myself. It is something I need to go back to again and again, in that sense, the exorcism gives me spring water and fresh, juicy orange slices as I run this race called life.

In other words, exorcism if used responsibility as I have shown can be nourishing to the autist soul.

That is *my eleventh authority being an autist Christian*, *exorcism as deconstruction*.

### School Studies to Learn about Life

Richard Foster writes about the role of study in ones spiritual development,

> Many Christians remain in bondage to fears and anxieties simply because they do not avail themselves of the Discipline of study. They may be faithful in church attendance and earnest in fulfilling their religious duties, but still they are not changed. I am not here speaking of those who are going through mere religious forms, but of those who are genuinely seeking to worship and obey Jesus Christ as Lord and Master. They may sing with gusto, pray in the Spirit, live as obediently as they know, even receive divine visions and revelations, and yet the tenor of their lives remains unchanged. Why? Because they have never taken up one of the central ways God uses to change us: study.[98]

Even through study or any other intellectual pursuit *is not* a substitute for a personal relationship with the Living God. Yes, many Christians and Jews oftentimes make the mistake of replacing personal intimacy with God, with impersonal intellectual pursuits. Assuming that God stop talking to mortals thousands of years ago and the only way they can experience the Voice of God is through their intellectual faculties, such as human reason, engaging in endless study of sacred and profane texts, without a direct encounter with the Divine. This of course in my opinion is one of the central mistakes of both Rabbinical Judaism and Scholastic Christianity. In reality, according to Lord Jesus Christ, "God is not the God of the dead, but of the living. You are badly mistaken!" (Mark 12: 26-28). Even today! God lives!

I am now going to make the case that study even through not a substitute for the Living God, does play a vital and integral role in ones faith and spiritual development and growth, however. Most certainly, study plays a vital and integral role, in the faith-life of my autist Christianity, with the Discipline of Study, playing, no small role in my liberation as an autist.

Mainly, the Discipline of Study helps me to learn about life, "the way things are" and why, coupled with what I can reasonably expect from life, how I can improve mine and others "lot in life." Study even helps me to celebrate and embrace life through helping me to better appreciate life.

In other words, "school studies," defined as structured, formalized and systematized learning versus the random consuming of information and experiences can help me to critically reflect upon and even empathically engage "all-reality," "the world-around-me" and "the world-in-me." This engagement with the world includes not only the human world, but also the nonhuman world and not only the nonhuman world, but also the spirit world, even God and my relationship with Him, encompasses my intellectual pursuit for the truth, which I am hoping will set others and myself free (John 8:32). Not just "freedom from oppression" (freedom from pain, suffering, fear and want, "creature comforts"), but also "freedom to participate" in the pursuit of creating a better world for all peoples and creatures (freedom to speak, write, teach and act, "living with dignity").

Many of the neurotypicals in my life have this strong category called, "life," which I do not have being a person with autism, mainly because I do not overgeneralize to such a degree about fundamental questions of existence. Many neurotypicals often make statements like, "Life is this…" "Life is that…" "In life…" "Life principles," are vague, universal, even metaphysical claims which I do not fully understand.

What neurotypicals define as "life" is not "life" in a biological sense or even in a human development sense. Neurotypicals are not even talking about life in a spiritual sense. The word life in this case is being used as a "code word" for survival. At heart, the metaphor of life, in this context, is being used as a gage of one's expectations, about what one can reasonably get out of their time Here on Earth. In other words, what one can "realistic" expect from their existence in this world, within the constraints of "what is," e.g., "life is unfair!"

Many neurotypicals come to these sweeping conclusions about the meaning of life, through engagement with life and life experiences, which for most Westerners is working and playing hard, dating, making and breaking friendships and the like, coming to the conclusion, that what they have been exposed to is "the way the world works" "the real world."[99] Outside the Western world, "life" also includes the Natural World and the Spirit World. Outside the Western world "life experiences" also includes initiation rituals into adulthood, hero's journeys, religious ceremonies, mystical experiences, pilgrimages, intimately knowing a particular place, interspecies communications, healing miracles, adventure, communal care, comradely, learning a cultural tradition and experiencing beauty, hospitality and stability.[100]

In many ways, the category called "life" is the twenty-first century's answer for superstition. Something someone beliefs in the absence of a confirmed truth. A false, incorrect belief! An error! A mistake!

At one time in human history, people had all kinds of "superstitions" about the nature of the cosmos and human being's place in it, mainly because their lives were dependent on a world, which they did not create, nor could they totally control or even completely understand.

As humans created cities and high civilizations, creating artificial environments in the process, humans could have more control over their own environment. Humans than designed the conditions and terms of their existence, within the constraints of these enclosures. So, when things went wrong, a fire, an explosion, it can no longer be blamed on the "gods" or some other mysterious supernatural entity. This is because when a disaster happens in a city, a fire, an explosion or the like, it just did not happen for some mysterious unexplainable reason, it was the result of human error or the like, so a person or group in their community can be held responsible for the action.

What went wrong all of a sudden can now be explained in terms of fallible human error, meaning it is within ones power to hold the guilty human party responsible for their actions, for the guilty party is a flesh and blood human being, like everyone, not a god-like force, immune to human powers of intervention, with the perpetrator's final vain appeal to the supernatural to dismiss any claims for justice and fairness, failing on unsympathetic ears. Hence, a supernatural explanation was no longer deemed necessary, to explain the significance of a tragedy. As a result, social justice-like movements began to emerge.

Now as twenty-first century human civilization progressed to a level of complexity, sophistication and power unattained by any other earlier human civilization, within the last five hundred years, human civilization itself has now become an epic force to contend with, in terms of its immense power not only over individual human lives and human communities, but even over the very cosmos, which to our ancestors, was a Universe which they did not even create or control or even understood, yet they were completely dependent upon this uncontrollable Universe, for their survival. In the twenty-first century, this wild and untamable Cosmos is now under a significant amount of human control.

As artificially created human systems like cities, globalized political economies and technology grids become more and more deeply entrenched in the order of the Cosmos, while remaining increasingly insular to herculean efforts by individuals and groups to effectuate necessary changes, in response to some of the most unfathomable injustices, sufferings and disasters in human history. Many neurotypicals, to avoid all-out insanity, are beginning to attribute almost god-like, supernatural powers, to socially produced, culturally constructed, human institutions, ignoring and dismissing over three centuries of socio-political theory which has adequately established that these forces have "the number of a person" (Revelations 13: 18) in a vain attempt to make sense of a seemingly all-powerful world civilization, heading toward a perceived inevitable destruction, where the individual is both powerless to do anything about it, yet is dependent upon such a broken system, which such an individual did not create, nor control, or even totally understands, yet like our ancestors, we are also dependent upon such an entity, which also is powerful, uncontrollable and unintelligible.

This new superstition is also compounded by the increasing isolation numbers of people are feeling from traditional systems of meaning such as religion and culture, friends and family, community and wilderness. The various religions, cultures and bioregions of the world have nourished and sustained the human race across countless geopolitical locales and time periods, emotionally, spiritually, even relationally for most of human evolution, through humanity's many trials and tribulations, victories and defeats, joys and desolations, hopes and despairs, births, deaths and rebirths, playing no small role in the survival of the human species, over the millennia. Adding a certain sense of meaning, significance, even order to people's lives. Helping people work through their hopes, dreams, and longings and mornings, when these too are dashed, helping people not to give up on surviving and reproducing. Inoculating individuals and whole groups of people, from anxiety, despair, worthlessness and other self-esteem problems, through ones religion and religious leaders, making it clear where everyone's place in the Cosmos was.

Even those at the lost rungs of society could be comfortable "in their own skin," for they knew who they were, what their place in their society and the greater cosmos was at all times, faithfully fulfilling their preordained destinies. Even such people enjoyed a certain sense of safety, stability and belonging, leading to inner peace, even sparks of happiness and joy.

Many in the twenty-first century people do not even have their religion to fall back on, as an anchor in a time of great turmoil, anxiety and uncertainty, to make sense of things and work through circumstances which are beyond their control. Even those of us who are part of a religion even a faith community, still do not have the emotional, ceremonial, moral, relational, cosmological and mythic coherence, comfort and stability that our ancestors had, enjoyed and were deeply nourished by, especially during times of adversity.

Oftentimes our living traditions, theologies and communities, are all too often riddled with corruption, inconsistencies, hypocrisies, heresies, abuse, insecurity, inferiority complexes and all around confusion and lackluster. Not to mention, constantly being highjacked by political propaganda, charity scams, spiritual fraud, fashionable ideas, nationalistic fervor and cults of personality on both the left and the right alike in America.

I would even be so bold to say that from my experiences, I have sadly encountered after years of aggressively searching, that there is not all that much True Christianity, left in existence, in our twenty-first century world. I mean True Christianity, not in the sense, that a particular faith communities has to believe and act just as I would personally want or demand, but True Christianity, in terms of trying to faithfully, authentically, sincerely, lovingly and consistently try to live the core tenets of the Christian Faith, discerned with an active, living, continuous engagement with the Holy Spirit, participating in the current works and projects of the Living God, who is very much alive, even in the twenty-first century. In otherwords, American Christianity has not only developed historical amnesia as many experts contend, I argue that American Christianity also has spiritual amnesia too.

Postmodern neurotypical humanity to fill the void of adapting to a pre-human, natural, sacred, Cosmos, replaced with mal-adapting to a manmade, artificial, profane cosmos of humankind's own making, combined with growing up in a world devoid of religious meaning, has resulted in the reemergence of superstitious ways of looking at the world. These superstitions meet three human spiritual needs: 1) To make sense of the senseless. 2) To muster some level of control over our own destiny. 3) To make a vain attempt to connect to a world, a reality, a power, beyond our current entanglements in despair, hopelessness, powerlessness, even fatalism.

Deep down, could it be that what I call, "pagan fundamentalism," is really a type of "holy longing" for something beyond our artificial dystopia, which is doing nothing less than breaking our spirits and destroying our hope for a better future. I am going to argue that not only is this, the case, but in such longing lies the hope for both the neurotypical and neurodiverse races alike.

What is this hope? There is still "a nice, big, round world" outside of humanity, which was not created by human hands and still remains beyond human control. By knowing this world, we can than reconstruct the lost meanings of religion, culture and nature, giving Natures and Cultures new meaning and purpose, forcefully affirming All Life in the process.

What is this world? This world is the Spirit World, otherwise known as the Kingdom of Heaven, the Kingdom of God, the New Jerusalem, the City of God, the New Earth, The Messianic Age or The Supernatural.

Where is this world? This otherworld encloses, encompasses, envelopes even permeates our world, trying to desperately revitalize our world with nonviolence and social justice, natural beauty and true love. For this is the type of world we live in: a world marked by its beauty, wonder and goodness. In other words, "Heaven" is the real, "real world." Heaven is the undergirding reality of our Earth, the process by which the Earth holds together, the Earth's true nervous system, not human beings.

Yet, how can we twenty-first century human beings get this "real world" experience, in a culture and time period where the resurgence in superstitious understandings of the world has become a virtual cottage industry. Between the intense popularity of such New Age approaches as "the Law of Attraction," where it is contended that people can control their seemingly uncontrollable external realities through changing their interior thought processes toward the positive, such as, if you think a traffic light turning green, it would will turn green. To Cable Networks featuring On-Demand horror movies, literally making every day of the year Halloween to the intense popularity of the "Left Behind" series to the widespread concern about a massive alien conspiracy and subsequent government-wide cover-up. Demons, devils, angels and even vampires are back with a vengeance. While, it is amazing that witchcraft, the occult, psychics, and tarot cards, are more popular than ever, despite thousands of years of monotheism and over five hundred years of scientific demystification.

Modern humans are more spiritually desperate than ever for dreams, visions and oracles, prophesies, revelations, miracles, epic battles between good and evil, a world where dragons and fierce monsters terrorize the locals and where chivalrous knights once again roam an enchanted landscape, rescuing villages from abject terror. Modern humanity is desperate for the whimsical, the enchanted and the mysterious. Modernity humanity is desperate for any sign, signal, even the slightest inklings that there is such a thing as The Supernatural. Wearingly holding out for a more powerful, more meaningful, larger realm that can lead modern humanity out of its prison of loneliness, alienation, meaninglessness and hopelessness, where one's greatest dreams, longings and desires are given life and one is delivered from endless adversity, suffering and darkness. There is definitely an audience for this recent rebirth of the Enchanted Garden through the now popular fantasy literature and film genre.

Yet, once the latest installment of the popular Harry Potter series is finished and put back on the shelf, once one saw the latest "Alison and Wonderland Movie" in 3D at the movie theater and after one has been to Disney World, umpteenth times, which provide only a facsimile of a transcendent world beyond machines and bureaucracies, one returns to their ordinary mechanistic, materialistic world. A world filled with problems without easy solutions, one crisis after another, endless busyness, endless commitments, sacrificing greatly for a life, one might not even want, frustrations, disappointments, compromises, personality conflicts, demands, pressure, stress, anxiety, embedded in a landscape of deadness, lifelessness, even physical isolation. The computer is dead. The fax machine dead. The flickering florescent light. Dead. All dead. All lifeless. The only sign of life-another human being. That is if you are fortunate enough, to even have that. We in the twenty-first century are imprisoned in a world of deadness. Cut off from life, living things, fresh air and sunshine, as well as beauty, mystery and adventure. Epic battles of good and evil have been replaced with ordinary struggles for negotiation and compromise through the endless drama of moral gray areas.

So, some neurotypicals have settled with the "consolation prize" of "that's life!" to fill the voids left behind by the absence of Nature, Spirit, religion, even humanity, in their lives, to meet their need to make meaning, to gain self-control and to hold onto the possibility that there is a larger spiritual even cosmic dimension to their existence. The word "life" then becomes such a sacred canopy, in a mechanistic, bureaucratized, manmade cosmos, which is fundamentally dehumanizing.

Life often becomes to the neurotypical, even the Christian neurotypical, their primary everyday connection to the possibility of their being a transcendent, larger world, which both encompasses and permeates their ordinary, seemingly meaningless reality. This particular vision of the transcendent might not be fair or even just. It is not even personal. And, there is not much love in it either. But at least, such a spiritual sentiment at least makes sense to the person. It can be controlled. Somewhat. And, it allows room for free choices. It provides the person the opportunity to learn rules and make certain choices in their own best interest within the constraints of these rules. It even leaves open the possibility for mystery. That what is happening to them is beyond their understanding, giving them vain hope, that what is happening to them, might in fact be part of a much larger plan, which they do not fully comprehend. It does nothing less than keeps alive that there is a God! Somehow, someway!

Yet, this Model of God leaves me as an autist, both spiritually and theologically wanting. The term "life" leaves me spiritually wanting, because chalking off to "that's life!" leaves me feeling profoundly unsatisfied. This is because the axiom "life is not fair" is a negative, pessimistic, even fatalistic, assessment of our world. It leads to me feeling hopeless and in despair. It makes me feel trapped. Doomed. With no end in sight! This leads me to sink even deeper into depression, darkness and desolation. It certainly does not help me. It only makes me feel worst. At best, this approach is counterproductive. It solves nothing. It fixes nothing. It does nothing less than trivializes the seriousness of my issues, making me feel resentful too. It certainly does not empower me. It just makes me feel terrible. It even makes me feel judged and misunderstood. This is just the spiritual problems.

Theologically, "life is unfair," even Christians spout this phrase, does nothing less than undermine my faith and hope for salvation in Jesus Christ. It does nothing less than makes me stumble in my faith. It makes me feel like that I am not saved. That no one is saved. That there is no such thing as salvation. I am damned. We are all damned. Our whole world is damned. We are just stuck with the world we have, with all its problems and brokenness. It even makes me feel like the world is literally a living Hell. It certainly does not make me feel "at-home" in the world.

By one saying "life is unfair," one is also implying that "God is not fair." Which is an unbiblical, even heretical statement about the God we confess as Christians to be a God whom we believe is good, loving, just and even righteous. This mentality does nothing less than "with wisdom and eloquence," empty "the Cross of Christ…of its power" (I Corinthians 16-18)" in my life. It makes me feel like my faith is "in vain." It extinguished "the flame of the Gospel" in my life. It causes me to stumble. It theologically confuses me.

Yet, I know deep down, that "life *is not* fair" *is not* true, neither metaphysically (statements about the nature of reality) or theologically (truth about God's world). This is because; I know from my studies of sociology that it is not "life which is not fair," life is neutral, whatever this vague term word "life" even means, it is "society which is not fair." Many unfair things in our world are not systemic to the Universe, but are the result of socially produced human institutions, which were created by human beings, usually for the self-serving purpose of empowering the ruling elites. There is nothing natural, cosmic or supernatural about these social institutions. These social institutions are nothing less than "arbitrary and capricious" human precepts, crafted for the purpose, for keeping the elite in power and in control of the "means of production."

Theologically, the axiom "life is unfair" is not even a monotheistic concept, contradicting the tenets of all three monotheistic religions (Judaism, Christianity and Islam) which categorically affirms and confesses God's justice and righteousness. In fact, the axiom, "life is unfair," comes from an axiom in Buddhism, taken out of its cultural and religious context. In fact, no less than the Dahlia Lama advocates this position to Westerners. One must not underestimate the power, influence and infiltration that Buddhism and other Eastern philosophies have on modern-day Western culture, particularly among the post-60s generations. Buddhist concepts and practices, have taken over the American landscape like wild fire. To fill the void left behind by monotheism. When these concepts and practices, infiltrate the Christian Church and get incorporated into the Christian religion, yet are fundamentally irreconcilable with central Biblical or Christian tenets, we have hearsay on our hands. Such hearsay can do nothing less than corrupt, destabilize even undermine the Christian message. It can cause many to stumble in their faith.

This situation is compounded by the fact that the pagan ancestry of many Christian civilizations, also believed in "gods" which were also unfair, violent and irrational. Western civilization is only insolated by a precious thin veneer of Judeo-Christianity, which keeps the Western world, barely above paganism and all the scapegoating and sacred violence, which goes along with it.

So, certain Buddhist understandings resonate well with the pagan Christian's ancestral soul, causing pagan mythology to be resurrected from thousands of years of extinction, where after thousands of years of being debunked, is now believed again, with a vengeance, usurping and corrupting the essential Christian message of love, justice and righteousness, in the process, causing much confusion in the process.

The spiritually starved Western soul leaches onto such a principle with everything it's got, creating a kind of "pagan fundamentalism," which is just as much a reaction to "Future Shock" as Islamic or Christian fundamentalism and just as dangerous, in no small way. With Buddhism used to recover pagan mythology in a demystified era, replacing the loving, just and righteous God of the Bible with the unfair, violent and irrational goddess of paganism, liken to the Great Whore (Revelations 17-19), prophesized in the Book of Revelations, who will enable the Beast, to unleash great evil on the world, by co-opting all peoples, by her seductive promise of false comfort, in a time of great human desperation.

Also, this newly recovered goddess archetype is not revitalized religious language signifying the glory and majesty of neither the Natural World nor is it a celebration of femininity or womanhood, but instead the metaphor of the goddess, as it stands today, is "irrelevant," "exclusive" and "harmful" religious language, legitimizing and perpetuating, an unjust social order. The mark of the beast is "a number of a person" (Revelations 13: 18) after all. Like prophesized in the Book of Revelations.

Now that we know that all this evil in our world is "a number of a person." We now have a place to begin to stop it. We now know that it is within the realm of plausibility that unfairness and injustice can be stopped. Or, at least reduced. It does not have to be that way. A more fair and just world is possible.

I have discerned all this about the meaning of life and our world, because unlike many neurotypicals, I do not rely solely on my life experiences, to learn about the meaning of life. Instead I rely on what I read in books and articles, what I learn in school and continuing education and what I hear in church, lectures and discussion groups, to learn about the meaning of life. This gives me a different perspective on the "way things are," which is sometimes radically different, than what most neurotypicals believe about their world and themselves and what is possible.

I of course, take very seriously my life experiences, even allowing my life experiences to both inform and formulate my ideas and worldview. Using my life experiences to ask questions about my life and my world. I even use my life experiences to formulate hypotheses about reality. I certainly try to discern patterns based on my life experiences, even trying to make meaning from them, in the process, learning from my life experiences.

Where I part ways with neurotypicals is that I do not judge the nature of reality with "what my eyes sees" and "what my ears hear," but instead through the lens of a spirit of righteousness, I judge the world-around-me and in-me, liken to the same manor Holy Scripture says our Messiah will judge the poor (Isaiah 11: 3-4).

Not to say that I am claiming to be the Messiah or God. I am certainly *not* the Messiah or God. I am a fallible, broken, sinful, mortal human being like everyone else.

What I am saying is that my methodology for attaining truth is liken to the depiction of the Messiah in the Bible, in that I am able to make meaning beyond the immediate circumstances, realities and superficialities of what I am being confronted by on a day-to-day basis. I know deep down like Saint Paul, that what I see will pass away and what I do not see is immortal (Hebrews 11: 6-8) and that what I am not fighting "is not flesh and blood, but principalities and powers" (Ephesians 6: 12). That what I am experiencing in my everyday reality is not all there is, all there ever was, all there will ever be or could be, at some time in the future. Things are not the way they are by accident or have they been like they are now, for all time, since the beginning of time nor are things done the same way across all groups of peoples, cultures and time periods. Instead, "the way things are" are the result of deeply entrenched social, cultural and historical forces, idiosyncratic to particular groups of peoples, regions of the world and time periods.

Part of the secret to me being a bully survivor and not succumbing to an abusive totalitarian environment is that I have understood profoundly, maybe even subconsciously, sense a young age, that there is a whole Universe, beyond middle school or whatever the captivity situation, I had to endure, since a young age. This is what helped me survive, physically, psychologically, vocationally, even spiritually. What kept my soul alive, was that deep down, I knew there was a whole world beyond my temporary, present circumstances and the sacred canopy given to me about "who am I?" and "who are they?," used to imprison, isolate and break me into conforming to my circumstances. Circumstances, which I found to be both dehumanizing and plain inaccurate (a distorted view of the world and myself).

My hope, that I would not be in this harmful and traumatic environment forever, did nothing less than helped me survive. I held onto the hope that one day I would be able to both deconstruct and refute this toxic sacred canopy given to me, replacing it with a richer, fuller, more satisfying sacred canopy. That I would not be in this place forever. Exposed to these same old corrupt ideas forever. I would not be existing in this state forever. I would eventually get out of this environment. Amount to something. Do something important. Be something important. Be respected. Become successful. Even become a respectable person in society. Making a difference. Making the world a better place. I only needed to survive and get out of this situation, somehow, someway. Fight with everything I got, holding onto hope, no matter what. Even, when success eludes me, I still keep going back to the endless well of school studies, to find out what went terribly wrong. What was thwarting my effort? How can I do things differently? What issue have I avoided addressing or working through? What is the snag? How do I get beyond my current impasse? Never blaming myself for things which are not my fault. But, even this question, is also investigated.

Now, that I am no longer, in school, I still engage School Studies. Accessing information, which was not available to me, when I was school, responding to these readings, through my writings, scholarships and critiques, telling me a very different story about the nature of reality than neurotypicals, "that a better world is possible!" Where I have rediscovered time and time again, that "lifelong learning" has the power to set me free, with "the truth," with "the truth" becoming my greatest "source of healing and empowerment," my greatest weapon of resistance against ableism, normalcy and neurotypicalism.

That is ***my twelfth and final authority being an autist Christian***, using my studies to learn about life, through ***secondary reflection***.[101]

This now completes my discussion of my twelve theological authorities, my twelve religious sacraments which I receive, to access the Living God, the sociosymbolic life of the Christian Church and my own spiritual history as a neurodiverse human. I go back, again and again, to these twelve authorities for "healing and empowerment." These twelve authorities are nothing less than my twelve "sources of healing and empowerment" which allow me to Ascent to Belief in God at all.

Now, for the rest of my autistic liberation theologian project, I am going to turn my attention to offer you concrete guidance on how my model of contextual, liberation theology could be integrated into your own "situation" and "context," whether you are a fellow autist like me, a cousin from another disability community, a member of another oppressed minority group, an environmentalist or animal activist, from a Christian or another World Religion group or you are a friend, family member, ally or caregiver of a brother or sister on the autism spectrum.

This final section will offer tips for those just getting started, concrete guidance for communities, existing models and success stories and the positive benefits of including and accommodating human beings on the autism spectrum.

**Chapter Four:**

**Pilgrimage Tips for Other Aspies Beginning Their Own Soul's Journey into God**

I am going to briefly discuss four key strategies which helped liberate my autistic spirit. These are four recommendations based on what was helpful for me.

First, some disclaimers!

- My wisdom is only as good as you are able to integrate my recommendations into your own personal situation and context. Remembering that each neurodiverse human is totally unique and will have to figure-out on his or her own what "works" and "does not work." My written wisdom *is not* a substitute for your own lived, embodied, personal experiences of being a full human being on the autism spectrum within the context of living within a particular social, cultural or geopolitical location which might be different then mine. For example, I am a man. There are many women on the autism spectrum too. For example, I come from a Judeo-Christian cultural background, autism cuts across racial, ethnic, cultural even religious boundaries. Autism even cuts across sexual orientation boundaries too. For example, Dawn Prince Hughes is openly lesbian. I live in the United States, there are also neurodiverse humans living in Canada, Mexico, Europe, Asia, Africa, Latin America, the Middle East, even in Australia. So by all means take a highlighter or a pen and mark all passages in this liberation theology which are relevant to your own particular situation and context and cross-out what *does not apply*.

- My wisdom is also not a substitute for working with a trained medical professional (doctor, nurse, councilor, psychiatrist or special education teacher). Nor is it a substitute for working with a licensed clinical social worker, therapist or psychologist. My wisdom *cannot* diagnose autism or any other secondary disorder either *nor is it* a substitute for prescription medications. So by all means, if you are having psychologically destabilizing reactions, put down my book immediately and get professional help. The role and gift of my wisdom *is* to supplement and complement conventional medical understandings and treatments for autism, to provide information and an argument and to tell my story. Any other claims about the role and use of this document is technically illegal! This book *is* a spiritual book, *not* a medical book!

**My First Tip-The Magic Words to Make It Stop:**

Your first step to coming to a Belief in God is to get your oppression symptoms under control and get to physical and emotional safety. Gandhi said "God would never dare approach a hungry man without bread."

As a neurodiverse human, your primary disadvantages in American society are wanting in terms of health care, education, employment and love. God's first priority with you is to get the life-giving health care, stimulating education, meaningful employment and love you deserve, before burdening you with morality and doctrine.

When I am talking about health care, I *am not* talking about "applied behavior analysis" which is more about "social control" (making you pleasing to privileged neurotypicals) than about your "personal healing." I am talking about you finding medical professionals which treat you with "dignity and respect," who treat you as a "whole person," who gives you a correct diagnosis, who you can rely on to authorize "reasonable accommodations" in school and employment situations, who can "advocate" for government disability services and are "safe" people to talk to during a crisis and who address secondary disorders *only.*

Secondary Disorders include anxiety, depression, Obsessive Compulsive Disorder (OCD), Post Traumatic Stress Disorder (PTSD), addictions, anger management and any physical ailments like insomnia, nightmares or myofascial syndrome. Anything else is imperialism!

When I am talking about a stimulating education I am talking about an education where you actually learn versus just doing "busy work," where you are exposed to the various academic disciplines from the natural sciences to the humanities not just learning a mere trade, where you receive "information about yourself and others," where you are being prepared to work in the field of your choice.

I am also talking about an education which gives you the "reasonable accommodations" entitled to you under the Americans with Disability Act (ADA) such as extended time on tests and papers, being able to take a test on a computer and/or in a quiet room and getting a peer note-taker for class lectures, so the "playing field is leveled" and you can perform at your optimum and reach your potential in life.

My academic training has been my greatest defense against becoming a victim!

When I am talking about meaningful employment, I am talking about finding non-discriminatory employment and volunteering opportunities. I am talking about employment and volunteer opportunities where you get "reasonable accommodations," where you are treated with the respect you deserve and where you are appreciated. I am talking about opportunities where you get a fair compensation for your "hard work" such as a "Living Wage" and enough money, services and benefits where you *are not* going to go hungry, thirsty or end-up on the street and are able to afford the medical services you need to function independently, at all. Where you get the legally required amounts of breaks, time-off and vacation time, where you can work in a physically and emotionally safe work environment, where you do not have to perform tasks which are unethical, illegal, unprofessional or make you feel morally uncomfortable in any way, where you can work in a profession you enjoy and are competent in.

All of the above is the minimalist standard for meaningful work! All of the above will add "meaning and purpose" to your life! Anything else is exploitation!

The minimalist standard for having "enough love" in your life *is not* being physically, emotionally, sexually, economically or financially abused or neglected in anyway. Having "enough love" means having other live, human beings in your life who accept you just the way you are and genuinely care about you, who also allows you to recipicate their acceptance and care. Having "enough love" means having at least one or two "stable relationships" in your life that you can depend upon during your "darkest hours" such as a family member, a best friend, caregiver or mentor, outside a professional relationship like a psychiatrist or therapist. Having "enough love" means being part of a nourishing community, having an animal companion, taking care of plants and having access to wild Nature. Anything less, is dehumanizing![102]

Yet, how do you do this when your health care providers, your educators, your employers and your own people are your oppressors?

One of the latest conflicts between the autistic pride movement and the mental health establishment is over the new DSM IV definition for autism where categories like "Asperger's" and "low functioning" are removed and everyone receives a singular diagnosis called "Autism Spectrum Disorder" whether you have an intellectual disability or you are have a genius IQ.

The mental health establishment's reasons for this change were to account for all the constellation of differences in symptoms, an admission that everyone on the autism spectrum are totally unique, individual human beings, who cannot easily be lumped into categories like "low functioning" or "high functioning" anymore, with the hope of developing more individualized treatments. The later can also be a problem too, as I will demonstrate. Some in the autism movement objected to removing the less stigmatizing Asperger's diagnosis and being "lumped in" with peoples with intellectual disabilities for obvious reasons.

Yet, in my situation, going from a Pervasive Developmental Disorder (PDD) to an Asperger's Syndrome diagnosis only "modestly reformed" my lot in life. I only got "partial healing" at best. Neurotypicals were having less severe reactions, my intelligence was respected and my "emotions" and "inner life" were being addressed for the first time in my entire life by the mental health establishment through using Cognitive Behavior Therapy to treat my anxiety and depression symptoms versus "Applied Behavior Analysis." Yet, there was a very serious flaw in both Cognitive Behavior Therapy and my Asperger's diagnosis, mainly neither one addressed trauma nor situation change.

Cognitive Behavior Therapy at-best helped me manage anxiety and depressive symptoms, at worst "set in motion" some of the worst psychological destabilization I have ever experienced in my entire life, before or since, to the point where I became non functional because this treatment assumes no prior traumatic history or active abuse situations.

It left very little room open to the possibility that my worst fears and longings might actually have a basis in reality, such as that I might be in an unsafe, untenable situation, that I was actually being abused, that I was living below my potential in life, that I had yet to have a good experience in certain areas of my life which most neurotypicals take for granted, that what clinicians were proposing were unrealistic, even dangerous. Most importantly, they wanted to blame everyone but society and god-forbid themselves for my past and present psychological problems. They wanted to blame my mother, "the refrigerator mother theory" revisited and revitalized. They wanted to blame it on my liberal arts education where I learned a non-psychological, non-medical, non-mechanistic, non-passivity narrative about myself and others, which frankly based on my horrific experience I am more inclined to trust and believe, for oppression is my experiences.

Most disturbing of them all, they blamed me for all my problems. They were all about "blaming the victim!" Where these so-call mental health experts were completely insular to the notion that it is in fact possible to change my situation even society, like over two centuries of critical social theory, nonviolent political activism and participatory democracy even existed, contradicting everything I learned in school, like making "superficiality," "heathenism" even "lying" into carnal virtues instead of noxious vices.

They just wanted me to "over function" even through "I will never feel good enough." They just wanted me to psychologically adjust "to worsening and worsening conditions." They just wanted me "to passively accept my fate in life." They had this philosophy "life is not fair!" and were all about instilling "learned helplessness!"

An Asperger's diagnosis has its own stigma issues such as the "geek" stereotype.

For example, the "geek" stereotype causes practioners, caregivers and ordinary people "off the street" to make the incorrect assumption that I am this math and computer whiz. In reality, I was a C math student in high school, I was an A history student throughout graduate school and I am just as bad with technology as any neurotypical. This is because I have a "performance" disability according to my latest 2005 neuropsychological evaluation, while scoring in the exceptional range on "memory" and above average on "abstraction."

The "geek" stereotype also causes neurotypicals to assume that I am this loner because I have an Asperger's diagnosis. In reality, I can get just as lonely as any neurotypical who does not "fit in," just ask anyone who has ever known me.

Also, the "geek" stereotype insists that I am "low functioning" social-emotionally. In reality, as anyone who has ever known me can attest, I have a much a higher emotional IQ than my diagnosis. Most importantly, the "geek" stereotype incorrectly assumes that I have no prior traumatic-abuse history.

Also, the "geek" stereotype seems to give neurotypicals the impression that I am already getting all these "wrap around services" and everything is just "hunky dory." In reality, I now have a PTSD diagnosis, I *am not* getting all the "help" I need and I continue to remain vulnerable to revictimization (because neurotypical society *has not* fully acknowledged abelism and normalcy nor has it sincerely reformed or changed their beliefs and practices).

Most disconcerting of all, an Asperger's diagnosis "funnels" me into very specific, prescribed social roles like being a computer programmer, a technocrat, a librarian or a hard scientist in much the same way in previous generations women were "funneled" into homemaking, nursing and secretarial pools. Where intelligent, well-educated, qualified, hard working, passionate women were "glass ceilinged" based on their gender alone. As a neurodiverse man, I feel "glass bottomed" out of the "helping professions" such as religion, theology, activism and teaching. Where the liberal arts establishment has made humanities and social science courses a "chilly classroom climate" for neurodiverse students and the "helping professions" have become neurologically chauvinistic.

Because of the new DSL IV diagnostic category "Autism Spectrum Disorder," I am getting individualized treatment for the first time in my entire life. But when I really started to make "real progress" was when I insisted on a PTSD diagnosis for once I got this diagnosis I went from being treated like "a mistake" to being treated like "a survivor."[103]

**This is "the magic word" to make it all stop: *I was abused! I am being abused!*[104]**

This is because "abuse" is something the mental health establishment takes very seriously and is obliged to investigate and take action on, *especially* if you are a minor, if you are a "ward of the state" or if you are no one's "legal guardian." Making an "abuse" accusation will lead to 100 % liberation from your medical abuser. Insisting on a PTSD evaluation will lead to your medical professional proactively trying to protect you from present and future "abuse" situations.

Also, there are psychological and physical medical treatments available just for "recovering" from "trauma" including certain types of medications, therapies, support groups, techniques and strategies. There are even treatments for "trust" issues too. Also "solitude," "assertiveness training," "self-esteem building," "safe environments," "healing relationships," "physical exercise," "music," "celebration," "acceptance," "finding socially acceptable outlets," even "intuition," "holistic medicine," "self-knowledge" and "getting information" are all clinically proven to manage your own violent behaviors such as "meltdowns" and "acting-up."[105]

If and only if, your medical professional still *does not* recognize your traumatic abuse history and you are *still* having all the symptoms of PTSD which are resistant to "emotional regulation," such as nightmares, insomnia, panic attacks, depression and unexplained physical symptoms like unexplained jaw pain, then you are ready for the "radical" option. To start to take responsibility for your own body, your own health and your own life and start systemically "firing" and "replacing" members of your own treatment team.

If you start to encounter intimidation, remember these three mantras:[106]

- ***I was abused! All abuse is against the law!***
- ***I have rights too! I deserve treatment!***
- ***"It's not my fault! It's not my responsibility!"***

Then remember your three legal rights:[107]

- ***If you are over the age of eighteen and you do not have a "legal guardian" you are here by choice, you are not legally obligated to be in therapy, psychiatry or in a program, unless "you are a threat to yourself or others" or there by a "court order."***

- ***For this reason, "Suicide is not an option!" In other words, when you share suicidal or homicidal thoughts or threats to a licensed medical professional or any other person in a position of authority, they are legally obligated to take action, meaning you forfeit your above rights! The good news, as the establishment better understands anxiety disorders, more and more practioners are able to make a distinction between a suicidal/homicidal thought and a threat or action. If you are going to "get out," you cannot come across as suicidal or homicidal in any way, anyways you need a strong "will to live" to survive and you need to be "nonviolent" for your case to be heard and won!***

- ***You are also entitled to confidentiality! It's the law! A therapist, psychiatrist or councilor cannot talk to an employer, a previous provider, other members of your treatment team, the press, the police, a community leader, a friend, a family member or even your own parents without getting your written permission first. So you can talk about your issues freely "without it coming back to bite you," even taboo subjects!***

- ***Your insurance company can also be a powerful alley! Insurance companies will not pay for treatments which are "not working." That's also a waste of their time and money too!***

These are your latent powers!

Also some other latent powers you have (your rights).

- A secular medical professional must absolutely respect your religious beliefs, political commitments and sexual orientation. A medical professional cannot change a client's religion, politics or sexual orientation.

- In America, know that you get to choose your friends, your community membership, your hobbies and interests even your identity.

Also, remember as you "take action" to also tell your abuse story and what you are planning to do, to a trusted confidant, so you do not "suffer in silence," so you get the help, guidance and comfort you need and you "break the silence" on your own abuse, so that your abuser does not go off to hurt another human being in your situation.

Congratulations! You did it! You are free!

You made the first and hardest step when making any lifestyle change! The first step!

Now you are ready for your next step into God!

**My Second Tip: First, Go Inward To God**

Now that you have began to "clear your deck" of negative, abusive, hurtful, oppressive, life-draining influences in your life and you are beginning to get everything you need and some of what you want, you are now ready to begin your mystical climb up Jacob's Ladder to "meet God face-to-face," your "source of healing and empowerment," remembering that you only have to take "one step at a time."

Your next step is to go to the place where you meet God, a place deep within your soul. According to ecofeminist, ecopsychologist Chellis Glendenning's classic study on "technology survivors" (humans who have survived "the side effects" of toxic chemicals and dangerous technologies), Glendinning found that "technology survivors" who had a personal relationship with the Living God were more likely to harness the healing and libratory benefits of spirituality than "technology survivors" who had an impersonal relationship with God through doctrine, tradition and community. In fact, "technology survivors" who saw God "as a metaphor for otherness" and relied on organized religion to meet all their spiritual needs, not only had their faith undermined when this crisis hit, they even became "entangled" in oppressive, toxic religions which further alienated and oppressed them, compounding their trauma in the process.[108]

So, how do you develop this personal relationship with the Living God?

First of all, I cannot make you reach out to God. Second, I cannot make God reach back to you. This is between you and your God. The gratuitous gift of God's Holy Spirit!

What I can help you with is to help you find the Voice of God in and amongst the mire of your own life through providing you with what is known in academic theology, philosophy and literary circles as a framework, which can be understood as a "grid," "a screen," "a matrix" or a "test" where you can run your ideas and experiences through a series of "constraints" to verify and falsify your experiences, liken to the scientific method in the hard sciences, helping to isolate the Voice of God from your own voice and the voice of society.[109]

The specific framework I am offering you is the story of Pentecost in the Christian Bible (Acts 2), where shortly after the Death, Resurrection and Ascension of Lord Jesus Christ, the Holy Spirit descended upon all the remaining disciples, emerging apostles and new converts, all at once, on a particular day, in a particular place in the Holy Land. The Holy Spirit descended upon these early Christians through speaking to all these Christians gathered together from different countries in their "own native language" (Acts 2: 8). This means if you were a Hebrew, God spoke to you in Hebrew. If you were a Greek, God spoke to you in Greek. If you were a Roman, God spoke to you in Latin. If you were an Arab, God spoke to you in Arabic. This is where the "speaking in tongues" tradition comes from, but in this framework, "speaking in tongues" does not mean reciting "strange utterances" from a language you know not of in a trance-like state, but God speaking to you in your "own native language" (Acts 2:8).

This means that if you are American, Canadian, British or Australian or from any other English speaking country, God will speak to you in English. This means that if you are Spanish, Mexican, Cuban, Peruvian or Chilean or from any other Spanish speaking country, God will speak to you in Spanish. This means that if you are Portuguese or Brazilian or from any other

Portuguese country, God will speak to you in Portuguese. This means that if you are from China or from any Chinese speaking country, God will speak to you in Chinese, even the dialect from your own region in China, for example God will speak Mandarin Chinese to you, if you are from Mandarin China. If you are from a particular African tribe in Botswana, God will speak the language of your tribe to you. Even if you come from an exiled country like Scotland or Whales, you are a Gypsy (aka Roma), you have a Yiddish background or you are a member of a First Nation in the Americas, God will even speak to you in the language of your ancestors, which explains why "speaking in tongues" is so important to many Christians today, especially as the Christian religion is becoming an increasingly multicultural religion.

Now that you have identified the language of your own country, it is time now to identify your "language of discourse," the language you use when talking about your interests, passions and the livelihood of your choice. God also talks to you through your "language of discourse" through giving you metaphors you can relate too. For example, if you are a scientist, God uses scientific metaphors when He explains things to you. For example, if you are an artist, God uses artistic metaphors when He explains things to you. If you are a writer, God uses writing metaphors when He explains things to you. If you are a historian, God uses history metaphors when He explains things to you. If you are a philosopher, God uses philosophy metaphors when He explains things to you. If you are a political activist, God uses political activism metaphors when He explains things to you. If you are a theologian, God uses religious metaphors when He explains things to you.

Finally, as a neurodiverse human, you also have a "sub-culture" language which we use to make sense of our situation and context, when we talk with other brothers, sisters and cousins, when we relate to those outside the community, when we deconstruct our oppressors and build our own sovereign culture. This is our very own "sociosymbolic life." For example, if you are deaf, you can communicate through sign language. If you are blind, you can learn how to read brail. If you are autistic, you can "think in pictures," communicate through "the written word," even communicate with Animals and the Earth.

God can even talk to us through our "alternative systems of meaning." For example, if you are deaf, God can communicate to you through sign language and you can actually See God. If you are blind, God can communicate with you through your sense of touch and He can give you oral instructions through audible voice. If you are on the autism spectrum, God might speak to you using certain metaphors and images; you could be receiving religious visions, you might find God's voice verbal and concrete, God might dictate messages to you, you might find God in created things, in your "extreme perceptions," you might have "good intuitions," engage certain types of spiritual experiences and God might even be speaking to you through animals, plants, even "inanimate objects," even All Creation.

In otherwords, using myself as a "model" and "case study," God speaks to me in American English, using ecological metaphors and species-inclusive language, verbally and concretely, out of the Whirlwind of All Creation and I find something of the Living God in what others dismiss as mere "inanimate objects." For me, "God is in the details!" And, "The Devil too!"

However God speaks to you, the most important thing to remember is that your revelation is private and personalized just for you (it can have public, political implications however). It's just that God needs to speak to you in your own language, for it's God's Will to make His various spiritual traditions "accessible" to all peoples, regardless of our diagnosis, disability standing, neurological difference or learning style. You too, "are welcomed at the table!" The Kingdom of God absolutely also includes you!

Once you have mastered the "second step," now firming "rooted" in the One, True God, firmly "anchored" in the Spirit of the Living God, you are now ready to begin to emerge from your shell and "make a leap" to the third rung on Jacob's Ladder where you will discover "vestiges" of the Living God in "the world around you."

"Vestiges" are the "evidence" that God in fact, "exists" and He is who He says He is (Mark12:26), the Creator, Sustainer and Redeemer of the Entire Universe, who is "gentle and humble in heart" (Mathew 11:9). The Christian tradition uses metaphors like "signs," "sacraments," "smoke" and "footprints" to explain these Vestiges of God found in our ordinary,

everyday, mundane world, where the Supernatural "sacred realities" mentioned in the Holy Bible are in fact embodied into the Natural "profane realities" of the Natural World and Human Beings, enlivening Nature and Culture with beauty, wonder and goodness, making our whole world, sacred and holy, in the process.

**My Third Tip-Going Outward**

I have found that some of the most persuasive arguments for the Existence of God can be found in the Natural World.

The first argument, taken from the late Paul Shepard, an ecopsychologist and deep ecologist who writes that, "Only when we accept risk as part of the price of having wild bears will we contain the irrational fears and thoughtless habitat destruction that result in the loss of bears from the wild."[110]

In other words, whether you believe in God or the Big Bang, you cannot escape the reality that we live in a world which *was not* made by human hands. Human beings did not create these "wild bears." Human beings did not create all the evolutionary ancestors of these "wild bears." Nor did human beings create the ancestral habitat of all these "wild bears," a vast, unbroken wilderness of colossal mountain ranges, rivers of ice, verdant alpine meadows, expansive evergreen forests and raging salmon runs. Something outside "human wisdom" made these bears and the alpine paradise which these bears call home. This "something" we believe as Christians is "really somebody." As Christians, we believe that this "somebody" is really God, the Creator, Sustainer and Redeemer of the Entire Universe.

The second argument for the Existence of God comes from early environmentalist Aldo Leopold, who tells the story in his classic *Sand County Almanac* about a boy who was brought-up atheist who came to a Belief in God "when he saw that there were a hundred-odd species of warblers, each bedecked like to a rainbow, and each performing yearly sundry thousands of miles on migration about which the scientists wrote wisely but did not understand. No 'fortuitous concourse of elements' working blindly through any number of millions of years could quite account for why warblers are so beautiful. No mechanistic theory, even bolstered by mutations, has ever quite answered for the colors of the cerulean warbler, or the vespers of the wood thrush, or the swansong, or---goose music. I dare say that this boy's convictions would be harder to shake than those of many theologians. There are yet born many boys, like Isaiah, who 'may see, and know, and consider, and understand together, that the hand of the Lord hath done this."

All the science in the world, that this little boy was being indoctrinated into at school, at work and at home, could not completely explain away "why warblers are so beautiful" even as science tried to explain to him the evolutionary functionality, adaptability and randomness of a "hundred-odd species of warblers." Science and reason could not explain why "evolution" selected "beauty" of all traits. Nor could all the science and reason in the world, explain why "the hundred-odd species of warblers" "came-out" so beautiful.

In other words, the reality of "beauty" imposed "doubt" into the child's otherwise perfect atheistic formation and upbringing. This is because this child just discovered the Existence of God.

This child discovered what Christians have been contending for Millennia from Saint Paul the Apostle to Saint Augustine of Hippo, from Saint Bonaventure of Bagnoregio to Saint Anthony of Padua, who linked the "Beauty of Nature" to nothing less than the Holy Spirit, the Third Person in the Holy Trinity, believing that God's Holy Spirit was embodied into All Creation, enlivening the sensory, material world with beauty and wonder (The Doctrine of the Incarnation).

Leopold in the mid-twentieth century used this argument to a declining Christian nation as an argument for why Americans need to preserve pristine wilderness areas and conserve the natural resources and sustainable traditions of our rural countryside, to make ascent to a Belief in God possible at all, in a world increasingly being marked by industrialization, urbanization, artificiality and non-belief.[111]

In other words, the Natural World is the "salient variable" in the "God versus Atheism debate," for the voices of Shepherd's "wild bears" cannot be as easily controlled by ideologues nor are they "moved" by mere "human wisdom."

Yet, as God onetime pointed-out to me, "Creation is the purist form of revelation." Yet, even our human nature even harbors evidence of God's existence and goodness.

One Vestige of God in humanity is the Bible, where despite millenniums of human-created, social constructions, being reviewed by thousands of eyes and umpteenth translations; it is nothing less than a miracle that any truth at all survived in the Holy Bible. Yet, it can be conceded that there is at least something of "the truth" left in the Bible. This is evidence that God's Holy Spirit worked through all the human beings who wrote the Bible transforming a mere "human document" into a "sacred text."

The Other Vestige of God in humanity is the Communion of Saints, where despite ten thousand years of human-Earth estrangement, there were still a core group of men and women who faithfully believed in the Existence of God to the death, who also brought about much healing in human relations, human-animal relationships and human-Earth relationships, in the process, because of their indomitable religious faith and intense religious experiences.

Once, you have contemplated the Mysteries of the Universe, you are ready to climb onto the fourth rung of Jacob's Ladder, as you continue your ascent to the Kingdom of Heaven, to meet your God. You do this by actually "going outside" where you meet God's Creation "face to face." When once you "go outside" into the sunshine, fresh air and impervious ground, you will have the opportunity to encounter real animals, real plants and real places, developing intense attachments to All God's Creatures, in the process.

## My Fourth Tip-Getting To Outside

To see real, live animals, plants and green places you *do not* have to go-out to a pristine wilderness area or even deep into the rural countryside, for as Saint Paul the Apostle says "But someone may say, 'How are the dead raised? With what kind of body will they come back? You fool! What you sow is not brought to life unless it dies. And what you sow is not the body that is to be but a bare kernel of wheat…but God gives it a body as he chooses, and to each of the seeds its own body. Not all flesh is the same, but there is one kind for human beings, another kind for animals, another kind of flesh for birds and another for fish. There are both heavenly bodies and earthly bodies, but the brightness of the heavenly is one kind and that of the earthly another. The brightness of the sun is one kind, the brightness of the moon another, and the brightness of the stars another. For star differ for star in brightness" (I Corinthians 15: 35-41). In otherwords, we "live, move and have our being" in God's Creation. We are surrounded by God's created beings. We are enveloped by natural bodies. We have to go no further than our own gardens, lawns and bodies to find wild Nature.

This means a real, live animal can be your animal companion, a bird at a birdfeeder, a squirrel in a birdbath, an earthworm on a sidewalk, a fish in a stream or a shrimp under a microscope. You can find real, live animals at the local zoo, aquarium, nature center, natural history museum or pet store. You can find real, live animals in your own backyard, in your own neighborhood, at birdfeeders, in birdbaths, in local city parks, around flowers and under microscopes. Once you encounter real, live animals, you can come see for yourself whether or not animal rights is a legitimate cause or not and develop your own relationship with animals independent of the various animal movements.

This means a real, live plant can be a maple tree which grows out of your apartment window, a pine tree you wake-up to every morning, a landscaped bed of roses in your neighborhood, a wild dandelion embedded in an otherwise manicured lawn, a clump of moss sandwiched into the cracks in a concrete sidewalk, a local forest, meadow or marsh. A real, life plant is even the rubber plant, pencil tree, succulent or orchid in your own apartment. You can also find real, life plants in your backyard, in your neighborhood, at a local park, in the local botanical garden, conservatory or zoological garden, under a microscope, even within your own house.

A real place is an abandoned woodlot, an overgrown meadow, a public park, zoo or botanical garden, the grounds of an historical home, the land of a local community church, a tranquil spot down by a river, the beech, the ocean, the campus of a university, the family farm, the city cathedral or wherever you stand on solid ground surrounded by living beings not created by human hands. A real place is wherever there is fresh air, natural sunlight, plants, animals and living soil. A real place is wherever you can see the Sun, the Sky and the Moon and the Stars above you, wherever you can see the soft dark soil below you, wherever you can see a plethora of plants and animals around you.

Once you stock your reservoir of real life experiences with real, live plants, animals and places, you can see for yourself whether ecology is a legitimate cause or not and you can develop your own personal relationship with the Natural World independent of the various environmental movements.

Make sure also "when you are out" to take in all of the emotional and spiritual safety of the Natural World, as well as all the beauty, wonder, comfort and stability found in All of Nature. When you go out into the wild, you will also find the acceptance and freedom your soul so longs for. When you step outside of civilization, you are free to be yourself. The Natural World can even help you identify a physical exercise you actually enjoy doing, exercise which does not feel like exercise at all, but relaxing stimulation and you might even find yourself, when you actually "go outside."

## My Fifth Tip-Reconnecting With Society

Once you have experienced personal healing, developed your own personal relationship with God and Nature and have contemplated the nature of the Universe and your place in it, you are now ready to rejoin human society.

When I talking about rejoining human society, I *am not* talking about "pretending to be normal" or "pleasing society" or "passing," I am instead talking about reintegration back into human society in a manner which respects the strengths and weaknesses of our autistic self, the prophetic gifts of neurodiversity and our very human need for companionship and signifigence. I am talking about rejoining human society in a manner which both respects our boundaries, our individuality, our independence, our health and our humanity, while allowing us to connect with each other, individual neurotypicals and neurotypical society at-large, in a more positive, empowering, life-affirming manor than the status quo.

For this to happen, I agree with ecopsychologist Chellis Glendinning that as trauma survivors, we absolutely "need safety."

When, I am talking about safety, I am not just talking about physical safety, although we need physical safety too. For example, our autistic side necessitates for health reasons that we absolutely need to be able to live in a safe neighborhood where we are less likely to become a victim of a violent crime such as rape, murder or assault or of a property crime such as a being pick-pocketed, burglarized or scammed. All three property crimes have happened to me personally. Dawn Prince Hughes was repeatedly raped in her childhood and youth years.

I am also talking about emotional and spiritual safety.

I define emotional safety as freedom from all forms of abuse (physical, emotional, financial, economic and sexual), bullying (physical, psychological and sexually suggestive), dysfunctional medical professionals ("using" and "manipulating" a patient for an ulterior motive, "doing cover" for someone/something else and giving unnecessary invasive treatments) and being able to "defend oneself" nonviolently from all abuse, bullying and dysfunctional medical professionals.

I define spiritual safety as not being coerced into a certain belief system, not being forced to participate in religious rituals you do not believe in, not being asked to do actions against your conscience, not being asked to breach your integrity in any way, not having to listen to other people use spirituality or religion to be nasty or to "get there way." I define spiritual safety as a comforting religious faith, a certain respect for tradition, ancestors and critical thinking, a welcoming, hospitable, respectful community and accessible, inclusive teachings for everyone. I define spiritual safety as freedom from all religiosity which excludes, marginalizes, separates, scapegoats, psychologically destabilizes, causes "bizarre experiences," inspires behavior which is a "threat to yourself and others," is overly rigid, legalistic, bureaucratic or graceless and does not include disability or neurodiversity.

I contend that the more physical, emotional and spiritual safety you can attain in your life, the more you will be able to engage in meaningful relationships with other people and contribute to society.

You attain such safety in such a fallen, broken and dangerous society by "questioning any and all authority." You *do not* "just passivity accept your fate." You *do not* "chalk it off" to "That's life!" or "life is not fair!" You *do not* tell yourself "don't question anything!" You *do not* "check your brain at the door!" You *do not* "just sit down and fallow those rules."

You become instead an "independent thinker," a "questioning believer," a "lifelong learner." You "feel deeply," you become "compassionately curious," you ask "lot and lots of questions," you "gather information," you "think for yourself" and you keep "digging for the truth." Most importantly, you start to "live the life of the mind," you start to become a "cultural critic," you start to "take action," you become "an activist" and you begin to "make a difference," working towards helping to "make the world a better place."

Once you reject "passivity" and start to "question any and all authority" and start to become an "historical actor" in the process, you will feel less like a powerless, helpless victim and more like the empowered "moral agent" that you are.

In turns out, despite fashionable political and spiritual rhetoric, we need both: *safety* and *democracy.* That safety versus democracy is another false dualism and false choice which needs to be challenged by postmodernity. You need both and you can have both.

Safety is a democracy-social justice issue, for not everyone in our democratic society is equally safe. Everyone needs physical, emotional and spiritual safety, so they can participate rationally, meaningfully, justly, even peacefully, in the democratic and social justice arenas. Anything else is violent!

Democracy is a safety issue for money, possessions and armaments do not keep us safe. Money, possessions and armaments keeps us secure (in control of our enemies). What keeps us safe (in control of our own lives) is our "good questions."

This is what has kept me alive all this time! This is how I survived! This is how I got out! This is how I made it do freedom! This is how I am becoming happy! This is how I am learning to trust again! This is how I am getting reintegrated back into society! This is my strategy! This is my greatest defense against becoming a victim!

**Chapter Five: On Welcoming Neurodiversity at the Table-My Letter to Ministers**

The late Roman Catholic priest and disability advocate Henri Nouwen writes about the proper role and place of disability within the Body of the Christ,

> The most honored parts of the body are not the head or the hands, which lead and control. The most important parts are the least presentable parts. That's the mystery of the Church. As a people called out of oppression to freedom, we must recognize that it is the weakest among us---the elderly, the small children, the handicapped, the mentally ill, the hungry and sick---who form the real center. Paul says, "It is the parts of the body which we consider least dignified, that we surround with the greatest dignity" (I Corinthians 12:23).
>
> The Church as the people of God can truly embody the living Christ among us only when the poor remain its most treasured part. Care for the poor, therefore, is much more than Christian charity. It is the essence of being the body of Christ.[112]

Nouwen made three vitally important theological-ethical claims about the role and place of disability and neurodiversity in the Body of Christ.

First, our disabled and our neurodiverse brothers and sisters absolutely belong in the Body of the Christ, the Christian Church universal. We are integral, vital even essential to the Life of the Church. Anything else is morally evil!

Second, including and caring for those of us who struggle with disability and mental illness issues is not a mere matter of Christian charity (aka "segregationist charity"), including and providing pastoral care and spiritual instruction to the various disability and neurodiversity communities is the Christian thing to do. Anything else is un-Christian!

Third, our disabled and neurodiverse brothers and sisters absolutely deserve the "preferential option." I define "preferential option" as being sided with in oppression situations, assuming the best in us in capacity debates and "going the extra mile" to make sure we too "are welcomed at the table." We are truly "welcomed at the table" when our unique gifts are used, appreciated, respected and welcomed by the Church and our "material well being" needs are taken into consideration, such as that the fact that we might be wanting in health care services, education, employment, safety and love, even those of us who live in the United States of America. Anything else is a threat to social justice and human rights everywhere!

Yet, how do you actually do this in practice? You might protest!

In the remaining section I am going to offer what I want personally as a full human being on the autism spectrum and what the disability community at-large wants politically from religious groups and peoples of faith. The later is especially important to include in this discussion, because much pain, dysfunction and oppression have been perpetuated in the disability community when one or two high profile individuals or organizations monopolize the disability-ability discussions. My particular disability community has been particularly hard hit by this unfortunate, tragic and unjust phenomenon.[113]

For example, I have had to pay a very heavy price personally and professionally as an Aspie animal rights activist for modest animal reformer Temple Grandin's stances in-favor of "humane" slaughterhouses and factory farms, because not only has she alienated my fellow non-disabled, neurotypical animal rights activists, the animal rights community mistakenly assumes that Grandin speaks for the entire autistic community on animal issues.

I also have an autism diagnosis; I also love animals and I also have the ability to empathize with animals like Grandin.

Unlike, Grandin, I am a lacto-ova vegetarian (I do not eat meat, fish or seafood). I believe factory farms and slaughterhouses, as well as practices like hunting and fishing need to be abolished. I am an abolitionist on hunting! I believe non-lethal, non-invasive, nonviolent alternatives absolutely need to be developed to test the safety of pharmaceuticals and to teach the field of academic biology. I believe unwanted and dangerous companion animals need to be rehabilitated, not murdered. I believe animal death is morally significant!

Another example is these "autism blogs" which are cropping up like virtual mushrooms in cyber-space. These "blogs" have done nothing less than further stigmatize, isolate and traumatize Aspie humans everywhere, through spreading dangerous stereotypes and taking hurtful positions which affect the lives of very real human beings on the autism spectrum, in our "real life" "offline."

One hurtful stereotype which these "blogs" are spreading around our non-disabled, neurotypical society is the whole "geek" stereotype.

I am a bully survivor! I was severally bullied from elementary school through high school, with the worst being in middle school and special education. In middle school, the bullies used to call me "a geek" as well as "a nerd" because I was on the autism spectrum. So everytime "Asperger" and "geek" are used together, I am revictimized.

Most seriously, "geek" does not honor who I am. I was barely a C mathematics student in high school. I am as good with computers as the average neurotypical. I was an A history student throughout high school and college. I graduated with a master degree from a respectable theological school in Boston with a 3.7 GPA. I am a Christian convert. I believe in the existence of God! I love the outdoors! I am a people person! I hate technology! I am a technological pragmatist! I do not worship technology! I do need community! I do need religion! I do need culture! God and Nature are my interests not mathematics and computers!

Another hurtful position which these "blogs" have taken is "siding" with the vaccine industry aka "Big Pharma" over the "autism-vaccine connection," just to make an identity politics statement about the natural-ness of autistic culture and to "lash-out" at autism parent groups. This militant position I have found personally hurtful, for I was one of the humans who had a medical reaction to vaccines in early childhood.

The recent government-industry study so-called findings that there *is not* a connection aside, this was the narrative I was told over and over again my whole life, growing-up. This position was taken before people like myself, had a chance to tell our stories, excluding our narratives from this discussion.

If these on-line "bloggers" would have listened to my narrative, they will have learned some statistically significant details about those of us in this situation.

First, I developed autistic-like symptoms, alongside the loose of muscle tone and motor coordination and language abilities after being put on a battery of mercury-laced vaccinations when I was still recovering from bronchitis by my childhood pediatrician. Shortly after I started developing unexplained physical symptoms, after my parents fired my childhood pediatrician, my new pediatrician discovers that most of my records were mysteriously missing, most likely shredded and destroyed. We will never know! In fact, there was so-much suspicious behavior, my family participated in a class action lawsuit for many years.

Such "bloggers" will discover that before the vaccines, I had above average language ability. Most compelling and disturbing of them all, they would have learned that these vaccines which caused unexplained symptoms in the early 1980s, when the word Asperger's was barely translated into the English language aside.

The "vaccine" incident meant because it was the early 1980s, "set in motion" a "violent socialization process" throughout my childhood which included horrific behavior modification regimes, colonial-style special education programs, "dysfunctional medical professionals" and a "restrictive environment" only appropriate for someone much "lower functioning" than a "high functioning" Aspie like myself. All this created the necessary "totalitarian environment" for giving me the same Post-Traumatic Stress Order (PTSD) as war veterans and rape survivors, in the process.

In terms of the government-industry study, I only ask you the following questions: Do you really trust the scientific integrity of the same "Big Pharma" who brought us "behavior modification" and "special education"? Knowing what you know about chemistry---do you actually believe that "mercury is safe"? Did it ever occur to you that the real reason why the "military-industrial complex" produced all this "scientific" evidence that "mercy is safe" is because not enough fellow autists have suffered to warrant taking mercury-laced vaccines given to infants and small children "off the market"? Could it be that the disparate causes of autistic parent groups and neurodiversity actually be another linked oppression? Could the real couplet in the autism struggle be neither "refrigerator mothers" nor "refrigerator children," but the reality that we live in a "refrigerator society," a society marked by loneliness, alienation and the decline of community, culture and stability? Could the increasing neuro-diversifying of "the human spirit" be an evolutionary response to the socio-planetary crisis? Could "abstraction" aka "neurotypicalism" no longer be an advantageous trait for human survival? Do you really want "Big Pharma" to domesticate our lives, our cultures and our futures?

For the above reasons, this is what I personally want from the Christian Church: that my personal story be heard and factor into the non-disabled, neurotypical Christian response to abelism, neurotypicalism and normalcy. For my own story to complement the collective stories of the various disability and neurodiversity communities, so that individual neurodiverse humans such as myself, whom you might meet in Synagogue, Church or Mosque will get the individualized, respectful treatment we deserve. Anything else is cannibalism!

Emotional cannibalism, a technical term in the Compassion Fatigue literature is anytime you might "rob Peter to pay Paul" such as dividing various oppressed minority groups into "deserving" and "undeserving" poor, pitting members of the same minority group against one another, "getting ahead" on "the backs" of other fellow comrades, putting "token minorities" and "token members" on a pedestal "to tear everyone else down," using your own oppression situation as an excuse for oppressing other oppressed people and so forth. Emotional cannibalism is usually a dysfunctional response to feeling powerless. This is why all individual sentient beings are entitled to rights! No exceptions!

### *What I Personally Need and Want From Religious Groups as a Christian on The Autism Spectrum*

### *To Get the Word "Selfish" Out Of Your Vocabulary!*
Many Christian Churches are increasing using the metaphor "selfish" to describe "sin" which I find very offensive, hurtful, oppressive and spiritually abusive.

This was because until very recently, the word "selfish" was used as a very derogatory word to describe autistic humans, in a time when the medical elite made the unfortunate incorrect assumption that human beings on the autism spectrum such as myself, "lack empathy." Equating "autism" with "lacking empathy" is a position which the neurodiversity movement has insistently refuted and the medical establishment has recanted, yet whose "residue" remains active in our popular culture at-large in the form of ignorance and stigma.

For example, teachers growing-up sometimes called me "selfish" when I was overly preoccupied with environmental and animal rights causes, for when they were talking about being "selfish" or that I "lack empathy" they were really saying that I was not concerned enough about "pleasing" very privileged non-disabled, neurotypicals from the upper socioeconomic classes in America.

This imperative also excluded other oppressed minority groups, the economic poor, the homeless, criminals and other outcasts in our society. In other words, "selfish" was being used as a code word for "middle class morality." Social justice or sustainability had nothing to do with it!

Now, my current mental health providers tell me to disregard this argument.

This word "selfish" not only impacts the disability community, it also impacts anyone who has felt like an "other" for any reason. According to psychologist Fielding in his book *Fitting in Is Overrated: the Survival Guide for Anyone Who Has Ever Felt like an Outsider* (Sterling First Edition, 2008) the word "selfish" is used as a "code word" for "non-compliance" especially with "compassionate people." In other words, "selfish" is used to intimidate "compassionate people" from following their destiny, calling us instead to meet "societal expectations" and preserve "the status quo" at all costs. A "sustainable and just Earth community" is diametrically opposed to what these "status quo affirmers" (to use the words of my later mentor, Dr. Philip Bosserman) are trying to accomplish. According to Fielding, the word "selfish" is used, because "compassionate people" find being accused of it "so irritating," "stopping us dead in our tracks" in the process.[114]

The "selfish" metaphor even negative impacts the very people who are part of these privilege classes themselves according to gender theologian Stephen Byrd. Byrd argues that increasingly "self love" is being equated with "selfishness" which he called "unfortunate." This is because men *do not* become less oppressive when they become "more compliant," work harder to meet "societal expectations" or when they are denied the ability to take care of themselves. Instead, men become more benign when they "under-function in public life," when they "follow their bliss" and when they can take care of their physical and mental health.[115]

In other words, the word "selfish" is "irrelevant," "exclusive" and "harmful" religious language for everyone. So when religious leaders address issues like social inequality and the planetary crisis, they need to watch their language about "disability" and "mental illness." Religious leaders must never use disparaging words like "selfish," "collective autism," "sacrifice," "orthopathy," "nuts," "crazy" "insanity," "madness," "deranged" and "schizophrenic," as metaphors to frame the most pressing ethical-moral issues of our time. Such language is spiritual abusive!

Religious leaders need to heed what my academic advisor in undergraduate, who also advises pre-medical students and those going into the various health professions said to me onetime when a similar issue came-up, "the problem with using medical terms when giving a speech is that you never know who is in the audience."

Since the "pulpit" is such a politically charged platform, the clergy absolutely must watch their language about "power," "privilege," "psychology," "critical social theory" "disability," "autism" and "mental illness." This is the first step toward having nonviolent, inclusive language for peoples of all kinds of different disabilities, physical and mental. Anything else is religious violence! This is non-negotiable!

### To Crip Christian Environmentalism!

Disability Studies scholar are using this word called "crip" to describe the process by which an academic discipline, political ideology, world religion or social movement can integrate the disability justice worldview into existing non-disabled frameworks.

An example of "crip" is my work with both the Journal Critical Animal Studies (JCAS) and Society for Disability Studies (SDS), where I have tried to address the disconnection between the various animal rights, autistic pride and disability justice movements over the highly abelist, neurologically chauvinistic animal rights movement and the highly anthropocentric, species chauvinistic disability justice movement. With the help of other disability and animal activists, I am working to reform both the abelist, neurologically chauvinistic ways of the animal rights movement and the anthropocentric, species chauvinistic ways of the disability justice movement.

We are accomplishing this by trying to include sympathetic disability and neurodiversity voices in our discussions and debates and through trying to find a "linked oppression" between speciesism (bigotry towards animals) and abelism (bigotry towards humans with disabilities). We are also accomplishing this through recovering the ecological, humane gifts of individual disabled and neurodiverse humans, naming the benefits of including disability and neurodiversity in ecological, animal rights debates and through exploring the interface between disability and species level privilege and oppression.  In other words, find a "win-win-win" resolution to this on-going conflict.

This is an example of how one could "crip" an ideology or movement.

There is no reason why a similar model cannot also be applied to the "conflict of interest" between the various disability justice movements and the various Christian environmental movements over such "inaccessible" and "exclusive" strategies as "community" and "internationalization."

In the Judeo-Christian Biblical stewardship movement the "conflict of interest" is that this branch insists on such high "professional proficiently standards" that it makes the Christian environmental life "inaccessible" to most Christians in the various disability and neurodiversity communities. For example, stewardship academic programs require unrealistic standards in abstract, scientific reasoning (such as meeting perfectionist level standards in mathematics, chemistry, physical and technician work). This approach excludes Bible based, doctrinally orthodox students who have impairments in mathematics, chemistry, physics and motor skills, but are gifted in the environmental humanities or social sciences, ecotheology, the creative arts, ecological ministry or political activism. Not all environmentalists are straight scientists! Such an approach significantly narrows your "pool" of sympathetic collaborators. So to "crip" the

Christian stewardship movement means having educational programs and professional and volunteer opportunities which appeal to a variety of learning styles, callings and ecological gifts.

In the Creation Spirituality/Process Theology branch of the movement, the "conflict of interest" is that they insist on unrealistically high "etiquette" standards which most spiritual humans on the autism spectrum cannot possible meet. To "crip" Creation spirituality is to actually "practice what you preach" and honor the ecological callings of those us who are called to directly engage, one-on-one, the Natural World through an unmediated, personal relationship and address the planetary issues which effect the planet directly such as institutional animal cruelty, the worldwide loss of biodiversity, urban sprawl, the domination of wilderness and localized litter problems, as well as the scientific study of the Natural World and global environmental change.

The conflict in the Christian Ecofemism/Eco-justice branch of the movement is they externalize environmental justice. They see environmental inequality as something which only happens to starving children in Africa or that environmental inequality only impacts certain very specific communities like women and those in lower socioeconomic classes. They do not properly acknowledge that there is much across the board environment inequality right here in America.

For example, anyone who has ever developed a serious illness or disability because of being exposed to a toxic chemical, a dangerous medication or an unsafe technology is a victim of an environmental injustice. Right here in America there is a huge disparity between the "environmental costs/benefits" of the superrich and ordinary citizens. Most of our sweat shop clothing, imported "sweets and beverages," "cheap food" and "big box" landscape was not all these "selfish consumers" demanding it, but where "behind closed revolving doors," from "the top down," from within the Corporate Class, anti-democratic decisions. In fact, many of the democratic processes in place which have the power to check ecological inequality in America have been severely weakened and compromised like not having strong militant labor unions, an insular enforcement branch in the Environmental Protection Agency (EPA), good American manufacturing jobs which have to meet American minimum wage and workplace safety standards and now multi-national corporations can legally call themselves "green," "natural," "sustainable," "local," "artisan," "homemade," "fair traded," and "humane."

To "crip" Christian ecojustice and ecofeminism is to *not* make assumptions or overgeneralizations about the life of ordinary people in America. To also speak-out against environmental inequalities in our own communities and to provide pastoral care to those personally effected by an environmental illness. To "crip" ecojustice and ecofeminism is to educate the public about the sinister origins of our "everyday products" and their "side-effects" and "risks" and to provide concrete alternatives, while doing "anti-oppression" in "communities at-risk." To "crip" Christian ecojustice and ecofemism is to be "open and affirming" to "technology survivors," to offer chaplaincy services to labor unions and to listen to the ecological autobiographies of the laity.

Such an approach, I contend does not upstage other legitimate planetary efforts for one of the benefits of making disability and neurodiversity an environmental justice issue is it takes away the "it happens to other people" mentality which is one of the ways environmental injustice gets perpetuated. Something like Love Channel is something which happens to working class people. Something like all these horrible earthquakes, super storm hurricanes and tsunamis happen to all these people in "the third world."

When in reality, something like Love Channel can easily happen to anybody, regardless of your social class: whether it is in the pesticide-laced fruits and vegetables you feed your family with, the vaccines you give your babies or even a Big Pharma birth control pill you take alongside your neighbor's organic, hormone free cow's milk, with a pristine cocktail of supplements from the local health store and a bedtime yoga ritual. When in reality, the plush penthouse office of a superrich C.E.O. in downtown Manhattan can get "hit" just as hard by a super storm hurricane as a fishermen shack in Haiti.

Such an approach could only lead to compassion, for you realize that this could be your mother grieving the unnatural death of one her children to leukemia like what happened in Love Chanel because of a deposit of synthetic chemicals under her child's elementary school and playground by the local employer. This could be your father grieving the loss of all he worked his whole life to attain, only to have his beloved family farm wiped out by a "fly by night" super flood caused by global climate change and the politicians being "too cheap" to pay for the proper public works infrastructure which would have saved your father's farm.

Such an approach is not even anthropocentric or speciesist, because to "crip," "localize" and "personify" environmental injustice is to check the twin tendencies to A) turn humanity into a god and B) develop an "uncritical humanism." Neither contention is desirable for Animals or the Natural World, leading to the Christian animal rights and Christian deep ecology branches also becoming "crip," in the process.

Yet, why am I still so dissatisfied with Christian churches and Jewish synagogues as an environmentalist and animal activist, despite all the "off the charts" successful "in-roads" the Christian environmental and animal movements have made in "houses of worship" and "secular environmental organizations" across America in the last decade. Despite words like "stewardship" and "community" becoming household names. Despite almost every local church and synagogue addressing the planetary agenda and speaking-out against "consumerism in North America" and settling the "jobs versus environment" debate once and for all with the Christian eco-justice movement. Settling the Lynne White debate once and for, where the planetary crisis is no-longer blamed on the Hebrew Bible and "dominion" no-longer means "domination" but "stewardship."

Although I applaud all these exciting breakthroughs, using "human-human community" as an intermediater to the Natural World is problematic, for I have much more deep seeded issues with "human-human community" than I ever will have going to Animals and the Earth directly. As a secular trained environmentalist, I really do not need religion or theology to teach me environmental ethics and morality. My atheistic and agnostic friends have taught me too well, that you do not need religion, let along Judeo-Christianity to live a moral life. That is what Kant, Batham and Mills are for. As a veteran, life-long committed environmentalist I really do not want to listen to the same privileged clergy try "to convince me to become an environmentalist," who just a decade or so ago tried to explain to me that "animals do not have souls!" and "deep ecology is pantheism."

I guess, I always have been and I always will be----a naturalist. I love the Natural World! That is the real reason why I became an environmentalist, an animal rights activist, a vegetarian, an ecotheologian, even a person of faith. I am like earlier Christian environmentalist Ennis Mills when I go out into the Natural World,

> Most men and women, boys and girls, go camping, just to go camping. They have a fair time. Others go chiefly because it gives them an opportunity to fish or hunt or take pictures. These campers are certain to have a good time. As I think of it now, after hundreds of camping trips, I went camping chiefly because I enjoyed watching the ways of birds and the habitat of animals. The rocks, the trees, and the flowers caused me to look again and again. So, too, did the mountain tops, the canons and the lakes. I enjoyed winter camping as well as summer camping and camping on deserts, plains, and forested mountains. I was ever excited to know *how a plant or animal came to be what it is and where it is.*[116]

In other words like Mills, the Natural World to me, is way more than pure pleasure or a place to exercise; the Natural World is also a source of theological revelation and spiritual subsistence, even a "source of healing and empowerment." As a naturalist, the Natural World spiritually and theologically to me is nothing less than a House of Worship, a church, a temple, a monastery, a friary, a religious order, a pilgrim matrix, a cathedral, a basilica, an initiation cave and a laboratory for learning a new "way of life" which is more in peace and harmony with Animals and the Earth.

This is the disconnection between naturalists such as myself and the Christian environmental movement. As Christian environmental writer Bill McKidden lamented when he wrote the forward to Ennis Mills' anthology of writings, "there are now many environmentalists, but few naturalists."[117]

The two main differences between a naturalist and an environmentalist are that A) a naturalist studies the ecology of a particular place like Rocky Mountain National Park or Deer Ridge. In other words, it's the naturalist, not the scientist, who studies the details of the Natural World. B) A naturalist "interprets" the Natural World from both a scientific (natural) and a cultural perspective (history).

The later was the real reason why I turned to the Christian environmental movement and the Christian Church, to get a Christian interpretation of the meaning of the Universe, the planetary crisis and my place in the Universe and in the planetary struggle. In my young life I have studied, experienced and suffered much in my relationship to the Natural World and other people, I already have become intellectually curious, scientifically literate and ecologically convinced to how the world works, now I wanted the Christian religion to interpret for me, what all this means. The role of culture! In other words, I was turning to religion not for moral guidance, but for spiritual guidance, even theological guidance.

Yet, the Judeo-Christian ecotheology field has yet to produce a single distinctively Judeo-Christian spiritual or theological insight which adds anything at all to secular discussions on the environment or animals, other than motivating religious people to become environmentalists. Part of the problem is that the Christian environmental movement has been so preoccupied with getting the Christian Church and individual Christians "on-board" with the planetary agenda, they have theologically and pastorally neglected the possibility that "another half could drop" too. Secular environmentalists like myself would start to turn toward Christian environmentalism for theological instruction, spiritual comfort and healing, even the salvation of our very souls.[118]

The Christian animal rights branch of this movement does get this possibility and reality however. Reverend Frank Hoffman is a practicing ordained Christian minister, a vegan and a very committed animal rights activist who has created an "on-line" Christian animal rights ministry (all-creatures.org) which is especially targeted toward providing pastoral care to the various animal movements. Providing not only information and arguments, but also inspirational animal stories, poems, photography projects and essays, inviting grassroots activists like myself to have a web page to give "visibility" to our animal ministries and moderating an on-line list serve.

You do not even need to be a Christian to be on the list serve, you can be Jewish, Buddhist, New Age even atheist or agnostic (the religious affiliation of most secular environmentalists and animal activists). He writes and publishes sermons each week tailored just for the animal movements. Each week, with his weekly newsletter, he has a special section called "good news for animals" where he posts a series of celebratory articles chronically "in-roads" the animal rights and environmental movement has made in reforming and changing our anthropocentric, speciesist society and culture.

All-creatures.org can serve as a model and success story for the entire Christian environmental movement, as well as a model for other "online," "in-person," "academic/professional" and "parish level" communities, a model which has "common ground" with the ecological learning styles and ecological gifts of your brothers and sisters on the autism spectrum.

In other words, to "crip" Christian environmentalism is to "blue" the secular environmental movements. To do nothing less than to address our own personal healing alongside preserving wilderness, abolishing factory farms and fighting climate change, through Christian environmentalists interpreting spiritual experiences to the secular environmental movement and celebrating spiritual values with the secular environmental movement.

### To Get That The Mind Is A Body Too!
The Christian religion has made two welcome neurodiverse "turns" in recent years.

One is a movement away from "language" based theology which was "too abstract," toward a more "metaphoric theology," with twenty-first century theologians taking a more literary approach to theological reflection using metaphors and stories to communicate spiritual values, versus the more mid-twentieth century theologians which took a more philosophical approach using mere logical arguments to communicate the Christian message.

Second, is a movement away from Platonic "mind-body dualisms" which saw the mind and the soul as disembodied and spiritual, while seeing our own physical bodies as other and inferior, leading us to both neglect our physical health and even denigrate our own bodies. Where now, as Christians we see both our bodies and our embodiment in the material world as sacred, holy and good. Both of these worthwhile endeavors give our autistic brothers and sisters a "foothold" in terms of making the theological method "accessible" and religious experience "intelligible," while sanctioning autistic realities, in the process.

Yet, there is still some Plutonic "residue" left in "metaphorical theology" and "body theology."

"Metaphoric theology" does not sufficiently account for "concrete realities" such as the human psyche and the details of Creation, reducing religious experience to a mere Ivory Tower "language came," leading to spiritual and theological confusion, ultimately to psychological and social destabilization, in the process. Becoming its own form of abstraction which makes it difficult for individuals to integrate themselves into a diverse commune (practical guidance) and next to impossible for social movements to critique and falsify theological claims (critical thinking), so cultural change can happen.

While "Body Theology" in an attempt to counter the extreme spiritualisms and abstractions of Plutonic and Neo-Plutonic philosophies and spiritualities, have gone to the other extreme and have reduced our humanity and the Natural World to mere material, privileging a person wanting materially in food, water or shelter ("deserving poor") over a person wanting psychologically in terms of safety, belonging, health care and self-knowledge ("undeserving poor"), going along disability/non-disabled, neurodiverse/neurotypical, physical disability/invisible disability lines, in the process.

Not realizing that modern brain science and modern psychiatry have established that most of the cognitive, emotional even moral and spiritual functions which Western religious and philosophical traditions have attributed to an immaterial, disembodied "mind" or "soul" are really functions of our "central nervous system." An organ system embodied into our physical body which is not only interconnected to and interdependent with every other body system in the human body, but also encompasses, even envelops our other body systems, with an intricate matrix of nerve cells embedded into literally every bone, muscle, blood vessel and organ in our physical body. Meaning that those of us who are in chronic physical pain, who are emotionally suffering, who feel lonely and alienated, who are being bullied and excluded, who are being denied appropriate health care, spiritual instruction and dignified work, who are stress-out, anxious and worried, who are depressed and ashamed, who are struggling with "compassion fatigue," who are not being treated with "dignity and respect," who are being exploited and intimidated, who are unhappy, who are dying alone, are just as deserving of loving attention and social justice as someone who is hungry, thirty or homeless.

Since autism effects men disproportionally to women, this means a well-dressed autistic man in an mental institution or trying to make it independently in society is also entitled to his feelings and having his feeling respected.

This is because a mind is a body too!

This means that taking care of a person's psychological and spiritual well-being is a "material well being" issue too.

This is because the brain is an organ just like the stomach, the heart or the lungs, meaning the brain also needs to be feed and renewed to work properly through quality sleep and stress management, through intellectual, creative and sensual stimulation, through engaging the spiritual disciplines and through exposure to fresh air, natural sunlight, healthy food, physical exercise, beauty, human touch, healing relationships and safe environments.

This is because Temple Grandin, who is also a bully survivor and a behavior scientist, refutes the notion that "sticks and stones might break my bones, but words can never hurt me!" by arguing that "words do hurt!"[119]

Meaning religious leaders also need to come-up with non-mechanistic, organic metaphors and religious symbols for the nervous system, which leads one to respect the various nervous systems of the planet.

For example, premodern words like "mind," "spirit," "soul," "living being," "life," "life blood" and "inner life" can be revitalized metaphorically *not* literally to describe the dynamitic interplay among our nervous, endocrine, reproductive, genetic and immune systems which leads to intelligence, emotions, desires, behaviors even spirituality and faith, which makes Transcendence possible.

Meaning, ecological metaphors like "system," "process," "living organism," "animality," "sentience" and "matrix" can be used to explain neurological phenomena.

Meaning, that Eternal Life even the Afterlife can be revitalized through the Nicean Orthodoxy "The Resurrection of the Body" through employing the archetypal "root metaphor" of "rebirth." That our being changes from a solid (body), to a liquid (soul), to a gas (spirit) when we die. That death is just another state of existence. That we do nothing less than expand out into the Universe when we die, where our energy, our vitality, our beauty, our charism becomes part of the Glory of God, where our spirits become "the wheels" in God's Chariot in the Prophet Ezekiel cryptic vision, traveling wherever God goes throughout this vast and great Universe (Ezekiel 1), helping God to restore balance in the Universe and new life to flourish.[120]

Meaning religious leaders do need to maintain their traditional ministries like the "Ministry of Healing the Sick," "Intercession," "Monastic Life," "Adult Sunday School," "Evangelism," "Missions," "Praise Worship," "Administering the Sacraments," "Spiritual Direction," "Spiritual Formation," "Lectionary," "Music," "Liturgical Calendar" and "Bible Studies" alongside more vanguard ministries like the various ecological, social justice, political activism, nonviolence, creative, academic and gender specific ministries which are cropping up in local churches like mushrooms after a downpour.

This is because; just because "religious experience" is "psychological," does not mean that it is not "real." Any more, than "myth means lie."

***To Become ADA Compliant and Fully Include Neurodiversity In Religious Leadership!***
When the Americans with Disabilities Act (ADA) was drafted in the 1980s, religious leaders lobbied for an exemption from ADA which was created to protect our disabled brothers and sisters from discrimination and give us "reasonable accommodations" to "level the playing field" so we could contribute to society and fulfill our potential in life.

I am briefly going to make the case that all religious institutions ***absolutely must become ADA compliant! That this exemption be removed!***

*Four Myths about the Americans for Disability Act (ADA)*

- *That you have to hire anyone with a disability regardless if their qualification?* No, you do not have to hire anyone with a disability regardless of their qualifications. ADA compliant means that you cannot discriminate against a qualified applicant based on a disability or diagnosis. No more, no less! *Expanding this to a religious context* means that no house of worship, private religious school, religious college, university, divinity or theological school or seminary or religious order or retreat center could discriminate against qualified applicants based on disability or diagnosis or any of our family members. In my proposed framework, the Christian Church absolutely will need to include all qualified disabled and neurodiverse brothers and sisters in Christ in all aspects of community life and church leadership from membership to clergy to monastic religious orders to missionary opportunities to theology professorships.

- *That "reasonable accommodations" means "undue hardship"?* "Reasonable accommodations" means "reasonable accommodations" like wheel chair ramps and extended time on tests. It *does not* mean lowering academic standards or tearing down multimillion dollar buildings. In a religious context, it would mean wheelchair accessible houses of worship, a sign language interpreter on special request, glutton free communion wafers, alcohol free communion juice, readily available worship materials and trained ushers who could offer assistance. Also exemptions from tithing requirements and/or non-financial tithing alternatives (e.g., volunteering) is also a critical "reasonable accommodations" for all those in the disability community receiving government assistance, are on a fixed income, are unemployed or underemployed or financially dependent on family members. Making religious institutions ADA compliant *would not* mean that religious institutions would be legally obligated to "change the culture" of the religion, whether it is the curriculum, obligations, traditions, rituals or language of a particular denomination, sect or religion. Just become non-discriminatory, a little less rigid, a little more accommodating and a little more "open minded." Although additional concessions would be welcomed!

- *That Americans with Disability Act (ADA) is un-economical?* One of the reasons for creating ADA was that it was calculated by economists that so much money each year is lost in our GNP (Gross National Product) because of discrimination, in terms of loss of work and productivity, additional psychiatric care, bad press and lawsuits. In other words, discrimination costs money! Discrimination is money lost when qualified workers cannot fully contribute to society based upon an insular institution or employer. Expanding ADA to include religious institutions means that our disabled and neurodiverse brothers and sisters will be available to contribute our time and talent to the Body of Christ through volunteering, paid employment, teaching and leadership, filling in for clergy, staff, volunteer, and laity shortages.

- *That Americans with Disability Act (ADA) only applies to those of us with physical disabilities?* No! ADA also applies to those of us who have what is known as an "invisible disability" including being on the autism spectrum, living with Down Syndrome, being dyslexic, having Attention Deficit Hyperactivity Disorder (AHDD), having a history of mental illness like bipolar or depression, being a trauma survivor with Post-Traumatic Stress Disorder (PTSD) or being blind or deaf. ADA also protects our family members from discrimination too. Applied to religious contexts, religions cannot exclude, discriminate, target or "discriminatory harass" or "create a hostile environment" based on an "invisible disability" like mine-Asperger.

### Three Myths about Government Disability Services

- *They are government handouts?* No, government disability services whether they are a monthly Social Security (SSI) check, Medicaid, the Nutrition Supplement Program (aka "food stamps"), Energy Assistance programs, Section 8 Housing or one time stipends for additional disability services ***are not*** government handouts. ***Uncle Sam does not give them out like candy!*** In fact, there is a very rigorous documentation process to get these services and many people who need them or may benefit from them, do not get them. Or, we get barely enough to function in society at all. All of us who get them, needed to go through an extensive documentation and application processes, to get them at all. Also, if you start to do significantly better financially, you become ineligible. For this reason, we are required to report additional income to the IRS.

- *People who get them are lazy?* Not true! In reality, everyone who gets disability services have been judged through an extensive review process to have a disability which makes us unemployable, temporally unemployable or not employable enough to be able to support ourselves financially all on our own. Some of us, have even chosen to use this stipend to follow our dreams through becoming independent, free lance artists and scholars and are actively engaged in volunteer community service, political activism and building relationships, addressing needs and issues which our conventional, market driven society struggles to address like institutional animal cruelty, the planetary crisis and globalized alienation. We desperately want to more actively engage the employment sector, but are forced into this predicament because of our discrimination based on disability. Like by religious institutions! You also *do not* get rich on disability services either! All those with a criminal record *or* are actively involved in criminal behavior are also automatically excluded from this process too! I had to go through an extensive criminal background check and a credit report check to get these services.

- *Disabled Americans are a burden to society?* Such an argument does not account for the reality that A) we also contribute much to society and B) that non-disabled Americans are also a burden to the disability community which I have talked about extensively throughout this liberation theology project.

### Three Myths about Neurodiversity

- *Don't all neurodiverse peoples have intellectual disabilities?* Intellectual disability is what they used to call "mental retardation," "low intelligence" or "low functioning."

Many of us with Down's, Fragile X Syndrome and even some of us on the autism spectrum fit into this category. Many of us with Asperger's, dyslexia, AHDD, learning disabilities, turrets or have a history of mental illness *do not* fit into the category "low intelligence" or "low functioning." In fact, many of us have "above average" to "exceptional intelligence." Many of us are college graduates, have been to graduate school, have worked in professional level jobs and live independently in society with minimum supports.

- *Aren't all neurodiverse people mentally deranged?* No! All of us from Down's and Asperger's to being Dyslectic are considered "competent," that is we are "clinically sane." Even those of us who have a history of mental illness are considered "competent" and "sane" when we are "psychologically stable." There are many "high functioning" peoples with mental illness, living independent, productive lives in society as a result of getting the right diagnosis, the right medication regime, receiving out-patient psychiatric care and developing management strategies.

- *Can neurodiverse people not do certain things?* No! The more the profession learns about the full diversity of neurodiverse peoples, they are learning that our diagnosis does not define who we are as human beings, whether it is our character or even our own potential in life. For example, my sister who currently works as a journalist for a Zionist organization called "United with Israel," in Jerusalem, had to write this article entitled "Disabled Israelis Serving Their Country with Pride." In her article, my sister talked about how the Israeli Army is welcoming Israeli citizens from both the physical disability and neurodiversity community into the country's mandatory military service program because many in the disability community did not want to use their disability as an "excuse" for not serving their country. This program has been a tremendous success! 20-year old Eliran Oster with only one arm became a charismatic military recruiter. A blind man, Oren Almog works in Israeli intelligence. Yuval Wagner remains wheel chair bound, yet Wagner has become an Israeli Air Force officer. 10 autistic Israel Lights even chose to serve in the IDF and the IDF accepted us. Many of these disabled veterans on active duty were suicide bomber survivors and disabled war veterans, while the autistic legion came out of a special program in Israel. My sister's article begs two critical questions. One, if we can be trained to become military soldiers to fight in a war, then we most certainly can be trained to serve communion and pray the rosary in a Franciscan fraternity? Two, if we can be trained to take enemy human lives on the battlefield, we most certainly can be taught how to save civilian human lives on the home front?[121]

What I have done in the above "thought experiment" is demonstrate that it's irrational, immoral, even unrealistic to exclude anyone, based on a disability or diagnosis from any aspect of religious life for any reason, physical or invisible. That it is in fact rational, moral and even realistic for American world religions to become ADA complaint. That it is possible, even desirable for Americans with disabilities to be included not only in worship and membership, but also in leadership, ministry and mission trips, as well as Christian academia even intentional communities like monasteries, convents and friaries.

Anything else is "irrelevant" and "harmful" to the various disability communities!

### *To Defend The Highest Ideals of the Christian Religion!*

Does this mean that we need to become anti-Christian, post-Christian or even post-Church to accommodate neurodiversity at the table? Absolutely not!

Mid-twentieth century Roman Catholic theologian G.K. Chesterton said in his biography of Saint Francis of Assisi that one of the reasons why Saint Francis was more peaceful, socially progressive, spiritual and environmental than many of his Medieval contemporaries is not because his theology, spirituality, cultural identity or moral code was radically different than anyone else in his time period, but that he actually defended the beliefs and values of his society.

He did not just right poetry like the troubadours and laurels of the twelfth and thirteenth centuries, he also "lived his song." Francis did not just write the "Canticle of Brother Sun," he lived under the Reign of Sir Brother Sun. Francis lived his everyday life under the Glory of God as a fighter, builder, lover and beggar. Francis did not just speak-out against poverty and injustice. Francis lived in solidarity with all those impacted by poverty and injustice, actually doing something about the problems of the world in his own community. Francis did not just preach the Gospel with mere words. Francis evangelized through his example, demonstrating what of the Kingdom of God is possible and attainable in such a fallen, broken world. Seeing how far his belief in the Holy Gospel and faith in the Living God would take him and the planet. Seeing what can happen when the highest ideals of Christendom are put into practice in real life. Ideals, which Saint Francis of Assisi contended were not only attainable, but also good and laudable. What his world needed most of all![122]

Francis's theological vision absolutely included all peoples with disabilities and all members of the neurodiversity communities.

For starters, there is no Medieval, Byzantine or Biblical word or explanation for autism, Asperger's or developmental disability. Yet, some scholars contend that Francis's follower Brother Juniper was on the autism spectrum.[123] While, Jessica Lee, a Disability Studies scholar studying deaf communities in Tanzania gave a fascinating presentation from the plenary session of the 2012 Society for Disability Studies (SDS) annual conference in Denver entitled "Re-mapping deaf-disability divides: Lessons from Tanzania" where Lee discovered that one of the reasons why those with invisible disabilities in this particular traditional African society were so stigmatized, was not because deaf brothers and sisters were seen as inferior, in fact the opposite, they actually saw their deaf brothers and sisters as physical and mental equals and misjudged "reasonable accommodations" as unfair "special treatment."

In Byzantine and Medieval societies, religious figures whom psychological historians have recovered as being on the autism spectrum, including everyone from Brother Juniper to the Holy Fools of Russia, also have noticed that their society praised them for their humility, simplicity and truth-telling abilities.[124]

This is because in premodern and traditional societies, neurodiverse humans are seen as equals, who are called to contribute to society using our strengths. Most likely a significant amount of the clergy and prophetic classes in premodern and traditional societies were on the autism spectrum or a member of another neurodiverse or physical disability community. In fact, everyone from Moses to Paul to Saint Augustine of Hippo to Saint Thomas of Aquinas to Saint Teresa of Avila complained about "this unexplained illness" which can only be remedied by cognitive or spiritual means. In fact, everyone from Saint Francis of Assisi to Lord Jesus Christ has had their sanity questioned at one time or another by historical contemporaries.

These suggestive examples have been systematized by the men's movements as the "wild man" archetype, by ecopsychogist Chellis Glendenning as the "wounded healer" archetype, by Aspie primatologist Dawn Prince-Hughes as the "ape-man archetype" and Temple Grandin uses what she calls "dresses like a slob" to recover historical figures in recent history which might have been on the autism spectrum like the late-animal rights activist Henry Spiro.

In fact, Grandin is so confident of this possibility that she mentors others on the autism spectrum to turn toward our heroes as role-models to help survive, for she contends that if we are attracted to particular figures in history, most likely they were autistic. While, Glendenning argues that one of the whole reasons for creating mental hospitals during the Enlightenment was to colonize those of us who "have the ability to experience non-ordinary consciousness" connected to "mystical experiences" which Glendenning argues are critical "sources of healing and empowerment" for "living more sanely and sustainability on this Earth."[125]

All of the above is conjunctive on my part, which as a liberation theologian I am absolutely entitled to recover the history of my people, the voices of our ancestors and place ourselves within the context of the human condition.

Having said this, what is an undeniable historical fact is that Saint Francis of Assisi did in fact overcome his fears and privileges surrounding the leaper outcasts of the middle ages. Overcoming millennia of stigma, taboos even local legal ordinances to such a point that Francis was able to touch, kiss even hug our brothers and sisters with leprosy. Where after Francis renounced all his worldly possessions, went to live in a leper colony outside the walls of the City of Assisi, where Francis ministered to the physical and spiritual needs of his beloved lepers, providing our lepers with both spiritual and physical healing.

In fact, when Francis started his own religious order with the blessing of the Christian Church, he required that all new brothers complete their novice year (training, initiation and formation period) in one of the local leper colonies. Providing a sense of disability literacy, spiritual equality even empathy and solidarity lacking in many of today's Christian disability ministries based more on "segregationist charity" than "social justice" and "equality."

Francis applied the Medieval chivalry value of "honor" (aka "human rights") to peoples with disabilities through not only giving us pastoral care and spiritual instruction, but also living among us, dinning with us and even eating from our bowls. Francis even applied his unique Model of God-World Relationships, "The Poor Christ" to disability, neurodiversity contexts. Where Francis saw all of us, whether we were a man or a woman, a disabled or non-disabled human being, neurodiverse or neurotypical, rich or poor, Christian or non-Christian, Jew or Greek, human or animal, plant or mineral as his beloved brothers and sisters in Christ, for we all emerged out of the same Creator God as he did, where all of us dwell within the Fountain of All

Good, the Streams of Living Waters which flows through God's own body. A Loving, Rational and Fair God who is personal and relational by nature, a Transcendent, Living, Just God who radiates through the Entire Cosmos in a spirit of beauty and wonder, sustaining our world with life and resurrection.

Yet, you might protest that we do not live in thirteenth century Medieval Italy? You might say we live in the twenty-first century? Hold your horse's---there will be a place for our twenty-century situation and context.

I am going to now identify two fragments from the tradition which I am going to contend does in fact have "relevance" to neurodiverse/neurotypical relationships within the twenty-century context of today's Christian Church. The first is the story of Merib-Baal in the Hebrew Bible (2 Samuel 4 and 9), the only story in the entire Bible about disability justice and disability responsibility. The second is Saint Anthony of Padua's (another follower of Saint Francis and Doctor of the Church) commentary on one of Jesus's healing miracles with lepers. I will use Sallie McFague's metaphoric theology method to recover, deconstruct and revitalize the original meaning of the problematic "sin-disability connection" in the Christian religion, making the case that the "sin-disability connection" is "irrelevant," "exclusive" and "harmful" religious language and explore the possibilities of using Anthony's commentaries for better integrating disability and neurodiversity experiences into the rest of the human condition within the Christian theological and spiritual context of the twenty-first century.[126]

### *Merib-Baal: A Better Model of Proper Disability/Non-Disabled Relations*

Merib-Baal, was King Saul's five year old grandson (one of the great kings of Ancient Israel), who survived Saul's and Jonathan's (Merib-Baal's father) tragic death. Yet with King David's impending cue over Israel, Merib-Baal's nurse helped Merib-Baal escape into exile, "but in their hasty flight, [Merib-Baal] fell and became lame" (II Samuel 4: 4).

Merib-Baal resurfaced many years later as a grown man when King David asked "Is there any survivor of Saul's house to whom I may show kindness for the sake of Jonathan?" (2 Samuel 9: 1). King David found Merib-Baal living in the household of one of Saul's servants where Merib-

Baal was still "crippled" (2 Samuel 9:2-6). When King David found Merib-Baal, the King said to Merib-Baal, "Fear not...I will surely be kind to you for the sake of your father Jonathan. I will restore to you all the lands of your grandfather Saul, and you shall always eat at my table (2 Samuel 9: 7). Merib-Baal's response, "What is your servant that you should attend to a dead dog like me? (2 Samuel 9: 8).

Unmoved by Merib-Baal's display of inferiority and self-hatred, our King aptly responded, "I am giving your lord's son all that belonged to Saul and all his family. You [Saul's servant turned Lord] and your sons and servants must till the land for him [Merib-Baal]. You shall bring in produce, which shall be food for your lord's [Merib-Baal] family to eat. But Merib-Baal your lord's son, shall always eat at my table" (2 Samuel 9: 9-10). Ziba, Saul's former servant, who now had fifteen sons and twenty servants of his own graciously accepted, "Your [Ziba] servant shall do just as my lord the king commended him [Merib-Baal]" (2 Samuel 9: 11).

The Biblical account ends with, "And so Merib-Baal ate at David's table like one of the king's son. Merib-Baal had a young son whose name was Mica; and all the tenets of Ziba's family worked for Merib-Baal. But Merib-Baal lived in Jerusalem, because he always ate at the king's table. He was lame in both feet." (2 Samuel 9: 10-13).

There are three critical principles of proper disability/non-disabled relationships which can be recovered from this delightful little "best kept secret" in the Holy Bible.

- There is nothing natural, inherit, cosmic, mythic or supernatural about disability. Disability like poverty, racism and gender inequality is also "socially produced." In Merib-Baal's case, his lameness was the result of being a civilian survivor of war. In my case, even through autism is a genetic condition, my symptoms were compounded by medical malpractice, violent socialization, bullying, stigma, discrimination, isolation, alienation, spiritual abuse and vocational disadvantage which a truly humane and progressive society should never have exposed a vulnerable member in society like myself, too. This means, ***the survival, welfare and dignity of all human beings with disabilities absolutely is the responsibility of a non-disabled society. This is non-negotiable!***

- *That all individual human beings with disabilities as well as the various disability communities at-large absolutely deserve social justice.* According to King David, social justice for humans with disabilities means a full investigation, acknowledgement, explanation and apology for any and all past atrocities which were in the not too distant past. Social justice for individuals with disabilities means providing for the basic material, emotional and spiritual well-being of all individuals with disabilities in the present and future, so our brothers and sisters with disabilities can live with dignity in the present and future. Social justice for individuals with disabilities according to King David means treating us as moral and spiritual equals and fully including us in non-disabled society.

- *That the "preferential option" absolutely needs to be given toward disability and neurodiversity. Religious groups must absolutely be in solidarity with every disabled and neurodiverse brother and sister and give the reality of the oppression of humans with disabilities the same respect and attention as any other minority group's liberation struggle. Disability and Neurodiversity absolutely must be on every religious group's social justice, anti-oppression agendas "worth its salts"! Anything else is part of the problem!*

So in essence, according to the exchange between King David and Prince Merib-Baal, proper disability/non-disabled relationships are based upon A) accountability, B) social justice and C) equality. These there Biblical disability principles I contend are good, laudable and completely relevant to our twenty-first century situation and context. They need to be intensified!

### Saint Anthony of Padua: Disability Is Part of the Human Condition

Saint Anthony of Padua, a Doctor of the Christian Church, follower of Saint Francis of Assisi and a man who suffered from a serious illness himself, having died at the age of only thirty-six years old, offers a fascinating commentary on Lord Jesus Christ healing the ten "lepers," "And as he [Jesus] entered a certain town, there met him ten men that were lepers, who stood far off, and lifted their voice, saying: Jesus, master have mercy on us. Whom when he saw, he said: Go, show yourselves to the priests. Go: show yourselves to the priests. And it came to pass, as they went, that they made clean" (Luke 17: 12-14).

Taking an allegorical versus literalist interpretation to Holy Scripture, Anthony uses "the ten lepers" as a metaphor for both "all sinners" and "the human race." Which is a curious even seditious interpretation of the "sin-disability connection" (the belief that disability is a punishment for doing something wrong, e.g., "mental illness is a sin" and "mental illness is demon possession"). A superstitious belief which the medical establishment, the disability studies field and the various disability and neurodiversity movements have full-heartily rejected as "irrelevant," "exclusive" and "harmful" religious language.

Yet, Saint Anthony not only uses "leprosy" as a metaphor for "sinners" (an abelist narrative), Anthony also uses "leprosy" as a metaphor for "the human race" (a crip narrative), juxposed in the same paragraph. In other words, Anthony uses a serious disability like "leprosy," a predominant disability in Anthony's thirteenth century world, as a metaphor for "the human condition."

In other words, Anthony is implying that disability and disease is in fact part of the human condition, after all, part of what it means to be human in a fallen, broken world. Disability *is not* "other," "them," "sub-human," or "more primitive" or "more childlike." Disability *is not* "demon possession" or "post-human." Disability *is* "us," "we," "humanity," "manhood" and "womanhood." Disability *is* "East of Eden" and "only human."

Anthony's interpretation of the meaning of disability begins to bring "disability experience" back down to "human scale," beginning the process of integrating disability into the rest of the human condition. Disability occurs because we live in an imperfect world marked by fallenness and brokenness. Disability occurs within the context of a disabled world. Disability is the preverbal "canary in the coalmine" that we live on a wounded planet. A planet wounded by human sin and evil.

This is what metaphoric theologian Sallie McFague contends is one of the signs of a truly powerful metaphor, where a mystic like Saint Anthony of Padua would use as a comparison, juxposed opposite words like "war" and "peace" or "God" and "Nature" to inspire new understandings of hackneyed concepts. For example, if a mystic wants us to gain a new understanding of "world peace," a mystic might use "war" and "military" metaphors to describe "pacifism" and "world peace," where we would "pull-out" "nonviolent resistance," creating a "narrow passage" between "pacifism" and "just war theory." If a mystic wants us to a gain a new understanding of "God's Creation," a mystic might use "God" metaphors to describe the "Natural World" and "Nature" metaphors to describe "God," where we would "pull-out" "The Doctrine of the Incarnation," creating a "narrow passage" between an "anti-nature monotheism" and a "misanthropic paganism."

I contend that Anthony in his "leper" analogy uses the "sin-disability connection" as a metaphor to describe "the human race," to get his thirteenth century audience to "pull-out" "the human condition," creating a "narrow passage" between "sin" and "disability" which acknowledges the "social construction of disability," in the process. Where disability is understood as a completely artificial, human created phenomenon; there is nothing natural, scientific, objective, value-neutral, cosmic, mythic or supernatural about the category "disability."

In other words, "the human condition" was the original Biblical-Medieval meaning of the "sin-disability" association. It was a premodern explanation for the "human costs" of "the sins of society."

According to McFague, when a religious metaphor leaves its original context (like Biblical times or the Middle Ages), the original meaning of this word is lost, leading the metaphor to have an opposite meaning than its original intended use. For example, the "sin-disability" metaphor was developed in a time period when many human beings did not enjoy good physical and mental health, so having a physical, mental or psychological disability meant "welcome to the human race!"

We now live in a society because of the scientific and industrial revolution, coupled with modern medicine where we have all the science and technology to make everyone physically and mentally fit and provide such health care to a significant number of the population (although not everyone). So a substantial part of human society is physically and mentally "fit," where those who of us who are not fully benefiting from modern medicine (those of us with conditions resistant to modern medical treatments and those who are uninsured or under-insured) automatically gain "minority" status. The "sin-disability" metaphor becomes "irrelevant," "exclusive" and "harmful," for this metaphor can then be used to justify the exclusion, persecution, exploitation and oppression of the disability "minority" group.

Religious language, according to McFague can be "revitalized" when the "root metaphor" (the undergirding reality which is the origins of the metaphor) and our current, contemporary situation and context is identified. I have already identified "the human condition" as the "root metaphor" for the "sin-disability" metaphor. Our current, contemporary situation of disability and neurodiversity within a twenty-first century context *is* marked by abuse, stigma and isolation at the hands of our own people (scapegoating). In other words, we are oppressed by our own families, our own communities, our own culture, in our own country and in our own homes. We are treated as strangers in our own country. Our neighbors are our enemies.

So, to "revitalize" the "humanity" metaphor for our disabled and neurodiverse brothers and sisters, some possible new "branch" metaphors which would integrate disability and neurodiversity back into the human race, could be to understand "humanity" to be more like an "assembly," a motley group of beings with a diverse set of strengths and weaknesses, who are all members of the same species. Or, like a "team" where everyone brings a unique set of gifts which complements and supplements each other's weaknesses, where each individual is called to cooperate with everyone else, to work toward the "common goal" of species survival.

The strength of these "disability-virtue" metaphors is that they have "common ground" with both the Biblical, Medieval religious language of our ancestors and today's science, psychology and critical social theory. Also the "disability-virtue" metaphor leaves "room" for Animals and the Earth too, also having "common ground" with "play" in "animal societies" and "mutualistic relationships" in "biotic societies."

In this model, disability will be associated with respect for the different virtues! Disability is a body of virtues needed for human survival and flourishing! Neurodiversity is another body of virtues necessary for human survival and flourishing!

Meaning the tradition is in fact "good news" for the "assembly" of disabled and neurodiverse humans after all!

If the Christian Church actually sticks to Christianity, they will be on the "right track" to better relationships with the various disability and neurodiversity "assemblies." As well as the "assembly" of All Life! Becoming a "win-win" winning "team" in the process![127]

In other words, what I personally need and want as one neurodiverse person of faith from religious groups is A) to get the word "selfish" out of their vocabulary, B) to appreciate that disability and neurodiversity is an "inconvenient reality" on the planetary agenda, C) to acknowledge the human psyche as embodied phenomena, D) to welcome disability and neurodiversity charisms in religious leadership and ministry opportunities and E) to come to the realization that disability justice is compatible with respect for the various Christian traditions and sound Christian doctrine.

### *What the Disability Assembly Might Want At-Large*

I am basing my observation on what the disability community at-large needs from the Christian Church, based on my attendance of a workshop entitled "Spirit & Pride: Reimagining Disability in Jewish and Christian Communities" at the 2012 Society of Disability Studies annual conference in Denver, Colorado. All of us came to similar conclusions based on discussions, debates and break-out sessions which I will discuss briefly.

### *We Do Not Want Charity, We Want Justice!*

No one who spoke in our workshop wanted "pity," "paternalism" or "segregationalist charity."

Everyone wanted to fully participate in religious life. Everyone wanted to be treated as a spiritual equal by non-disabled religious. Everyone wanted to contribute to faith community in a meaningful manor.

Everyone agreed that religious groups have been oppressive to the various disability assemblies. Yet, everyone agreed that we would benefit from perusing spirituality and religious life. Meaning, none of us were going to give-up on spirituality or religion.

Everyone agreed that "liberation theology" and "social justice" is the appropriate "means" for making "in-roads" with religious groups.

In other words, we, "the disabled," want to be treated with respect.

### *There Is More To Accessibility Then Mere Wheelchair Ramps!*
Although all of us absolutely insist on "reasonable accommodations" like handicap accessible sanctuaries and gluten free communion wafers.

All of us agree that to make houses of worship truly accessible to all peoples with disabilities, there are definitely some deeper cultural changes religious groups will need to make, like an "accessible theological method" and "ability inclusive language."

### *Act Locally!*
All of us had concerns that social justice has become "internationalized," becoming just another form of escapism, in the process. We asked the question, are American religious institutions really bringing theology "down to earth" by fixating on starving children in Africa or peace in the Middle East? Or, is this just another way of being otherworldly?

All of us are concerned that the religious establishment seems more concerned about oppressed non-disabled people at the other end of the world, than disabled people in their own congregations.

Our objection parallels Harper in her occult civil rights classic *To Kill A Mockingbird* who in her parable about racism and segregation in the American South, had this one scene where the local high school got the students all worked-up about the evils of Nazism and the Holocaust, but did not even mention all the racism and injustice right in her own Deep South community. My high school honors English teacher used this scene as a parable about the dangers of hypocrisy. In other words, Harper's parable is not denying the evils of Nazism and the Holocaust, she is more speaking-out against our impulse to psychologically project, deflect even redirect our feelings of moral outrage as a "defense mechanism" against feeling a certain way, having to change or god-forbid, wreck too much havoc in our lives, like confronting the bigot within, instead of accusing everyone else of it.

This reprehensive sample of the disability community is making a similar argument. We are not denying that poverty and inequality in Africa or violence and wars in the Middle East are important issues and injustices. In fact, the Society for Disability Studies (SDS) community at-large *absolutely* is in solidarity with oppressed minority groups everywhere. Including how disability also effects and impacts different minority groups from the various gay, lesbian and transgender assemblies in North America to disability assemblies in the various African nations. We are actively in dialogue with every movement from the women's movement to the animal rights movement.

In fact, even this very workshop was made-up of men and women, members from the various physical and invisible disability assemblies, Jews and Christians and peoples from all over the world.

Our argument than is not that global peace and social justice issues are not important, but that organized religion in their quest to "love humanity" absolutely must "love human beings" to truly become compassionate, just and nonviolent.

This absolutely also includes "loving" all individuals with disabilities in your own congregations.

When Jesus was asked "who is my neighbor?" Jesus did not offer a Plutonic ideal of "neighborly-ness." Nor, did Jesus use examples of suffering and injustice in Rome or Athens. No, Jesus told the parable of the "Good Samaritan," the story about the "compassion" and "humanity" of a member of an oppressed minority group right here in the questioners own community. Jesus does not just bring theology "down to earth," Jesus brings theology "close to home" too.

So, religious would be wise to take a hint from the secular environmentalist slogan, "think globally, act locally!"

Remembering the historical reality that trying to "run the lives" of peoples at the other end of the world is how colonization, slavery, racism, bigotry, paternalism and chauvinism happened in America and continues to be justified even tell this day a-broad. Although more subtle than in the past. Peoples around the world, from various First Nations to many Latin American countries, from modern-day Israel Lights to the Arab world to Africa to Southern Asia, really *do not* want Western "charity" or "intrusion" in their lives and culture; instead they want to "just be left alone." America *is not* "the policeman of the world." Such a mentality is world domineering, nothing less than the Roman Empire revisited and completely oppressive. Left over colonialist residue! Neo-colonialism!

### *The Moral Imagination as Libratory Praxis for Disability Justice!*

We also agreed that our "imagination" is our "way into" the Judeo-Christian tradition, through creatively envisioning possible ways to integrate our "disability experiences" into our religious faith and our relationship to faith community. The workshop leaders offered two proposals as a "place to begin" to answer this waver.

*The Christian proposal* was to use the late-disability liberation theologian Nancy Eisland's vision of the Disabled God as a metaphor for further theological reflection on disability. Nancy Eisland developed this metaphor based on two different religious authorities:

- *The Resurrection of Jesus Christ:* The reality that Jesus survived a complete death on the Cross, with His wounds intact. Where there are parallels between the Resurrection of Christ and the embodied experiences of living with a disability. Such as going through a death-rebirth process and becoming a survivor. Surviving and flourishing, without being cured or fixed. In other words, "[God] is a survivor too!" A Christology (beliefs about Jesus Christ) which Eisland insists is consistent with Early Church Teaching.

- *Feminist Christology:* A belief coming out of postmodern feminist theology, which is gaining momentum in the Christian Church, that the Incarnation is more than merely accepting that "Jesus is God" or that "Jesus is the Son of God" or even believing in the "Historical Jesus." Feminist Christology insists that the Incarnation is nothing less than the Physical Manifestation of God, embodied into All Creation. Where the Historical Jesus is a non-literal parable about "God-World relationships" and "the Meaning of the Body." Where Eisland "crip" feminist Christology of the Disabled God, gets Christians to also respect and celebrate imperfect disabled bodies and to acknowledge bodily diversity.

In the process, Eisland links and systematizes two fragmented Christian doctrines, The Doctrine of Incarnation and the Doctrine of Resurrection, revitalizing the Caledonian Orthodoxy that Jesus Christ is both "Fully Man" and "Fully God." This is because Eisland has revitalized the Resurrection through recognizing that Christ is *both* the physical embodiment of the Living God (God's humanity) *and* has the power to survive death (God's divinity) because of her embodied, disability experience. The later is missing in feminist Christology, preserving more of the tradition in the process. In other words, the Disabled God metaphor illuminates that Jesus Christ is both Fully Creature and Fully God at the same time, placing Eisland on solid Nicean grounds.

*The Jewish proposal* was given by one of the workshop leaders who is both a Jewish rabbinical student and uses a wheelchair (Julia Watts Beiser). Beiser gave one of the most fascinating and promising proposals in my opinion. She offered one of the most fascinating exegesis on the very cryptic Ezekiel I passage where the Prophet Ezekiel received a prophetic vision of God traveling through the Heavens in a Chariot being pulled by the same Four Creatures (ox, eagle, lion and man) who appeared in the Christian Bible in the Book of Revelations, which the Jewish mystical tradition insists you need to be at-least thirty years to understand. When I listened to her disability criticism of Ezekiel I, I was beginning to understand.

Beiser made the case that the Chariot was a Wheelchair. That God travels around the Universe like a woman in a wheelchair, in a spirit of passion and vitality. As a disabled guy, I had more a masculine imagine of God being this Roosevelt-like figure who lived with a serious disability, but who rose to be a great world leader, who not only had great inner strength to personally survive, most importantly, he actually gave strength to an entire non-disabled nation. Even beyond! A civilization seriously weakened by Nazism. Roosevelt offered nothing less than the rooted moral vision and decisive political action necessarily to get out of the Great Depression and win World War II. I see many of these same attributes in God.

I contend that such an interpretation of Holy Scripture is not isogesis (projecting your own self-serving bias onto scripture) but actually has an historical precedent for two reasons.

*First*, the rabbinical student's novel insight does have "common ground" with the Psalmists in the Hebrew Bible where "Heaven" is "God's thrown" and "the Earth is God's footstool" (Psalm 132:7; Isaiah 66:1).

In fact, when I visited the vibrant, watery oasis smack in the middle of the desolate Judean Desert, Ein Gedi National Park in Israel, the place where King David fled from King Saul and some believe David was inspired to write many of the Psalms in the Hebrew Bible, I saw this magnificent waterfall shaped like a thrown. When I looked above this crystalline freshwater waterfall I saw stark canyons and vast sapphire skies above me, inhabited by a flock of wild ravens. Around me, I saw groves of date palms, thickets of desert brush and marshy blocks of papyrus, giant cattails and common reeds as "thick as thieves." Behind me, I saw wild rock badgers play and wild ibex roaming around the ruins of an ancient Jewish settlement dating all the way back to the time of David and Saul, thousands of years ago.

When I gazed into the veil of this life-giving waterfall, because of the fall's unique geological, hydrological and ecological structure, this one waterfall literally encompassed plants from two completely opposite regions of the world. These falls enveloped both the mosses from the temperate regions of the world and the Sodom's Apples (a member of the milkweed family, what the Bible calls "gall") a plant found mostly in African tropical savannahs. Yet, both the mosses and the galls are native to this bioregion, with flocks of red and green dragonflies hovering all around.

This one thrown-veil waterfall is actually part of a stream of life-giving water, an entire watershed of cascading, interlocking waterfalls and crystalline pools, which eventually overflow into the Dead Sea, with origins in an underground river, right smack in the middle of a vast and sublime desertscape.

This was a scene right out of Psalm 104 (The Sabbath Psalm) or Psalm 148 (The Ecology Psalm). One can only imagine how the ancient Israel Lights were inspired to their belief in One God, who fairly rules the Earth from the Heavens in a Fiery Chariot, where the Universe is being perpetually created by an Invisible God, who sustains His Creatures, where All Creation is enveloped by God's Reign.

*Second,* it also makes sense that the Chariot is a Wheelchair, because by your thirtieth year, you would most likely have had your first "run-in" with death where you discover your own mortality and the fragility of all life. In fact, in the ecological tradition, there is documented evidence that Thoreau, Muir, Mill and Anzsel Adams all went through a maturing periods in their early thirties. Also, Saint Augustine of Hippo went through a similar process in his early thirties.

In other words, the taboo against reading Ezekiel I until your thirtieth birthday now begins to make more sense, Ezekiel I was considered "mature reading" for it presupposed a certain amount of life experiences and formation into adulthood, like almost dying, losing a love one, struggling with a disability or a serious illness, discovering your limits and so forth.

The Fiery Chariot is a non-mechanistic, sacred metaphor and a message of empathy and hope which anyone who has ever wrestled with a disability or serious illness can easily relate to. Reading the first chapter of Ezekiel is not for the temporally-able!

Also, the Chair metaphor, unlike the Wounds of Christ metaphor, is a metaphor of disability transcendence and embodiment which shares "common ground" with Judaism and other World Religions and secular spiritualities alike. Meaning Jews, Muslims, First Nations, Hindis,

Buddhists, Pagans and New Agers who also live with a disability can also recover their own theological and spiritual visions and reflect critically on their own religious or spiritual traditions.

For example, in the Muslim religion, all Muslims are required to "Submit to God" even in the face of great suffering and hardship. In an Islamic context, the Chair metaphor means that the Will of God is bounded by the limits of God's existence and we are bounded by God's limits. We cannot venture outside God's limits.

In many First Nation societies there are countless stories of the Universe being created through mistakes and mishaps which explain both the inherent limits and imperfections of our world.

Despite my gripes with Eastern religions, I do agree that suffering including disability, disease and death is a realistic expectation in a fallen, broken world. I do still part ways, for as a Judeo-Christian and a Westerner, I insistently believe that suffering *is not* deterministic. Suffering can be remedied through social justice, nonviolent resistance, personal responsibility, spiritual guidance and Divine help. You do not need to passively accept your fate in life.

In a since, what I have done is establish Eisland's "Disabled God" as an archetype, which according to Yunnan psychology are "common human experiences" which are universally recognized through certain reoccurring dreams and "root" metaphors regardless of the culture or time-period, because these archetypes are embodied into our instinctual, mammalian minds. The Disabled God is one such archetype.

Ecopsychologist Chellis Glendenning names this the "Wounded Healer" archetype, the "common human experience" of an imperfect, unhealed person being able to heal others and create beauty. The "Wounded Healer" archetype is also connected to the "death-rebirth" archetype which sees much healing and beauty in and amongst such an imperfect, broken, wounded world.

In Christianity, these archetypes appear as The Disabled God, the New Earth, the Communion of Saints and The Martyrs. In Judaism, these archetypes appear as the Footstool of God, the Promised Land and the Messianic Age.

In many pagan religions, this archetype is deeply connected to morality lessons, healing rituals and life cycles, as well as the "green man" and "wild man" archetypes. In Nature-based religions, these archetypes appear in the form of stories and statements about the nature of the Universe and human beings place in it.

All of these religious specific metaphors than can be connected to the "embodiment" archetype, "the world is a living organism," as different models of disability transcendence, embodiment and relationality, whether you understand the meaning of disability to be a resurrection, rebirth, revival or a cosmic reality or just making the best of a bad situation, recovering an archetype gives you a framework to make subsequent improvements or improvisations on the insufficiency of these existing models of disability. This is one methodology for effectuating cultural change!

So, what I have done here is provide disabled and non-disabled people of faith, a framework for integrating our own disability experiences back into our various religious traditions, so our disabled brothers and sisters can experience nourishing religious community and a meaningful religious faith, giving our lives meaning and purpose, in the process.

**Chapter Six: On Listening to Neurodiverse Voices---What Neurodiversity Wants To Tell Us**

Ecopsychologist Chellis Glendenning writes,

> In light of the tenuous condition of our earth, technology survivors have a special mission. They present the most sticking personal illustration of the consequences of modern technological development. And they have the most passionate voices to describe these consequences….Their prophesy begins as a challenge to the psychological defense mechanisms that keep us from thinking about technological threats…On the surface, the key to surrounding defense mechanisms is simple. It is an admission of vulnerability. More than other people, technology survivors feel vulnerable before the forces of technological development and use…Such psychological breakthroughs, while undergone by technology survivors out of necessity, are required by all of us all if we are to muster our efforts towards collective survival. This is the most impassioned message that technology survivors want to tell us. With their hearts and minds, they understand the implications of *not* making such changes in consciousness about technology, and they understand the personal challenges involved in making them. Above all, they know that such change demands courage and creativity. After making them, technology survivors are left with a sense of fragility in technological society. They have been left exposed to an uncertain future. They have also been left with a state of unqualified honesty. Such a state can become a source of strength and transformation. Stripped down, as [pesticide-poisoned anthropologist] Joan Westcott says, to "the ground rules for essentials," technology survivors are open to new perceptions and new ways.[128]

Like the technology survivors of the great environmental disasters of the late-twentieth century, the survivors of Love Canal, Woburn, Three Mile Island, nuclear weapons testing in the American Southwest during the Cold War and the countless survivors of pesticide outbreaks, medication side-effects and other chemical hazards and dangerous technologies across the country, which Glendenning describes in her 1990s book, we as neurodiverse humans in the early twenty-first century are the second wave of technology survivors, who also hold great promise for offering an ecologically prophetic message, the faithful backing of the planetary sustainability effort, where our stories directly link the personal to the political to the planetary, putting a human face on an overwhelming abstraction, the planetary crisis.

We as neurodiverse humans are technology survivors in that we have survived mercury laced vaccines, dangerous medications with serious side-effects, invasive medical procedures, dysfunctional medical professionals, an overstimulating, disorienting built environment, a volatile, ailing civilization, noise pollution, light pollution, florescent lights and human overpopulation, just to name a few. This is not to mention surviving all of the toxic, dysfunctional social institutions which mark industrial and post-industrial society from an intellectually compartmentalized educational system to a rigid, dualistic, hierarchical, authoritarian religious political economic system to a medical caste system to a professional meritocracy to dehumanizing bureaucracies to a violent socialization process into adulthood to atomized housing to a sedentary lifestyle, leading to the loneness, alienation, anxiety, depression, hopelessness, futility, addictive consumerism, empty leisure and glaring physical health problems which most neurodiverse humans struggle with. We are violently allergic to modern Western civilization.

We also, like the first wave of technology survivors are acutely aware that we need clean water, fresh air, sunlight, nutritious food, restorative sleep, appropriate health care, a healthy, life-giving, beautiful environment, dignified relationships, meaningful work, an illuminating education, a comforting religious faith, self-determination and large tracts of undeveloped wilderness and farmlands for our personal survival.

We also get that our personal survival *is not* dependant upon a manicured lawn, total environment buildings, fossil fueled electricity, agribusiness food, sprawling concrete jungles, unlimited children, a high powered job which makes tons of money, fear-based religion or making every Animal and All the Earth useful to human beings or an all-powerful military-industrial complex.

We are not wedded to consumerism as our source of happiness. We also make a strong distinction between "freedom of conscience" and "creature comforts," "sovereignty" and "property holding," "self-care" and "self-absorption" and "bigness" and "greatness."

I contend that an ecological model of disability and neurodiversity *does not* negate disability or autistic culture; because each of these "clusters" became their own disability culture and each of these technology survivors have militantly rejected abelism and normalcy, in the process.

Remembering that no culture is ever really natural, disability or autistic culture is no exception. All culture is a social construction. The whole point of human culture is to help foster human survival and flourishing, to interpret, celebrate and maintain our place in the Universe through knowledge, religion, morality and the arts.

So in other words, in this section, I am going to apply Glendenning's recovery of the prophetic message which "technology survivor want to tell us" to a neurodiversity context. In this chapter, I am going to showcase the positive benefits of including neurodiversity and individual neurodiverse humans on various religious, social and planetary agendas. I am going to recover the various ways which neurodiversity can grow, enrich and enliven these worthwhile existing efforts. The main benefit of including neurodiversity, to quote from Westcott, "…throughout history it has been the outcasts—the victims---who have the great potential for prophesy and vision."

Glendenning writes, "One of the questions I asked forty-six survivors I interviewed was: 'If you could tell the world one thing about your experience, what would it be?" All forty-six survivors want non-survivors "to know that the prevailing beliefs about technological development and use serve nether life or hope. The notion of technological progress is the first to go… Nor, in many technology survivors' minds, is the primacy of the technological solution adequate… To many technology survivors, the ethos of human mastery over nature is revealed as ultimately destructive… Many survivors, through generalizing their experience of dehumanization through a technological event, came to see that the accepted social belief in the mechanization of life is responsible for mass dehumanization."

In other words, the four key themes of the "technology survivor worldview" include A) rejection of technological idolatry, B) rejection of technological solutions, C) rejection of anthropocentrism and D) rejection of mechanistic cosmology.

These four themes I contend also appear in the "autistic worldview."

Animal scientist Temple Grandin challenges the technological and economic rigidity of factory farm practices, speaks out against the limits of abstraction and compartmentalization, deconstructs anthropocentrism from a scientific perspective through her contributions to the animal intelligence research program and has spent her entire life developing a non-mechanistic model of animal behavior.

Primatologist Dawn Prince-Huges deeply questioned the "arbitrary and capacious" changes to her social, natural and built environments in the "name of progress" as a child. She then went onto to question her own militant agnosticism and libertarian individualism in young adulthood, opening her own heart up to spiritual experiences and the role of relationships and community. Where Prince-Hughes also surrendered her powers over to Animals and Nature, where she let a troop of captive gorillas guide her on how to "live more sanely and sustainability on this Earth." Where Prince-Hughes also helped recover, preserve and revitalize the missing "personalism" link of non-mechanistic, organic cosmology, leading to the "re-humanizing" of not only human beings and humanity, but also "re-humanized" aka "re-personalized" Animals and the Natural World.

Political activist Jim Sin Clair has spent his life trying to deconstruct how modern biomedicine is being used to colonize and domesticate neurodiverse humans. He also militantly rejects a medical technological fix for the autistic condition which does not respect our humanity. He even questions Temple Grandin's insider reforms of factory farms and slaughterhouses, comparing them to "humane" forms of human execution like hanging and the lethal injection, definitely seeing a contradiction between Grandin's purported love of animals and her willingness to kill them. In the process, Clair has rejected animal welfare, in favor of animal abolition and veganism. Clair in other words, has made it his life work to create and articulate a non-mechanistic model of autism.

As a naturalist and person of faith, I have expanded this discussion to also include Faith and Nature. I definitely have grave concerns about the idolatrous dangers of marrying technology to ideology which technological optimism has attempted to do. I contend that a pragmatic use of technology is compatible with a demythologized ecological critique of technology. I *do not* believe that a mere technological fix is going to sustainably resolve the planetary crisis. I belief we do need to address the "root causes" of the planetary crisis, we do need social, cultural, political, economic and lifestyle change. I belief as humans we do need to let go of needing to control everyone and everything in our environment. I believe in the intrinsic value of all Animals and the Earth. I believe that the Universe possesses aesthetic and spiritual properties.

I have made it my life work to seek-out "situations of inherent worth," "to seek after every green thing," to recover the "slime mold" of Judeo-Christianity, to heal the human-animal and human-Earth bonds, to live right with Animals and the Earth in a spirit of peace and harmony, to identify "reasons for hope," to search for the first signs of the New Earth, to research and develop compassionate, humane, ecological solutions to the planetary crisis and institutional animal cruelty, to revitalize and articulate the non-mechanistic vision of progress embodied in Judeo-Christianity's Apocalyptic, Messianic and Medieval traditions, to live my everyday life under the Glory of God and to devote my entire life to praising, worshiping and serving my Lord, the Love of My Life.

In other words, we the neurodiverse, bring the various planetary movements, the necessary ecological worldview for living sustainably, justly, nonviolently and harmoniously with Animals and the Earth in an age of planetary crisis and animal enslavement. We have a non-anthropocentric anthropology. We have an organic cosmology. We have a holistic worldview.

Unlike the worldviews of our premodern ancestors and First Nations around the world today, ours was developed within the constraints of our present context of planetary crisis, globalized alienation and institutional animal cruelty. Meaning our worldview is uniquely equipped to provide the necessary ecological response, because our ecological vision is not bound to a very specific place, it is versatile without becoming rootless; our worldview preserves the wildness of our artificial world, breaks down the First/Second nature, wilderness/civilization dualism, sanctions human participation and interspecies communications, re-humanizes humanity, re-animates animals, re-personalizes the Natural World and transubstantiates technology into a tool to serve all life, while respecting and preserving the aesthetic, intellectual, spiritual and democratic values of world civilization, in the process.

Most importantly, our sustainable worldview respects animals and animal rights and keeps alive the possibility of positive human participation in the web of life and interspecies communications in a globally colonized world, colonized by a modern Western civilization who is noted for its violent, exploitive, domineering, manipulative relationship with Animals and the Natural World, making the return to being "hunters and gatherers" not tenable for the planet nor is such a return desirable for animals either, getting a "blood thirsty" gun sub-culture instead of sustainability or nonviolence.

Our worldview does keep intact however, respect for specific places, communities and natural elements, respect for local cultures and traditions, respect for individuality, respect for individual freedom, interests, solitude and access to beauty and wild Nature and respect for grassroots democratic processes and local economic systems, not to mention the Earth at-large.

Yet, the stories, traditions, cultural artifacts and ancestral biocultural landscapes of First Nations and Premodern peoples around the world, do need to be preserved at all costs, to provide models of subsistence living and because it is the right thing to do. The self-determination of First Nations peoples today do need to be respected and tolerated at all costs like the "right to hunt."

Yet, in this sustainability worldview, just because those in very specific cultural situations need to be able to hunt, that does not mean we also need to become hunters. Nor, does that mean that if privileged white Europeans start hunting, then all of a sudden things like climate change, human overpopulation and extinctions will go away. Just look to the British, French, Belgium, Spanish, Russian and American Empires for an example, European cultures marked by a strong hunting culture. Nor does this mean that the model of hunting in First Nations is a viable model for Westerners in a twenty-first context. Nor does every "right to hunt" claim need to be taking equally seriously. For example, Makah ceremonial whale hunts *must not* be put on the same plain as privileged white people in rural America claiming a "right to hunt" or Japanese or Norwegian whalers in violation of international treaties or yesterdays peasant classes aka today's merchant classes in modern-day England and France feeling entitled to hunt like nobles in the Middle Ages.

Even such ceremonial whale hunts absolutely need to be subjected to the same government oversight, regulations and limits as other hunters, meaning it cannot be an automatic process. It absolutely needs to be scientifically investigated whether existing whale populations and their long-term sustainability can even handle being hunted at all. The same with wild seals too.

Not to mention: male bonding, women's liberation, recreation or sports, an acceptable activity for troubled youth, eradication or population control, preserving rural culture, commercial uses, appeals to the United States constitution and "ethical hunting"---being all considered illegitimate reasons for allowing the practice of hunting or fishing to continue at all, in this ethical-moral framework.

The only people who should be allowed to hunt or fish in this day and age are oppressed minorities in very specific situations like Native Americans and academic trained government managers implementing very specific policies which absolutely need to be defended through academic scientific and public democratic processes also open to the animal rights community. No more, no less!

Hunting should never be instilled on younger generations. Hunting is not how we solve wildlife pest problems either.

Remembering that animals are colonized peoples too!

Until about the time of the Great Depression of the 1930s, cows, pigs and chickens happily roamed cage free across verdant pastures and sovereign barnyards until merely for money reasons, were ripped out of their happy habitats and homes to be warehoused in de-animalizing, mechanized indoor stalls, isolated from the Natural World and each other, where they are now feed the cannibalized remains of their comrades in concentration-camp style factory farms and slaughterhouses.

Until about the last five hundred years when English colonialists invaded and colonized my bioregion, the Piedmont Plateau, early English explorer Captain John Smith cited grizzly bears and bison, right here in Central Maryland. Now locally extinct! While, in the last two centuries alone, Passenger Pigeons and Carolina Parakeets were so numerous that they eclipsed the sky of my bioregion, now they are extinct. All to provide sporting pleasure to very privileged white men and fancy plumbs hats for very privileged white women. Non-human oppression---not the same thing! Becoming a hunter is sustainable! It's part of a sustainable culture! Give me a break!

Yet, the autistic sustainability worldview does attempt to preserve the most mature elements of the "hunting and gathering" archetype like the need for male bonding, masculine empowerment by women and men alike, respect for human movement, humor, play, travel and acceptable outlets for aggression, a functional ecological niche for human beings, preserving the spirituality and religiosity of rural culture, subsistence human-scale local agriculture and aquaculture, the right to resist tyranny, interspecies communications, wildlife conflict resolution and the need to dwell in wide-open wild and bucolic spaces.

The autistic sustainability worldview provides physically intimate male friendship as an alternative to hunting for male bonding.

Non-blood sports like mountain climbing, boating, hiking, backpacking and ball games as alternative modes for masculine empowerment for men and women alike.

Pilgrimages, day trips, travel opportunities, activism, religion, hobbies, celebrations, having a sense of humor, political activism, creativity, the arts, volunteering and employment, physical exercise, athletics, gardening, harvesting edible and medicinal plants and good self-care, self-determination, self-formation and self-esteem, the joy of learning, solitude and independent thinking provides alternative venues for human movement and relaxation.

Civil disobedience, questioning authority, speaking truth to power, organizing a movement, participating in democratic processes, attending demonstrations and vigils, petitioning leaders, running for public office, boycotting, the martial arts, assertiveness training, self-esteem building and growing your own fruits, vegetables and herbs, are all alternative ways to exercise your third amendment, your "right to assemble militias" *not* "bear arms."

Practices of ecological nonviolence, direct ecological healing, self-mortification, grassroots political activism, ecological leadership, human-animal reconciliation, interspecies communications, wildlife conflict resolution, interspecies friendship or companionship, science studies, naturalist pastimes and becoming an artist, becoming attached to a particular piece of land or bioregion, defending the planet and engaging sensuality in moderation are all non-exploitive ecological practices where you can not only participate in the web of life, but you can actually constructively and productively contribute to and give something back to the biotic community, according to the autistic sustainability worldview.

A worldview which also has recovered the positive benefits of living sustainability with the natural elements and living creatures beyond our wisdom and control, as well as the positive benefits of living benignly, harmoniously and peacefully with "all the animals of the field," even the positive benefits of stewarding unpeopled wilderness and wild areas. Mainly, living a sensual, meaningful, life-affirming, embodied, sacramental, safe, warm, rich, comforting, exciting, free existence surrounded by beauty, wonder, love, warmth, goodness, meaning, purpose and provincial care like Adam and Eve in the Garden of Eden, creating a "moral equivalent to hunting" and a post-gunfighter America, in the process.

Glendenning then asked her sample of technology survivors the question, "If they have a vision of a society that uses technology in safe, beneficial ways. I discovered that dissatisfaction with current technological ideologies leads many to contemplate a different kind of a world, a world in stark contrast to the one they know. Not surprising, their visions derived directly from their own positive experiences of coping. The survivors I interviewed paint a picture of a society based on a sense of personal responsibility, respect for spiritual reality, service to others, and concern for the future…Together they present a new and decidedly nontechnological foundation for modern society."

The same can also be said about neurodiverse humans. The main difference between the vision of the earlier technology survivors and neurodiverse minorities today, while technology survivors add a "nontechnological foundation for modern society," we neurodiverse survivors offer a non-anthropocentric "foundation for modern society." I am going to "paint a picture" of the world we want to live in, using the above criteria as a framework.

**Excelling in the Nonhuman Sector: Taking On Personal Ecological Responsibilities**

Grandin, who has a PhD and is a professor of animal science at the University of Colorado-Fort Collins, is using her autistic gift to recover the silenced voices of animals in capacity. Grandin has very successfully made significant "in-roads" in very pragmatically reforming institutionally cruel practices like factory farming and zoos from the inside, opening up dialogue about animal welfare with multinational corporations like McDonalds. Getting one half of all slaughterhouses in America to adopt minimalist animal welfare standards and has patented many countless inventions and interspecies communications techniques to reduce animal pain, suffering, fear and boredom within the constraints of factory farms and slaughterhouses. In the process, she has eliminated the most egregious, gratuitous acts of animal cruelty in many factory farms and slaughterhouses.

Where "down on the factory farm," at least on a growing number of factory farms, it is no longer possible for multinational agribusiness tycoons and their employees to do whatever they want to animals. Grandin has gained enough power, respectability, persuasiveness and trust, that she can impose "absolute limits" on what many McDonalds factory farms and slaughterhouses can and cannot do to their own animals, showing big agriculture that animal cruelty is not only "bad morals" but also "bad for business," where not only is she not kicked-out, McDonalds actually listens to her, even fears her animal welfare audits.

While settling the "do animals have emotions debate?" once and for all. Strengthening the scientific foundation for animal sentience, necessary for the rational argument for animal liberation, complementing the works of comparative psychologist Jeffery Mason, population biologist Mark Bakeoff, cognitive biologist Donald Griffin, ornithologist Alexander Sketch, primatologist Jane Goodall and many others.

Dawn Prince-Hughes, who also has a PhD, has used her autistic gift to recover the individual identities of gorillas in relationship to gorilla community, applied to improving the quality of life for captive gorillas which cannot be released back into the wild and gathering additional evidence for the theory of human evolution.

One of her most startling discoveries is the "ape as a parody of human nature" belief in the Middle Ages and "Back to Nature" movements and autistic personalities today are tapped into the archetype which Prince-Hughes calls the "ape man" archetype, which can also easily be construed as connected to the "wild man" archetype which the men's movements have recovered and the "hunter/gatherer" or "caveman" archetype recovered by the ecopsychology movement, also a potential retrieval device for recovering "autism in history." This part of our minds and our bodies might be nothing less than the missing evolutionary link that could connect us to the shared common ancestor of the other hominoid apes like gorillas, chimpanzees and orangutans, insistently contended by evolutionary biologists and physical anthropologists alike, a potentially major scientific breakthrough in understanding human evolution and animal intelligence.

Prince-Hughes's second most startling scientific discovery was that she discovered that the captive gorilla troupe she studied also engaged in simple religious rituals, what Prince-Hughes calls "The Rain Dance," named after a similar phenomena observed by world-renowned primatologist Jane Goodall with wild chimpanzees in Africa. Both Prince-Hughes and Goodall agree that this ritual is connected to "rites of initiation" liken to "initiations into adulthood" in many traditional, Nature-based societies around the world involving ceremonial rituals, mythic representations and mentoring by elders, to help young people adapt to the difficult conditions for surviving in the wild and to reduce fear, when ensuring such adversity.

From observing "religious rituals" in her beloved gorillas, Prince-Hughes began to understand the "role of religion" in her own life to reduce fear, cope with adversity, to take calculated risks and to live in community. From there Prince-Hughes came to "Belief in God," embracing a very Incarnational-Personalistic Model of God-World Relationships which has "common ground" with Judeo-Christianity, in the process.

I have used my autistic gift to live a life of mystical communion, public service and green living.

I currently mystically commune in a spirit of fraternity with the God of the Bible, the Communion of Saints (Saint Francis of Assisi, Saint Anthony of Padua, Saint Bonaventure, Brothers Rufono, Juniper, Bernardo, Sylvester, Leo and Friar Wolf), the Archangels in Heaven (Saint Michael, Saint Rafael and Saint Gabriel), Sister Moon, The Sabbath Queen, Animals and the Earth.

I have become a life-long committed environmentalist, animal rights activist, interdisciplinary environmental studies scholar, academic theologian and professional writer. I have both undergraduate environmental degrees and graduate theology degrees. I have become a multiply published author. I have become a grassroots environmental leader. I have become a canvasser. The modern translation of a mendicant beggar!

I am a lacto-ova vegetarian. I do not eat meat, fish or seafood. I do not own a car or have a driver's license. I do not hunt or fish. Nor, do I attend rodeos or circuses. I do not invest in the stock market.

I do recycle and turn off lights I am not using. I do grow plants without pesticides and synthetic fertilizers. I do provide food and water for wild birds. I do clean-up litter in local streams. I do spend much time each week outside in wild Nature. I do engage in interspecies communications. I do buy organic and locally grown produces when possible. I do use public transportation when possible. I do fast from computer work on the Jewish Sabbath. I do vote. I am a registered voter.

I also have completely eliminated ordering in delivery pizzas and Chinese food within the last year. I have almost completely eliminated eating at fast food restaurants within the last year. I have significantly reduced eating-out at fine dining restaurants in the last year. I have significantly reduced my television watching time. I have lost weight. I am getting more exercise. I am in significantly better physical health than a year or so ago. I have made progress in my emotional and spiritual health in the last year too. I am overall in a much healthier and happier place than I have been.

I do pray for the planet, receive ecological guidance from the Creator, continue to read, study and travel, engage society, develop meaningful relationships and I am persistently working towards making God's "beautiful world," beautiful again.

**Under-functioning in the Human Sector: Tying Our Fate into an Unknown God**

Everyone wants to believe in a God who is on our side and is altogether like us. The reality of the matter is that we did not create God. Nor did we choose to be created, nor did we choose the created form of our existence. We did not even choose to create the other creatures we share our world with. We live in a world marked by otherness. This otherness can be described as Transcendence or Mystery using metaphors like "container," "enclosure," "encasement," "skin," "matrix," "tapestry," or "boundaries," as well as "sprit world," "afterlife," "immortality," "logos" or "natural law" which describes the non-material, non-scientific, natural, invisible, subjective frontiers of the Universe like beauty, wonder, love, goodness, justice and peace.

Temple Grandin has used the possibility of God's Transcendence as an opportunity to use religion as an opportunity to decode and cultivate the virtue of goodness, helping Grandin to develop more meaningful relationships with other people, in a world marked by mystery. Prince Hughes has used God's Transcendence to grow in both her own self-examination and healing and her relationship to other Humans, Animals, the Earth and the Cosmos.

I have a more relational view of God's Transcendence where God is my "guide dog" through the challenges of my social and built environment, my "interpreter" of the Mysteries of the Universe, my "teacher" of life, my "mysterious friend" who "fills the void" of my loneness and emptiness. God is my "beautiful trail" through a fallen, broken world. God is my gentle Shepherd, who leads me through desolate valleys, prepares a "beautiful table" before my greatest fears, who "bind and tends" my wounds and gives me refuge, comfort and hospitality.

God is my fierce and decisive King, who provides for all my needs like a brooding father bird, who satisfies my deepest longings like a wolf godfather, who boldly and faithfully leads me to mountain tops, lush green meadows and life-giving waters like a bullfrog leading his hundreds of tadpole children, with the consistency of the womb of a male seahorse, who cleanses the bitterness of my sinful nature with a vinegar and hyssop doused sea sponge, with the personal attention of a father minnow and his hundreds of children.

God is my Rock and my Redeemer! God is my stony fortress, my crag, my cave, my hiding place, my wild sanctuary, my desert paradise, my wilderness home. God is not only my confessor, my consoler, my pastor, my priest, my spiritual director, my teacher, my liberator, my savior, my healer, God is also my friend. God is the love of my life. I love the Lord!

My experience of God has parallels with some Native Americans who experience God as the Creator of the Universe, a kindly wise elder who they can approach for guidance or just enjoying spending time with. My experience also parallels how many Biblical Jews and the Christian mystics of late-antiquity and the middle ages also experienced God's Transcendence, a personal relationship with the God outside oneself, where one meets the Transcendent God deep within your own soul, oftentimes in the wilderness, always outside of civilization.

The social and ecological benefits of experiencing such a personal relationship with God (love-based) coupled with a respect for Spiritual Realities like Heaven, Hell, The Afterlife, Angels, Demons, Ancestors, Saints and Redemption and so forth (mystery based), is that a love-and-mystery based religion gets you beyond both self-serving rationalizations and burdensome shoulds, leading to not only an authentic conversion experience and actual spiritual growth, but also respect for all those who are not like yourself. Even to the point, where you celebrate the beauty and wonder of the diversity of All God's Creation.

A belief in a Trinitarian God gets one to respect "others," to draw you into the beauty and wonder of "others" as "Creatures of the Same God" to use Reverend Andrew Linzey's words, letting go of the need to control everyone or everything in your environment, in the process. Recognizing that we did not create our world, nor does our world belong solely to us. God also created the world for the sake of our enemies and our animals and plants.

Living under the Reign of the Sovereign God will not only deflate our egos, our grandiosity, our seriousness, our inflated sense of self-importance and our need to control and manipulate others and outcomes in a non-self denigrating manor leading to inner peace, perfect joy, moral integrity and personal sovereignty, but also such a belief, will deflate our bellies, our appetites, for believing in and communing with such a personal, personable, loving, good, down-to-earth, powerful, stable, sensual God will give you a key to happiness which does not need consumerism. When you live your everyday life under the Glory of God, your everyday mundane existence will be enlivened and animated with meaning and purpose, peace and joy, excitement and adventure, beauty and wonder, passion and desire, mystery and magic, sensuality and rootedness, even hope, idealism and optimism. The Glory of God then would become a "non-material treat," a mystical Banquet, which would give you much pleasure and reward for all your hard work within the constraints of a planet with diminishing natural resources and unjust distribution.

In essence, Grandin, Prince-Hughes and I all have this "holy longing" to want to engage the Mysteries of God and to live a more meaningful, purposeful deliberate existence in such an enchanted, beautiful, good world, embracing our humanity and our creaturely nature along with all life. We get at an unconscious and not so unconscious level that our survival, our reproduction, our happiness, our health and our legacy are depended upon the God of the Bible, the Living God, The Holy Trinity, the Creator, Sustainer and Redeemer of the Entire Universe who is both all-powerful and all-good and everywhere present and perfect in love, where we have accepted our flesh-and-blood God, who is present to us, in both spirit and body, an intelligence outside of human wisdom, but made intelligible through human experience.

In other words, we have trusted the revelation available to us and have entered the Mysteries and Majesty of the Living God and have found much healing, happiness, liberation and human dignity, even faith, in the process.

**Defying the Empathy Stereotype: Setting Ourselves Up As Paragons of Compassion**
One way other disability teams have countered the abelist stereotypes of non-disabled peoples is through setting themselves up as the paragon opposite of their stereotype, such as defying the laziness stereotype by setting themselves up as a paragon of the Protestant work ethic.

Some of us, on the autism team; have countered the abelist stereotype that people on the autism spectrum lack empathy, by setting ourselves up as paragons of compassion.

Temple Grandin has devoted her entire life to community service, education, teaching, mentoring and reforming the system. Prince-Hughes has devoted her entire life to ape advocacy, writing for publication, teaching at a university, mentoring and being a good partner and a good mother.

I have devoted my entire life to environmental and animal rights activism, writing for publication, academics, community service, voluntary simplicity, helping others, critiquing and changing the system, being a good son, brother and friend, being a good descendent, ancestor and elder, being a good steward of "God's earthly household," being a good husband to God's animals, being a good groundskeeper of God's lands, speaking truth to power and living in peace and harmony with Animals and the Earth.

This is how we have defied our "stereotype of being human," through showing the types of compassion and empathy autistic humans are capable of and that autistic humans are just as compassionate and empathic as anyone else, especially if you count compassion and empathy to also include animals, the Earth and oppressed minorities as morally significant and not limit your compassionate/empathic consideration just to privileged, non-disabled neurotypicals in the upper socioeconomic classes.

**Creating Earth in Heaven: Our Descendents Have Called Us Too!**
I have already talked in *Have Mercy On Me, An Ecological Sinner* (Create Space Independent Publishing Platform, 2012) about how I have accepted and embraced my Medieval Franciscans who I loved and admire so much as my adopted ancestors in the spirit of ecopsychologist Chellis Glendenning being absolved by her Native American mentor of all the shame and stigma of her people's tragic, oppressive history (Glendenning is a European). Glendenning's mentor did this by telling Glendenning that she *is not* defined by the behavior of her immediate biological ancestors, but instead she can look to her evolutionary genetic connection to the entire human species even to all life for a sense of belonging and cultural identity. When Glendenning did this,

although her horrific memories of traumatic abuse and sense of political responsibility for her people's history were still there, she did discover a newfound sense of stability, rootedness, belonging, identity and inner peace in her life which she had not known earlier until her true ancestors called her.

Although my personal memories of being shamed based on my disability are still here and I still struggle with "double consciousness" and "contaminated self" issues, I have discovered newfound freedom, individuality, systems of meaning making, religious rituals, guidance, comfort, healing, self-knowledge, love, grace, acceptance, mercy, honor, signifigence, joy, hospitability, warmth, friendship, understanding, affirmation, strength, courage, humor, whimsy, maturity, insight, sensuality, beauty, purpose, humanity, life-affirmations, balance, happiness, simplicity, creativity, rest, peace, empathy, passion, male bonding, even initiation into adulthood and manhood when I accepted a bunch of Medieval Franciscans as my ancestors and they accepted me as one of their descendents.

Yet, the Native American tradition insists that you can not only have a relationship with your ancestors, you can also have a relationship with your decedents, those who come after you. Yet, even though I have discovered my "hidden history," which to use the words of my late mentor Dr. Phil Bosserman: "you are in good company!" There are many people like myself throughout history. Yet, this still did not address the realities of my twenty-first century situation and context, let alone the future. I was still living in the past, for the present was so unbearable and my future still bleak.

Then something really amazing started to happen. My parents took my on this magnificent vacation to Portland, Oregon to help me heal from "Compassion Fatigue" after a series of several very embittering, disillusioning professional disappointments, revictimizations and impasses which was a "terrible time" in my life, which led to a very serious "personal crisis."

I knew Portland, Oregon was noted as a mecca for anything green: the environment, local, animal rights, vegetarian, vegan, social justice, peace, political activism, bohemian culture, sustainable living and ecological planning. I knew beforehand that Portland was noted for its locavore restaurants and cafes, vegetarian and vegan options, environmental zoning, sustainable architecture, public transportation system, spacious city parks, planetary political activity, communitarian spirit and ecological vanguard. That is why we wanted to go, along with staying at the famous Timberline Lodge at Mount Hood, the Columbia River Gorge (rich in environmental history and unique natural beauty), the famous port of Astoria and Oregon's sublime coastline.

No book or travelogue prepared me for how friendly and down-to-earth Portlanders were. I have never been to a city or a country anywhere in the world, where locals were so hospitable, helpful even downright "out-going" to strangers. I do not say this lightly. It is not like I have never been anywhere before.

I have been to Jerusalem, Rome, Natanya, Geneva, Nassau, Seattle, Chicago, Santé Fe, Denver, Baltimore, Phoenix, Tucson, Scottsdale, Tulsa, Pittsburg and New York City. I lived in Boston for three and a half years in graduate school. I grew-up thirty minutes from the White House outside Washington D.C. I have traveled to Florida four times. I have traveled to Canada three times. I have traveled all over Italy and Israel. I lived on the Delmarva Peninsula of Maryland for four years in college. I completed a summer course in upstate Michigan. I have been to Yellowstone, Grant Tetons, The Grand Canyon, Waterton Glacier International Peace Park, Acadia National Park, Rocky Mountain National Park and I have explored the Colorado Plateau, New Mexico, Arizona, West Virginia and the Bahamas. I even have been to the West Bank. I even have explored neighboring Washington state twice for two different summer courses in college visiting everywhere from Seattle to Mount Saints Helens to Olympic National Park to Mount Rainer to Mount Baker to Puget Sound to the Pacific Ocean.

None of these places could even approach Portland in terms of hospitability and human scale.

Not only will strangers off the street help give you directions when you are lost or even engage a deeper conversation with you about your spiritual lost-ness, I was expecting to see this futuristic city lacking in beauty. Instead, Portland looked like a set off a classic American western with perfectly preserved Victorian, Italianate and Queen Anne's houses and flats. Portland had alleys and pocket parks resembling nineteenth century Paris. Docked in the Willamette River was a real riverboat which looked liked a set in the classic movie "Showboat." Downtown Portland had roaring 1920s hotels with 1920s hospitality and the rusted oriental ruins of Portland's once sprawling Chinatown, one of the largest in America, at one time.

Portland's Chinatown is currently being restored by civically minded Portlanders into one more bohemian district. For example, you can visit a Chinese Garden built above a weedy parking lot, recreating an entire Chinese scholar's garden from the Ming Dynasty period in mainland China. This American rendition of a Ming scholar's garden includes a traditional tea house surrounded by a waterfall, a stunning aquatic garden filled with pedigree carp, enveloped by a matrix of plants and rock formations native to China, recreating the major geographic regions of China right here in America. Portlanders also maintain one of the largest and best examples of a Japanese Gardens outside Japan.

Along the Willamette Riverfront, Portland's most unusual historical preservation effort preserved the various public works buildings and industrial revolution era bridges along the river, right in downtown Portland, in one of Portland's most famous, popular and beloved city parks. Giving Portlanders and Back Easters alike a reminder of where our water comes from and where our sewage goes, alongside a lesson in modern engineering history.

So Portlanders definitely see respect for their local culture, traditions and ancestral past as compatible with working towards creating a sustainable and just civilization in the present and future.

One of the most fascinating and exciting experiences I had in Portland was when we visited the famous Vaux swift roost at a Portland elementary school. We were hoping to take in the thousands of swifts who fly into roast in the chimney of a certain elementary school every night in the month of September. We thought that some might think that we are a little weird coming with our binoculars to watch swifts funnel into a chimney at an elementary school. So, when we saw hundreds of people parked-out in lawn chairs and blankets and a baseball game in process, we were all set to head back to our hotel, assuming all the birds were scared away by the baseball event.

Walking back to our car, we made an astonishing discovery when we ran into some of these fans.

All of these hundreds of screaming, raving fans were not here to see the baseball game; they were here to watch the swifts funnel into the chimney, like we were.

In fact, we learned many Portlanders come here, every year, for the entire swift season, to watch these swallow-like creatures gather into a whole galaxy of birds, only to swirl into a tiny manmade chimney with the precision of figure skaters and the elegance of ballerinas, all choreographed in three dimensions, with the Heavens as their stage, in a dance extravaganza more sophisticated than any human counterpart.

In fact, the year we visited, the National Audubon Society was there canvassing the event and the elementary school PTA was selling pizza and soda as a fundraiser, while a prowling red tailed hawk was upstaging this award-winning event, stalking these avian divas, while being cheered and booed along by his human fans, like at a major football event. It was almost as though birdwatching was made the official sport of Portland. This happening gives new meaning to the Shakespearian axiom "the world is a stage." It was such a hopeful, life-affirming event! I have never seen anything like it, before or since.

This is not to mention all the classic sustainability efforts of Portland, like having some of the toughest zoning in the country against sprawl, a public transportation system second to none, preserving an old-growth temperate rainforest within city limits, having a whole museum dedicated to the history of forestry, a whole citywide matrix of pocket parks and common areas, a whole tapestry of bicycle paths and biking lanes, farmers markets galore, locavore restaurants, even preserving as a public park, the only extinct volcano (Mount Tabor) found in a major metropolitan area, in the lower forty-eight states. Not to mention, Portland's famous slogan "Keep Portland Weird!"

I am still challenged by our challenging times, I am still haunted by the ghosts from the past, but now for the first time in my entire life I have a sense of optimism for the future which has been a constellation of day dreams, solidified into something in the twenty-first century which I can confidently believe in and embrace. Environmentalism!

In fact, as of May of 2013, I became a Portlander!

I relocated cross-country to be part of this nourishing political community which I have been searching my whole young life for.

My decedents have finally called me!

**My Two "Dreams for the Earth": The Peaceable Kingdom and the Messianic Age**
Since I wrote *Have Mercy on me, an Ecological Sinner* (Amazon.com, 2012), I have seen for myself, several "shoots" of the Peaceable Kingdom "spouting" from "the stump of Jesse," offering me "foreshadows" of the impending Messianic Age, giving me "reason for hope" for the planet in peril, that we truly live in a "world without end." Mainly, the fact that "nothing has happened" apocalyptically, the "end of the world" has not happened, we are still here, at all, despite over five hundred years of globalized colonization, two world wars, a half century of nuclear cold war and umpteenth terrorist rebellions and countless environmental disasters is nothing less than a miracle, a testimony that we truly live under a "state of grace." Where we are not only surviving under post-Apocalyptic conditions, we are beginning to thrive in post-Messianic conditions.

One "sprout from the stump of Jesse" in my life was my beloved "white as snow" parakeet Brother Spirit who I was blessed by for over a year-and-a-half, who took the place of my late parakeet Brother Mordecai (see http://www.all-creatures.org/church/grmindir-md-ss-salomon.html, for more information). Already I had successfully taught Brother Mordecai and his mate Sister Golda catechism (knowledge necessary for salvation) and they responded quite positively in a spirit of peace, play and trust as though they understood.

I even made it even further with Brother Spirit and Sister Golda, to a point that Brother Spirit started "preaching back at me." He often signaled to me the parts of my "Parakeet Eucharist" (see, *Have Mercy on me, an Ecological Sinner)* that he was most interested in, aptly, "Saint Francis's Sermon to the Birds." He also signaled to me when he has had enough. He even had the audacity to "bade" me when I spent too much time at the computer and when I watched too much violent television. Both looked forward to the Eucharist every day as a kind of "non-material treat." He even "bade" me to feed them with the Eucharist (seed and water) even when they do not eat right away. That is now much they looked forward to this "non-material treat." During this ritual, Sister Golda sometimes snuggled up against the edge of her enclosure nearest to me like a dog and sometimes like in humans; she has to gently remind her mate to pay attention during a religious service. In other words, I have trained my parakeet companions how to "say grace."

Not only has Brother Spirit "preached back," Brother Spirit has improvised the Christian interspecies communication tradition by preaching sermons to other wild birds in our neighborhood from the families of goldfinches, purple finches, mourning doves and juncos who visited our thistle feeder to the Carolina wren who sang outside our balcony to an American Crow and Fish Crow who frequently passed through, to a roast of house sparrows across the commons, even the chorusing seventeen-year cicadas and crickets last summer (most likely mistaken as more birds).

Brother Spirit has even developed a contact call for God, which is reciting the calls of species of birds Spirit has mimicked from a cockatiel at the pet store to goldfinch, junco and mourning dove calls when the birds *are not* present, like when I mention God's name in the Eucharist Rite, where Brother Spirit sometimes would gives his litany of bird calls. In other words, God's name in parakeet literally translates "Order." "God" is "The Source of Life." "God" is "The Creator."

I contend that such an endeavor *does not* undermine my bird's "wildness," in fact, I am empowering them to reclaim a part of their "wildness" lost to captivity, mainly inspiring them to forge interspecies friendships with wild birds, like parakeets do in the wilds of Australia who travel around the Outback desert in these massive mixed flocks of parakeets and zebra finches.

In fact, the same year as I released *Have Mercy On Me, An Ecological Sinner* (Create Space Independent Publishing Platform, 2012), National Geographic editor Jennifer Holland released her compilation of documented cases (many from respectable scientific sources) of interspecies friendships liken to what Holy Scripture and Medieval hagiography contend is possible between species (see, *Unlikely Friendships: 47 Remarkable Stories from the Animal Kingdom* (New York: Workman Publishing, 2012).

In fact, Temple Grandin and Mark Bekoff even spoke on the respectable PBS series *Nature*, calling this compilation of case studies on interspecies animal friendship "one of the most important discoveries in animal intelligence in recent years," a promising frontier for a "whole new field of scientific research." Corroborating my hypothesis from the beginning that the interspecies miracles of the Peaceable Kingdom and of the Communion of Saints were describing real historical events and real naturalistic phenomena and I knew from the beginning that I was dealing with a "lost knowledge" issue, that the interspecies miracles could not be dismissed as easily, as mere superstition.

Yet, none of these case studies included a study of interspecies friendship in the wild, although the studies did include not only members of similar species making friends, but also friendships between animals of different orders, friendships between predators and prey, larger and smaller animals, domestic and wild animals, able-bodied and disabled animals, even between humans and animals.

Yet, I have witnessed two suggestive interspecies friendships at Deer Ridge. One was between a wild buck and a wild red fox. The other was between a wild deer heard and myself.

Not to mention witnessing at Deer Ridge the already scientifically accepted phenomena of songbirds traveling around in multi-species flocks for mutual survival in the winter, which animal friendship literature contends is the evolutionary value of friendship, mutual physical survival. Like safety in numbers, providing each other with physical warmth, fostering a "will·to live" in uncertain situations and helping individuals and species survive and reproduce during times of mutual crises like natural disasters. This is my second "sprout from the stump of Jesse."

That interspecies friendship between animal and animal and humans and animals is possible in the wild. I witnessed twice at Deer Ridge, my majestic white-tail deer buck in close proximity to the little red fox who also lives at Deer Ridge, traveling around the forest together in silence, like a dog protecting a heard of sheep. I first saw them together at one of the quartzite beaches of the little stream who runs through the heart of Deer Ridge, connecting Deer Ridge to the Chesapeake Bay watershed, passing through the stream crossing in search of food. I saw the two together again on another day, almost a quarter of a mile downstream, in this expansive biological corridor, traversing the hardwood and laurel outcroppings above one of Deer Ridge's amphibian vernal pools, in search of food.

This is a wild heard of white-tailed deer who lives at Deer Ridge and a red fox is as wild as it gets "back-east," being one of the few wild dogs who stills exist east of the Mississippi River, the others being the gray fox, the coyote and a small assembly of reintroduced red wolves in North Carolina. So the "wolf lying down with the lamb" is a real phenomenon. It turns out that our Biblical, Byzantine and Medieval ancestors were right, that the Natural World is as much defined by "cooperation" as it is by "competition," "mutual aid" as much as by "red tooth and claw," being vindicated by postmodern, animal behavior science.

According to comparative psychologist Jeffery Mason, the main difference between "taming" and "domestication" is that "domestication" is "forced" on an animal by human coercion through involuntary training and genetic manipulation, while "taming" is "earned" through a human behaving in such a way that the animal actually begins to start to trust the human being. Mason contends that almost every animal can be "tamed."

So it is within the realm of "scientific plausibility," that I have been accepted by the deer of Deer Ridge, despite Enos Mill's observation that wild deer are untamable, because of their deep seeded fear of deer hunters.

Despite, deer hunting being allowed on near-by state park land, the deer herd of Deer Ridge *do not* run away, when they run into me on Deer Ridge land, nor do they freeze in fear in fright either, nor do they attack me.

Instead, they gently looked-up at me, acknowledging my presence and continue doing what they are doing. In fact, one day when I was at Deer Ridge, the two young bucks continued playing in the non-tidal freshwater marsh, even bucking each other's antlers, in my presence. Yet, when other visitors approach them, they run away in "fear and dread." So the deer can definitely tell the difference between humans who are safe and humans who are unsafe. The deer *have not* lost their fear of deer hunters. They know! In fact, an animal being able to tell the difference between individuals is a phenomenon corroborated by Grandin.

In fact, as I have "cleaned-up" all the trashy isores and tacky pollution in Deer Ridge, Deer Ridge is becoming a more inviting home for our white-tail deer family, where our deer are beginning to feel more comfortable on Deer Ridge land, where hunting *is not* allowed because of its proximity to residential development, making Deer Ridge their permanent family home. Where Deer Ridge became a deer sanctuary during this year's managed hunting season, escaping sharpshooters at the local state park within walking distance of the local elementary school, where my entire deer herd survived this last winter's hunting season, where my buck's two sons welcomed two does into Deer Ridge and started a family of their own, bringing a whole nursery of fawns into this world.

Where Deer Ridge has not only become a deer sanctuary after I have cleaned-up the tacky pollution, for targeted, bullied and scapegoated white tailed deer, but also a sanctuary for declining native wildlife. Deer Ridge has also become a wildlife sanctuary for shad and rainbow trout, migratory songbirds, spawning frogs, butterflies, dragonflies, damselflies and fireflies and native bees.

Since I became my clean-up efforts about a year and a half ago, I have also noticed the natural die-off of invasive plants like garlic mustard, bamboo and hydrilla and the sprouting of new native plants, funguses and slime molds left dormant in the primal seed and spore bank. This I contend is because litter was not only becoming like another invasive species which was not only taking up space, but slowly poisoning the forest, the field, the wetland, and the stream, by leeching pollutants. Removing the litter gave the forest-field-wetland-stream complex newfound strength.

Where "every leaf" in this emerging, healthy, flourishing forest-field-marsh ecological complex became a "carbon sink," fixing greenhouse gases, carbon dioxide ($CO_2$) out of the atmosphere, transubstantiating carbon dioxide into life-giving oxygen ($O_2$), for the "healing of the nations," helping to counter "climate change," in the process. Which has also got to help the property value of the local neighborhood, for a "community forest" is economically worth more than a tacky "dump," where with time, my neighbors are beginning to see Deer Ridge, less as a garbage dump and more like a community resource which everyone can enjoy and cherish.

Now, the value of community is beginning to make more sense. Community *is not* this top-down utopian ideology for regulating human behavior and policing the bellies and genitals of individuals, developed in cliquish, elitist, anti-democratic committees based on scapegoating, cannibalism, hierarchy, dualism, institutional rigidity and insularity, religious and cultural violence, judgementalism, domination, manipulation, control and to be frank, sociopathic narcissism, the colonialist, imperialistic, mechanistic residue of Christian communitarianism.

No, community is the instinctual, primordial human need to be loved and to love, our natural human need for safety, belonging, participation and purpose, a super-archetype sharing "common experience" with animal societies and the relational, interconnected, interdependent nature of the Universe solidly grounded in biophysical reality and in very real places around the world. I agree with ecopsychologist Chellis Glendinning that a lap top computer *is not* a substitute for community and a hamburger at an airport *is not* culture. I also add that a bureaucracy *is not* a substitute for love, that giving money to non-profit organizations *is not* a substitute for being a good neighbor and legalism *is not* spirituality. Mainly, you are still "bowling alone!"

So I am no-longer intimidated by moralistic and repressed self-righteousness, self-projecting pastors and priests who have excluded a qualified applicant like myself, from their ranks just because I have a disability and I was an earlier environmentalist before it was accepted and adopted by the Christian Church, to have "the gall" to lecture to me about environmental and social ethics. How dare they? They lost that right a long time ago!

These clerical insiders say they are all about community, yet they are systematically destroying communities across America with their grandiose, utopian, "ivory tower" ideologies, caring more about the "outcomes" of certain special interest political agendas like homosexuality and abortion than church unity and educating the laity and opening-up dialogue about these issues.

These clerical insiders say they care about the peoples of the Geographic South, yet these same clergy are using the same methodologies used to justify the colonization, enslavement and economic poverty in the Geographic South in the first place, to argue for social justice. These clergy also take sides in highly complicated "regional conflicts" like the Israeli-Palestinian conflict basing their positions on propaganda, spin, limited information, partial truths and no direct experience, in true nineteenth century colonialist missionary spirit of trying to "run the lives" of other groups of people, at the other end of the world. In true "white man's burden" spirit, not trusting the moral agency of peoples in cultures which know how to be a "real man" more than any of these parlor revolutionaries and religious bureaucrats could ever be.

Where one Roman Catholic sex abuse scandal even occurred on an Indian Reservation, meaning these male priests seem to target not only little boys, but little boys who come from a disadvantaged minority group like being a member of a First Nation, an underdeveloped nation like Ireland or a deaf school in Wisconsin, leading to the multiple oppression of male minorities in the Christian Church.

All of these privileged religious insiders would get farther with their causes, if they open-up these discussions to a wider audience, like to the various disability and neurodiverse communities, like to the various ecological and animal rights movements, like to younger generations, like to the laity, like to Christian converts and persecuted Christians. Like expanding interfaith dialogue to include other religions like all sects of Judaism, New Age, Neo-Paganism, First Nations, the various Eastern religions, African animalism, even atheists and agnostics, not just perseverate on Buddhism and Islam in the spirit of the Baal-worshipers of Biblical times and the Lombard heretics of the Middle Ages.

Basing interfaith dialogue instead not on idol-worshiping, but on conflict resolution, in the true patristic-scholastic fashion of Saint Augustine of Hippo and Saint Thomas of Aquinas, as well as Apostles Peter and Paul and Church Fathers Gregory, Ambrose, Patrick, Gerome, Columbia, John of Damascus and Anthony of the Desert. Basing interfaith dialogue on trying to reconcile our Christian faith with our life in a non-Christian world with the goal of searching for ways to include outsider Christian converts in the "life of the church" and for Christians "to live as peacefully as possible" with peoples of other faiths, the "spirit" of the scholastic tradition in our twenty first century context. Now we are an anarchist territory!

One of the main differences between communitarian anarchy and libertarianism is that libertarianism economically emancipates individual consumers to a life of self-interest without institutional invention from government bureaucracies, while communitarian anarchy emancipates individual consciences to a life of moral agency without institutional invention from any bureaucracy whether it's government, industry, the military, the police or organized religion, where order is kept and the "common good" maintained through emancipated moral patients working together in a spirit of cooperation, mutuality, altruism, nonviolence, consensus and civic responsibility, creating spontaneous, highly localized, place-based, non-hierarchical, non-dualistic, directly democratically elected, role-based equalitarian social institutions, also including the margins of society.

One of the main differences between communitarian anarchy and communism is that communism insists on an intrusive state who enforces rigid, prescriptive rules of human conduct and moral and legal responsibility on individuals, does not respect the individuality of each and every person, calls for mass conformity and denies individual civil liberties like freedom of dissent and freedom of religion. Communitarian anarchy respects democratic ideals, individuality and the role and place of spirituality and religion, as well as culture, creativity, education, family, friendship and proximate community, in human life.

So when I am talking about communitarian anarchy, I *am not* talking about communism or libertarianism. Nor am I talking about an unrealistic, imaginary utopian society. In fact, I am talking about something that already exists, in at least one Christian community in Spain for almost a hundred years, in Christian Amish and Mennonite communities for over two hundred years, in many First Nation societies around the world, in countless animal societies, in some sects of Judaism, in hunter/gatherer Western nations until about 10,000 BC, in the Golden Age of Rome and Greece, in some periods of Biblical Israel, the Early Christian Church, in some Medieval communes, in Calvin's Geneva and even today in some of our educational and religious organizations, support groups, community organizing collaborations, neighborhood associations, grassroots movements, labor unions and farmer's markets.

Meaning that the role of the Christian Church, being in the unique position of Separation between Church and State, can use its religious freedoms and political distance to create viable, living, practical, tenable and I would dare say, realistic models of sustainability, justice, nonviolence, grassroots organization, participatory democracy, rootedness, place, continuity, hope, faith, joy, beauty, healing and most importantly---love. Inspiring through example, the larger secular society to divest from globalized imperialism and world domination and continue investing in the future evolution of all life and world peace through providing a compelling spiritual vision, a theological praxis, a pastoral sensibility, practical guidance, formation and spiritual disciplines, reflection, prayer and religious rituals, historical literacy and most importantly---faith. In other words, demonstrate the type of planetary healing which is possible.

One human being in the twenty-first century who embodied, practiced, devoted his entire life to, even lived, even implemented, such a communitarian anarchist vision, was my late-mentor Dr. Phil Bosserman, who I had the honor of collaborating with. Bosserman was involved in the civil rights movement before it became the "political correct" thing to do, having personally known Dr. Martin Luther King Jr. before he became a household name, when he still worked in obscurity, attending the same theological school, where both men became ordained Methodist ministers. Afterwards, King trained Bosserman and his wife Carol.

Bosserman also served in the Peace Corp in the former French Congo where Bosserman personally met Albert Switzcher like my own father, who also met Switzcher when my father participated in Switzcher's Crossroads Africa program. Bosserman met Switzcher, when Bosserman almost died in Africa and had to be hospitalized; Bosserman was hospitalized in Switzcher's hospital in Gabon. Bosserman, as a life-long committed ideological pacifist, returned to America and became involved in the anti-Vietnam war movement, having the opportunity to develop friendships with both Collin McCarthy and the Bergon Brothers.

Unlike a significant amount of war resisters from the 1960s era, who developed Compassion Fatigue and dropped out of public life, Bosserman who was a onetime professor of "Leisure Studies," used his theological and sociological training (Bosserman was a professor of sociology), his pastoral sensibilities, his activist training and travel experiences to systemize his historical experiences into a coherent worldview, paradigm, ethical-moral framework and academic discipline.

Bosserman systemized the disparate student movements of the 1960s (the African-American civil rights movement, the anti-Vietnam war movement, the free speech movement and the women's movement), the Holocaust and the nonviolent resistance of the righteous gentiles, the two World Wars, the dropping of the first nuclear bomb on Japan, earlier pacifist and abolitionists movements of the nineteenth century, the various pacifist traditions in Christianity from Quakerism to Franciscanism, peaceful and compassionate insights from various World Religions and over two hundred years of critical social theory in academic sociology into a coherent worldview, paradigm, ethical-moral framework and academic discipline which Bosserman called "Conflict Resolution."

Bosserman was one of the first academics to elevate student anti-war movements and anti-oppression efforts of the 1960s to the level of an academic discipline, to be brought in-house into the academy as a legitimate and respectable endeavor. Where Bosserman helped found at my Alma Marta, the conflict resolution center and taught courses like "Sociology of Conflict and Nonviolence," helped to create the "Conflict Analysis/Dispute Resolution" minor which I have, which later developed into a full major and now a full master degree program.

Students in this very focused interdisciplinary program take both a variety of electives from a menu of approved courses in the various social science departments like sociology and psychology to the various humanities departments like philosophy and literature and a core practica of skill related courses and internship opportunities to work in the field at the interpersonal, regional or global levels. Such a course prepares students to work as peer mediator trainers in public schools, courtroom mediators, labor negotiators, work for a non-profit organization, become an activist/organizer or pursue a career in diplomacy. Such a course can also serve as background and a practical framework for a whole variety of vocations in environmental studies or animal studies, the ministry, law, medicine, public policy, lobbying even psychology and business, bringing a humanistic, liberal arts, ethical-moral, holistic perspective to these fields.

By pioneers like Bosserman bringing social justice, political activism and nonviolence up to the level of a worldview, academic discipline and body of skills ("conflict resolution") versus a mere ideology (like "pacifism" or "just war") or a specific community (like anti-racism or women's liberation) or a movement (like anti-Vietnam war), for the first time, we now have a framework which is equipped to address the most pressing issues of our times, not to mention making the activist life, anti-oppression and nonviolent resistance accessible to all peoples in current and future oppression situations like disability and neurodiversity.

Bosserman, as a result, was equipped to address post-1960s issues like the possibility for a nuclear armistice in the 1980s, environmentalism, animal rights, corporatization, globalization, political apathy, homosexuality and spirituality in the 1990s and was in solidarity with emerging new social movements of the Post Nineleven, Bush years like the emerging anti-globalization, anti-capitalism, planetary and twenty-first century anti-war efforts resisting the Iraq War, The War in Afghanistan, the Patriot Act, Guantanamo and anti-terrorism witch hunts targeting innocent Muslim Americans, as his health allowed, until he finally died of dementia in 2011.

Bosserman, as a result, was absolutely supportive of and in solidarity with my environmental, animal rights and disability activism, as well as supportive of my Christian faith and Jewish identity. He understood me and I could be myself. He made me feel special, worthwhile and respectable. I felt like a grown man around him. I have never met a human being who was such an empathic and humble listener to my story and my ideas, before and since. Bosserman genuinely felt I had something to offer and wanted to learn from me. He sponsored my writing of *Creation Unveiled* (Xulon Press, 2003) and wrote my forward. Bosserman and his wife Carol even came up to attend my graduation from graduate theological school from Andover Newton Theological School, outside Boston in 2006.

So it was no wonder that this last November in 2012, the new Dr. Bosserman Conflict Resolution Center was unveiled by the current women president of the university and his life was celebrated by a campus wide event, being eulogized by local politicians, attended by professors, collogues and former students and peace core comrades and family members, a personal letter from Archbishop Desmond Tutu to Bosserman was displayed, along with Bosserman's countless academic and popular articles which he wrote. (I even discovered he even wrote a blub linking a "healthy self-esteem" to conflict resolution and nonviolence). It was ironic than how my mother and father, who both attended this event with me, were "blown away" that the man who befriended and mentored their son, being extraordinarily generous with his time and energy with me, was so high-powered and revered in the community. As my father pointed-out to me, "You never would have known this when you meet him. He was so modest."

Bosserman was able to do all this without ever berating his students, creating a super-competitive environment, cannibalizing other people, pitting one minority group against another, being judgmental, adversarial or overly-moralistic, being overly cynical, skeptical, workaholic, slave driving, negative or nihilistic, overly pessimistic, fatalistic or morose or being self-righteousness, self-absorbed, authoritarian or controlling or intimidating or contemptuous in any way or coming across stronger than he had too.

Bosserman is a testimony to what an ordinary farmer's son from Kansas can accomplish in terms of "making a difference." Bosserman is a testimony of the type of change which is possible, which an individual concerned citizen can effectuate, which is really what the communitarian anarchy model is all about--- direct, participatory, grassroots, human-scale democracy.

This model of democracy is the form of governance that is truly accessible to a person like me, a model of community which truly includes me and a model of community which I can contribute to in a responsible, nonviolent, meaningful and productive manor. Where at this event I also had the opportunity to network with former professors and rekindle some old flames and bring back some positive memories of a time in my life when I was the most happy around other people.

Also, during this time I was also reunited with Wounded Healer, the Canada goose with a broken wing I befriended and prayed with in *Creation Unveiled* (USA: Xulon Press, 2003). Over nine years later, Wounded Healer was still alive. His wing had pretty much healed. He was still with his mate. Wounded could even fly short distances. Wounded even remembered me and displayed all the progress he has made in the decade or so, when we last parted ways.

Luna Two, the magnificent old-growth Scarlet Oak which we in the Environmental Studies Association (ESA) had famous environmental political activist Julia Butterfly Hill personally dedicate in her honor when we welcomed Hill to our campus to share a meal and give a teach-in was still there too, despite all of the growth and development of the campus, along with my beloved loblolly pine stand, the Henry David Thoreau statue donated by a former environmental studies professor and the gazebo with rocking chairs where we used to meet.

Where at this very spot with so many good memories, I encountered a third "sprout from the stump of Jesse," a magnificent red tailed hawk, a common grey squirrel and my first sapsucker woodpecker peacefully making improvised contact calls to each other, which animal friendship contends is possible, peacefully sitting among each other's company. They were all friends.

Some might say that all this is becoming too attached to a particular scientific theory or a few antidotal subjective experiences. Yet, subjectivity, creativity even romantic whimsy is the whole point. This is my "Dream for the Earth."

That the vision of the Peaceable Kingdom in Isaiah 11 in the Hebrew Bible of a multi-species society which values all life is a viable model of proper human-Earth relationships to work towards in our twenty-first century context of planetary crisis globalized alienation and institutional animal cruelty. That it is still possible for the Earth to make a full recovery from the planetary crisis as contended by the various Judeo-Christian Apocalyptic, Messianic and Medieval traditions. These are my two "Dreams for the Earth" as one neurodiverse Christian on the autism spectrum.

This is what neurodiversity and Judeo-Christianity adds to environmental ethics:

- That it is a *false choice to choose which lives are worth saving based upon inherent capacity when in reality all lives have something to contribute and can be saved.* You do not need to choose between saving individuals or saving community, saving humans with intellectual disabilities or saving chickens, caring for animal companions or feeding starving children in Africa, clean water or food banks, jobs or the environment and so forth. Such an environmental ethic is militantly non-dualistic.

- That *respect for the liberties of individual humans and animals alike is compatible with a sustainable and just civilization.* When I am talking about individual civil liberties, I *am not* talking about consumerism. I am talking about the freedoms necessary to sustain a democratic society and for everyone to be able to live with dignity. These freedoms include not only freedom from hunger, thirst, nakedness, sickness, homelessness and ignorance. These freedoms also include freedom of speech, expression, travel, press, religion, conscience, the right to vote, the right to organize movements of nonviolent resistance and the right to petition leaders. I also contend that self-preservation, happiness, love, safety and self-determination are also necessary for living with dignity. Such an environmental ethic is militantly democratic.

- That *the value of nonviolence is compatible with a sustainable and just civilization.* We absolutely need beautiful experiences, the arts, spirituality, religion, culture, history, interspecies communications, outside time, leisure time, frequent breaks, travel, rest, humor, fun, celebration, mourning, non-exploitive relationships and meaningful work as a substitute for consumption. We absolutely need the unique gifts of each individual for planetary survival as much as the preservation of the system at large, where individuals bring the unique ecological gifts of diversity, critique, innovation, specialized niches and the future evolution of life. We absolutely need to find the functional ecological niche of human beings in the Natural World, so we will be able to quench our deep longings for participation and communion, "dwell in situations of inherent worth," be able to give back to the planet, pull our ecological weight and be able to adapt to "life in the wild," living within the constraints of natural selection. Human beings need to also be able to live nonviolently with Animals, the Earth and each other to fulfill our ecological job of reducing "red tooth and claw," in a world marked by natural evil, if human beings were to become extinct. Beginning to heal the anthropogenic ecological damage already done in the planet, in the process. For example, in the process of reclaiming my functional ecological niche in Deer Ridge through interspecies communications, prayer and contemplation and an aesthetic appreciation of the Natural World, I also ended-up picking-up the garbage dumped into this little stream by other human beings. Such an environmental ethic is militantly romantic.

- *Animal Rights and Deep Ecology is compatible with world peace and social justice.* Such an environmental ethic contends that not only is there a positive correlation between social injustice and environmental degradation (environmental racism, classism, sexism and abelism). There is also a positive correlation among violence, environmental degradation and animal cruelty. For example, there is a positive correlation between domestic violence and animal cruelty, bullying and sports hunting, dog fighting and crime. A positive correlation between wars and ecological destruction, environmental pollution and dangerous technologies. A positive correlation between the objectifying of the Natural World and the demeaning of women, colonization, abelism and normalcy even the culturecide and genocide of various oppressed minority groups. Meaning that the "War on Nature" is an act of violence with humanitarian implications. Such an environmental ethic is militantly relationship-centric.

A crip, neuro-diversified Christian environmental ethic adds a philosophical foundation to eco-justice, a conflict resolution foundation to environmental ethics, a biocentric/ecocentri foundation to social ethics, a social ecology foundation to scientific ecology and a distinctively Christian foundation to Christian environmentalism.

**Conclusion:**

**Everybody's God----Toward a Libratory Theology of Neurodiversity and the Need for a Dialectic Spirituality**

Classical Latino liberation theologian Gustavo Gutierrez said,

> Only through concrete acts of love and solidarity can we effectively realize our encounter with the poor and exploited and, through them, with Jesus Christ.[129]

"Who is God?" According to Gutierrez, God *is not* merely the god of the rich and powerful. God *is also* the God of the poor and the oppressed everywhere. God is the "champion of the oppressed." The Christian God it turns out is really Everybody's God. This is because every rock, river, mountain, ocean, plant, animal, planet and human being all comes from the same primordial source---God, the common ancestor of all life. This is because every rock, river, mountain, ocean, plant, animal, planet and human being is under the authority of the Living God, the Sustainer and Redeemer of the Entire Universe. This is because the Christian God is a loving, caring, personable, "down to earth" God at-heart. God cares about individual people alongside caring for the Cosmos at-large. God *does not* use "individuals" as "means to an end." God instead sees each individual creature as both having "intrinsic value" and is fundamentally "irreplaceable." God takes a personal interest in all His Creatures, wants a personal relationship with them; God wants to work with all of us "one-on-one" and meet each and every one of us, "face to face."

"Where is God?" According to Gutierrez, we find this God in the poor and oppressed everywhere. In other words, we find the Christian God in the beliefs and practices of the poor and oppressed everywhere, in the strength and spirituality of "the multitude." God exists in the margins of society. God dwells in the borderlands. God lives in the shadows. In other words, Yahweh is the People's God. This is what some modern-day Franciscans call the "Poor Christ." God's embodiment in broken, disabled, diseased, neglected, imperfect and unwanted bodies both in the poor and oppressed everywhere and in the parts of ourselves we are ashamed of.

"How do we pray to God?" According to Gutierrez, we *do not* just feed the hungry and liberate the oppressed, mere acts of charity, nor do we patronize the oppressed with empty platitudes, we instead are called to listen to the stories of the oppressed, to let the oppressed teach us Gospel, to help us recover True Christianity and learn a "new pattern of living." In other words, we are called to treat the oppressed as spiritual equals who *are not* reducible to profane material, but sentient beings who need to be treated with "dignity and respect" and have something to contribute and not necessarily as "cheap labor."

I also contend this also goes for Animals and the Earth. Just like we consider it morally wrong to reduce women to material (pornography), I consider it wrong to reduce Animals or Nature to mere material too (eco-pornography). Why cannot an animal or a plant or a place also be viewed in non-materialistic, subjective, spiritual, personalistic, virtuous terms?

I contend the Doctrine of the Holy Trinity (personal relationships) alongside the Doctrine of Incarnation (embodiment) preserves the subjective, non-material, spiritual, personalistic, virtuous nature of Animals and the Earth which is my "***key insight***" or "***relative absolute***" about the nature of the Universe as an Aspie: "***Creation is structured in Triune form.***"[130] The Holy Trinity is the totality of all the different individual, distinct, autonomous creatures of the Universe, who have the potential for balance, harmony and to live as one, brooded over by the One, True God, the "over soul" of the Entire Universe, who both cares for individual sheep and shepherds the entire flock. In other words, the early Christian Church developed the Trinitarian Model through cosmologically integrating the attention to the Details of the Universe and the Content of Creation in paganism (polytheism) with the insistence in Judaism on the goodness, oneness and transcendental nature of God (monotheism). I contend the Holy Trinity can be made intelligible to a twenty-first century audience through the metaphor of an ecosystem. God is an ecosystem!

This is my revelation from the Poor Christ as one ordinary oppressed person.

Yet according to Glendenning, most oppressed minorities *are not* able to access their unique beliefs and practices, like I have, because they have been systematically "cut-off" from the "land of their ancestors" because of Western colonization. Groups like Native Americans, Latinos and Africans have been especially "hard-hit" because illiteracy makes it impossible to learn their history from books and many of them have preserved their history as oral tradition on the "land of their ancestors," the very land they have been exiled from.

Although, Glendenning praises the Christian Church for teaching faith, for Glendenning contends that we need all the faith and courage we can muster to solve the pressing moral issues of times. Glendenning also contends that the Christian Church also needs to teach history too, to help dislocated, dispossessed peoples recover their history aka their stories, their unique "bottom-up," "inside-out" religious beliefs and practices. In other words, to have a truly authentic Christian faith, a truly life-changing Christian conversion experience and to be truly a relevant spiritual witness to the issues of our times, we also need both historical literacy and respect for our ancestors and traditions, alongside being taught mere faith, good works and how to be-in-the-world. We need to reconstruct church history.

I contend as neurodiverse humans, the history we have been exiled from *are not* locked-up on a piece of land belonging to our ancestors, but history we have been locked-out of by organized religion. Although, I have been able to recover my autistic spiritual history through studying books. I am still locked-out of the embodied, lived, communal, relational, place-based history of the various world religions. Organized religions still interprets their traditions in manors which make the "living traditions" inaccessible, exclusive, irrelevant, even disparaging toward me as a disabled human on the autism spectrum. Organized religion still latently and blatantly excludes disabled and neurodiverse humans from religious rituals. Organized religion still *does not* sanction disability and neurodiverse realities, leading to much confusion, loneness, suffering, disorientation, instability, stigma and emptiness in my life, in the process.

Yet, I have a relationship with the Living God and with the Communion of All Saints within the context of Animals and the Earth which can stand on its own and is my "source of healing and empowerment" for "living more sanely and sustainably on this Earth."

This is our history. To use my late mentor Dr. Bosserman's popular saying, "we are in good company!" Even as we feel alone in space, we are not alone in time. A prophet, a saint, a wise person went through something similar to us. Our situation is not unique!

We are not alone in space either, for we are "in the wilderness [for many days], tempted by Satan, and [we are] with the wild beasts; and the angels [wait on us]" (Mark 1:13). Our humanity is affirmed! We find solace! Solitude! Rest! Comfort! Consolation! True and Perfect Joy! Even freedom!

The historical context of our ancestors was the margins! The tradition was written from the margins! By the outcasts! The poor! The oppressed! The disabled! The neurodiverse!

Our ancestors were the masses! The multitude! The people!

This is the "good news" about Christianity!

Christianity professes and confesses a "down to earth" God who welcomes and includes everyone! God is the God of everyone!

There is definitely a contradiction between American Christianity and the Christianity of our common ancestors.

I am going to summarize this project, by briefly applying Marxist dialectic materialism to the history of world religions, to not only show that there is a positive correlation between who controls the "means of production" and who controls the "socio-symbolic life" of a religion or culture, but actually recover the two distinct spiritualities of the oppressed and the oppressors, with the goal of creating a dialectic spirituality, adding a special spiritual sensitivity lacking in Marxist analysis. I contend that understanding neurodiversity social history, the anthropological reasons for economic inequality, internal European colonialism and First Nations outside of North America is a possible solution to better understanding the real reasons for economic inequality, bigotry and colonization in North America. I am going to use this conclusion to articulate the need for a libratory theology of neurodiversity and a neurodiverse Model of God.

Karl Marx in nineteenth century Germany developed his classic theory about the patterns of human history at the macro-level, to "pull-out" a critical social theory which explained the origins of economic inequality, deconstructed capitalism as fundamentally anti-democratic, hypocritical and oppressive and reconstruct industrialism in more egalitarian, morally consistent and empowering terms. Of course, Marx's predictions of the future did not come to pass and many of his ideas when implemented were an unmitigated disaster for obvious reasons. Yet, many contemporary, postmodern scholars like my late mentor Dr. Phil Bosserman did contend that Marx did provide an excellent critique of capitalism which is still relevant today. I would go further and say that many of Marx's predictions did come true, in reality; his predictions came to pass through evolution instead of revolution. Also, I contend that Marx's ideas would have worked in reality, if his detractors also respected democratic, spiritual, religious, creative, psychological and ecological values, listened better to the stories of the very commoners they were trying to help and "let-go" of this need to "control outcomes."

I am also going to use classic Marxist analysis despite all these emerging Christian critiques of capitalism in Christian environmental and social justice circles, because Pope John Paul II is no Carol Marx. Mainly what is lacking in the former Pope's critique of capitalism, immanent in Marx's critique, is staying focused on blaming the problems of capitalism on the capitalists themselves ("The Corporate Class") and on the capitalistic economic system itself, with a focus on collective, society-wide change, not "soft targeting" ordinary people for all the problems of the world or burdening individuals with all this personal change without also providing a changed society which provides individual citizens the supports and strength necessary to sustain personal transition from a hierarchical society to an egalitarian society.

In other words, in this model, the Marxist critique of the Christian critique of capitalism than is that the eccisioastic critique of capitalism leaves in-tact the neoclassical residue of psychological reductionism and social conservativism, the same logic used to blame the economic poor for their own poverty. A toxic critique of capitalism based on "blaming the victim," "achievement ideology," "scathing critiques" and "modest reforms" instead of religious leaders basing their critique on "stigmatizing society," "hope and empowerment," "discerning the signs of the times," "systemic evil" and "basic change." Such a critique betrays a certain unconscious bias toward liberalism aka modernism.

The Marxist model of human history and economic change contends that the origins of economic inequality is perpetuated through a dialectic struggle between who controls the "means of the production," "whoever has the gold rules," where whosoever ends-up controlling the "means of production" becomes the oppressor and whoever *does not*, becomes the oppressed.

In classical times, the "masters" controlled the "means of production" and "the peasants" became the oppressed, until the "peasants" revolted and gained control of the "means of production." In Medieval Times, the "peasants" became the "lords" and the "aristocrats" became the "serfs." The "serfs" than revolted and became the "merchant class." With the rise of modernity, the "merchant class" became the "capitalists" and the "lords" become "the poor" again. Marx predicted that "the economic poor" would rise-up against the "capitalists" and regain control of the "means of production." Where if the "educated people" like himself can educate "the masses" about the origins of inequality, that the latest "journeymen" to use Mark's words would words, can this time work towards a more fair and just egalitarian society for everyone, through creating order through "socialism" and freedom through "anarchy."

There is a serious flaw in Marx's logic however. Mark still *did not* account for the reasons why different classes were able to gain control of the "means of production" at different points in history or why the oppressed were successful and unsuccessful at different points in history at overthrowing their oppressors. Who exactly were these oppressors and oppressed people and journeymen? What motivated them to act? What exactly where their advantages and tactics? For the answer, we turn to feminist theory, environmental history and mimetic theory.

Feminist theory unlike Marxist analysis is equipped to address the lingering question of power which was the downfall of the various communist, socialist and anarchist movements. In fact, it is a safe generalization to make, that power is the downfall of all worthwhile movements. Even when the oppressed do get control of the "means of production," there is still the lingering Christian anthropological question of human nature, that human beings have an inherent sinful nature past from one generation to another whether it is genetic or cultural. That the oppressed are still stuck with the residue of their own sinful nature which gets magnified when they win, which my father who is retiring from over thirty years of public service with the federal government said when I shared Sharon Welch's project with him, "you need a fundamentally different skill set, you are expected to start implementing your ideas."

According to Sharon Welch, these "skill sets" for leadership do involve compromise, careful . listening, acknowledging your own limits and weaknesses, managing conflict and disagreement, creatively responding to imperfection, uncertainty, chaos, contradiction even mistakes, watching your language about power and relinquishing your need to "control outcomes." According to Welch, once minority groups like women, master these mature leadership virtues, there is no reason why women and other minorities group *cannot* become strong, benign, fair and just leaders.

So the first step as disabled and neurodiverse journeymen and journeywomen, to truly moving into the third millennium and beyond the mistakes and tragedies of the second millennium is to recognize our own "sinful" human nature as full human beings who happen to be oppressed at this point in history, to celebrate our victories whenever we win an "in-road" no matter how modest in neurotypical society marking the "milestone" from being an exile to becoming a power-holder and to learn all the "social skills" necessary to prepare us to become "servant leaders" once we win.

Now we have taken "social skills" into activism/organizing territory and activism/organizing territory into religion territory. Who are the oppressed, the oppressors and the journeymen and women; it turns-out "at the end of the day" are "only human." We are all fellow human beings. Yet this still does not explain, the origins of inequality, to which we turn to environmental history and mimetic theory for the answers.

Environmental historians contend that when the human population outstrips the inherent scarcity of natural resources found in the Nature (there is only a finite amount of energy in the world for a finite amount of human beings "carrying capacity") this striping of natural resources leads to intraspecies competition in human society like wars, conquests and other types of oppression, when individual groups of humans fight over the dwindling natural resources necessary for human survival and reproduction. Environmental historians link human overpopulation in about

10,000 BC in the "Fertile Crescent" of the eastern Mediterranean region to both the transition in Eurasia from being "hunters/gatherers" to becoming "farmers/herders" to becoming "city/states" and the rise of oppressive ideologies in the West including anthropocentrism, speciesism, neoclassicism, patriarchy, classism and imperialism.

Ideologies with historical origins in Hellenistic civilizations, which are still an integral part of Western culture and thought and are used by modern-day societies to justify the practices causing the planetary crisis like capitalism, industrialism, bureaucracy, hierarchy, dualism, domination, conquest, exploitation, control, manipulation and violence. Environmental historians attribute the collapse of classical civilizations like Ancient Greece, Rome and Egypt to exhausting natural resources caused by human overpopulation. The neoclassical ideologies *did not cause* human overpopulation and resource depletion in ancient societies, however; instead ideologies and civilization building were developed to create order and stability in an unsustainable society, where environmental historians contend that *both* "subsistence living" *and* "human population control" are necessary to have a truly sustainable *and* just society.

That "subsistence living" is necessary for living sustainably with the Earth, while "human population control" is necessary to make such an austere society---fair, just, peaceful, tenable, palatable, livable and doable for the greatest amount of people, freeing-up the necessary resources needed for every human being to get everything we need to survive, reproduce, flourish, be happy and live with dignity.

I contend that "human population control" *need not* be attained by abortion or contraception; "human population control" can also be attained by no sex outside marriage, keeping monogamous marriage vowels, taking a vow of celibacy, eliminating human trafficking and other forms of prostitutions, adopting disadvantaged children, avoiding artificial copulation, breast feeding when possible, becoming literate of the responsibilities of parenthood, educating girls and women, teaching your children about human sexuality and its responsibilities and political and economic gender equality for women.

Environmental historians contend that both "hunter/gatherer" and "farmer/header" societies are compatible with living sustainably with the Earth and fairly, justly, harmoniously and peacefully with each other, because such societies live in close communion with the Natural World, a world marked by beauty, sensuality, mystery, personal relationships and observable limits.

Environmental historians contend that this was the historical context of the mythic, archetypal Garden of Eden and subsequent Fall mentioned in the Hebrew Bible and today's Jewish and Christian environmental circles. The Garden of Eden in this interpretation symbolizes not a literal garden, but the proper human-Earth relationships which occurred at one time in Western history when Eurasians still lived in caves as "hunters/gatherers" in the times following the end of the last ice age before 10,000 BC, for a period of several million years. The Forbidden Fruit, The Serpent and The Fall *are not* to be taken brutally literally, but are really parables about human-Earth estrangement and the mythic-poetic remembering of a time when human beings lived in harmony with the Earth as "hunters/gatherers" in the wilderness and how human overpopulation and resource depletion "ruined everything."

Where in this model, the "means of production" *are not* moral-neutral or power-neutral, but that the types of technologies and ideological frameworks we use to survive and reproduce, actually plays an active role in shaping the development of world civilization and the quality of our relationships with Animals and the Earth. For example, in this model, a barter system is more sustainable than a paper/plastic/wireless money system, because paper/plastic/wireless money introduces a level of abstraction and objectification of natural resources, the Natural World and each other, lacking in a more concrete, place-based, personalistic, relational barter system. A paper/plastic/wireless money system leads humans to live beyond their means, overinvest, over borrow, make mindless financial decisions, not separate need from want, develop unrealistic and untenable economic policies and business practices, dismiss ethical-moral consequences, not take personal responsibility for their own financial stewardship and use others as "means to an end" instead of an "end in itself," in other words, "cheat the system," because our economic system has become so abstract, dislocated, disembodied, complicated, hyper-specialized, compartmentalized, homogenized and impersonal.

So in other words, according to environmental historians, the second step, we Aspie journeymen and women need to take is to question the "means of production" themselves, to investigate if our inventions and innovations are ethically and morally tainted. Gandhi said, "science without humanity" is one of "seven deadly sins of the world." All of us neurodiverse humans are in a unique position to critique and change our current broken industrial, market-driven economic systems, because our propensity is away from the abstract, toward the concrete, the mundane, the detailed, the practical, the realistic and the personal. Those on the autism spectrum with specialized scientific and applied science training are in a unique position to offer concrete critiques of the risks and externalities of specific technologies, to research and develop concrete and practical ecological, humane and socially responsible solutions and invent new technologies and economic systems which are more in harmony with Animals, the Earth and each other.

In other words, actually implementing the planetary agenda, not just sitting around and talking about it! Actually doing something about the planetary crisis, other than debate climate deniers because as Aspies we have this unusual gift of being able to both engage in unskilled manual work through working with our hands in the material world and are able to analytically and critical reflect on our mundane, everyday worlds, at the same time, leading to analytical engagement with concrete reality.

Most neurotypicals, are either/or, leading to both compartmentalization of labor and a class-based society based on merit. We have a "sense of wonder" toward the mundane, seeing something of the sublime, the divine and the infinite in our "world-around-us." As an Aspie, like Saint Paul, I only have to go as far as my own garden, to sense God's existence and goodness.

I need both the rootedness and stability of the mundane (my food) and faith, reason, beauty and creativity to wash down my "daily bread" (my drink) to fell happy and whole, at peace and in-love with all life, "at-home on this Earth," a Caledonian, sacramental world which is both Fully God and a Creature of God, at the same time. Where I am intimately aware at every turn, no matter what I do, no matter how mundane, base or worldly, that I live in a "Sacramental Universe" where I *cannot* keep from praying and Praising the Lord. I have found Jesus Christ in All of Nature.

Jesus Christ is the Physical Manifestation of God in "the world-around-us," who is also the Redeemer of the Entire Universe. Out of mere biophysical, naturalistic phenomena, I "pull-out" all of the Supernatural claims of Christendom embodied into our material world, like the mind being embodied in the brain and all of literature, poetry, art and music coming out of the dynamic interplay among biochemical reactions, nerve firings and sense organs in the human body which transcends itself to become a member of all the beauty, wonder, goodness, love and glory of our animate Universe, the Living God, the Intelligence of our Universe.

Yet, this still does not provide a guarantee that if we learn from all the mistakes of world history, live in reality, engage the Natural World and live our lives in a spirit of acceptance, humility, grace, love, joy, careful listening and a reverence for all life, that the political and religious movements of the twenty-first century will be any more benign than the one's of the twentieth century.

This is because the "road to hell is paved in good intentions!" This is because "old habits die hard!" This is because our bonds to our sinful human nature run very deep indeed. This is because such a communitarian anarchist society is fundamentally unnatural. That our primal needs for safety, belonging, stability and order diehard, that it is very hard to be peaceful or loving or forgive or even act in our own self-interests, if we fundamentally do not feel safe, are lonely or alienated, if we feel disoriented or lost or chaotic ourselves. These are deep emotional longings which defy logic or reason, even self-interest. They seem almost instinctual even natural.

According to Girardian theology (aka mimetic theory) that our hominoid brains (our vermis) has genetically evolved in early human history as an adaptation to help us work together toward mutual human survival through channeling our animal-like propensities toward individual self-interest through a form of collective violence which French intellectual Rene Girard calls "sacred violence" or "scapegoating." Getting the majority self-interest bearers to mob together against all the evolutionary weak (mostly fellow humans with disabilities in their own society) or ineffective leaders in a given society (like kings, queens and so forth) to drain their violent, self-absorbed impulses like venom in a rattlesnake. This creates the necessary self-sacrificing order and altruistic cooperation in a given society necessary for human survival over and against a challenging natural environment.

Such a social order was justified through the institution of organized religion which created legitimizing narratives, cultural norms/taboos and human sacrifice cults to justify and perpetuate scapogoating individuals and groups at the margins of society, to create social order and a cooperative spirit for everyone else. In other words, the whole archaic religion project, which none of today's World Religions and secular societies are immune from the contaminating residue of the superstitious religions of the Stone Ages. Meaning it is no joke, when liberal-progressives make jokes about fundamentalists "living in the stone ages." There is actually a "grain of truth" to this religious joke! Today's religious, philosophical, cultural and ideological traditions, according to Girardian Theory have unconsciously preserved the superstitious, sacrificial, scapegoating violent residue of Stone Age religions. This is why many non-western traditional religions still exclude animals, disability, neurodiversity, outsiders and Westerners, even tell this day. We are their scapegoats!

In other words, in the Girardian model, the oppressed are the scapegoats, the oppressors are the majority group and the "means of production" is one's individual psyche energy, the sociosymbolic life of a given society and a society's individual and collective relationship to a challenging natural environment needed for collective survival and reproduction.

The Good News, according to Girardian theorists, is that there was one religious narrative which emerged in the human consciousness which *was not* based on scapegoating but on the systematic deconstruction and renunciation of culturally-sanctioned violence. This religious narrative was none other than the Christian Bible (aka New Testament).

This was the most startling, ironic and promising discovery Girard made. Especially since at the time, Girard was an agnostic, who assumed that because of Christianity's violent histories of crusades, inquisitions, witch hunts, genocides and conquests, that Christianity was one more human sacrifice cult. Until Girard started researching the tradition and applying his critical social theory to the Christian tradition.

The crux of Girard's discovery was that the Holy Gospels told the scapegoating narrative of Stone Age religions backwards and upside down. The story was told from the point of view of the scapegoat (aka "the oppressed" aka "the minority" aka "the outsider") instead of "the mob" (aka "the oppressors" aka "the majority" aka "the insiders"). Aka Jesus Christ, a condemned man on a Roman Cross, a member of a colonized people (the Israel Lights) at the height of Roman occupation of the entire Mediterranean basin and beyond, an illegitimate child rejected by his own people, "a minority within a minority."

In the Christian narrative, not only was Jesus a member of a colonized group, an illegitimate child rejected by his own people and a criminally condemned man on a Roman cross, Jesus was also a God, Jesus was also Christ, "the anointed one," the Promised Messiah, the Savior of the Entire World.

In fact, in the writing of Christian Sacred Texts and the ritual reenactment of the Passion of Jesus Christ in Christian liturgical art and religious rituals, Christians call their God "victim." Victim *not* Victor is the primary "root metaphor" for God in the Christian religion.

This "set in motion" a whole series of historical events in Western civilization, among believers and non-believers alike, which continues to destabilize traditional modes of social organization, even tell this day, leading to the re-emergence of psychological instability, competitiveness, adverserialism, extreme individualism, social chaos and mass-violence in modern society.

This is because the Story of Jesus Christ has very successfully pulled-off the demystification of evil to such a point, that humanity now has the ability to both self-critique culture and have empathy for the oppressed, an illumination which according to Girardian scholars already existed in a more immature form in Ancient Israel and Ancient Greece, which reached maturity with the advent of Christianity.

I would also contend that Ancient India and Persia, ancient Celtic societies, some traditional African societies like Ethiopia and Nubia (modern day Algeria), many First Nations societies like the Lakota, Dine, Navaho, Cherokee, Seneca and Aztec in North America and some of the aboriginal tribes of Polynesia, Micronesia, Indonesia, Australia and New Zealand, as well as Mongolia and Tibet, also were undergoing their own demystification of oppression processes.

In other words, the demystification of evil, the ability to self-critique one's own culture and having empathy for the oppressed is Jesus's gift to the Earth Quilt. Creating a viable, living, operational model of communitarian anarchy, over two millenniums and counting of Christian exprerimentation and implementation of Jesus's "Dream for the Earth" of an inverted hierarchy, where the strong *do not* conquer the weak, instead, the strong take care of the weak.

The Holy Gospels offers us a more positive, life-affirming, nonviolent outlet for human aggression than scapegoating, domination and oppression through giving us a life of good works, where we help other people and make the world a better place for everyone, giving our own lives, meaning and purpose, through restoring beauty to the world, in the process, our moral and religious self-interests. Our very real human need and longing for signifigence! Self-actualization!

Yet, Girardian scholars have also discovered a very serious flaw in the Gospel Life model. That once all of the oppressed and marginalized have successfully taken control of the "means of production," they become just like their oppressors. They start scapegoating and oppressing their former oppressors as a form of revenge, leading not only to the preparation of cycles of violence, but worse, with every new revolution, further destabilizing, even eroding away at, the very social structures, human beings have depended upon for thousands of years, for safety, order, stability and belonging, with the Christian narrative still at-work at the unconscious level.

One example, Girardian Theorists use, is the historical reality that one of the first heresies in the Christian Church was anti-Semiticism, wanting to scapegoat all Jews for the Cruxifixation of Jesus Christ. I would also add that it was also no accident that Gnosticism was another early Christian heresy, wanting to scapegoat Pagans for the persecution of early Christians, through trying to violently expunge all of the non-monotheistic elements of pagan religion and culture like pantheism, naturalism, henotheism and animalism, through hatred for the body and the material world, through becoming excessively otherworldly and disembodied, through burning down "sacred groves" and through "burning" medicine women as "witches," once Christians gained Christian control of the pagan empire, hence, all of the scapegoating of Animals and the Natural World in Christendom.

With such polarization of human society, planetary annihilation through world wars, genocides, nuclear holocausts, environmental disasters, terrorist attacks, spree killings, cultural meltdowns, communal disintegrations, invasions, civil wars and all around dystopia is becoming more and more of a possibility, if left unchecked.

Originally, I was counting on the Girardian movement to offer "repenting of all your sins" and "accepting Jesus Christ as your Lord and Savior" as an alternative strategy for engaging in anti-oppression and nonviolence, other than the current inadequate strategies of political correctness and trying to undermine our religious beliefs which we depend upon for our sanity, as well as a potential Christian apologetic to the "ecological complaint against Christianity."

I am saddened to report that many Girardian scholars have come to the cynical conclusion that most modern-day people *are not* ready for the Way of Jesus. Instead, many Girardian scholars are questing the validity of anti-oppression and nonviolence as a legitimate enterprise, purposing a revitalization of archaic religion, with scapegoating and all, accomplished through "affirming the status quos" in our religions and cultures, "at all costs." Taking such a position is unfortunate!

Such a position, I maintain *is not* desirable for humans with disabilities, nonhuman animals and the nonhuman world who have yet to enjoy a proper liberation, being forced to watch every other minority group get all this justice while we go without, is very hurtful, unfair, hypocritical and embittering. We need to let our Lord Jesus Christ finish what He started over thousand years ago. "Jesus is the Answer!" There is no other way!

We are so far beyond going back to the way it was in the past! It's too late! Too much un-repairable damage has been done!

The "good news" is even though we might not be ready for the Way of Jesus, the Gospel Life, nor is it possible for us to do the Sermon on the Mount by our own weak human will-power, we *do not* have to do it all on our own, nor do we have to use Jesus as a viable example or model on how to live our lives.

This is because, Jesus not only died on the Cross, Jesus also has Risen from the Dead, was Resurrected, was Reborn in the Tomb of the Earth and Ascended to the Heavens to be healed, empowered and renewed by The Grandfather.

Our Grandfather is nothing less than the Source of All Life, the Creator of the Entire Universe. Our Creator God, our Papa in Heaven, is also the Intelligence of the Universe, "The Mind of God," the true nervous system of our world. Where "The Mind of God" has been giving our world beauty, order, safety, stability even peace and harmony through the laws of physics, chemical bonds, genetic codes, mutualistic relationships, providential care and "non-ordinary states of consciousness" since of the beginning of time, over two billion years ago, with over two billion years of experience of nonviolently, justly, fairly and beautifully ordering the Entire Universe.

Only for Jesus to Return Again at the First Pentecost of the Early Church as The Christ, The Resurrected Messiah, having dissipated out into the Universe, as the Holy Spirit, who is here for as long as it takes, to restore balance to our planet and help all Life on Earth to survive and flourish for All Time, Eternity.

It turns-out, sometimes God has to shake our world-up, to get healing and reconciliation we *did not* even think was possible, "sometimes God has to almost kill us to teach us something," giving us "reason for hope" that "these things have to pass" to "not dismay" and "endure tell the end" with the promise of redemption for all those who "faithful endure," in other words, we are called as Christians to "practice radical patience." Remembering the Christian axioms "for mortals it is impossible, with God all things are possible" (Mathew 19: 26) and "I can do all things through [God] who strengthens me" (Philippians 4: 12-14).

You might protest that such a vision is escapist, otherworldly even fundamentalist or cultish, yet from a disability Christology perspective such a vision is accepting of our limitations, is mundane, realistic, even pragmatic, because saying "Christ has Risen" means calling God "a survivor." Where many disabled Christians find solace not only in an embodied God who is a "victim" (The Passion of Jesus) but also in a God "who is a survivor too" (The Resurrection of Christ).

To put this reconstruction in Girardian terms, the Resurrected Christ is a scapegoat who survived! In more Disability Studies terms, Jesus Christ "is a survivor too!" In more interfaith terms, Jesus is a "Wounded Healer!"

In more ecological, animal rights terms, Redemption symbolizes all the "rebirth" or "regeneration" in the Natural World. New live coming out of old. New islands erupting out of cooling underwater volcanoes and dying coral reefs! The riot of wildflowers after a forest fire! The natural succession of an overgrown farmer's field into a mature oak-hickory forest! When an endangered species like the Bald Eagle comes back from the brink of extinction to repopulate the Earth again! When robins and wood thrushes still sing their ethereal songs in springtime! Despite everything, when increasing choruses of frog and toad species refuse to let an impending extinction intimidate them from singing through yet another growing season in the various temperate regions of the world! Whenever the sun still sets and rise over and over again "in its own accustomed fashion," congratulations, you just discovered the Resurrection of the Body.

In other words, as long as we are alive at-all, there is always the possibility for a better future, for all involved. "Despair" is a complete "non-starter!"

Environmentalists and animal activists would be wise to take a hint from our military troops who believe that "failure is not an option!" We cannot just "give up the ship!" That is Spaceship Earth! Not now! Not when our Wilderness Home needs us more than ever, to be there, to help all the animals, plants, microorganisms and bioregions of the Earth through "their darkest hours," putting All the Animals and All the Earth on their own "road to redemption," the Great Rebirth, the Resurrection of All Life, the Messianic Era, the Cosmic Revival, the "next level" in human and planetary evolution, reclaiming our rightful ecological place in the Universe as Nature's healers, in the process, where Christ's Holy Spirit is understood as the Immune System of the Earth, "who fights for life." Allowing individuals and collectives to heal and regenerate.

Now "Christ as Mediator" begins to make more sense. We *do not* need all these mediators whether they are priests or popes, oppressed minority groups, the Natural World, other human beings or even the angels and saints in Heaven, let alone the Historical Jesus or the Holy Spirit, to communicate with our Creator God.

The Risen Christ, God Himself, is our "mediator" between priests and popes, the peoples of the borderlands, Animals and Nature, other humans and a whole litany of idols, to quote from Bonheoffer, "we do not have to face our enemies alone."

In this model, Christ is neither the Cosmic Persecutor of Calvinism, nor is He the Cosmic Plaintive of the whole mid-twentieth century project, nor is He the Cosmic Public Defender of the Emerging Churches, no, Christ Is The Docket!

Integrating two metaphors, one from the Western conflict resolution field and the other from Native American spirituality, where "Christ as Mediator" is understood as the matrix, the environment, the container, the place, where justice, "right relationships," can occur. Where "Christ as Mediator" is our "Beautiful Trail" from "womb to grave" to help us through conflict, adversity and uncertainty, keeping us safe, stable and sane, compassionate, fair and nonviolent, where we will find the Sabbath rest our soul so longs for and like Saint Francis of Assisi, will receive the necessary guidance from our Living God, directly, without confusion and very personally, after much prayers, supplications and holy longings on how to live the Gospel Life and fulfill God's Commandments in a fallen, broken world marked by traumatic novelties like Francis encountered over seven centuries ago.

All we have to do is Ask God and an Answer will be given to us. We need to "dwell in situations of inherent worth," we need to dwell in the Kingdom of God, to be able to implement the Way of Jesus, at all. The "good news" is that the Kingdom of God dwells within the context of a fallen, broken, suffering world. Read the chapters before and after Isaiah 11's "The Peaceable Kingdom" in narrative context. Read the Book of Revelation, more carefully and you will see.

In other words, we the oppressed *are not* the Poor Christ, but our sociosymbolic life keeps alive the theological vision of the Poor Christ, "Jesus Christ Liberator" in the Judeo-Christian tradition, becoming the generic, universal spirituality of the oppressed everywhere. A "bottom-up" spirituality of "healing and empowerment" for all those from the margins of society, Black Coffee for the Masses! Where the "role of religion" is to make one sober, deal with reality and work towards revolutionary reforms and changes in our society and culture.

Where the primary thing that the Disabled God metaphor adds to the Poor Christ model is a libratory reconstruction of the Resurrection of Jesus Christ, where in this model the Cruxifixation was an act of solidarity with the oppressed everywhere contended by classical liberation theology, while the Resurrection gives the oppressed, a powerful message of hope, solace, survival and endurance. Our abusers *do not* get the last word on the destiny of our lives, our present and future, nor do they get any say in how we define ourselves, name ourselves, give our own lives meaning and purpose or proceed from victimization.

Through Christ's Dying and Rising from the Dead, we develop resilience, "indomitable spirits." Even though we *do not* get "cured" of disability, we can make a "full-recovery" from disability when we integrate our disability experiences and realities into our stories and our humanity, when we learn how to manage our symptoms, learn to trust ourselves and other people again and when we are able to authentically re-integrate ourselves back into human society as dignified "moral agents" applying our "real world" disability life experiences to solving our own problems and providing our own unique responses to the most pressing moral issues of our times.

What autistic liberation theology adds to the "Disabled God" metaphor is a libratory reconstruction of Doctrine of the Holy Trinity, where God is much more than "what we need god to be." God *is not* our "imaginary friend," a "socially constructed" ideology to argue and manipulate at all, a "human invention," a "rhetorical device," a "projection of ourselves," "the story of our community" or the "totem pole" of our tribal identities. God *is not* the "goodness of humanity." Not everything which "just happens" is from God. Not everything we do as Christians is God's Will. Just reciting a mechanical Prayer to God *does not* mean God has answered or that anything we say afterwards speaks for God. We *are not* "God's representatives Here on Earth." We *do not* "create god in our own image and likeness." We *are not* called to "Be Jesus." God *is not* a "brother." We *are not* God!

Autistic liberation theology actually takes seriously the Biblical insistence that "my thoughts are not your thoughts, nor are your ways my ways" (Isaiah 55:8). Drawing from the "root metaphor" of "mystery" in much of the "inside-out" autistic studies literature (our sociosymbolic life), an autistic Model of God insists that the Will of God is completely wild, undomesticated and autonomous, insisting that God is beyond human control and *is not* defined by "human precepts" (Mathew 15: 9).

Yet, unlike many impersonal Eastern mystical approaches, autistic mysticism in "good company" with much of the personal Nature mysticism of Western religions also insists that this "mystery" is "intelligible," "knowable" even "personable" and "down to earth." "The word became flesh and lived among us" (John 1: 14). We are atheistic to both "the angry god" of fundamentalism and "the distant, critical god" of liberalism and postmodernity. We are confessional to the loving, mysterious, personal, living God of the Bible.

This is because our "hard won" "pragmatic experiences" of learning to "cope" in a world not created for us, has forced us to relinquish our need to control everyone and everything in our environment, leading us to respect the rights of our neighbors and enemies alike, mainly their inhalable "right to exist for their own sake." This reality made us more open to the possibility of God's Transcendence.

This is also because we *have not* had the privilege of just being able to "live with the question." We still needed answers to all "the mysteries of life." Our pragmatic survival is dependent upon it. We had to engage this Mystery! We had to be like the Arthurian Knights of the Round Table and step through "the mysterious mist" to the "mystery ship" to get "wisdom" and "guidance" from the Christian nuns abroad the ship. We as autistic mystics have to contemplate the

Mysteries of the Universe in a more pragmatic and mundane and I would have dare say, scientific manor, then neurotypical mystics, like "finding-out who the killer is in a murder mystery," like a "spy on a reconvene mission" like "putting together a 5000 jigsaw puzzle." We had to become pilgrims! Sojourners! Travelers passing though! There was no other way! This reality also made us more open to the possibility of God's Imminence.

This is because we ourselves "live, move and have our being" in "invisible realities," that is the nature of autism, "an invisible condition." You cannot see it, touch it, taste it, smell it or even hear it, yet it exists. It is very real indeed! We *are not* defined by our physical, temporal bodies, even our physical, temporal minds, nor are we completely defined by secular realities such as "peer pressure," leading us to becoming dreamy dreamers. Yet, still "bracketed" by physical, temporal and secular realities, like running up against our limits, we *are not* totally free and uninhabited to "create our own reality," forcing us instead to "change reality," becoming innovators and implementers, in the process. Practical idealists! Peoples of action! This reality made us open to the possibility of the existence of the Invisible God!

Such a traditionalist, "high" Christological formulation of our "pragmatic experiences" with the Living God as full human beings on the autism spectrum, which is much more transcendental and personalistic, than all the "limbo, limbo, limbo, how low can you go" Christology which marks the liberation theology tradition in both South and North America alike, I contend is our greatest gift to this worthwhile endeavor.

The autistic Model of God gives "oppressed-oppressors" everywhere, whether you are a middle class white woman in the United States who is also struggling as a single mother in a depressed economy, part of the emerging African-American upper classes yet still suffering from the traumatic memories of a segregationist childhood and youth, come from a wealthy Latino family in a country still marked by poverty and colonization, a financially comfortable yet persecuted homosexual, a privileged white male who also had an abusive father or was drafted into an unpopular war like Vietnam, or an underprivileged white male like myself, where I have been repeatedly bullied, stigmatized, patronized and discriminated against based upon disability and diagnosis, the "best of both worlds."

Autistic liberation theology, on the one hand, acknowledges our own oppression situations and our own very real human need for "love and solidarity" through confessing and professing a very personal, loving, intimate God. Yet, on the other hand, autistic liberation theology also acknowledges our own fallibility and our own very real "shadow side," as well as the inherent worth and intrinsic value of others through confessing and professing also a fair, just, sovereign God.

Such a non-dualistic, nuanced and I dare say, universalized liberation theology, which militantly rejects dividing the oppressed into "deserving" and "undeserving" and is militantly nonviolent is uniquely equipped to both liberate us from our "contaminated self" through God's grace and unlock our mutualistic, altruistic, heroic potential for living a life of good works and helping other people.

The strength of this model is that it provides a "detour" around "god is on our side!" "We are in the hands of an angry god" and "god is too busy" which has marked American Judeo-Christianity all too often, where the Living God of the Bible instead wants to "mediate" our conflicts and help us all work toward "win-win-win" solutions to all our problems, giving all of us, everything we need and some of what we want, restoring balance, order and harmony to the Universe, in the process. Where God will not rest until all of this is accomplished!

*Autistic liberation theology* in essence, *insists* that ***The God of the Bible is really Everybody's God! There Is Only One God! There Is No Other! God's Houses of Worship Are Not Your Own Private Property! God's Houses of Worship Belong to God Alone! We All Live Under God's Reign! We Do Not Control Access to God! We Do Not Determine Who Is In And Who Is Out! We Do Not Determine Who Goes To Heaven And Hell! Who Is Saved or Not! Who Gets Communion and Who Does Not! God Is The Only True Judge! Our God Chooses To Save Whoever He Chooses To Save! Calls Whoever He Chooses To Call! Our God Unilaterally Chooses Through Gratuitous Grace To Welcome All Who Are Hungry, Thirty and Weary to His Table! Lord Jesus Christ in the Holy Gospels Is Pretty Darn Clear About This! Read Your Bible! In God Alone, Is To Be Found All Power, Glory and Authority! All Of***

*Us Mortals Will Have To Stand Before God! All of Us Can Rest In God's Goodness, Fairness and Infinite Love! Grace Be With You! Go In Peace!*

## Bibliography for Further Study

### Disability Studies:

- Americans With Disabilities Act (ADA): www.ada.gov.
- Tammy Berberi, http://disstudies.org/biographies/tammy_berberi/. Currently my mentor in Society for Disability Studies (SDS), Dr. Berberi is now the president of SDS. Berberi is also an associate professor of French and director of the program at the University of Minnesota-Morris. Berberi is an example of a person with a physical disability working in one of the liberal arts fields.
- Nancy Eisland, *the Disabled God: Toward A Libratory Theology of Disability* (Nashville: Abington Press, 1994). The classic work in disability liberation theology.
- Martha Nussbaum, *Frontier of Justice: Disability, Nationality, Species Membership* (Cambridge: The Belknap of Harvard University Press, 2006). For an example of the "dependence" argument which is fashionable in many Christian theological and secular philosophy and liberal arts circles. Written from a non-disabled perspective.
- Rachel Salomon, "Disabled Israelis Serving Their Country with Pride" in United with Israel, 11/25/2012, http://unitedwithisreal.org/disabledirsaelis-serving/. Rachel is my biological sister and as of the time of this publication is finishing-up her Master's Thesis in Middle Eastern Studies at Ben Gurian University in Israel. My sister also has two bachelor degrees from University of Maryland-College Park in political science and international relations and has already completed her Master degree (coursework) at Ben Gurian University. My sister currently is a dual citizen of Israel, lives in Israel with her husband and current works for a non-profit Zionist organization in Israel as a journalist.
- Society for Disability Studies (SDS): www.disstudies.org. An international organization and the primary professional society servicing the emerging disability studies field, disabled professionals, academics, activists and artists and non-disabled scholars and activists addressing disability and disability studies issues. In addition to an active website, phone directory and list serve, SDS also sponsors an annual academic conference each year in a different location, several smaller regional or specialized conferences, an academic peer reviewed journal, a newsletter and a series of scholarships and awards. I am currently a member of the Society for Disability Studies (SDS).
- Society for Disability Studies (SDS) Annual Conference in Denver, 2012: http://disstudies.org/annual-conference/2012-conference/.This was the conference I presented at. Learn more about the presentations, panel discussions and workshops and disability scholars featured in my book, as well as any other topics of interests. Use this also as an opportunity to get a feel of a typical SDS annual conference.
- Sunaura Taylor, http://sunaurataylor.org/events-and-projects/. To find out about my friend and collaborator, disability animal activist Sunaura Taylor. Do know in advance that there is some mature content on her website.

- Tanya Titchkosky, *Disability, Self and Society* (Toronto: University of Toronto Press, 2003, 2006, 2011). For an excellent scholarly introduction to the disability studies research program and field written from an "inside out" perspective, as well as guidance on how to integrate "disability experience" into "the embodiment," critical social theory, multiculturalism, other social agendas, communitarianism, inclusive language efforts and anti-oppression.
- C. Wolfe., (Spring 2008) "Learning From Temple Grandin or, Animal Studies, Disability Studies and Who Comes After The Subject," New Foundations, pp. 110. For a secondary source in a peer reviewed academic journal. Written from a non-disabled perspective.

**Neurodiversity:**

- Boundy, K, (2008) "Are You Sure, Sweetheart, That You Want to Be well?' An Exploration of the Neurodiversity Movement," Radical Psychology, http://radicalpsychology.org/vol17-1/boundy.html. See, for a secondary source and a sympathetic endorsement of the neurodiversity perspective by a feminist theorist who links neurotypicalism and normalcy to patriarchy and colonialism.
- Daniel Dombrowski, *Babies and Beasts: The Argument from Marginal Cases* (Chicago: University of Chicago Press, 1997). For an in-depth study of the content of Peter Singer's controversial "Argument from Marginal Cases" (AMC) and where Singer is coming from.
- Rab Houston and Uta Frith, *Autism in History: The Case of Hugh Blair of Borgue* (Malden, Massachusetts: Blackwell Publishers Inc., 2000).
- Thomas Balsame and Sharon Rosenbloom, *Souls: Beneath and Beyond Autism* (New York: NY: McGraw Hill, 2004).
- Jim Sinclair, (1998) "A note about language and abbreviations on this site," http://web.archive.org/web/2008060624118.
- Jim Sinclair, (1998), "If you love something, you don't kill it," http://web.archive.org/20080330071836/web.syr.edu.~jisincla/killing.htm.
- Jim Sinclair, (1988), "Some Thoughts on Empathy," http://web.archive.org/web/2008625050027/web.syr.edu/~jisincia/empathy.htm.
- Steven Shore, *Reflections from a Different Journey: What Adults with Disabilities Wish All Parents Knew*, ed. by Stanley D. Klein, Ph.D., and John D. Kemp (USA: McGraw Hill, 2004) 54-59, "The Autism Bomb."
- Bruce Wiseman, *Psychiatry: The Ultimate Betrayal* (Los Anglos: Freedom Press, 1995).
- Shomer Zwelling, *the Public Hospital of Williamsburg, Virginia, 1773-1885* (Colonial Williamsburg Foundation, 1963).

**Temple Grandin's Project:**

- Temple Grandin, *The Way I See It: Revised and Expanded-2rd Edition: a Personal Look at Autism and Asperger's Syndrome* (Future Horizons, 2011).
- Temple Grandin, *Thinking In Pictures, Expanded Addition: My Life With Autism* (Vintage, 2010).
- Temple Grandin and Catherine Johnson, *Animals Make Us Human: Creating The Best Lives For Animals* (Mariners Book, 2010).
- Temple Grandin and Catherine Johnson, *Making Animals Happy: How to Create the Best Lives for Pets and Other Animals* (Bloomsburg Publishing, 2009).
- Temple Grandin and Kate Duffy, *Developing Talents: Careers for Individuals with Asperger's Syndrome and High Functioning Autism, Expanded Edition* (Autism Asperger's Publishing Company, 2008).
- Temple Grandin, *Humane Livestock Handling: Understanding livestock behavior and building facilities for healthier animals* (Storey Publishing, 2008).
- Temple Grandin and Catherine Johnson, *Animals in Translation: Using the Mysteries of Autism to Decode Animal Behavior* (Harvest Books, 2006).
- Temple Grandin and Sean Barron, *the Unspoken Rules of Social Relationships: Decoding Social Mysteries through the Unique Perspective of Autism* (Future Horizons, 2005).
- Temple Grandin and Margaret Scariano, *Emergence: Labeled Autistic* (Warner Books, 1996).

**Dawn Prince-Hughes's Project:**

- Dawn Prince-Hughes, *Songs of the Gorilla Nation: My Journey through Autism* (Broadway, 2005).
- Dawn Prince-Hughes, *Expecting Teryk: An Exceptional Path to Parenthood* (Swallow Press, 2005).
- Dawn Prince-Hughes, *Gorillas among Us: a Primate Ethnographer's Book of Days* (University of Arizona Press, 2001).
- Dawn Prince-Hughes, *the Archetype of the Ape Man: The Phenomenological Archeology of the Relic Hominoid Ancestor* (Disscertation.com, 1st Edition, 2000).

**Chellis Glendenning-A Figure All Disability Scholars and Activists Need to Be Familiar With:**

- Chellis Glendenning, *Chiva: A Village Takes On the Global Heron Trade* (New Society Publishers, 2005). A case study of a man in Glendenning's bioregional community in New Mexico, who Glendenning befriended, who is both a hereon attic and drug dealer, but also an economically poor America who is of Algerian, Hispanic and Dine origins, who Glendenning tried to help, befriend and rehabilitate. Glendenning demonstrates that severe long-term abuse, trauma, oppression, injustice and inequality are the real root causes of addiction, overconsumption and psychopathology, not individual private "selfishness" or "bad genes." Glendenning, both a licensed psychotherapist and a political activist also refutes the spurious argument that healing from a serious addiction or mental illness is solely a matter of personal responsibility and private psychology adjustment, acknowledging social and economic inequality right here in the United States, statistically documents and accessibly communicates through a powerful story how the mental health establishment and the dominant society really *does not* want us to be successful in our personal healing and treatment goals and that all this so-called "help" out there is really about "social control" not "personal healing." Through her own discernment and some poignant success stories right in her own community of Chiva, New Mexico, Glendenning gets to the "bottom" of addiction and mental illness through arguing for the direct treatment of traumas, integration between conventional and holistic medicine, talking about religion and politics, attentiveness to the healing environment, community involvement and development, historical, ancestral and ecological literacy, social and cultural change, the role of direct action grassroots political activism, making respect for clients non-negotiable, healing the Human-Nature bond, nurturing intimate long-term contact with the Natural World, a life-affirming culture, a functional society, a comforting religious faith, even prayer, intercession and a direct, personal relationship with the Living God and the Communion of Saints.

- Chellis Glendenning, *Off the Map: An Expedition Deep into Empire and the Global Economy* (New Society, 2002). Another case study from Glendenning's own bioregional community of the New Mexican red rock desert involving the conflict between a Native American/Latino community who wanted to live on the land of their ancestors and environmental groups/the federal government who wanted to preserve this portion of desert as a protected wilderness area. Glendenning argues in solidarity with the traditional land-based community of New Mexico against her own environmental movement, arguing that the current wave of the environmental movement lacks experience with and direct ties to the biotic community, that "globalization" is really a "code word" for "multi-national corporations," that "the global community" is a "myth" which is really a "green wash" and "blue wash" job with colonialist, imperialist, capitalistic, mechanistic, technological optimism residue which is further dislocating and alienating groups of people already living sustainably with the Earth and homogenizing the diversity of humanity based on a distorted, second-hand view of the Natural World filtered through mass media which denies the existence of details and overstates "red tooth and claw." Glendenning also acknowledges that ordinary Americans *are not* to blame for America's imperialistic foreign and domestic policies, for Glendenning makes a strong distinction between ordinary Americans and the Global Corporate Class, a fundamentally anti-democratic neo-colonialist elite group of superrich internationally syndicated and connected corporate, government, military and religious leaders who run our business, government, military and religious establishments. That most modern-day

Americans and Europeans are also colonized peoples, such as peoples from Scotland, Ireland or Whales, Jews, Muslims, Africans, women, immigrants from Southern and Eastern Europe, peoples from the Middle East or Asia, Native Americans and peoples with disabilities and neurodiverse humans. The only difference between Western colonized peoples and the colonized peoples of the Geographic South is that we were colonized first, longer and from within by unconscious, pragmatic anti-democratic forces from within our own civilization going all the way back to the whole domestication and civilization-building projects of ancient Greece, Rome, Egypt, Babylon, Persia and Mesopotamia, intensified in the late Middle Ages and early Modernity during the Age of Exploration, coming to a pass in the mid-twentieth century. Glendenning recommends that ordinary Americans wanting to address planetary issues need to first seek healing from their own oppression situations, then carefully listen to the stories and voices of colonized peoples from the Geographic South to learn a new "pattern of life" which is sustainable and in harmony with the Earth and then develop our own unique creative original ecological solutions based upon our reactions to knowledge of our own and other's oppression situations and through directly engaging the Natural World and embracing the Earth as our home, where we act on behalf of the planet, at the grassroots, local, land-based levels, creating our own sovereign, sustainable Western culture, in the process. Environmentalists and political activists absolutely must have direct personal contact with the Natural World and the groups of humans we are trying to help.

- Chellis Glendenning, *My Name Is Chellis Glendenning and I am in Recovery from Western Civilization* (Shambhala Press, 1994). This book absolutely saved my life when I was going through a very serious personal and professional crisis a few years ago. This is the book of Glendenning, which I quote from most frequently in my recent books. Mainly, Glendenning's gift to me was threefold A) called me to be attentive to the role of my natural, social and built environments in my own healing pilgrimage and inspired my move from the "concrete jungle" to a place in the outer suburbs close to wild Nature where I could begin to heal and have precious breathing space from a dysfunctional, oppressive society to think and regroup. B) Identified safety as a neglected need in my life. I needed physical, emotional and spiritual safety as a trauma survivor and oppressed minority to function and make progress at-all in my healing, growth and lifework. As well as identified "safety" as "a driver" and "root metaphor" in many conservative agendas and can explain at least some of their bizarre behaviors and extreme rhetorical posturing in many of today's conservative movements. Many Westerners fundamentally *do not* feel safe. C) Validated my insights about interspecies communications, the "shadow sides" of modernity, postmodernity, New Age religion, paganism, classical civilizations, globalization, some Eastern religions and organized Christianity, as well as my insights about disability social history, neurodiversity, neurotypicalism and normalcy, even my own spiritual and mystical experiences. In the process, providing the "missing link" in my research, scholarship, writing and my life and lifework. Her book worked, while many other "self-help" programs have failed me, mainly because she has training, experience and expertise in *both* psychology *and* critical social theory, is both a *therapist* and a *political activist*, who is *both* psychologically literate *and* sociologically savvy, involving not only the psycho-medical model in my healing process, but also the integrated, interdisciplinary perspectives of academic sociology, anthropology, history and political science, critical social theory, critical environmental studies, ecofeminist theory, first nations studies, aesthetics even spirituality and religion. This is the Glendenning book I recommend you start-out with.

- Chellis Glendenning, *When Technology Wounds: The Human Consequences of Progress* (William & O Marrow Company, 1990). This earlier Glendenning book although addressing the very specific situations of "communities at-risk" like Love Channel and Woburn in the 1970s and 1980s as well as individual Americans who survived a dangerous technology like a medicine with "side effects" with a focus on the long-term psychological effects of peoples who have survived a serious technology-induced illness such as cancer, infertility or mental illness, I contend has relevance to 2013 discussions and debates about global and inner city environmental injustices, the social construction of disability, the deconstruction of normalcy, the "green washing" and "blue washing" in the medical model of disability and why and how, and a model of how the validity of neurodiversity and disability cultures can be reconciled with a belief in the social construction of disability. A voice, work and argument which must not be lost in a stream of all-new information coming in on environmentalism and the planetary crisis. There is a rigger of scholarship, intellectual depth, moral nuance and humane compassion for her readers, written in a time when we environmental activists had to "earn our strips" in the academy and in society, lacking in much of today's bombastic, self-righteous, highly polemic, politically polarized, propaganda-like, fashionable ecological diatribes. Her work also provides a pragmatic, realistic model of personal healing and political empowerment for both individuals with disabilities and the various disability and neurodiversity communities and movements at-large. Glendenning is also a technology survivor and child abuse survivor herself.

**Neurotheology and Ecopsychology:**

- Andrew Newburg, MD and Mark Waldman, *How God Changes Your Brain: Breakthrough Findings from a Leading Neuroscientist* (Ballantine Books, 2010). For an excellent introduction to all the mounting evidence showing that there is a positive correlation between our religious beliefs, practices and experiences and the renewal of our nervous system. Such an approach *does not* scientifically proof the existence of God nor does it invalidate the truth-value of religious claims through tracing spirituality and religion back to scientifically measurable embodied, naturalistic phenomena in our brains and nervous systems. But, for the first time ever, we can actually study scientifically, "religious experience" as "human behavior," taking theology as "faith seeking understanding" to the next level, where we can use the tools, methodologies even discoveries of science to better understand what exactly our traditional beliefs and practices are actually accomplishing, answering every child's "so what?" once and for all. Not to mention, pastors and theologians now having for the first time a methodology and a framework for falsifying our religious claims, recovering how exactly the "shadow sides" of our religious traditions impact how we treat other people and ourselves and better focus sermons and worship services to get the intended outcome. Also, for the first time ever, we now have a scientific framework for explaining the timeless role of religion in human society and culture, through recovering the adaptive value of "religious experience" to human survival and reproduction throughout the history of our species, situating "religious experience" into an evolutionary context. Such an approach could revolutionize historical-critical scholarship through understanding how the human mind has changed throughout time and across sociocultural and geopolitical contexts. Not to mention to better understand "the role of religion" in the present and future, attain more meaningful statistics about religion in America and even make predictions about the future of our religion and start making strategic plans for our future today. Although their negative non-scientific opinions on Judeo-Christians are weak, as well as their discussion of how all the world religions are basically the same, their ignorance of denominational continuity in Christianity overstating the differences between Protestants and Catholics, their unrealistic, unfair standard of basing religious tolerance on how willing you are to date a person of another faith, putting interreligious dating on the same plain as interracial dating. Most Christians would agree that it is fairer and more realistic for two Christians of different races to date and become married, than for a Christian to date a Buddhist. There are too many irreconcilable differences when different religions are involved, mainly making an intimate life-long commitment to somebody who has fundamentally different beliefs and values than you is just a recipe for divorce. It takes a very special couple to pull something like this off like Harvard Christian theologian Harvey Cox marrying a Jewish woman and raising their children in both traditions, where both still practiced their religion, while sharing with each other their own religious traditions and rituals. Not to mention that it's "loaded" to put intra-religious dating on the same plain as religious hate crimes. It is much easier to pull something like this off between parent and child and brother and sister, like in my case, where a family relationship by its very nature, assumes much lower, less rigid expectations of other members being like yourself or agreeing with you and much higher stakes for conflict resolution and reconciliation. You can respect other people's religious freedoms without dating them. This I attribute to the scientist's involved New Age bias, theological illiteracy and nativity about the particular challenges facing people of much less education, wealth and other privileges as themselves, especially in matters of social justice, oppression, religious persecution and culturecide. Also, their survey questions were also poorly framed, leading to them coming to the wrong conclusions, for you had to answer them in such a way that it may not reflect what you actually believe, also one of the problems with belief.net, although belief.net can identify your religious fit more accurately than these surveys. So as you read this book, make sure to integrate their scientific findings, only, with your own accustomed religious tradition and what you know to be true about your religion. Remembering there are other options to be religiously nonviolent than New Age religion like interreligious pluralism, religious sovereignty, Separation between Church and State and interfaith dialog and collaboration on public issues like the planetary crisis.

- *Ecopsychology: Restoring the Earth, Healing the Mind* ed. by Theodore Roszak, Mary Gomes and Allen Kanner (Sierra Club Books, 1995). For an excellent introduction to ecopsychology, important theorists and practioners in this field and short essays by different scholars and activists writing about the intersection between clinical psychology and critical environmental studies. Also a good book to document abelism, neurotypicalism and normalcy in the environmental literature like using "mental illness" metaphors like "collective autism" and "madness" to describe ecologically destructive behaviors like "consumerism," "denial" and "being self-absorbed." Based on an out-of-date DSL IV definition of autism without any awareness of in-depth study of autistic neurology and treatment nor in this particular essay was there a sign that the author was familiar with the "inside-out" neurodiverse, disability justice perspective on autism and others mental illnesses which is anything but "consumeristic," "phony" or "self-absorbed." It has been established by the medical establishment, the various neurodiversity movements and the disability studies field at-large that humans with an autism diagnosis like myself are materially ascetic, honest to a point of a fault, altruistic hard workers and hyper-compassionately sensitive to the "world-around-us." Know that as a life-long committed neurodiverse environmentalist, I absolutely resent the implications. If ecopsychology is going to be updated and revitalized, this time it is going to have to go "crip," involving the full diversity of ecological auto-biographies and prophetic ecological voices in the various neurodiversity and disability communities and movements, as well as the ecological stories, voices and arguments of disability studies scholars and disabled academics, artists and activists. The various disability communities absolutely must be given both oppressed minority status and silenced voice status and be treated like any other oppressed minority by environmentalists and Christian environmentalists alike.

- Esther Sternberg, M.D., *Healing Spaces: the Science of Place and Well Being* (United States: self-published, 2009). For a more up to date study in ecopsychology, incorporating new knowledge in neurology, holistic medicine and medical history, also expanding the discussion to also include physical health and medicine, preventive medicine and exercise physiology, even landscape architecture and city planning and some discussion of Christian Church history and the medicinal and therapeutic benefits of certain Christian religious rituals and houses of worship like smelling Frankincense and

Myrrh, walking a Labyrinth, even the healing elements endemic to the Franciscan Holy City of Assisi---mainly a balanced harmony among light, beauty, nature and places of prayer. This book also gives readers concrete guidance on how to identify such "healing spaces" in our own lives, how to turn our own homes, hospitals, institutions and communities into "healing spaces," what exactly do we feed our senses with which actually leads to healing, wholeness and wellness and what specific spiritual practices actually lead to physical and mental healing, wellness and wholeness according to scientific evidence. Also this work independently scientifically corroborates Glendenning's contention that there is a positive correlation between an individual being in a beautiful, healthy, functional physical environment and personal healing and wholeness. The right physical environment is in fact a very scientifically and psychologically real "source of healing and empowerment." This book also integrates the reality that most of us live in the city through helping us take advantage of such places right in the city or suburbs, utilize natural and cultural elements, as well as certain spiritual and other holistic practices available to us all at little to no cost and through calling our religious, medical, employment and housing institutions to design buildings and grounds which are more conducive for healing and wholeness.

**Critical Theory and Political Activism:**

- Appelbaum, R. and Chambliss W., *Sociology: a brief introduction* (New York: Longman, 1997).
- Phillip Bosserman, *More of Us Than You Think: The Searchers for a Post-Capitalistic Society* (Writers Publisher Collective, 2003).
- Josephine Bellaccoma, *Move the Message: Your Guide to Making a Difference and Changing the World* (Lantern Books, 2004).
- Center for Conflict Resolution at Salisbury University, http://www.conflict-resolution.org/.
- Greaves, R., and Zaller. R, *Civilizations of the World: The Human Adventure, Third Edition* (New York: Longman, 1997).
- Judith Herman, M.D., *Trauma and Recovery: The aftermath of violence-from domestic abuse to political terror*, (United States of America: Basic Books, 1992 1997).
- George Lakeoff, *Don't Think of an Elephant: Know Your Values and Frame The Debate-The Essential Guide for Progressives Including Post-Election Updates* (Chelsea Green Publishing, 2004).
- George Lakeoff and Mark Johnson, *Metaphors We Live By* (Chicago: University of Chicago Press, 1980 2003).
- Paul Loab, *Soul of a Citizen: Living with Conviction in Challenging Times* (St. Martin's Griffin, 2010).

- Jay MacLeod, *Ain't No Making It: Aspirations and Attainment in a Low-Income Neighborhood* (Westview Press, 2008, 3<sup>rd</sup> Edition).
- President Barak Obama, "The 2013 State of the Union," http://www.whitehouse.gov/state-of-the-union-2013?utm_medium=email&utm_source=obama&utm_content=httpmybarackobamacomWatchtheInteractiveSpeech&utm_campaign=em13_20130213_jm_ndi&source=em13_20130213_jm_ndi/.
- Salisbury University, CADR---Conflict Analysis and Dispute Resolution, http://www.salisbury.edu/cadr/.
- Salisbury University, "Welcome to Sociology," http://www.salisbury.edu/sociology/.
- Hedrick Smith, *Who Stole the American Dream?* (Random House, 2012). For an example, that there is economic inequality right here in the United States, that there is in fact such a thing as the Corporate Class, that the Middle Class in America *is not* what it used to be like it was 1950s and that a strong Middle Class is critical to sustaining a democratic society.

**Theological Literacy and Liberation Theology:**

- Saint Anthony of Padua, *Sermons for Sunday and Festivals-Volume II* (Italy: Aedizioni Messaggero, 2007).
- *Francis and Clare: The Complete Works (The Classics of Western Spirituality)* trans. and ed. by Regis Armstrong, O.F.M. CAP.
- Saint Bonaventure, *Bonaventure: The Soul's Journey into God; the Tree of Life; the Life of Saint Francis (The Classics of Western Spirituality)* trans. by Ewert Cousins (New Jersey: Paulist Press, 1978).
- Dietrich Bonheoffer, *the Cost of Discipleship* (Touchstone, 1995).
- G.K. Chesterton, *Saint Francis of Assisi* (Empire Books, 2012).
- John Cobb, Jr. and David Ray Griffin, *Process Theology: an Introductory Exposition* (Philadelphia: Westminster Press, 1976).
- Ross Douthat, *Bad Religion: How We Became a Nation of Heretics* (New York: Simon & Simon, 2012).
- Richard Foster and Emile Griffin, *Spiritual Classics: Selected Readings on the Twelve Spiritual Disciplines* (Harper One, 2000).
- Richard J. Foster, *Celebration of Discipline: The Path to Spiritual Growth*, (Revised Edition, San Francisco: Harper San Francisco, A Division of Harper Collins Publishers, 1998).
- *Francis of Assisi-The Founder: Early Documents II* ed. by Regis Armstrong, O.F.M. Cap., J.A. Wayne Hellmann, O.F.M. Conv., and William Short, O.F.M. (New York, London, Manila: New York Press, 2000).

- Jan Johnson, *Enjoying the Presence of God: Discovering Intimacy with God in the Daily Rhythms of Life* (Colorado Springs, Colorado: NavPress Publishing Group, 1996).
- Brother Lawrence, Frank Laubach, *Practicing His Presence: One of the Great Pieces of Christian literature of all Time* (Jacksonville, Fl: The Seed Sowers, MCMLXXIII).
- Vladimir Lossky, *The Mystical Theology of the Eastern Church* (New York: St. Vladimir's Seminary Press, 2002).
- Daniel Migliore, *Faith Seeking Understanding: an Introduction to Christian Theology* (Wm. B. Earbman's Publishing Company, 2004).
- Henri Nouwen, *the Wounded Healer: Ministry in Contemporary Society* (New York, New York: Doubleday, 1972).
- Mercy Oduyoye, *Hearing and Knowing: Theological Reflections on Christianity in Africa* (Maryknoll, New York: Orbis Books, 1986).
- Michael Pakaluk, *Other Selves: Philosophers on Friendship* (Indianapolis, Indiana, Hackett Publishing Company, 1991).
- James E. Reed and Ronnie Prevost, *a History of Christian Education* (Nashville, Tennessee: Broadman & Holdman Publishers, 1993).
- Caryle Fielding Steward, III *Soul Survivors: An African American Spirituality* (Louisville, Kentucky: Westminster John Know Press, 1997).
- Neale Donald Walsch, *Conversations with God: an uncommon dialogue-Book 1* (New York: G.P. Putnam's Press, 1995 1996).
- Sarah York, *Pilgrim Heart: The Inner Journey Home* (San Francisco: Jossey-Bass A Wiley Company, 2001).

**Ecological Literacy and Animal Literacy:**

- *Environmental Ethics: Convergence and Divergence ed.* by Susan Armstrong and Robert Botlzer (McGraw Hill, 2003).
- Catocton Wildlife Preserve & Zoo, http://cwpzoo.com/.
- Donald Griffin, *Animal Minds: Beyond Cognition to Consciousness* (University of Chicago Press, 2001).
- Institute for Critical Animal Studies (ICAS), http://www.criticalanimalstudies.org/.
- The Jane Goodall Institute, http://www.janegoodall.org/.
- Jennifer Holland, *Unlikely Friendships: 47 Remarkable Friendships from the Animal Kingdom* (New York: Workshop Publishing, 2011).
- The Humane Society of the United States (HSUS), http://www.humanesociety.org/.
- People for the Ethical Treatment for Animals (PETA), http://www.peta.org/.
- *Animal Rights and Human Obligations (Second Edition)* ed. by Tom Regan and Peter Singer (Pretence Hall, 1989).
- Salisbury University, ENVR Environmental Studies Program, http://www.salisbury.edu/environmentalstudies/.

- Salisbury University, Department of Biology, http://www.salisbury.edu/biology/.
- Salisbury Zoological Park, http://www.salisburyzoo.org/.
- Smithsonian's National Zoo, http://nationalzoo.si.edu/.
- Tufts University, MS in Animals and Public Policy, http://www.tufts.edu/vet/mapp/.

**Environmental History:**

- *The Great New Wilderness Debate* ed. by J. Baird Caldecott and Michael Nelson (University of Georgia Press, 1998). For an introduction to the history of the conflict between the conservation/preservation wilderness movements of earlier environmentalism and the emerging environmental justice movements of today. Also places the idea of wilderness into an international, multicultural context. Basis for some of the historical claims in this book.
- Robert Booth Fowler, *The Greening of Protestant Thought* (The University of North Carolina Press, 1995). Basis for some of the historical claims in this book, as well as critique of the Christian environmental movement.
- J. Donald Hughes, *Pan's Travail: Environmental Problems of the Ancient Greeks and Romans* (The Johns Hopkins's University Press, 1996). Basis for some of the historical claims in this book.
- Shepherd Kretch III, *The Ecological Indian: Myth and History* (W.W. Norton and Company, 2000). Basis for some of the historical claims in this book.
- Carolyn Merchant, *the Death of Nature: Women, Ecology and the Scientific Revolution* (Harpur One, Reprint Edition, 1990). Basis for some of the historical claims in this book.
- Roderick Nash, *Wilderness and the American Mind* (Yale University Press, Forth Edition, 2001). One of the classic works in environmental history with a focus on the conservation/preservation movements in the United States in the nineteenth and twentieth century. Good introduction to the history of the earlier environmental movement and the history of the idea of wilderness.
- Michael Northcott, *the Environment and Christian Ethics* (Cambridge University Press, 1996). Basis for some of the historical claims in this book.
- Mark Stoll, *Protestantism, Capitalism and Nature in America* (University of New Mexico Press, 1997). Basis for some of the historical claims in this book.
- Chive Pointing, *A New Green History of the World: The Environment and the Collapse of Great Civilizations* (Penguin Books, Revised Version, 2007). Another classic in the environmental history field which focuses more on global environmental history which identifies possible root causes of the planetary crisis and puts the conflict between wilderness and civilization in historical perspective.

**Natural History:**

- Edward Abby, *Desert Solitaire* (Touchstone, 1990).

- Edward Armstrong, *Saint Francis: Nature Mystic-The Deviation and Signifigence of the Nature Stories in the Franciscan Legend* (University of California Press, 1970).
- *The Wilderness Reader* ed. by Frank Bergon (University of Nevada Press, 1994).
- Richard Cartwright Austin, *Baptized into Wilderness: A Christian perspective on John Muir* (Creekside Press, 2nd Edition, 1991).
- Robert Bly, *News of the Universe: Poems of Twofold Consciousness* (Sierra Club Books, 1995).
- Rachel Carson, *Silent Spring* (Houghton Muffin Company, Anniversary Edition, 2002).
- Rachel Carson, *the Sense of Wonder* (Harper Reprint, 1998).
- Rachel Carson, *the Edge of the Sea* (Mariner Books, 1998).
- Annie Dillard, *Pilgrim at Tinker Creek* (Harper Perennial Modern Classics, 2007).
- Annie Dillard, *Holy the Firm* (Harper Perennial, Revised Edition, 2008).
- Aldo Leopold, *A Sand County Almanac: with Essays on Conservation from Round River* (New York: Ballantine, 1949 1953 1966).
- Alan Hodder, *Thoreau's Ecstatic Witness* (New Haven & London: Yale University Press, 2001).
- Kevin Koch, *the Driftless Land: Spirit of Place in the Upper Mississippi Valley* (United States of America: Southeast Missouri State University Press, 2010).
- Michael Strutin, *Discovering Natural Israel: From the Coral Reefs of Elliot to the Emerald Crown of Mount Carmel* (Jonathan David Publishers, 2001).
- Enos Mills and John Dotson, *Radiant Days: Written by Enos Mills* (Salt Lake City: University of Utah Press, 1994) with forward by Bill McKidden.
- Joan Maloof, *Among the Ancients: Adventures in the Eastern Old-growth Forests* (Ruka Press, 2011).
- John Muir, *the Wilderness World of John Muir* ed. by Edwin Teale (Mariner Books, First Edition, 2001).
- Petr Kropotkin, *Mutual Aid: A Factor in Evolution* (Create Space Independent Publishing Platform, 2012).
- Albert Schweitzer, *the Animal World of Albert Schweitzer: Jungle Insights into the Reverence for Life* trans. by Charles Joy (Kissinger Publishing Company, 2007).
- Henry David Thoreau, *Walking* (Create Space Independent Publishing Platform, 2011).
- Henry David Thoreau, *Walden, Civil Disobedience and Other Writings* (Norton Clinical Editions) (W.W. Norton & Company, 2008).
- E.O. Wilson, *Biophilia* (Harvard University Press, Reprint Edition, 1984).

**Christian Ecotheology, Animal Theology and Science Theology:**

- The American Scientific Affiliation, http://network.asa3.org/.
- Andover Newton Theological School, http://www.ants.edu/.
- Au Sable Institute of Environmental Studies, http://ausable.org/.

- Ian Barbour, *Religion and Science (Gifford Lecture Series): Historical and Contemporary Issues* (Harper One, 1997).
- The Boston Theological Institute, http://www.bostontheological.org/.
- Ilia Delio, O.S.F., *A Franciscan View of Creation: Learning to Live in a Sacramental World* (St. Bonaventure, NY: St. Bonaventure University, 2003).
- Thomas Kuhn, *the Structure of Scientific Revolutions: 50th Anniversary Edition* (University of Chicago Press; Fourth Edition, 2012).
- Reverend Andrew Linzey, *Why Animal Suffering Matters: Philosophy, Theology and Practical Ethics* (USA: Oxford University Press, 2009).
- Reverend Andrew Linzey, *Creatures of the Same God: Explorations in Animal Theology* (Lantern Books, 2009).
- Reverend Andrew Linzey, *Animal Rites: Liturgies of Animal Care* (Scm, 2000).
- Reverend Andrew Linzey, *Animal Gospel* (Westminster John Knox Press, 1999).
- Reverend Andrew Linzey, *Animal Theology* (University of Illinois Press, 1995).
- *The Little Flowers of Saint Francis* ed. by Heywood (Vintage Spiritual Classic, 1998).
- The Mary T. and Franklin L. Hoffman Foundation, http://www.all-creatures.org/.
- Sallie McFague, *a New Climate for Theology: God, the World and Global Warming* (Minneapolis: Fortress Press, 2007).
- Sallie McFague, *Life Abundant* (*Searching for a New Framework*) (Minneapolis: Fortress Press, 2000).
- Sallie McFague, *Super, Natural Christians: How we should love nature* (Minneapolis: Fortress Press, 1997).
- Sallie McFague, *Metaphoric Theology: Models of God in Religious Language* (Philadelphia: Fortress Press, 1982).
- Elizabeth Morison, *Beasts Factual and Fantastic (Medieval Imagination)* (J. Paul Getty Museum; 1st edition, 2007).
- Jurgen Moltmann, *God in Creation* (Fortress Edition, 1993).
- Max Oelschlaeger, *Caring for Creation: an Ecumenical Approach to the Environmental Crisis* (New Haven and London: Yale University Press, 1994).
- Holmes Ralston III, "Does Nature need to be redeemed?" *Horizons in Biblical Theology* (1994) 158.
- Steven Bouma-Predinger, *For the Beauty of the Earth: a Christian Vision for Creation-Care* (Grand Rapids, Michigan: Baker Academic, 2001) 148.
- The John Templeton Foundation, http://www.templeton.org/.
- Sir John Templeton, *Possibility for One Hundred Fold More Spiritual Information: The Humble Approach in Theology and Science* (The Templeton Foundation Press, 2000).
- *Beasts and Saints* ed. by Helen Waddell and illustrated by Robert Gibbings (Pook Press, 2010).

- Stephen Webb, *Jesus Christ, Eternal God: Heavenly Flesh and the Metaphysics of Matter* (Oxford University Press, 2011).
- Stephen Webb, *the Dome of Eden: A New Solution to Creation-Evolution* (Cascade Books, 2005).
- Stephen Webb, *On God and Dogs: A Christian Theology of Compassion for Animals* (Oxford University Press, 2002).
- Stephen Webb, *Good Eating (The Christian Practice of Everyday Life)* (Brazos Press, 2001).
- Stephen Webb, "Ecology versus the Peaceable Kingdom: Toward A Better Theology of Nature," *Soundings,* Spring/Summer. 79. 1996: 239.
- Terrence White, *the Book of Beasts: Being a Translation from a Latin Bestiary of the Twelfth Century* (Dover Publications, 2010).

**Feminism:**

- Judith Herman, M.D., *Trauma and Recovery: The aftermath of violence-from domestic abuse to political terror*, (United States of America: Basic Books, 1992 1997).
- Sharon Welch, *Sweet Dreams in America: Making Ethics and Spirituality Work* (New York: Roughage, 1999).

**Menism:**

- Stephen Byrd, *the Men We Long To Be: Beyond Lonely Warriors and Desperate Lovers* (Wipf. & Stock Pub, 2009).
- Sam Keen, *Fire in the Belly: On Being a Man* (Bantam, 1992).
- Jeffery Mason, *The Emperor's Embrace: Reflections on Animal Families and Fatherhood* (Pocket Books, 1999).
- Robert Moore and Douglas Gillette, *King Warrior Magician Lover: Rediscovering the Archetypes of the Mature Masculine* (United States: Harper San Francisco, 1990).
- Richard Rohr O.F.M., *From Wild Man to Wise Man: Reflections on Male Spirituality* (Ohio: St. Anthony Messenger Press, 1990 1995 2005).
- Daniel Jay Sonkin, Ph.D., *Wounded Boys Heroic Men: a Man's Guide to Recovering from Child Abuse* (Massachusetts: Adams Media Corporation, 1998).

**Great Literature:**

- Julia Alverez, *In the Time of the Butterflies* (Algonquin Books, 2010).
- Charlotte Bronte, *Jane Eyre* (Wilder Publications, 2009).
- Charles Dickens, *Great Expectations* (Dover Publications; Unabridged Edition, 2001).
- Ralph Ellison, *Invisible Man* (Vintage, 1995).
- F. Scott Fitzgerald, *the Great Gatsby* (Scribner, 2004).
- Fyodor Dostoevsky, *the Idiot* (Simon & Brown, 2011).

- Nathanael Hawthorne, "The Birthmark" http://www.online-literature.com/hawthorne/125/.
- Homer, *the Odyssey* (Simon & Brown, 2012).
- William Golding, *Lord of the Flies* (Century Edition) (Perigee Trade, 2011).
- David Guterson, *Snow Falling On Cedars* (Harcourt, Brace, 1994).
- Herman Hesse, *Siddhartha* (Dover Publications, 1998).
- Victor Hugo, *Les Miserable* (Create Space Independent Publisher, 2013).
- Victor Hugo, *the Hunchback of Notre Dame* (Signet Classics) (Signet Classics, 2010).
- Harper Lee, *To Kill a Mockingbird* (Harper, 2010).
- George Orwell, *Animal Farm and 1984* (Houghton Muffin Harcourt, 1st Edition, 2003).
- William Shakespeare, *Othello* (Simon & Simon, 2012).
- George Bernard Shaw, *Pygmalion* (Dover Theft Edition, 1994).
- John Steinbeck, *Grapes of Wrath* (Penguin Classics, 2006).
- John Steinbeck, *Of Mice and Men* (Frontal Lobe Publishing, 2011).
- Thornton Wilder, *Our Town* (Harper, 2003).
- Richard Wright, *Native Son* (Harper Perennial Modern Classics, 2003).


**Recommended Self-Help Books:**

- Stephen Byrd, *the Men We Long To Be: Beyond Lonely Warriors and Desperate Lovers* (Wipf. & Stock Pub, 2009).
- Leonard Felder Ph.D., *Fitting In Is Overrated: The Survival Guide to Anyone Who Has Ever Felt Like An Outsider* (Sterling, 1st Edition, 2008).
- Chellis Glendenning, *Chiva: A Village Takes On the Global Heron Trade* (New Society Publishers, 2005).
- Chellis Glendenning, *Off the Map: An Expedition Deep into Empire and the Global Economy* (New Society, 2002).
- Chellis Glendenning, *My Name Is Chellis Glendenning and I am in Recovery from Western Civilization* (Shambhala Press, 1994).
- Chellis Glendenning, *When Technology Wounds: The Human Consequences of Progress* (William & O Marrow Company, 1990).
- Peter Hauri PhD and Shirley Linde, *No More Sleepless Nights* (Willey, 1996).
- Carol Lloyd, *Create a Life worth Living: A practical course in career design for artists, innovators, and others aspiring to a creative life* (United States of America: Harpur Perennial, 1997).
- Paul Loab, *Soul of a Citizen: Living with Conviction in Challenging Times* (St. Martin's Griffin, 2010).
- Aphrodite Matsakis, Ph.D., *Trust After Trauma: A Guide to Relationships for Survivors and Those Who Love Them* (Oakland, California: New Harbingers Press, 1998).

- Robert Moore and Douglas Gillette, *King Warrior Magician Lover: Rediscovering the Archetypes of the Mature Masculine* (United States: Harper San Francisco, 1990).
- Sam Keen, *Fire in the Belly: On Being a Man* (Bantam, 1992).
- Richard Rohr O.F.M., *From Wild Man to Wise Man: Reflections on Male Spirituality* (Ohio: St. Anthony Messenger Press, 1990 1995 2005).
- Lewis Smedes, *Shame and Grace: Healing the Shame We Don't Deserve* (Harper One, 1994).
- Lewis Smedes, *Forgive and Forget: Healing The Hurts We Don't Deserve* (Harper One: 2007).
- Daniel Jay Sonkin, Ph.D., *Wounded Boys Heroic Men: a Man's Guide to Recovering from Child Abuse* (Massachusetts: Adams Media Corporation, 1998).

**Publication List of Author:**

- Daniel Salomon, http://www.all-creatures.org/church/grmindir-md-ss-salomon.html.
- Daniel Salomon and Steven Salomon, "Wounded Healer," all-creatures.org (2013).
- Daniel Salomon, "An Ecological Survey of Deer Ridge," all-creatures.org (2013).
- Daniel Salomon, "Homily: On a Wing and A Prayer," (Saint Mark Presbyterian Church, 2012) available at http://www.all-creatures.org/church/grmindir-md-ss-salomon-2012-homily.html.
- Daniel Salomon, "Disability and Animals: Building Coalitions" panel member at the Society for Disability Studies (SDS) Annual Conference in Denver, 2012: http://disstudies.org/annual-conference/2012-conference/.
- Daniel Salomon, "Glossary," http://www.shelfari.com/books/27033223/Have-Mercy-on-Me-An-Ecological-Sinner-How-the-God-of-the-Bible-H?amatc=kdp-c (2012).
- Daniel Salomon with forward by Dr. Mark Heim, *Have Mercy On Me, An Ecological Sinner: How The God of the Bible Helped Me Rise Above Compassion Fatigue And Not Give-Up On The Ecological Struggle* (Create Space Independent Publishing Platform, Kindle Edition, Amazon.com, 2012).
- Daniel Salomon, "A Eulogy to a Parakeet: Mordecai's "Soul's Journey onto God," all-creatures.org (2011).
- Daniel Salomon, "Animal Rights and Autistic Pride: Let's Heal the Rift," *The Scavenger* (2010).
- Daniel Salomon, "From Marginal Cases to Linked Oppressions: Reframing the Conflict between the Autistic Pride and Animal Rights Movements," *Journal of Critical Animal Studies* VIII, Issue ½, 2010 which can be accessed through http://www.all-creatures.org/church/grmindir-md-ss-salomon.html.
- Daniel Salomon, *Human-Animal Reconciliation: Franciscan Faith-based Interspecies Communications and Its Implications for Wildlife Management* (Kindle Edition, Amazon.com, 2008).

- Daniel Salomon with forward by Dr. Mark Heim, *Christian Environmental Studies: toward a Graduate Program* (Create Space Independent Publishing Platform, Kindle Edition, Amazon.com, 2008 2012).
- Daniel Salomon with forward by Dr. Philip Bosserman, *Creation Unveiled: the Implications of Girardian Theory to Environmental and Animal Issues* (Xulon Press, Kindle Edition, Amazon.com, 2003 2010).
- Daniel Salomon, *Rachel Carson in Carteret County, North Carolina: A Journey to "The Edge of the Sea"* (Rachel Carson Council, 2007).

---

[1] Daniel Migliore, *Faith Seeking Understanding: an Introduction to Christian Theology* (Wm. B. Earbman's Publishing Company, 2004) 15-18.

[2] Ibid.

[3] Steven Bouma-Predinger, *For the Beauty of the Earth: A Christian Vision for Creation-Care* (Grand Rapids, Michigan: Baker Academic, 2001) 148.

[4] Daniel Migliore, *Faith Seeking Understanding,* pay closest attention to 1-19, "Chapter 1: The Task of Theology."

[5] Nancy Eisland, *the Disabled God: Toward A Libratory Theology of Disability* (Nashville: Abingdon Press, 1994) 20-23, "Accessible Theological Method."

[6] Ibid.

[7] Ibid, 25-29 "Coming to Terms."

[8] Ibid, 23-25 "The Social Construction of Disability" and 31-48 "Chapter Two: Bodies of Knowledge."

[9] Rab Houston and Uta Frith, *Autism in History: The Case of Hugh Blair of Borgue* (Malden, Massachusetts: Blackwell Publishers Inc., 2000) 163-165.

[10] Steven Shore, *Reflections from a Different Journey: What Adults with Disabilities Wish All Parents Knew*, ed. by Stanley D. Klein, Ph.D., and John D. Kemp (USA: McGraw Hill, 2004) 58.

[11] The concept of "God neurons" from: Andrew Newburg M.D. and Mark Robert Waldman, *How God Changes Your Brain: Breakthrough Findings from a Leading Neuroscientist* (Ballantine Books, 2010) 8, 16, 17, 20, 26 and 36.

[12] Dawn Prince-Huges, Ph.D., *Songs of the Gorilla Nation: My Journey through Autism* (New York: Harmony Books, 2004) 152-153.

[13] Nancy Eisland, the *Disabled God*, 20-21.

[14] James E. Reed and Ronnie Prevost, *a History of Christian Education* (Nashville, Tennessee: Broadman & Holdman Publishers, 1993) 82.

[15] Steven Shore, *Reflections from a Different Journey: What Adults with Disabilities Wish All Parents Knew*, ed. by Stanley D. Klein, Ph.D., and John D. Kemp (USA: McGraw Hill, 2004) 54-59, "The Autism Bomb."

[16] George Orwell, *Animal Farm* (Orlando, Florida: Harcourt Brace & Company, 1945) 118, "All animals are equal, but some animals are more equal than others."

[17] For an explanation of "Blue Washing and "Green Washing" sec Josephine Bellaccomo, *Move The Message: Your Guide to Making a Difference and Changing the World* (New York: Lantern Books, 2004) 171-172 "Anticipate the Power Holders' Defense."

[18] For an example of how this can done: see Sharon Welch, *Sweet Dreams in America: Making Ethics and Spirituality Work* (New York and London: Routledge, 1999) Pay particular attention to "Chapter 3: Learning to See Simultaneously Yet Differently" 52-82 and "Chapter 4: The Art of Ambiguity" 83-118. For an example of a Disability Studies argument that "disability experience" needs to be taken seriously as a sociological phenomena, that "disability" needs to be understood as an oppression, social justice issue and that disability impacts one social location see Tanya Titchkosky, *Disability, Self and Society* (Toronto Buffalo London: University of Toronto Press, 2006 2011).

[19] Nancy Eisland, *the Disabled God*, 13.

[20] See, Ralph Ellison, *Invisible Man* (Vintage, 1995).

[21] See, Jay MacLeod, *Ain't No Making It: Aspirations and Attainment in a Low-Income Neighborhood* (Westview Press, 2008, 3rd Edition).

[22] Richard Foster and Emile Griffin, *Spiritual Classics: Selected Readings on the Twelve Spiritual Disciplines* (Harper One, 2000) quote from "Introduction," xi, where you can read the whole quote.

[23] Temple Grandin and Catherine Johnson, *Animals In Translation: Using the Mysteries of Autism to Decode Animal Behavior* (New York: Scribner, 2005) 294-296.

[24] Peter Burger quote taken from Max Oelschlaeger, *Caring for Creation: an Ecumenical Approach to the Environmental Crisis* (New Haven and London: Yale University Press, 1994) 84.

[25] Dawn Prince-Hughes, *Songs of the Gorilla Nation*, 224.

[26] Word Choice from Ibid, 11.

[27] Caryle Fielding Steward, III *Soul Survivors: An African American Spirituality* (Louisville, Kentucky: Westminster John Know Press, 1997) 13-15.

[28] Dawn Prince-Hughes, *Songs of the Gorilla Nation,* 26.

[29] Sallie McFague, *Super, Natural Christians: How we should love nature* (Minneapolis: Fortress Press, 1997) 112-113, 116, 116-117.

[30] Rachel Carson, *the Sense of Wonder* (Harper Reprint, 1998) 54.

[31] Ibid, 54.

[32] Ibid, 56-57.

[33] "The Land Aesthetic" by J. Baird Callicott in *Environmental Ethics: divergence and convergence* (New York, NY: Mc-Graw-Hill, 2004) ed. by Susan J. Armstrong and Richard G. Botzler, 137.

[34] Temple Grandin and Catherine Johnson, *Animals In Translation: Using the Mysteries of Autism to Decode Animal Behavior* (New York: Scribner, 2005) 294-296.

[35] For an example see, Chellis Glendenning, *My Name Is Chellis Glendenning and I Am in Recovery from Western Civilizations* (Boston: Shambhala, 1994) read entire book for an eye opening, life-changing, enlightening, empowering spiritual breakthrough of personal healing which is very affirming of the neurodiversity perspective. For another example see Sharon Welch, *Sweet Dreams in America: Making Ethics and Spirituality Work* (New York: Roughage, 1999) read entire book, Welch uses this belief in a "non-dualistic view of good and evil" effectively and responsibly as a complementary model to the moral absolutism of Judeo-Christianity to help twenty-first century activists act with integrity in a world increasingly being marked by ethical "gray areas." Naming this archetype inspired by Saint Anthony of Padua, *Sermons for Sunday and Festivals-Volume II* (Italy: Aedizioni Messaggero, 2007) 366. Anthony taps into this archetype through the "opened root" Biblical illusion in Job 29: 19 as a metaphor for the "infusion of grace." I use Anthony's metaphor to name the "common human experience" of early environmentalist Aldo Leopold's lament that "we kill the things we love." This is connected with the extra-Biblical belief found in many pagan, Eastern and First Nations societies that it is in fact possible to love someone else and exploit even kill them at the sametime.

[36] Temple Grandin, *Animals in Translation*, 17.

[37] Ibid, 30-31.

[38] Ibid, 296-297.

[39] See, Temple Grandin and Catherine Johnson, *Animals Make Us Human: Creating the Best Lives for Animals* (Mariner Books, 2010) "core emotional systems" 3, 5, 7, 8, 20, 23, 64, 75, 103, 192, and 210.

[40] Temple Grandin, *Animals in Translation*, 57.

[41] See: Tom Regan, "From *The Case For Animal Rights*" in *Environmental Ethics: Convergence and Divergence* ed. by Susan Armstrong and Robert Botlzer (McGraw Hill, 2003) "Inherent Value and the Subject-Of-A-Life Criterion" 315-316. Sallie McFague, *A New Climate For Theology: God, The World And Global Warming* (Minneapolis: Fortress Press, 2007) "Are We The Only Ones Who Matter?" 46-48. Stephen Webb, "Ecology versus the Peaceable Kingdom: Toward A Better Theology of Nature," *Soundings,* Spring/Summer. 79. 1996: 239. Stephen Webb, *the*

*Dome of Eden: A New Solution to Creation-Evolution* (Cascade Books, 2005). Holmes Ralston III, "Values in and Duties to the Natural World" and "Environmental Ethics: Some Challenges for Christians" in *Environmental Ethics* ed. by Armstrong and Boltzer. For an example of how humanistic philosophers like Kant and Bentham are used by animal ethicists see, *Animal Rights and Human Obligations (Second Edition)* ed. by Tom Regan and Peter Singer (Pretence Hall, 1989). For an example of how humanistic philosophers like Bentham and Locke are used by environmental ethicists see "From *Should Trees Have a Standing? Toward Legal Rights for Natural Objects"* (550) by Christopher Stone, "Environmental Ethical Issues in Water Operations and Land Management" (574) by Cheryl Davis and "From *Politics of the Earth"* (580) by John Dryzek in *Environmental Ethics* ed. by Armstrong and Boltzer. For a more detailed discussion see my books available at Amazon.com: *Creation Unveiled* (Xulon Press, 2003 2010), *Christian Environmental Studies: Toward A Graduate Program* (Amazon, 2008 2012), *Human-Animal Reconciliation: Franciscan Faith-based Interspecies Communications and Its Implications for Wildlife Management* (Amazon, 2008) and *Have Mercy On Me, An Ecological Sinner: How The God of the Bible Helped Me Rise Above Compassion Fatigue And Not Give-Up On The Ecological Struggle* (Amazon, 2012).

[42] Temple Grandin, *Animals in Translation*, 51-52.

[43] Concept of "Primary" and "Secondary Consciousness" from Donald Griffin, *Animal Minds: Beyond Cognition to Consciousness* (University of Chicago Press, 2001).

[44] John Perry, *Knowledge, Possibility, and Consciousness* (Cambridge, Massachusetts: The MIT Press, 2001) 15.

[45] Temple Grandin, *Animals in Translation*, 57.

[46] Ibid, 7.

[47] Dawn Prince-Hughes, *Gorilla Nation,* 92-94.

[48] Thomas Balsame and Sharon Rosenbloom, *Souls: Beneath and Beyond Autism* (New York: NY: McGraw Hill, 2004) 82.

[49] Robert Moore and Douglas Gillette, *King Warrior Magician Lover: Rediscovering the Archetypes of the Mature Masculine* (United States: Harper San Francisco, 1990) "The Divine Child" 15-27.

[50] For an argument for why the Caucasian women's movements of twenty-first century North America needs "to watch their language about power" see Sharon Welch, *Sweet Dreams in America: Making Ethics and Spirituality Work* , "Preface" xi-xxiii, "Chapter 1: Virtuosity" 1-26 and "Chapter 2: Frustration and Anger Do Not A Politics Make" 27-51. Also preeminent feminist theologian Sallie McFague agrees that homosexuality *is not* the most urgent issue of the twenty-first century; global climate change is the most urgent issue in the twenty-first century, while remaining "non-judgmental" and "accepting" of both homosexuality and homosexuals. See: McFague, *A New Climate for Theology,* 1 & 36. Sallie McFague, *Life Abundant (Searching for a New Framework)* (Minneapolis: Fortress Press, 2000) "Epilogue" 203-204.

[51] For a similar argument see Ross Douthat, *Bad Religion: How We Became a Nation of Heretics* (New York: Simon & Simon, 2012) 288-291. To read what major thinkers throughout history in the West thought about male friendship, including philosophers in Ancient Greece, Rome and Medieval Times see *Other Selves: Philosophers on Friendship* ed. by Michael Pakaluk (Hackett, 1991).

[52] Steven Bouma-Prediger, *For the Beauty of the Earth: A Christian Vision for Creation-Care* (Grand Rapid, Michigan: Baker Academic, 2001) 168-169.

[53] Phrase taken from Rab Houston and Uta Frith, *Autism in History: the Case of Hugh Blair of Borgue* (Oxford, UK: Blackwell Publishers Ltd., 2000) 43.

[54] For an example of the naming and argument against "normalcy" by a Disability Studies scholar see Tanya Titchkosky, *Disability, Self and Society*, 64-128 "Chapter 3: Mapping Normalcy: A Social Topography of Passing" and "Chapter 4: The Expected and Unexpected."

[55] For source material see my article: Daniel Salomon, "From Marginal Cases to Linked Oppressions: Reframing the Conflict between the Autistic Pride and Animal Rights Movements," *Journal of Critical Animal Studies* VIII, Issue ½, 2010 which can be accessed through http://www.all-creatures.org/church/grmindir-md-ss-salomon.html. For additional elaboration of this argument applied also to ecological and Christian environmental and animal rights contexts see my book, *Have Mercy on me, an Ecological Sinner* (Amazon, 2012). Cited for the entire section: Sharon Welch, *Sweat Dreams in America*, Temple Grandin, *Animals Make Us Human*, Dawn-Prince Hughes, *Songs of the Gorilla Nation* and Andrew Linzey, *Why Animal Suffering Matters: Philosophy, Theology and Practical Ethics* (USA: Oxford University Press, 2009) "Chapter Two: How We Minimalize Animal Suffering and How We Can Change" 43-72.

[56] George Lakoff and Mark Johnson, *Metaphors We Live By* (Chicago: The University of Chicago Press, 1980, 2003) 24.

[57] Ibid, See Chapter 4.

[58] Dawn Prince-Hughes, *Songs of the Gorilla Nation*, 25.

[59] Dawn Prince-Hughes, *Songs of the Gorilla Nation*, 203.

[60] For Lakeoff's full articulation of progressive Christianity from a cognitive science perspective see, George Lakoff, *Don't Think Of An Elephant: Know Your Values and Frame The Debate-An Essential Guide For Progressives* (Chelsea Green, 2004) 102-103.

[61] Brother Lawrence, Frank Laubach, *Practicing His Presence: One of the Great Pieces of Christian literature of all Time* (Jacksonville, Fl: The Seed Sowers, MCMLXXIII) 72.

[62] Ibid, 9-10.

[63] Jan Johnson, *Enjoying the Presence of God: Discovering Intimacy with God in the Daily Rhythms of Life* (Colorado Springs, Colorado: NavPress Publishing Group, 1996) 72, 68.

[64] Neale Donald Walsch, *Conversations with God: an uncommon dialogue-Book 1* (New York: G.P. Putnam's Press, 1995 1996) Introduction.

[65] Glendenning, *My Name Is Chellis*, 34.

[66] Chellis Glendenning, *When Technology Wounds: the Human Consequences of Progress* (New York: William Marrow and Company, 1990) "God's Help" 163-170.

[67] Carol Lloyd, *Creating a Life worth Living: A practical course for artists, innovators, and other aspiring to a creative life* (United States of America: Harper Collins Publishers, 1997) "Mystic" 80-82.

[68] Andrew Newburg M.D. and Mark Robert Waldman, *How God Changes Your Brain: Breakthrough Findings from a Leading Neuroscientist*, 51. For examples of the autistic propensity to personify inanimate objects (with implications for spirituality, religion and theology) see Dawn Prince Hughes, *Songs of the Gorilla Nation*, 3, 19 and 49. For an example of how an autistic human can channel, refine, develop, mature and nuance this propensity toward a more focused, rigorous academic, scientific end (with implications for spirituality, religion and theology), see Temple Grandin and Catherine Johnson, *Animals In Translation*, "Animals From The Outside In," 9-16, "Seeing The Way Animals See: The Visual Environment," 16-23, "What People See and Don't See," 24-26, "Animal Superstitions" 98-100, "Do Animals Have True Cognition?" 243-260, "Words Get In The Way" 261-272, "Do Animals Talk to Each Other The Way People Do?" 272-307 and 333.16.

[69] See, Alan Hodder, *Thoreau's Ecstatic Witness* (New Haven: Yale University Press, 1993) "Pagoda Worship" 134-139.

[70] Richard Rohr O.F.M., *From Wild Man to Wise Man: Reflections on Male Spirituality* (Ohio: St. Anthony Messenger Press, 1990 1995 2005), "Chapter 6: Male Initiation" 31-36.

[71] For a similar argument and usage of "God the Father" see, Richard Rohr O.F.M., *From Wild Man to Wise Man: Reflections on Male Spirituality* (Ohio: St. Anthony Messenger Press, 1990 1995 2005).

[72] See, Jeffery Mason, *The Emperor's Embrace: Reflections on Animal Families and Fatherhood* (Pocket Books, 1999).

[73] Mercy Oduyoye, *Hearing and Knowing: Theological Reflections on Christianity in Africa* (Maryknoll, New York: Orbis Books, 1986) Chapters 7 & 11, 90, 92, 94-95 and 139.

[74] John Cobb, Jr. and David Ray Griffin, *Process Theology: an Introductory Exposition* (Philadelphia: Westminster Press, 1976) Chapters 1& 3, 13, 14, 16-18, 21, 22-24, 24-26,26-28, 29, 41-43, 47-48, 52-53, 54-57 and 57-61.

[75] Jurgen Moltmann, *God in Creation* (Fortress Edition, 1993) 81 and 82-83.

[76] To learn more about my relationship with God see, Daniel Salomon, *Have Mercy on me, an Ecological Sinner* (Amazon, 2012). Daniel Salomon, *Christian Environmental Studies* (Amazon, 2008 2012). Daniel Salomon, *Creation Unveiled* (Xulon Press, 2003 2010).

[77] "The Assisi Compilation," *Francis of Assisi-The Founder: Early Documents II* ed. by Regis Armstrong, O.F.M. Cap., J.A. Wayne Hellmann, O.F.M. Conv., and William Short, O.F.M. (New York, London, Manila: New York Press, 2000) 209, Chapter 104.

[78] For an example of my exegesis see Daniel Salomon, *Christian Environmental Studies: toward a Graduate Program-Revised Expanding Edition* (Amazon, 2008 2012).

[79] Carol Gray and Abbie Leigh White, illustrated by Sean McAndrew, *My Social Stories Book* (London and Philadelphia: Jessica Kingsley Publishers, 2002, 2003, 2004) 17.

[80] "Nature in Industrial Society" by Neil Evernden, in *Environmental Ethics: divergence & convergence-Third Edition* ed. by Susan Armstrong and Richard Botzler, (New York, NY: McGraw Hill, 1993 1998 2004) 196, 199.

[81] Sallie McFague, *a New Climate for Theology*, 126.

[82] Holmes Ralston III, "Does Nature need to be redeemed?" *Horizons in Biblical Theology* (1994) 158-162, "7. Cruciform Creation."

[83] Ilia Delio, O.S.F., *A Franciscan View of Creation: Learning to Live in a Sacramental World* (St. Bonaventure, NY: St. Bonaventure University, 2003) 21-22.

[84] See, Michael Strutin, *Discovering Natural Israel: From the Coral Reefs of Elliot to the Emerald Crown of Mount Carmel* (Jonathan David Publishers, 2001).

[85] Nancy Eisland, *the Disabled God*, 22.

[86] Aristotle, "Nicomachean Ethics: Books VII and IX," ed. by Michael Pakaluk in *Other Selves: Philosophers on Friendship* (Indianapolis, Indiana, Hackett Publishing Company, 1991) 37, 1158a viii 5.

[87] Sarah York, *Pilgrim Heart: The Inner Journey Home* (San Francisco: Jossey-Bass A Wiley Company, 2001) 24.

[88] See, Daniel Salomon, *Have Mercy On Me, An Ecological Sinner* (Amazon, 2012). Also see, Daniel Salomon, "Homily: On a Wing and A Prayer," (Saint Mark Presbyterian Church, 2012) available at http://www.all-creatures.org/church/grmindir-md-ss-salomon-2012-homily.html.

[89] See story of Tower Oaks in Daniel Salomon, *Have Mercy on me, an Ecological Sinner* (Amazon, 2012).

[90] Henri Nouwen, *the Wounded Healer: Ministry in Contemporary Society* (New York, New York: Doubleday, 1972) 71-72, 72-73.

[91] Temple Grandin, *Animals in Translation*, see "Freedom from Fear" section, 193-.

[92] Francis of Assisi and the early Franciscans, "The Later Rule," in *Francis and Clare: The Complete Works (The Classics of Western Spirituality)* trans. and ed. by Regis Armstrong, O.F.M. CAP. And Ignatius C. Brady, O.F.M. (New York: Paulist Press, 1982) 139, Chapter III. 1-6.

[93] Ibid, 14-18, 152.

[94] Saint Bonaventure, *Bonaventure: The Soul's Journey into God; the Tree of Life; the Life of Saint Francis (The Classics of Western Spirituality)* trans. by Ewert Cousins (New Jersey: Paulist Press, 1978) 289, Chapter 11, 13-24.

[95] Sallie McFague, *a New Climate for Theology*, 109.

[96] Cited for whole section. For an introduction to Girardian Theory see my book, *Creation Unveiled: the Implications of Girardian Theory to Environmental and Animal Issues* (USA: Xulon Press, 2003 2010). For an introduction to neurotheology see, Andrew Newburg M.D. and Mark Robert Waldman, *How God Changes Your Brain: Breakthrough Findings from a Leading Neuroscientist* (Ballantine Books, 2010). For a discussion of the libratory benefits of exorcism for oppressed minorities and why more peaceful Christian virtues and rituals such as humility, forgiveness, self-denial, sacrifice and excellence *are not* desirable for oppressed minorities in North America such as African-Americans, Native Americans, Latinos, Asians, Jews, women, homosexuals and peoples with disabilities see Sharon Welsh, *Sweet Dreams in America*. See Chellis Glendenning, *My Name Is Chellis and I am in Recovery from Western Civilization,* for an example of the recovery of the personification metaphor in Nature-based societies around the world including in Eurasian civilizations, in the history of Western civilization and in human evolution. For the limits of forgiveness and the need for alternative rituals from a psychological perspective, as well as a robust legal definition of abuse, see Daniel Jay Sonkin, Ph.D., *Wounded Boys Heroic Men: A Man's Guide to Recovering from Child Abuse* (Massachusetts: Adams Media Corporation, 1998) "Forward" iv-x, "Introduction: Child Abuses and You," xi-xiv, "Chapter 1: Wounded Men, Wounded Boys," 3-25, "Chapter 2: Preparation for Your Journey,"26-42, "Chapter 3: The Abuse and The Wounds," 43-66, "Chapter 4: Breaking Denial: "I Was Abused As A Child," 67-84, "Chapter 9:Making Peace With Your Abuser," 172-189, "Chapter 10: Making Peace With Your Self," 190-200, "Epilogue: Wounded Heroes," 201-205 and "Appendix V: The Hero's Journey" 225-226. For a more nuanced, mature argument for forgiveness and what forgiveness *is not* read: Lewis

Smedes, *Shame and Grace: Healing the Shame WeDon't Deserve* (Harper One, 1994). Lewis Smedes, *Forgive and Forget: Healing The Hurts We Don't Deserve* (Harper One: 2007). Also see Dietrich Bonheoffer, *The Cost of Discipleship* (Touchstone, 1995) "Part One: Grace and Discipleship," 41-102, "Costly Grace," 43, "The Call to Discipleship," 57, "Single Minded Obedience," 79, "Discipleship and the Cross," 86 and "Discipleship and the Individual" 94. For an argument for political activism see Paul Loab, *Soul of a Citizen: Living with Conviction in Challenging Times* (St. Martin's Griffin, 2010). To learn about the "sin-disability connection" in Christianity and its impact on secular Western culture see Nancy Eisland, *The Disabled God*, "Disabling Theology," 70-75,93 and 101. For an example of the positive, responsible role of negative emotions in one's Christian faith see Saint Anthony of Padua, *Sermons for Sunday and Festivals-Volume II* (Italy: Aedizioni Messaggero, 2007) "On weeping: *Thine eyes are doves*" 245-246, "On compunction: *I will water thee with my tears,*" 263-264 and for positive bitterness see "Blessed are the eyes that will see, in bitterness of heart, the face of Jesus Christ, swollen with blows and smeared with spittle; for they will see that *on which angels long to gaze* (1Pt. 1.12), glorious in the courts of the heavenly Jerusalem. *He shall see in joy* (Job 33.26), as to say, if a man will first see thee, in bitterness of heart, the face of Jesus Christ as it was in the Passion; then later he will see it in joyfulness of mind such as can neither be expressed nor restrained, as it is in eternal blessedness," 329.

[97] Judith Herman, M.D., *Trauma and Recovery: The aftermath of violence-from domestic abuse to political terror*, (United States of America: Basic Books, 1992 1997) 15, 172-73, 181.

[98] Richard J. Foster, *Celebration of Discipline: The Path to Spiritual Growth*, (Revised Edition, San Francisco: Harper San Francisco, A Division of Harper Collins Publishers, 1998), 62 – 63.

[99] For further discussion on this topic see Carol Lloyd, *Create a Life Worth Living: A practical course in career design for artists, innovators, and others aspiring to a creative life* (United States of America: Harpur Perennial, 1997) "The Dangers of Abstractions," 28-31.

[100] See, Chellis Glendenning, *My Name Is Chellis Glendenning and I am In Recovery from Western Civilization*. Chellis Glendenning, *Off The Map: An Exploration Deep into Empire and the Global Economy* (New Society Publishers, 2002).

[101] See, Daniel Salomon, *Have Mercy On me, An Ecological Sinner* (Amazon, 2012). Also see, Chellis Glendenning, *When Technology Wounds: The Human Consequences of Progress*. Chellis Glendenning, *My Name Is Chellis and I am In Recovery from Western Civilization*. Chellis Glendenning, *Off The Map: An Exploration Deep Into Empire and the Global Economy*. Chellis Glendenning, *Chiva: A Village Takes On The Global Heron Trade* (New Society Publishers, 2005). Sam Keen, *Fire In The Belly: On Being A Man* (Bantam, 1992). Henri Nouwen, *the Wounded Healer: Ministry in Contemporary Society* (New York, New York: Doubleday, 1972). Max Oelschlaeger, *Caring for Creation: an Ecumenical Approach to the Environmental Crisis* (New Haven and London: Yale University Press, 1994). J. Donald Hughes, *Pan's Travail: Environmental Problems of Ancient Greeks and Rome* (Maryland: Johns Hopkins University Press, 1996). Paul Loab, *Soul of a Citizen: Living with Conviction in Challenging Times* (St. Martin's Griffin, 2010). Ross Douthat, *Bad Religion: How We Became a Nation of Heretics* (New York: Simon & Simon, 2012). Sallie McFague, *Life Abundant* (*Searching for a New Framework*) (Minneapolis: Fortress Press, 2000).

[102] For an argument for why human beings *need* safety to "live with dignity" see Chellis Glendenning, *My Name Is Chellis and I Am in Recovery from Western Civilization,* "Where Is That Beautiful Trail?" 137-143. For a discussion on the difference between "cure" and "healing" see, Glendenning, *My Name Is Chellis,* "Chapter 10: Moose Becomes Me," 131-133 and 133-137 "Attraction to Wholeness." For a realistic framework for healing, management and responsibility see Aphrodite Matsakis, Ph.D., *Trust After Trauma: A Guide to Relationships for Survivors and Those Who Love Them* (Oakland, California: New Harbingers Press, 1998) "Chapter 14: To Significant Others" 305-342. For arguments for why human beings *need* love, community, friendship, distance, psychological wholeness, a healthy self-esteem, individuality, faith, hope, grace, spirituality or religion, meaningful work, participatory democracy, political empowerment even celebration, humor and some pleasure and reward see: Paul Loab, *Soul of a Citizen: Living with Conviction in Challenging Times* (St. Martin's Griffin, 2010). Henri Nouwen, *the Wounded Healer: Ministry in Contemporary Society* (New York, New York: Doubleday, 1972). Sam Keen, *Fire in the Belly: On Being a Man* (Bantam, 1992). Stephen Byrd, *the Men We Long To Be: Beyond Lonely Warriors and Desperate Lovers* (Wipf. & Stock Pub, 2009). Also see, Chellis Glendenning, *When Technology Wounds*. For a contemporary argument for why human beings need contact with the Natural World see Chellis Glendenning, *My Name Is Chelsea, Off the Map* and *Chiva*.

[103] For an example of the "geek" stereotype see Temple Grandin, *Developing Talent: Careers for Individuals with Asperger Syndrome and High-Functioning Autism-Updated and Expanded Addition* (Autism Asperger's Publishing

Company, 2008). To show why such an approach based on "passing" and "assimilation" is dangerous to all peoples with disabilities see, Tanya Titchkosky, *Disability, Self and Society*, "Chapter 3: Mapping Normalcy: A Social Topography Of Passing" 64-94 and "Chapter 4: The Expected and Unexpected" 96-128. To corroborate that a person with a disability can have a capacity and functioning-level beyond their diagnosis see, "Chapter 2: Situating Disability: Mapping the Outer Limits" 46-62. For an explanation and a deconstruction of peoples with disabilities being referred to as "mistakes" see "Disability and the Background of the Ordinary" 8-17. For a discussion of the "challenge" of loneliness which all "outsiders" face in the United States whether we are neurodiverse, have a physical disability, are a women in a male dominated field, a homosexual from an older generation, a stay-at home mother in a working girls world, an introverted church worker, a dreamy innovator, an aspiring artist, an African American, a Latino, a child abuse survivor, or just plain not "fit in" and are looking for an alternative to "passing" and "assimilation" see Leonard Felder Ph.D., *Fitting In Is Overrated: The Survival Guide to Anyone Who Has Ever Felt Like An Outsider* (Sterling, 1st Edition, 2008). For an example of the peculiar forms of losses, oppressions and inequalities "technology survivors" like myself experience and have to overcome see Chellis Glendenning, *When Technology Wounds*, "Wounds," 41-42, "Discovery" 43-52, "Loss of Health" 53-58, "The Victim" 59-55, "Loss of Heroism" 79-86, "Uncertainty" 87-97, "Responsibility" 98-114, "The Taboos" 115-116, "We Don't Know The Wounds" 117-120, "Psychological Taboos" 121-131 and "Social Taboos" 134-147.

[104] Phrase adapted from Daniel Jay Sonkin, Ph.D., *Wounded Boys Heroic Men: a Man's Guide to Recovering from Child Abuse* (Massachusetts: Adams Media Corporation, 1998) "Chapter Four: Breaking Denial: 'I Was an Abused Child" 67-84.

[105] For documentation and recommended self-help books on post-traumatic stress disorder (PTSD)—definitions, symptom lists, problem analysis frameworks, healing exorcizes and guidance for dealing with mental health professionals and understanding the treatment process see "further reading" section under "recommended self help books," "feminism" and "menism" in appendix.

[106] See, Daniel Sonkin, *Wounded Boys Heroic Men*, "Chapter One: Wounded Boy, Wounded Men" 3-25 "Chapter Three: The Abuse and the Wounds" 43-64 and "Chapter Four: Breaking Denial" 64-84.

[107] Read the waiver you have to sign when you got into see a psychological therapist, a psychologist, a social worker or a psychiatrist on your first intake appointment for more information about your rights. Also ask your parent or parents, councilor or case worker or significant other if they are your "legal guardian." If not, you have the same legal rights as any other non-disabled, neurotypical adult in the United States. If you live in another country, check for equivalent wavers, laws and regulations. Know your rights within the constraints of the laws of your own country. This option will only work if you live in a democracy. If you live in a non-democratic country, the key to resisting is to A) accept that your abuse happened and you did not deserve to be treated this way even if you cannot change your external circumstances, B) put your own safety, survival and self-care first, C) identify the exact limits of your own powers and D) name your own powers and use them when appropriate.

[108] Chellis Glendenning, *When Technology Wounds: the Human Consequences of Progress* (New York: William Marrow and Company, 1990) "God's Help" 163-170.

[109] See, Sallie McFague, *Life Abundant*. Also see, Sallie McFague, *Metaphoric Theology: Models of God in Religious Language* (Philadelphia: Fortress Press, 1982).

[110] In Chellis Glendenning, *Off the Map*, 65.

[111] Story found in Aldo Leopold, *A Sand County Almanac: with Essays on Conservation from Round River* (New York: Ballantine, 1949 1953 1966) 230-232.

[112] Henri Nouwen, *Bread for the Journey* (Harper San Francisco, 1997). Expert from Henri Nouwen Society, "Daily Meditation" (11/2/2012) email_lists@henrinouwen.org.

[113] Tanya Titchkosky, *Disability, Self and Society*, "Reading Disability Studies" 42-45.

[114] Leonard Felder, PhD., *Fitting In Is Overrated*, 116-120.

[115] Stephen Byrd, *The Men We Long To Be: Beyond Lonely Warriors and Desperate Lovers,* "Losing Ourselves To Find Ourselves: Faith" 123-126.

[116] Enos Mills and John Dotson, *Radiant Days: Written By Enos Mills* (Salt Lake City: University of Utah Press, 1994) 16.

[117] Ibid, "Forward by Bill McKidden."

[118] An example of how this could be done see Kevin Koch, *The Driftless Land: Spirit of Place in the Upper Mississippi Valley* (United States of America: Southeast Missouri State University Press, 2010).

[119] Temple Grandin, *The Way I See It: A Personal Look At Autism and Asperger's* (Future Horizons, First Edition, 2008), 118.

[120] For "root metaphor" of "rebirth" see Alan Hodder, *Thoreau's Ecstatic Witness* (New Haven & London: Yale University Press, 2001) "Chapter Three: Redeem This Wasted Time" 102-130. For my vision of afterlife see, Sharon Welch, *Sweet Dreams in America*, 43-51.

[121] Rachel Salomon, "Disabled Israelis Serving Their Country with Pride" in United with Israel, 11/25/2012, http://unitedwithisreal.org/disabledirsaelis-serving/.

[122] See G.K. Chesterton, *Saint Francis of Assisi* (Empire Books, 2012).

[123] For an example see Rab Huston and Ute Frith, *Autism in History*, 99.

[124] Ibid, "Chapter 4: Autism and its Relevance to the Case of Hugh Blair" 97-131.

[125] For men's movement examples see: Robert Moore and Douglas Gillette, *King Warrior Magician Lover: Rediscovering the Archetypes of the Mature Masculine* (United States: Harper San Francisco, 1990). Sam Keen, *Fire in the Belly: On Being a Man* (Bantam, 1992). Richard Rohr O.F.M., *From Wild Man to Wise Man: Reflections on Male Spirituality* (Ohio: St. Anthony Messenger Press, 1990 1995 2005). For Chellis Glendenning see *My Name Is Chellis*. For Dawn Prince-Hughes see, *The Archetype of the Ape-Man* (USA: Destination.com, 2001). For Temple Grandin's discussion of Henry Spiro see *Animals Make Us Human,* 256-257. Also see Temple Grandin, *Developing Talents*, 67-68.

[126] For the details of McFague's method of theologian reflection see *Metaphorical Theology: Models of God in Religious Language*.

[127] Saint Anthony of Padua, *Sermons for Sunday and Festivals-Volume II* (Italy: Aedizioni Messaggero, 2007) 379-380.

[128] Chellis Glendenning, *When Technology Wounds*, "What Technology Survivors Want To Tell Us" 199-209. Cited for entire section.

[129] Chellis Glendenning, *Chiva,* 132-133.

[130] Vladimir Lossky, *The Mystical Theology of the Eastern Church* (New York: St. Vladimir's Seminary Press, 2002)44-46.

Printed in Great Britain
by Amazon